MW01274006

FIRE AND SWORD

Fire and Sword

Sorley Boy MacDonnell and the
Rise of Clan Ian Mor, 1538–1590

J. Michael Hill

The Aegis Press
Fort Worth

Published in 1993 by

AEGIS PRESS
P.O. Box 9420
Fort Worth, Texas 76107

© J. Michael Hill 1993

ISBN 0-9637142-0-1

All rights reserved. No part of this publication may
be reproduced, stored in a retrieval system, or
transmitted in any form or by any means, electronic,
mechanical, photocopying or otherwise, without
prior permission in writing from the publisher.

Maps by Applied Academic Services
Cartography Department

Originally published in Great Britain
by The Athlone Press

Aegis Press is a Division of
Applied Academic Services, Inc.

For James Edwin Hill,
my father

A Note on Dates

In 1582 the introduction of the Gregorian calendar (New Style) on the Continent did not affect the British Isles, which continued to use the Julian calendar (Old Style). The Julian calendar was ten days behind the new Gregorian calendar. In the British Isles 25 March began a new year with the Julian calendar, while 1 January marked the change on the Gregorian. For the present study, all days and months will be Old Style, but 1 January will denote the beginning of a new year.

Contents

List of Maps

MacDonnell Genealogies

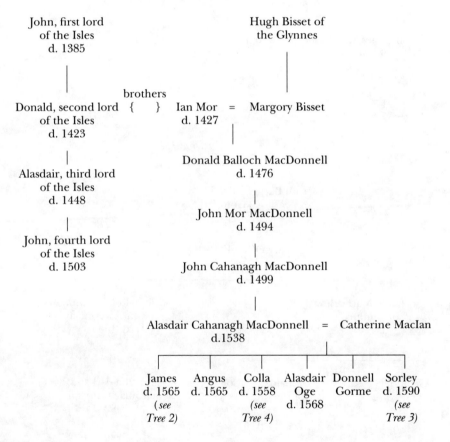

1.   Lords of the Isles and Clan Ian Mor

John, first lord
of the Isles
d. 1385

Hugh Bisset of
the Glynnes

brothers

Donald, second lord {   } Ian Mor = Margory Bisset
of the Isles   d. 1427
d. 1423

Alasdair, third lord
of the Isles
d. 1448

Donald Balloch MacDonnell
d. 1476

John Mor MacDonnell
d. 1494

John, fourth lord
of the Isles
d. 1503

John Cahanagh MacDonnell
d. 1499

Alasdair Cahanagh MacDonnell = Catherine MacIan
d.1538

James	Angus	Colla	Alasdair	Donnell	Sorley
d. 1565	d. 1565	d. 1558	Oge	Gorme	d. 1590
(see		*(see*	d. 1568		*(see*
Tree 2)		*Tree 4)*			*Tree 3)*

2. *Dunyveg MacDonnells*
1565–1626

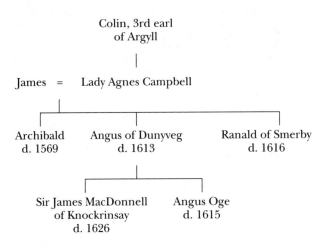

Colin, 3rd earl
of Argyll

|

James = Lady Agnes Campbell

Archibald   Angus of Dunyveg   Ranald of Smerby
d. 1569   d. 1613   d. 1616

Sir James MacDonnell   Angus Oge
of Knockrinsay   d. 1615
d. 1626

3. *Antrim MacDonnells*
1590–1644

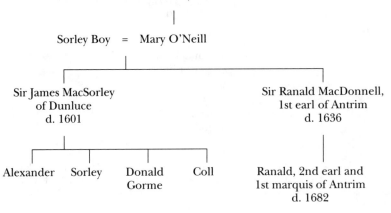

Con Bacagh O'Neill,
earl of Tyrone

|

Sorley Boy = Mary O'Neill

Sir James MacSorley   Sir Ranald MacDonnell,
of Dunluce   1st earl of Antrim
d. 1601   d. 1636

Alexander   Sorley   Donald   Coll   Ranald, 2nd earl and
Gorme   1st marquis of Antrim
d. 1682

4.   *Colonsay MacDonnells*
     1558–1644

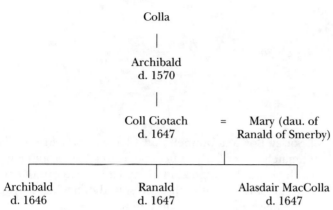

Colla

|

Archibald
d. 1570

|

Coll Ciotach   =   Mary (dau. of
d. 1647   Ranald of Smerby)

Archibald   Ranald   Alasdair MacColla
d. 1646   d. 1647   d. 1647

Preface

The story of Sorley Boy MacDonnell and Clan Ian Mor in the sixteenth century is ultimately one of a private association – a prominent Gaelic clan – against the centralized, quasi-modern Tudor state. In our own day the break-up of the Soviet empire, the unresolved difficulties surrounding European unity, the various ethnic and nationalistic crises in eastern Europe, and the general devolution of political power into smaller units suggest a trend away from the impersonal, centralized, bureaucratic, technocratic state and toward a more personal, regional, or local type government.

In order to protect their independence from an ambitious, increasingly impersonal and powerful English state, the leaders of Clan Ian Mor undertook an aggressive campaign of territorial expansion. They became a pan-Gaelic power with holdings in both Ulster and the western Highlands and Isles of Scotland. Under the leadership of Sorley Boy, Clan Ian Mor's two branches, the Antrim (Irish) and Dunyveg (Scottish) MacDonnells, beat back the English and their Gaelic allies and preserved the family's independent political base, especially in northeastern Ireland, until the mid-seventeenth century.

Though four centuries past, Sorley Boy MacDonnell's struggle reflected the same desire for local self-rule that we increasingly see in today's world. It was firmly grounded in the concept of private community – a tribal unity based on kinship (both blood and fictive), hierarchy, honor, and land. The MacDonnell family's primary nemesis was the Tudor state, the modern, formal, bureaucratic, and imperialistic nature of which was rooted in the contrary concept of public society. History teaches that the plight of the private community or association in the larger order of things is indeed perilous. On the one hand, when Leviathan is weak, the private association faces endemic violence and disorder, as a power vacuum seeks to be filled either by local rival associations, or by other large, imperialistic powers. On the other hand, when Leviathan is strengthened, the private association must struggle to keep control over its own resources and identity. During the sixteenth century, Clan Ian Mor faced the latter situation, as the organizing principle of the English state itself changed from one grounded largely in the ideas of community to one based increasingly on the paradigm of public society.

This book could not have been written without the efforts of many persons. For their generous financial assistance, I would like to thank Mr. Ellice McDonald, Jr., honorary High Commissioner of Clan Donald USA, Inc.; Dr. and Mrs. Forrest McDonald, the University of Alabama; Dr. Bernerd C. Weber, Professor Emeritus, the University of Alabama; and Dr. Willa Lowe and the Steering Committee for the Stillman College Mellon Endowment Project for Faculty and Curriculum Development.

I am indeed fortunate to have had several scholars, both within and outside my academic field, agree to read various drafts of the manuscript. I would like to thank Dr. Kenneth Nicholls, Cork University, Dr. Jeremy M. Black, University of Durham, Dr. Forrest McDonald, University of Alabama, and Dr. Grady McWhiney and Dr. Robert T. Maberry, Jr., Texas Christian University, Aegis Press, and Applied Academic Services, Fort Worth, Texas. I very much appreciate their many suggestions, general and specific, that saved me from numerous errors and improved the finished work.

Others to whom I owe thanks for various reasons include Dr. Stewart J. Brown, University of Edinburgh; Dr. Jane Dawson, University of Edinburgh; Dr. Alexander Murdoch, Edinburgh; Dr. Donald Frazier, Texas Christian University, Aegis Press, and Applied Academic Services; Dr. John M. Dederer, New Haven, Connecticut; Dr. Cordell Wynn, President, Stillman College; Professor Aubry Womack, Stillman College; Mr. Robert Heath, Stillman College; Mr. Alasdair Hawkyard, London; Mr. John Milner, Clan Donald USA, Inc.; Mr. Malcolm MacDonald, Tuscaloosa, Alabama; Ms. Patricia Henderson, the University of Alabama Gorgas Library; Mr. Robert C. Galbraith, High Commissioner, Clan Donald USA, Inc.; Mr. John W. McConnell, Winters, California; Mr. and Mrs. Edmund Black, Ballycastle, N.I.; and Dr. Daniel Gillis, Philadelphia, Pennsylvania. I especially would like to thank Mr. Brian Southam and The Athlone Press, London.

Special thanks and love are reserved for my wife, Sara D. Hill, and my daughters Elizabeth, Emily, and Mary Kate.

The efforts of many have made this book possible, but its errors and shortcomings are solely the author's responsibility.

J. Michael Hill
Tuscaloosa, Alabama

Prologue

Nemo me impune lacessit
No one wounds me with impunity.
            The motto of the Scot

The precipitous Antrim headlands in northeastern Ireland afford a spectacular view of the Scottish coast, the southern Hebrides, and the nearby island of Rathlin. It was here on the cliffs overlooking Murlough Bay in July 1575 that Sorley Boy MacDonnell watched several English vessels ply the North Channel waters. Were they headed for Rathlin's southeast shore or for Ballycastle Bay on the Irish mainland? Sorley had placed the clan's women and children on Rathlin for safety while his army remained on the Antrim shore awaiting an English advance overland. Soon it became apparent that the enemy ships under Sir John Norris, one of Elizabeth I's best Irish soldiers, were bound for Rathlin, and Sorley Boy had to decide whether to hold his ground or to rescue the women and children. He chose to keep his army on the mainland. It was, from a military standpoint, the correct decision; but the abandonment of his non-combatants to slaughter on Rathlin Island caused Sorley much grief.

The scenario is played out in a letter from Walter Devereux, earl of Essex, to Sir Francis Walsingham, the queen's principal secretary:

> I do now understand this day by a spy coming from Sorley Boy's camp, that upon my late journey made against him he then put most of his plate . . . and the children of most part of the gentlemen with him, and their wives, into Rathlin, with all his pledges, which be all taken and executed . . . in all to the number of 600. Sorley then also stood upon the mainland of the Glynnes, and saw the taking of the island, and was likely to run mad for sorrow, tearing and tormenting himself . . . and saying that he then lost all he ever had.[1]

Sorley Boy never forgave the English for the Rathlin massacre. Thereafter, his attempts to hold and expand the Antrim MacDonnells' enclave in Ireland became a personal quest that reflected the Scot's motto: *Nemo me impune lacessit.*

Sorley Boy's career parallels the rise of the Antrim MacDonnells.[2] No family played a greater role in the sixteenth-century Gaelic heartland, and no man loomed larger within Clan Ian Mor (Clan Donald South) than Sorley Boy, or Somhairle Buidhe (*c.* 1510–90). Along with his elder brothers – in particular James, Alasdair Oge, and Colla – Sorley carved out an enclave in the Glynnes and the Route along the northeastern coast of Antrim and held it against the Gaelic lords of Ulster and the best deputies and generals the Tudor monarchs could put into the field. And though Sorley and his kin suffered reverses, under his capable direction the MacDonnells overcame disasters that would have thwarted lesser families.

Sorley and his brothers were descended from the union of Ian Mor MacDonnell, younger brother of Donald, second lord of the Isles, and Marjory Bisset, heiress of the Antrim Glynnes, at the beginning of the fifteenth century. During that century the Antrim MacDonnells (also known as the MacDonnells of Antrim and Islay) became the most dynamic branch of Clan Ian Mor. Sorley Boy's grandfather, John Cahanagh MacDonnell (d. 1499), and father, Alasdair Cahanagh MacDonnell (d. 1538), built a power base in the Glynnes after the fall of the lordship of the Isles in 1493 that served as a refuge from the troubles that plagued the Scottish Highlands and Isles in the sixteenth century. The rise of Clan Campbell forced the MacDonnells to look more and more to the safe haven of the Glynnes. It was here in Ireland that the MacDonnell brothers, barring only James, the eldest and heir to the lordship of Dunyveg and the Glynnes (the main Scottish branch of Clan Ian Mor), learned from their father the political, diplomatic, and military skills necessary to expand the family's territorial holdings after mid-century. In 1558 Sorley was appointed Captain of the Route (fertile lands lying west of the Glynnes) by brother James. The enclave prospered under Sorley Boy's firm hand, despite the signal defeat inflicted on the MacDonnells at Glentaisie in 1565 by Shane O'Neill. James's subsequent death while in Shane's custody left Sorley as the family's acknowledged leader in Ireland.

By the mid-1560s Sorley and his family faced a precarious political situation. His chief adversaries – the English in Ireland and Shane O'Neill – sought to make him their ally or at the very least each wanted to prevent him from joining forces with the other. But Sorley saw in both parties obstacles to his ultimate objective – royal recognition of his own lordship in the Antrim Glynnes and the Route. As long as O'Neill lived, the MacDonnells feared another Glentaisie; as long as the English could readily find Irish allies, advance their territorial claims through "surrender and regrant", and keep out foreign interlopers, the MacDonnells might be restricted to the northeastern extremity of the island and thus politically neutralized. In either case, their future would be bleak. Shane's death at MacDonnell hands at Cushendun in 1567 removed one major threat. As for the English, they were woefully unprepared militarily, as events showed, to deal with the harsh exigencies of Gaelic irregular warfare, at least until Elizabeth despatched to Ireland her best general, Charles Blount, Lord Mountjoy, in the last years of her reign. Though the Antrim MacDonnells would suffer the Rathlin massacre and further tragedies, they never swerved from Sorley Boy's goal of procuring royal recognition to their claims in the Glynnes and the Route. Finally in 1586 old Sorley, negotiating from a position of strength, received a patent of denization granting him control over these areas.

The story of Sorley Boy and his kinsmen is, in part, that of a family, the most fundamental, private, and enduring of human institutions, struggling with limited resources against a growing English-dominated state that threatened to overspread the entire British Isles. From England's perspective, control of Ireland in the new era of power politics was viewed as a geopolitical necessity. Indeed, both the Roman Catholic Antrim MacDonnells and the Protestant English saw Ulster as a threat when it was in anyone else's hands but their own. Such a situation was a natural outgrowth of the politics of the Catholic Counter-Reformation.

At mid-century, England was a second-rate power at best, with a population of fewer than 4 million and with naval and military forces that compared unfavorably with those of her major continental rivals. England, like Clan Ian Mor, had long been active in Irish politics, but only after 1534 did the Tudor monarchs begin to see the island as a problem requiring a coherent strategic policy. Henry VIII's objective during his reign (1509–47) was to secure Ireland and prevent the Valois or Spanish Habsburg dynasties from using it as a forward base of operations from which to harass English trade or even to launch an invasion. There was a good deal of debate in government circles regarding the best method of controlling Ireland. Successive lord deputies and lieutenants vacillated between policies of conquest and colonization and of reform and conciliation toward the Gaelic Irish. At Elizabeth's accession in 1558, the policy of conquest and colonization triumphed and Ireland thus became a regular theater of war for England.

During Elizabeth's long reign (1558–1603), Ulster was beset by a continued influx of "New English' merchant-adventurers who gave focus to Gaelic hostility. These zealously Protestant *bodagh Sasonagh*, or "bodach Sassenach", quickly became England's political and military elite in Ireland, displacing the Anglo-Irish, or "Old English" Catholics. Having the state as well as their own abundant private resources behind them, the New English in Ireland were able eventually to destroy the traditional lords of Ulster. The O'Neills of Tyrone and the O'Donnells of Tyrconnell were extended families much like the Antrim MacDonnells, and as such were no match for the organizational and technological weight of the Tudor state. By the early seventeenth century both families had been emasculated as a result of an unsuccessful war against Elizabeth (1593–1602). Nonetheless, the Gaelic Scots and Irish normally stood up well against English armies, at least on the tactical level. And such success, though usually of limited strategic value, was quite remarkable considering the disparity of resources between the combatants. Barnaby Rich, an English officer and an astute observer of military affairs, marveled that the Gaels

> hath neither mint to make pay, shipping to transport, . . . no manner of provision, no store, nor store-houses furnished with munition, powder, shot, pieces, pikes, armoury, weapons, nor with a number of other engines and implements belonging to the war, without which a war cannot be maintained. . . .[3]

Burdened by such deprivations, only the Antrim MacDonnells, of all the Gaelic families of Ulster, were able to hold the English at bay and retain their lands and political influence into the seventeenth century. And the fact that the pro-Royalist MacDonnells of Antrim controlled the strategic northeastern portion of Ulster at the outbreak of the War of the Three Kingdoms gave Charles I a most valuable recruiting ground, as the 1644–5 campaign in Scotland would demonstrate.

It is not my intention to interject into this study historiographical arguments that would disrupt the flow of the story. If a historiographical debate is germane to my argument, it will be discussed in the appropriate note at the chapter's end. I am quite familiar with the works of those who have written widely on similar topics in early modern British history, from the Rev. George Hill's *An Historical Account of the MacDonnells of Antrim* (1873) and G. A. Hayes-McCoy's *Scots Mercenary Forces in Ireland (1565–1603)* (1937) to the more recent works of Karl Bottigheimer, Ciaran Brady, Nicholas Canny, Jane E. A. Dawson, Steven Ellis, Hiram Morgan, and David Stevenson, among others.[4] My objective herein is to elucidate for both specialist and generalist a complex series of events that attended the rise of Sorley Boy and the Antrim MacDonnells as the most dominant Gaelic power in Ulster and parts of the southwestern Highlands and Isles of Scotland in the last half of the sixteenth century. To accomplish this I have attempted: 1) to take a balanced historical view of an important part of the "Celtic fringe' and the various characters who shaped its development; 2) to tackle a specific and somewhat neglected Gaelic topic and fit it into the general British and European historical scheme; 3) to assesss the connections between Gaelic Ireland and Scotland; and 4) to explore generally the impact that MacDonnell military and political success had on English–Gaelic relations from the 1580s to the 1640s.

Chapter One
Clan Ian Mor in Antrim to 1538

Ni h-aoibhneas gun chlann Domhnaill.
There is no joy without Clan Donnell.

During the sixteenth century the Scottish branch of Clan Ian Mor – the MacDonnells of Dunyveg – reached its nadir and the Irish branch – the MacDonnells of Antrim – its zenith. The younger sons of Alasdair Cahanagh, especially Sorley Boy, made their mark primarily in Ireland while their grandfather, father, and elder brother James were more instrumental in the affairs of Scotland. To put this illustrious family's history into proper perspective, first it is necessary to trace the development of Clan Ian Mor in Scotland. Since the fourteenth century the lordship of the Isles had been the locus of MacDonnell power in Scotland, a "kingdom within a kingdom" that threatened the authority of the Scottish crown. Because of its territorial extent and large manpower resources, the lordship was by far the most powerful Scottish political entity in the late medieval period. Traditional connections between the western Highlands and Isles (particularly Islay, Kintyre, and the coastal fringes of Argyll) and Ulster grew stronger in opposition to the increasing political ambitions of both Edinburgh and London. The resulting triangular struggle between Lowland Scotland, England, and the Gaelic heartland would have important consequences for Clan Ian Mor.[1]

Prior to the establishment of the MacDonnell lordship by John, first lord of the Isles (d. *c.* 1385), several important Scottish mercenary families, most notable the MacDonnells, moved into Ulster and other parts of Ireland. These *gallóglaigh* families initiated the migration of Scots (i.e. "Irish" of "wild" Scots) back to Ireland and aided the native Irish chiefs in regaining their lands from the Anglo-Norman invaders. The movement of *gallóglaigh* families to Ireland occurred amid the turbulence associated with the Scottish Wars of Independence in the late thirteenth and early fourteenth centuries. Most accounts depict the typical *gallóglaigh* as a hardy warrior of great size and strength armed with a Lochaber axe and large two-handed sword, and clad in a coat of mail that extended to the knee. They were, without doubt, the most dependable body of troops that served under the Gaelic Irish chiefs before the sixteenth century. The *gallóglaigh* migrations ended with Edward Bruce's invasion of Ireland in 1314, but they left a legacy of Scottish settlement and military service that would serve as the impetus for two more major migrations from the Hebrides in the fifteenth and sixteenth centuries.[2]

The MacDonnells' prominent position in the Gaelic heartland and their influence in the affairs of Scotland drew the English into the region. From its inception the lordship of the Isles viewed Edinburgh as a greater threat than distant London. Consequently, John, first lord of the Isles, and his son and successor Donald, allied themselves with the English, casting a covetous eye on the Scottish throne.[3] While London seemed unconcerned with the presence of Scottish mercenaries in Ireland in the fifteenth century, it did recognize the lordship's military strength and its potential threat to the Scottish crown. Perhaps, too, the English sensed the political ambitions of the MacDonnell lords. Donald, second lord of the Isles (d. 1423), had been educated at Oxford, and subsequent events suggest that he may have gone there to cement an alliance against the Scottish king. The arrest in 1427 by James I of Donald's son and political heir Alasdair, third lord of the Isles, signaled an open break with Edinburgh. The battle of Harlaw (1411) might have been an attempt by Donald not only to secure the earldom of Ross, but also to win the Scottish crown. Donald of Harlaw was, after all, a grandson of Robert II of Scotland, and could have made a valid claim to the throne. This dramatic episode – in essence an Edinburgh–Finlaggan (the lordship's "capital" on Islay) struggle for the crown – increased suspicion and hostility between the Scottish monarchy and the lordship of the Isles. For the remainder of the fifteenth century Edinburgh attempted to create a balance of power in the west by fostering discord between the dominant families there, while the English continued to seek an accord with the MacDonnell lords.[4]

In 1427 James I seized forty Highland chiefs, including Alasdair, third lord of the Isles (d. 1448), a move that worsened relations between the MacDonnell chief and the Scottish crown. Alasdair, though, was not long detained. Upon his release he struck back with the aid of his able and impetuous cousin, Donald Balloch (d. 1476), who severely defeated royal forces at the first battle of Inverlochy in 1431.[5] Inverlochy and Harlaw, unlike most medieval battles between the crown and rebel forces, resulted in significant defeats for Edinburgh. The regime, however, quickly moved to quell the insurrection, and Donald Balloch fled to Ireland, leaving Alasdair alone to face Edinburgh's wrath. For the rest of his days the third lord of the Isles worked to form alliances with disaffected opponents of the Scottish monarchy, a policy that his successor John enthusiastically pursued.[6]

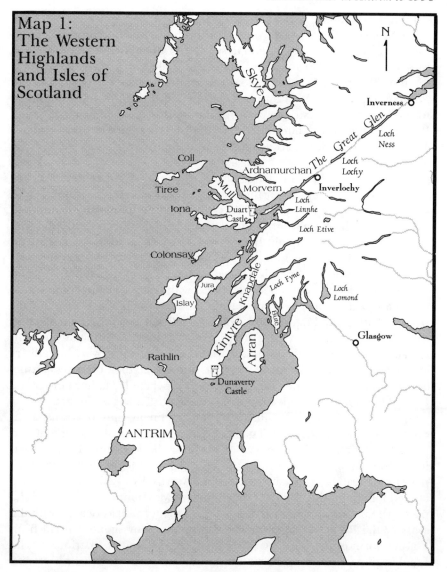

Map 1:
The Western
Highlands
and Isles of
Scotland

N

Skye

Inverness

Loch
Ness

Coll

Ardnamurchan

Loch
Lochy

The Great Glen

Tiree

Mull

Morvern

Inverlochy

Iona

Duart
Castle

Loch
Linnhe

Loch Etive

Colonsay

Jura

Knapdale

Loch Fyne

Loch
Lomond

Islay

Kintyre

Bute

Glasgow

Rathlin

Arran

Dunaverty
Castle

ANTRIM

John, fourth (and last) lord of the Isles (d. 1503), quickly challenged the authority of the Stewart dynasty. In the 1450s he offered protection to the renegade earl of Douglas and despatched Donald Balloch from Ireland with a force of 5,000 men and a fleet of galleys to harass the crown's interests along the Argyllshire coast. Responding, James II created Colin, fourteenth chief of Clan Campbell, earl of Argyll in 1457. John submitted to the king rather than face a firm Edinburgh–Campbell alliance. James II soon died, however, and the lord of the Isles' pretence of loyalty faded.[7] Thereafter, John became engaged in a foolhardy conspiracy against the Scottish throne.

John of the Isles' conspiracy against the Scottish crown centered on the Treaty of Westminster–Ardtornish (1462). John would receive English gold in return for becoming Edward IV's vassal and for providing an army to serve against the Edinburgh regime. If this scheme succeeded, John, the earl of Douglas, and Donald Balloch would lay claim to most of Scotland north of the Firth of Forth. It was obvious that John of the Isles would bear the military burden. He may have been willing to go to such lengths to gain the throne of Scotland. John's open break with James III caused immediate problems for Edinburgh, which was unprepared to face such a potentially strong alliance; the English king, however, refused to send sufficient aid to the lord of the Isles, and the enterprise got off to an inauspicious start. In all fairness to Edward IV, John behaved timidly, turning over the military enterprise to his son, Angus Oge. While Angus Oge took Inverness Castle, afterwards there was little else to do except proclaim his father king of the Isles and wait for either his English ally or Scottish adversary to act.[8]

In the mid-1470s the Scottish government finally moved against John of the Isles and Angus Oge. The Westminster–Ardtornish agreement had proved to be an ill-advised piece of work for the lordship. When judged in the context of fifteenth-century Scottish politics, including the increased power and visibility of Clan Campbell in Argyllshire, John should not be faulted for attempting to arrest the waning of MacDonnell hegemony. The pact with Edward IV failed partly because of the turmoil associated with the Wars of the Roses in England, which prevented any significant aid from flowing north of the Borders. John, then, faced losing his patrimony. The Edinburgh parliament declared him a traitor and confiscated his estates, but these territories (except Knapdale, Kintyre, and the earldom of Ross which were annexed to the crown) were returned to him in 1475–6 in exchange for his submission. He also was reinstated as lord of the Isles, but found loyalties among his clansmen divided between him and his son, Angus Oge. The two MacDonnell leaders met in a naval engagement off the point of Ardnamurchan. The battle of Bloody Bay (*c.* 1481) witnessed Angus triumphant and signaled the growing weakness of John's hold over the lordship.[9]

The final forfeiture of the MacDonnell lordship of the Isles came in

1493.[10] In the late 1480s John again sought an alliance with the English. The Scottish king quickly learned of the negotiations and stripped the lord of the Isles of his title and estates. The painful end to a golden age of Celtic society in the Hebrides dragged on until 1503, when John died destitute in a common dwelling house in Dundee.[11]

The demise of the lordship of the Isles actually had begun in the first quarter of the fifteenth century with the divergent interests of Donald, second lord of the Isles, and his younger brother, Ian Mor MacDonnell. Since the lordship's inception, Clan Donald and associated septs had been firmly within the Scottish national community, despite their opposition to the crown. But the split between Donald and Ian Mor MacDonnell moved a significant part of the family effectively outside that community even before the remnant lordship was banished in 1493. Donald's attraction to the affairs of the Scottish mainland contrasted with Ian Mor's attraction to the affairs of the Glynnes of Antrim in northeastern Ulster. The geographical split between these brothers brought on a decentralization of power within the lordship and the subsequent fragmentation of authority among the various branches of Clan Donald. The demise of the MacDonnell lordship forced the descendants of both Donald and Ian Mor to play their own hand outside the Scottish national community in the sixteenth century. By keeping the MacDonnells on the fringe, Edinburgh had refused them a legitimate role in Scotland's political development.[12] But because of the efforts of Ian Mor, Ireland beckoned many Clan Donald refugees.

The MacDonnells of Antrim originated through the marriage of Ian Mor MacDonnell (d. 1427) to Marjory Bisset. He was the second son of John, first lord of the Isles, and she the daughter of Sir Hugh Bisset and heiress to the Glynnes of Antrim. The Bissets had obtained territory in the Glynnes in the mid-thirteenth century from the de Courcy earls of Ulster. The union of Ian Mor and Marjory Bisset about 1400 opened the way for the second large migration of Gaelic Scots into Ireland, which consisted mainly of settlers from the southern branch of Clan Donald.[13]

Ian Mor MacDonnell's attraction to the Glynnes of Antrim resulted from several factors, chief of which was his position as a younger son of the lord of the Isles. The sons of Donald, his elder brother, stood in line ahead of him in succession to the lordship. Though he was designated as Donald's "tanister", Ian Mor realized after the birth of his brother's first male child that he would have to seek his fortune elsewhere.[14] Before he acquired title to the Bisset lands in Antrim, Ian Mor already possessed the constableship of Dunyveg Castle in Islay and the castles of Saddell and Dunaverty in Kintyre.[15] The addition of the Glynnes of Antrim gave him a place of refuge from the shifting fortunes of Scottish politics, and upon the death of his father-in-law, Ian Mor became known as the lord of Dunyveg and the Glynnes. At the time of his own death at the hands of the Clan

9

Campbell in 1427, Ian Mor had established a firm foothold in Ulster for his progeny.[16]

The death of the first lord of Dunyveg and the Glynnes caused a large-scale migration of MacDonnells to the Antrim shores. In the aftermath of Inverlochy (1431), Ian Mor's son and heir, Donald Balloch, second lord of Dunyveg and the Glynnes, fled there to escape the clutches of the Scottish king. Donald's ability to shield himself from the wrath of James I attests to his father's wisdom in establishing a MacDonnell refuge in Ireland. Aided by the O'Neills of Clandeboy, with whom Donald Balloch arranged a marriage alliance, he quietly strengthened his hand until the death of his cousin Alasdair, third lord of the Isles, near mid-century. Thereafter, Donald Balloch emerged from the wooded Glynnes to assume once more an active role in the fortunes of what now can properly be called Clan Ian Mor.[17]

By the middle of the fifteenth century it is not difficult to trace the parallel rise and decline of Clan Ian Mor and the lordship of the Isles, respectively. While Donald Balloch was a fierce and capable heir to the first lord of Dunyveg and the Glynnes, Alasdair and John (the third and fourth lords of the Isles) proved to be quite the opposite in character. The future of the Gaelic heartland thereafter lay in the capable hands of the descendants of Ian Mor MacDonnell. The aftermath of the Westminster–Ardtornish treaty provides a good example of the contradictory fortunes of the two branches of Clan Donald. While John fourth lord of the Isles, never recovered from the failure of the enterprise against James III, Donald Balloch, by far the greatest military threat to Edinburgh, escaped with his territories intact and his reputation among his followers unblemished, despite charges of treason. He retired to his lands in Islay where he died in 1476 at a ripe old age, acclaimed as the greatest MacDonnell warrior of his day.

After the death of Donald Balloch, Clan Donald South entered a period of relative inactivity until the final forfeiture of the lordship in 1493. Donald's successor, John Mor MacDonnell, third lord of Dunyveg and the Glynnes, did not long survive his father and played only a minor role in the family's affairs. The Antrim MacDonnells remained aloof from the struggle between John of the Isles and Angus Oge in the 1480s and the uprising of Alasdair of Lochalsh in 1491.[18]

The upheaval surrounding the final forfeiture of the lordship gave rise to the dynamic fourth lord of Dunyveg and the Glynnes, John Cahanagh MacDonnell (d. 1499), grandson of Donald Balloch. Following the lordship's demise, the western Highlands and Isles fell into confusion, as each clan sought to project itself into the power vacuum. Clan Donald itself split into the Dunyveg-Antrim branch in the south and the Sleat, Glengarry, Clanranald, Keppoch, and Glencoe branches farther north. The king of Scots also intervened in hopes of exerting a measure of royal authority in an area where his predecessors had had precious little.

Indeed, James IV quickly journeyed westward to receive the submissions of the lordship's former vassals. John Cahanagh was one of the first chiefs to greet the Scottish monarch. James IV knew all too well how crucial this island warrior's aid would be in securing the crown's interests in the west. In hopes of winning Dunyveg's support, James knighted him and granted him a charter to former MacDonnell lands in Islay and Kintyre, excepting the fortress of Dunaverty on the strategic Mull of Kintyre.[19]

John Cahanagh's loyalty to the Scottish crown stopped where his family's interest began; consequently, James IV's decision to garrison Dunaverty Castle forced Sir John's hand. Dunaverty was the most important point on the Kintyre peninsula for intercourse with northeastern Ireland. The strongpoint lay less than twenty miles by water from the Antrim headlands and served as an important staging area for the movement of troops from Scotland to Ireland. The royal seizure of Dunaverty also stung the pride of MacDonnell, since the fortress had been a traditional family possession. In short, when James IV occupied the castle in July 1494, John Cahanagh immediately set about to re-establish his own authority there. He and his sons stormed the castle moments after the Scottish king sailed away and in full view of their sovereign master (so the story goes), hanged the constable of Dunaverty from the walls.[20]

John Cahanagh's assault on Dunaverty began a period of decline for MacDonnell fortunes in Scotland. James IV, on the forfeiture of the lordship, had moved rapidly to establish the royal presence in the southwestern Highlands. He had occupied Dunaverty and Tarbert castles with strong garrisons (including artillery and skilled gunners), and apparently had not expected any immediate trouble from the MacDonnells. Furthermore, James and his predecessors (at least since 1457) had courted the Clan Campbell as a counterweight to the MacDonnells. But as James sailed away from the Mull of Kintyre in the summer of 1494, he was powerless to avenge John Cahanagh's insult.[21] He knew, however, that Archibald Ruaidh ("the red"), second earl of Argyll, who had succeeded his father in 1492, would be eager to pursue the outlawed MacDonnell chieftain.

The Scottish king's employment of Argyll to hunt down John Cahanagh and his sons turned out to be a stroke of good fortune for Clan Campbell in the short run, but, oddly enough, for Clan Ian Mor in the long run. For the time being, however, things looked gloomy for the lord of Dunyveg. Argyll turned for assistance to a kinsman of John Cahanagh, John MacIan of Ardnamurchan. MacIan's family was locked in a dispute with Clan Ian Mor over certain lands in Ardnamurchan. Nonetheless, he enjoyed Sir John's trust, and Argyll knew this might present MacIan with an opportunity to seize the MacDonnell leader unawares. Shortly before the storming of Dunaverty, James IV had granted MacIan a charter for part of Islay, a scheme the king of Scots undoubtedly designed to foment discord between these two branches of Clan Donald. John Cahanagh and his family spent considerable time at their residence at Finlaggan, and it was there that MacIan finally laid hold of his prize.[22]

There is some dispute as to the date of and circumstances surrounding the capture of Dunyveg and his sons, and, even more importantly, exactly whom MacIan handed over to the king in Edinburgh. First of all, it is unclear whether the MacDonnell leaders were captured and executed in 1494 or in 1499. Most contemporary annalists posit 1499 for the execution year. Among them, the Four Masters noted that in October 1495 "Alexander, the son of Gillespick MacDonnell . . . was slain by John Cahanagh, son of John, son of Donnell Ballagh. . . ."[23] Sir John, then, appears to have been active in Ulster affairs well after 1494. There is also some question whether MacIan took the MacDonnell outlaws by force or by trickery. Whatever the case, once in Edinburgh they were cast into prison, tried, and executed. Another royal grant in Islay to MacIan in March 1499 speaks inconclusively of "the taking, transporting, and handing over to us of our rebels. . . ."[24] Considering the strength of John Cahanagh's position in Islay, it is unlikely that MacIan tipped his hand. Rather he probably convinced Sir John to make amends with the king in person, especially since it had been five years since the Dunaverty affair. Once Sir John and his sons were away from their followers they were seized and transported under guard to the capital. There is also some doubt that John Cahanagh's father, John Mor MacDonnell, was among those executed on the Boroughmuir in Edinburgh. It is clear that Sir John and at least two of his sons fell victim to the treachery of MacIan of Ardnamurchan in 1499.[25]

The fate of John Cahanagh points up the consequences of the breakdown of a political unit the size of the lordship of the Isles. When this type of dislocation occurs, power is usually diffused among smaller groups – in this case, the individual clans that had formed the lordship – which results in heightened tensions within the vacuum and the intervention of more powerful outside forces. With the demise of the lordship and the extension of royal power by Campbell proxy, the Edinburgh regime temporarily filled the void in the western Highlands and Isles. The Scottish crown managed a precarious hold on this area until the latter half of the sixteenth century, when English pressure forced a changing of the guard and the creation of another vacuum not so readily filled. Clan Ian Mor was fortunate to have had a place of refuge on the Antrim coast when the lordship fell and John Cahanagh perpetrated his misdeeds. The family appeared to have reached its nadir amid the resulting confusion. Into the breach, however, stepped Alasdair Cahanagh MacDonnell, the eldest son of Sir John Cahanagh, and without question the most able chieftain in the illustrious history of his family to that time.[26]

Alasdair Cahanagh MacDonnell (d. 1538) began his tenure as fifth lord of Dunyveg and the Glynnes on his family's lands in Antrim. His father's execution and the pro-Campbell policies of James IV caused a floodtide of Scottish emigration into the Glynnes around 1500. As the eldest surviving son of John Cahanagh, Alasdair found himself banished from Scotland and his family's lands there expropriated by the crown. The exodus of Clan Ian Mor from the southwestern Highlands and Isles to the Glynnes of Antrim, in retrospect, proved fortunate for Alasdair Cahanagh and his sons. While their Scottish patrimony lay forfeit for much of the first half of the century, the MacDonnells established a firm foundation in Ireland. There they held their own against the native Irish, the English, and their Scottish rivals. The fierce and independent-minded MacDonnells flourished so well in northeastern Ulster that they set in motion changes that altered the balance of power in that region for the next century.[27]

Alasdair Cahanagh's strong position in Ireland immediately after his father's death did not deter MacIan of Ardnamurchan, who crossed the North Channel in pursuit. A MacDonnell history contained in *The Book of Clanranald* conveys that MacIan "expended much wealth of gold and silver in making axes for the purpose of cutting down the woods of the Glens, in the hope that he might be able to banish Alexander, son of John Cathanach, out of the Glens and out of the world."[28] MacIan's invasion of the Glynnes did not result in the destruction of Alasdair Cahanagh; rather it brought about an alliance between the houses of Ardnamurchan and Dunyveg when Alasdair married MacIan's daughter Catherine. The marriage ended the feud, but more importantly, it was extremely fruitful. From this union came the next generation of MacDonnells, including Sorley Boy, under whose leadership the family continued to expand its territories and influence in the Gaelic heartland.[29]

Alasdair Cahanagh's marriage to Catherine MacIan allowed Clan Ian Mor to establish a permanent presence in the Antrim Glynnes. Alasdair occupied Dunanynie Castle, the ruins of which overlook Ballycastle Bay, commanding a breathtaking view of the North Channel and the Scottish islands and mainland beyond. It was at Ballycastle (*Bailecaislein*), or Mairgetown as the English called it, that the clan's galleys landed with troops and supplies from Kintyre, Islay, and the southern Hebrides.[30] Dunanynie Castle marked the seat of MacDonnell power in Ulster in the early sixteenth century, but the dynamic Alasdair Cahanagh soon moved southward to establish coastal strongholds at Cushendun and Red Bay. The best indication of his intentions to build a permanent Scottish settlement centered on Ballycastle Bay was the adoption of Bunnamairge Friary as the principal MacDonnell burial-place.[31]

The projection of MacDonnell power into the northeastern corner of Ulster depended both on the establishment of a permanent coastal settlement and on the ability to navigate the treacherous seas separating Ireland from the Scottish Highlands and Isles. Norse invaders had established a seafaring tradition in the Hebrides during the early Middle Ages. Life

13

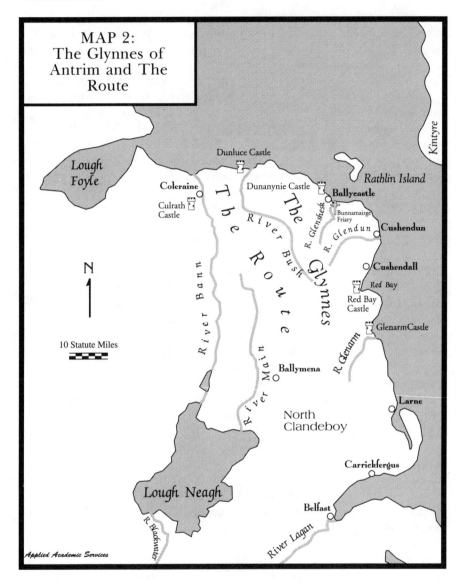

MAP 2:
The Glynnes of
Antrim and The
Route

Lough
Foyle

Kintyre

Dunluce Castle

Coleraine

Culrath
Castle

Dunanynie Castle

Rathlin Island

Ballycastle

The Bush

The Route

River Bush

R. Glenshesk

Bunnamairge
Friary

R. Glendun

Cushendun

The Glynnes

Cushendall

River Bann

N

Red Bay

Red Bay
Castle

10 Statute Miles

River Main

R. Glenarm

Glenarm Castle

Ballymena

North
Clandeboy

Larne

Carrickfergus

Lough Neagh

Belfast

R. Blackwater

River Lagan

Applied Academic Services

there indeed could not flourish without reliable water transportation. The Hebridean galley was certainly the most important piece of technology that Alasdair Cahanagh and his contemporary island chiefs possessed. The typical war galley – often inaccurately called a *longfhada* or *birlinn*[32] – was a modified version of the Viking longboat, having a single mast amidship rigged with a square mainsail. The vessel could be powered by the wind or by the force of some two dozen oars. Little has been written about the Hebridean galley, but its importance is evidenced by the frequency with which it appears on the armorial coats of Highland families and on the sculptured monuments of the western Isles.[33]

Since the Scots were firmly entrenched in the Antrim Glynnes and able to navigate the North Channel waters, Alasdair Cahanagh's stock rose in the eyes of both London and Edinburgh. Young Henry VIII, whom Alasdair considered for a short time as a possible ally, was advised that if he did not expel the Scots they would soon drive him "from his whole seignory of Ulster".[34] It was not long before Alasdair pursued just such an anti-English policy. James IV of Scotland then made an abrupt *volte-face*, returning to a conciliatory stance toward the Highland chiefs. Facing a worsening situation with England on the Borders, the Scottish king sought to lure the clans away from an alliance with Henry VIII. James knew that Alasdair Cahanagh could draw English resources into Ulster and away from the Borders or could threaten his own western flank if war should come. Though the Scottish monarch never formally exonerated the MacDonnells of Dunyveg for the Dunaverty affair, he hoped to portray the English as the greater threat to their interests. To this end, James encouraged MacDonnell emigration to Ireland. Continued good relations between the Scottish crown and Clan Ian Mor and its allies might have permanently altered the nature of Edinburgh–Highland politics. But before such a pattern could be established, James IV and most of his nobility (including several important Highland chiefs) lay dead on the bloody heath of Flodden in 1513.[35]

Alasdair Cahanagh's position *vis-à-vis* both Edinburgh and London improved considerably after Flodden. He no longer faced the uncertainty of dealing with James IV nor the pressure to form an alliance with Henry VIII. The new Scottish king, James V, seemed anxious to establish better relations with the Dunyveg MacDonnells, and the youthful English king was engaged on the continent against his French counterpart, Francis I. Alasdair Cahanagh, then, enjoyed a good deal of latitude in conducting his family's affairs. James V's accommodating policy permitted Alasdair to return to Scotland much stronger than when he had left it some two decades before. The MacDonnell chief's return to his native shore resulted in his restoration to royal favor, but he did not forget that Clan Campbell also enjoyed a privileged position under the new monarch.[36] Immediately after Flodden, James V appointed Colin Campbell, third earl of Argyll, "justiciar, sheriff, coroner, bailie, and chamberlain of Kintyre and Knapdale, south and north."[37] In 1513, then, Argyll was the most powerful lord in the Hebrides. The new regime's lack of stability after Flodden, coupled with the conciliatory signals it sent both to Clan Donald and Clan Campbell, almost guaranteed that the interests of the two families would clash. And with England, the only power that could police the region, occupied on the continent, an Argyll–Dunyveg feud appeared likely.[38]

Alasdair Cahanagh's strength in Antrim and the western Highlands and Isles rested partly on the employment of itinerant mercenaries, or "redshanks." These heavy infantry troops swarmed to Ulster during the campaigning season and augmented MacDonnell forces, but were late-comers when compared to the *gallóglaigh*. The redshanks marked the last great migration of Scots to Ireland in the sixteenth century, hiring themselves out mainly to the Antrim MacDonnells and their Irish allies. Redshank troops, in fact, were a chief's most valuable asset during the sixteenth-century struggles in the Gaelic heartland.[39]

The conflict between Alasdair Cahanagh and the house of Argyll initially centered on the attempt of Sir Donald Galda, chief of the Lochalsh MacDonalds, to revive the defunct lordship of the Isles shortly after the death of James IV. Donald, who seized Urquhart Castle on Loch Ness in November 1513, was joined in the uprising by the Duart MacLeans and the Dunyveg MacDonnells. Argyll and MacIan of Ardnamurchan moved quickly to quell the troubles, but because of the weakened state of the Scots' military after Flodden, they employed diplomatic means to restore order. The Lochalsh "rebellion", though of little political consequence, clearly illustrated that Clan Campbell now served as the crown's policeman in the Gaelic west. Alasdair Cahanagh soon learned that Argyll's paramount concern was to further the interests of his own family at the expense of the MacDonnells.[40]

Alasdair Cahanagh wisely made his peace with Argyll after the extension of *de facto* Campbell hegemony over former MacDonnell territories in the Hebrides. MacIan's death in 1519 caused Alasdair to agree to a bond of gossipry with Sir John Campbell of Cawdor (Calder or Caddell), brother of Colin, third earl of Argyll. The MacDonnell chief received the greater part of the old Dunyveg estates in Islay and the island of Colonsay in return for acknowledging Campbell as his overlord and agreeing not to harm MacIan's survivors who resided there. Each leader also agreed to serve as godfather for the other's children. Alasdair Cahanagh's pact with Campbell of Cawdor was not a submission, but rather a realistic reaction to the prevailing situation in the Hebrides.[41] In 1517 Argyll had been appointed Lieutenant of the Isles with authority to "treat with the Islesmen for the remission of their crimes", Alasdair Cahanagh being the notable exception.[42] Rather than face the formidable Edinburgh–Campbell alliance, the Dunyveg chief turned his attention to the affairs of Ulster.

Troubles with Clan Campbell in the Hebrides after 1520 sharpened the importance of the MacDonnells' Ulster refuge. From the Antrim Glynnes Alasdair Cahanagh worked to extend his influence southward and westward. In 1522 Irish annalists reported the outbreak of war between the O'Neills and O'Donnells. Alasdair joined the conflict, first on the side of the O'Neills, but in 1524 he reportedly stood ready to assist both Irish families. Whatever the case, the MacDonnell chief obviously became deeply involved in the warfare and politics of Ulster (and even Connacht) in the 1520s, thus establishing an important precedent for his successors.[43]

During his active stint in Ulster affairs in the 1520s, Alasdair Cahanagh never forgot the importance of his family's traditional holdings in Scotland; therefore, when the opportunity arose in 1528 to challenge Campbell hegemony in the Hebrides, MacDonnell struck. Without warning, Argyll had withdrawn recognition of the MacDonnell claim to lands in Kintyre granted by the Regent Albany in 1522. The king of Scots also ordered other revocations in 1528. Alasdair Cahanagh suspected Campbell complicity from the start, and with the MacLeans and others he ravaged Campbell territories. By summer 1529 the western Highlands and Isles were in open rebellion. Argyll appealed to James V for aid to put down the uprising, but little came. Instead, in early 1530 Edinburgh attempted to arrange a ceasefire with Alasdair Cahanagh. MacDonnell wasted no time in seizing the opportunity to make his case against Argyll to James V. Over the next two years Alasdair Cahanagh proved himself a shrewd diplomat.[44]

Alasdair's demonstration of strength and his willingness to negotiate in 1530–1 apparently convinced James V to establish a balance of power in the west between MacDonnell and Campbell. Edinburgh's position should have been clear to Argyll and Campbell of Cawdor in the previous year when the king had ignored their requests for military aid. Scottish officials suspected Argylll and Cawdor of using their positions (and the government's resources) to further Campbell interests in the west. Upon Argyll's death in 1530 and the accession of his son, the fourth earl, Archibald Campbell, the king began planning a royal progress to the Isles for the winter of 1530–1. The journey's goal would be to quell hostilities and bolster the crown's influence among the clan chiefs.[45]

To further crown policy in the west the king increased the power of Alasdair Cahanagh at the expense of the new earl of Argyll. Alasdair decided in 1531 to open negotiations with James V before the king provided Argyll with military support. Dunyveg, having gone over Argyll's head, was granted a royal pardon and safe conduct to meet the king at Stirling, where he submitted in early June. Alasdair received title to his family's lands in Kintyre and the Isles as payment for his pledge to act as the crown's agent for keeping order and collecting taxes and rents in those areas. To ensure his loyalty, Alasdair Cahanagh gave his eldest son and heir James as hostage.[46]

The MacDonnell chief so impressed James V that Argyll became alarmed and brought a number of wild, unsubstantiated charges against Alasdair. Since Flodden, the Campbells had made numerous enemies within Scottish ruling circles because of their self-aggrandizing policies in the Highlands and Isles. Argyll's behavior contrasted markedly with that of the cool-headed MacDonnell. The more the Campbell chief raved about his bogus list of Alasdair Cahanagh's crimes, the deeper the dungeon he dug for himself. When Argyll could not substantiate the charges against his adversary, he was publicly disgraced and quickly fell from favor with the crown. Allowed to retain his vast Argyllshire estates, he nonetheless lost authority in the Isles to Alasdair Cahanagh.[47]

Alasdair Cahanagh's restoration of Clan Ian Mor to prominence in the affairs of Scotland marked a shift in the prevailing alliance system and balance of power in the Gaelic heartland. Relations that had been complicated under the lordship of the Isles now became even more so. For the remainder of the century the affairs of the western Highlands and Isles and of Ulster would become more and more intertwined because of a power struggle between the English and Scottish crowns and their continental allies and enemies, the various Dublin administrations, the native Ulster Irish, the earls of Argyll, and, most importantly, Clan Ian Mor.

The forceful return of the MacDonnells to Scottish politics in the early 1530s brought a temporary peace to the Gaelic west. Though he tried, Argyll failed to move closer to the London government. Good relations between James V and Alasdair Cahanagh continued in 1532, as the latter caused trouble for the English by invading Ulster with 8,000 troops, an unusually large force for the time and place. More importantly to Alasdair, the invasion increased his own influence westward into Tyrconnell and Connacht. Given his possession of a powerful army and the goodwill of James V, it is not surprising that MacDonnell consolidated his position as lord of Dunyveg in the 1530s.[48]

After having regained his lost patrimony in Scotland in 1531 and invading Ireland the following year, Alasdair Cahanagh spent most of the remainder of his life in Ulster. His eldest son and heir James remained at the Edinburgh court under the stern tutelage of William Henderson, dean of Holyrood. James V realized the value of the MacDonnell alliance and thus sought to perpetuate it through influencing Alasdair's successor. MacDonnell's younger sons – Angus, Colla, Alasdair Oge, Donnell Gorme, and Sorley Boy – ranged far and wide with their father as he tended to his affairs in Ulster. The English and the native Irish chiefs quickly recognized that Alasdair Cahanagh and his sons posed a threat to their own positions. And since the MacDonnells' star was rising in the Hebrides as well, the family's source of redshank recruits appeared secure. The continued influx of Scots mercenaries into Ulster assured that the Antrim MacDonnells would possess the means to challenge all comers in the north of Ireland. As

Alasdair Cahanagh aged, it became clear that his younger sons would seek their fortunes in Ulster, since the elder James stood to inherit his father's Scottish possessions. In fine, the situation in Ulster at Alasdair Cahanagh's death in 1538 looked favorable for the growth of Clan Ian Mor's power both there and across the North Channel.[49]

Between the establishment of the lordship of the Isles in the fourteenth century and the death of Alasdair Cahanagh in 1538, Clan Ian Mor had become a crucial link joining the southwestern Highlands and Isles of Scotland to Ulster. The various migrations from the Hebrides to Ireland were closely related to its fortunes. MacDonnell claims of hegemony in the area resulted in frequent disputes with the Scottish crown, a situation that the English were oftentimes quick to exploit. The resulting struggle with the Edinburgh regime gradually weakened the lordship's hold in the west and helped to bring about its demise in 1493. Before the lordship fell, however, the mantle of MacDonnell leadership had passed to Clan Ian Mor.

The post-1493 rise of Clan Ian Mor marked a fateful transfer of power to a family – the MacDonnells of Dunyveg and the Glynnes – well positioned to benefit from the chaos. In 1500 the family already enjoyed control over a strategic portion of northeastern Ireland, territory that provided both a refuge and a staging area for further expansion either westward into Ulster or eastward back into Scotland. John Cahanagh MacDonnell and his son, Alasdair Cahanagh, laid solid groundwork for Clan Donald influence in Antrim. Moreover, the latter's superb diplomatic maneuvering in the 1530s re-established the family's influence in the southwestern Highlands and Isles. But Alasdair Cahanagh's most important and lasting contributions were his offspring, most notably his eldest and youngest sons, James and Sorley Boy MacDonnell.

Chapter Two
Into The Maelstrom:
James MacDonnell and the
Gaelic Heartland, 1538–50

> Clan Donald with him in full numbers
> As oaks that overtop the oakwoods;
> Of Ireland's warriors and Islay's mercenaries
> Men they are, strenuous, excelling.

Tadhg Dall O hUiginn

To survive in the rough-and-tumble Gaelic world demanded toughness of mind and body; to prosper required something more, something best described by the Yiddish term "chutzpah" – effrontery, impudence, or gall. The younger sons of Alasdair Cahanagh had been trained as warriors, their education being entirely military.[1] Their martial careers continued to flourish in the service of James MacDonnell, sixth lord of Dunyveg and the Glynnes. As James's lieutenants from 1538 to 1551, Sorley Boy and the others developed the skills that made the Antrim MacDonnells the dominant Gaelic family in Ulster in the last half of the century.

As the eldest son of Alasdair Cahanagh, James MacDonnell early on was groomed to succeed his father as chief of Clan Ian Mor. The year of James's birth cannot be determined, but in the early 1530s he studied under the dean of Holyrood at the Edinburgh court of James V. Since Alasdair Cahanagh and Catherine MacIan were married about 1500, it seems likely that James would have been born shortly thereafter. If indeed he was born in 1501, James could have been no more than thirty years of age when he arrived in Edinburgh.[2]

James MacDonnell's presence at the Scottish court in the 1530s gave the Edinburgh regime an opportunity to influence the future affairs of Gaelic Scotland. Under the dean of Holyrood, the MacDonnell heir learned to read and write – knowledge that most Highland chiefs lacked – and to move with confidence in courtly circles.[3] The crown's interest in MacDonnell *fils* stemmed from a desire to continue good relations with Clan Ian Mor after the passing of MacDonnell *père*. James V hoped to increase his own power in the west of Scotland by constructing a viable balance between MacDonnell and Campbell.[4] Young James MacDonnell weighed heavily in the king's plans. While at court, the Dunyveg heir met his future wife, Lady Agnes Campbell, daughter of Colin, third earl of Argyll, and sister of Archibald, the fourth (and present) earl.[5] The legality of James's marriage in 1545 has been questioned on the ground that Lady Agnes had already wed the sheriff of Bute;[6] nonetheless, she was always publicly acknowledged as James's wife, and the marriage proved a wise political move by Edinburgh, since it secured MacDonnell's loyalty to the Scottish crown.[7] Regardless of whether the union of James and Lady Agnes gave advantage to the Stewart dynasty, the match undoubtedly was the dominant matrimonial alliance in the Gaelic heartland until the widowed Agnes married Turlough Luineach O'Neill in 1569.

After the death of Alasdair Cahanagh in 1538, there is little question that James V expected the new lord of Dunyveg to follow his father's good example of harassing the English in Ulster. Indeed, just as young James assumed the mantle of leadership, the English moved to banish the Scots from Lecale in eastern Ulster. It is likely that Dunyveg's younger brothers, including Sorley Boy, had been involved there and elsewhere. In autumn 1538 Lord Deputy Leonard Gray entered Lecale and took Dundrum Castle, a fortification he described as "one of the strongest holds that ever I saw in Ireland, and most commodious for defense of the whole country of Lecale, both by sea and land. . . ."[8] Like most pre-Elizabethan English forays into Ulster, Gray's did not permanently alter the balance of power. The campaign did, however, point up Dublin's sensitivity to the presence of Scots in Ulster. Dundrum's strategic position controlled access to Lecale by land and sea. Both Gray and the Scots understood as much, which made the castle a plum of some note. It was the Dundrums of Ulster, or more precisely the points of coastal access, that both the MacDonnells and the English saw as the keys to controlling the province from without.

James's initiation into the nefarious realm of Ulster politics was softened by his brothers' first-hand experiences there. While James had remained insulated from the treachery and confusion that pervaded relations between the English, the Scots, and the native Irish, the younger MacDonnell brothers had plunged in headlong with their father. At Alasdair Cahanagh's death they were already battle-scarred veterans of a struggle about which their new chief knew very little. Ulster often shook as the provincial Gaelic heavyweights – the O'Neills of Tyrone and the O'Donnells of Tyrconnell – squared off against one another or, as had become more common by the late 1530s, against the English. The ambitions of lesser families such as the MacQuillins, the O'Cahans, the

Magennises, and the Clandeboy O'Neills, among others, fueled an already inflammatory situation. In fact, the blood-soaked pages of contemporary Irish annals reveal a province plagued by almost continuous strife.[9] The triangular contest that would dominate sixteenth-century Ulster politics had begun to take shape just as James MacDonnell came into his Irish inheritance.

Gaelic Ulster and the English Pale, though posing little threat to one another in the first third of the sixteenth century, stood as natural competitors. In the previous two centuries Gaelic Ireland had experienced a cultural revival that had reversed many of the effects of the Norman conquest. With assistance from Hebridean *gallóglaigh* families, the Ulster chiefs had regained much of their lost territory and put the Anglo-Normans on the defensive. Only the lack of Gaelic political unity had kept the Palesmen from being swept into the Irish Sea. But now, as the Tudor dynasty began to solidify its position within the British archipelago, the emerging English merchant-state loomed as a challenge to Gaelic hegemony in Ulster. The Gaels' greatest advantage was their style of warfare – irregular, guerrilla tactics carried out on the rugged and familiar terrain of their homeland. And since there was virtually no political or economic infrastructure for the English to strike, the Scots and Irish presented elusive targets. Ulster indeed deserved its reputation as a graveyard for the careers and bones of English generals. Despite the difficulties of campaigning in Ireland, however, by the 1530s the English had gained a tenuous foothold in Ulster.[10]

To English eyes, Ulster was as strange and barbarous a land as Africa or America. Though not far from England's western ports, and accessible overland through the Pale, the northern province remained a safe haven for the development of an unadulterated Gaelic society. This society was pastoral and politically fragmented between rival family groupings in which alliances changed as often as the winds. Tales of Celtic lawlessnesss abounded in the Pale and were dutifully passed on, no doubt embellished, to London. The English in Ireland understandably were both awestruck and revulsed by the Gaels' unsettled and often violent way of life. But it must not be forgotten that they were reporting scenes foreign to their more "civilized" mien and manner.[11]

Ulster was an undeveloped, rough-cut marchland or frontier that in the sixteenth century represented the largest single unit in the Gaelic heartland. Based on the *tuath*, the central political unit usually covering 300 or more square miles, a tribe or family was ruled by an *oir rioght* (*urraight*) or sub-chieftain, through the strength of his freeholders and *gallóglaigh* and redshanks. The sub-chieftain's troops were maintained by a system of *buannacht*, or a levy of rations and goods from the local populace. Above the *oir rioghtha* and their *tuatha* stood the chiefs (*ceannfine*) of the great ruling families – the O'Neills of Tyrone and the O'Donnells of

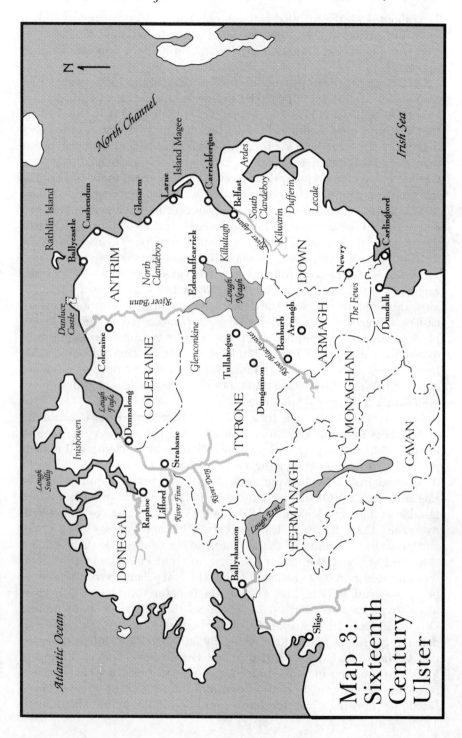

Map 3:
Sixteenth
Century
Ulster

Tyrconnell – who controlled a "country." These chiefs, in theory, relied upon the "rising out" of their sub-kings; thus the struggle for power in Ulster frequently depended on the loyalty and military prowess of the *oir rioghtha*.[12]

Gaelic localism, disunity, and internecine strife in the 1530s made Ulster a target for English meddling. The two great chiefs of the province, Con Bacagh O'Neill (d. 1559) and Manus O'Donnell (d. 1563), the driving forces behind the Geraldine League, became the first victims of a policy that from 1534 onwards defined the Irish problem as internal rather than external. The Anglo-Irish aristocracy had never managed to govern Gaelic Ireland effectively. By the sixteenth century, then, these Old English families were vulnerable to being pushed aside by a more aggressive wave of New English adventurers. In the previous century the house of York had demonstrated the strategic import of Ireland, and now Henry VIII feared the island might become a target for a continental foe.[13] Consequently, he sought to dominate it, thus ushering in a new era of violence.

London's plan for controlling Ulster had originated in the 1470s when England formed an alliance with the O'Neills. In the absence of a resident lord, the only way to curb the growing power of the Scots and Irish in eastern Ulster was to accommodate the province's ruling family. In the previous decade London had given up trying to persuade an Englishman to take the earldom of Ulster.[14] But by the 1530s the Tudor dynasty, aided by the crafty earls of Kildare, had established some measure of influence over the O'Neill chiefs. After 1534, however, the English king desired an even firmer hold over Gaelic Ireland.

The subjugation of Gaelic Ireland required a much greater expenditure of resources than the English had been willing (or perhaps able) to risk before 1534. Instead of pursuing costly military actions, Henry VIII initially preferred to negotiate with the O'Neills and O'Donnells. In the 1530s these great Irish lords had put aside their differences and united against England. But Con O'Neill began to drift towards an accommodation with London at mid-decade; Manus O'Donnell, too, swore fealty to Henry VIII. By spring 1538, however, Con reasserted his authority as the O'Neill and preyed upon some of the northern towns of the Pale. Con Bacagh alone did not have the military strength to conduct anything more than sporadic raids. In fact, Felim O'Neill, chief of Clandeboy, was said to be as powerful as Con. Like O'Neill chiefs before and after, Con knew when to parley and when to fight, and in the late 1530s both he and O'Donnell realized that even together they stood almost no chance of defending Ulster against the English. By late July 1538 Dublin observed that O'Neill and O'Donnell had joined Gerald Fitzgerald in an appeal for aid to the king of Scots. Indeed, the MacDonnells had landed 2,000 redshanks on the Irish coast, ostensibly in support of the proposed Geraldine uprising. The redshank invasion solidified the MacDonnell hold in northeast Ulster, but did nothing to further the cause of the Irish chiefs.[15]

London's blueprint for containing the Ulster Irish involved keeping out the Scots and driving a wedge between Con O'Neill and Manus O'Donnell. The latter objective would be accomplished by promising English protection to each in return for submission to the policy of surrender and regrant. For such a device to be effective, however, both chiefs first had to be dealt with in the field. Throughout 1539 Lord Deputy Gray pressured O'Neill in Tyrone. That Con failed to restrict English movements through his territories suggests that his MacDonnell redshanks were more concerned with consolidating their own position in northeastern Ulster than with protecting their ally's headquarters at Dungannon. Thus the Antrim Scots remained aloof from the conflict for the time being. Gray revealed Con's weakness in February with a fire-and-sword descent upon Dungannon, which the once-mighty O'Neill barely eluded by slipping away into the cold Ulster mist. Con O'Neill finally struck back after bringing together Manus O'Donnell, the Clandeboy O'Neills, and a small contingent of Scots from the Glynnes.[16] In late November O'Neill threatened to invade the Pale's northern marches. Gray thwarted the attempt and "pursued them to a ford called Ballyhoe near the border of Ferney, where he slaughtered many of them and put the rest to flight, on 2 December [1539]."[17] After the battle of Bellahoe the Ulster chiefs began earnest peace talks with Dublin.

In the early 1540s the English employed a heavy hand against the Ulster chiefs to hasten the policy of surrender and regrant. In truth, however, Henry VIII knew that if O'Neill and O'Donnell proved recalcitrant, Dublin would be hard-pressed to subdue Ulster without significant increases in money, men, and arms. And since he wished to rule Ireland with as little expense and trouble as possible, Henry sought first to bluff and then to cajole the chiefs into submission. Meanwhile, the Antrim Scots remained the wild card in Ulster politics. As long as they stood aloof with an open North Channel at their backs, the MacDonnells made it necessary for England to commit military and naval forces permanently in northern Ireland. Not surprisingly, English officials desired a swift agreement with O'Neill and O'Donnell so that the Scottish threat could be isolated and dealt with in its proper turn.

Neither Con O'Neill nor Manus O'Donnell seemed to have been aware of England's Ulster problems in the early 1540s. While Con vacillated between submission and defiance, as he had done previously, Manus quickly reached an agreement with Dublin in mid-1541. The Privy Council in faraway London, unaware of O'Donnell's submission, wrung their hands and suggested that Henry VIII placate the Ulster chiefs. Sir Thomas Cusake, who became Lord Chancellor of Ireland in 1550, advocated bestowing lands and honors upon the Ulster lords. Each side, acutely aware of its own and equally ignorant of the other's weaknesses, advocated appeasement.

O'Neill, had he possessed the requisite military and diplomatic skills and a reliable spy network, might have seized the moment. He dallied, however, and allowed events to control him. As the autumn leaves turned, so did the fortunes of the great house of O'Neill.[18]

Over the next year England mobilized her superior military, organizational, and administrative strength and forced Con Bacagh O'Neill to negotiate from an uncharacteristic position of weakness. In early October 1541 Lord Deputy Sir Anthony St. Leger (d. 1559) reported to the king that he had persuaded many of the native Irish to oppose O'Neill. Con undoubtedly realized that his position was untenable, and in December he wrote an agonizing letter to Henry VIII begging forgiveness and favor. Correspondence between Ulster, London, and Dublin continued throughout the winter of 1541–2 and into the following spring. Both Con and Manus O'Donnell desired to be created earls – the former of Ulster, the latter of Sligo. Neither, however, could argue his case from a position of strength; thus Henry refused to entertain their requests. When in late spring 1542 the captain of O'Neill's *gallóglaigh* went over to the English with most of the chief's fighting strength, Con had no choice but to submit.[19]

The story of Con Bacagh O'Neill's humiliating submission to Henry VIII at Greenwich in autumn 1542 is well known to students of Irish history. Con's new title, earl of Tyrone, bore a heavy price – the loss of his traditional Gaelic title and the prestige and influence it commanded among his people. As the first O'Neill to go to England, he kneeled before Bluff King Hal and agreed to conditions similar to those that Manus O'Donnell had accepted the previous year. In return, Con was allowed to hold his lands in Tyrone of the king and to pass them on to his English-designated (but illegitimate) heir Matthew (Ferdorcha) O'Neill, the newly created baron of Dungannon. Succession problems between Con's sons alone proved enough to almost destroy the O'Neills of Tyrone in the coming generation. For now, though, the once proud and haughty O'Neill returned to Ulster a humbled and broken old man, destined to live out the remainder of his days as an impotent vassal of the English monarch.[20]

Con O'Neill's submission in 1542 stands as Henry VIII's greatest success in Gaelic Ulster. Beginning in the mid-1530s, London had installed an English Lord Deputy and provided him with the military and financial wherewithal to ensure greater centralized political control in Ireland. This suggests that Henry VIII, through an able Lord Deputy wielding sufficient power, sought to extend a firmer grip over Ulster than could be achieved by the policy of surrender and regrant. Henry's goal was to subvert the Irish military system, which was based on the *gallóglaigh* and redshank tradition. The submission of the two greatest employers of Scots, O'Neill and O'Donnell, convinced England that she could secure the services of a mercenary army to be billeted upon the Irish people. England faced a twofold problem: she apparently did not understand 1) that the Gaelic mercenary system in Ulster was actually controlled from Scotland; and 2) that those forces that heretofore had served O'Neill and O'Donnell had now thrown in their lot with more reliable employers in Ireland.

The submission of Con Bacagh O'Neill and Manus O'Donnell allowed for a reduction of the English garrison in Ireland to 500 regulars by late 1542. Despite the failure to subvert or gain control of the Scots mercenary system there, England appeared unconcerned about the outright conquest of Ireland or a Gaelic resurgence in Ulster.[21] Before the late 1550s the Tudors did not see Ireland as worthy of conquest.[22] Gaelic Irish society perhaps was not yet sufficiently sophisticated to be governed by the English system. Most English officials saw persuasion and education, rather than coercion, as the proper way to bring order to Ireland.[23] Obviously, then, and for whatever reasons, the submission of O'Neill and O'Donnell opened the way for the Tudors to implement an Ulster settlement based on economy of force. Ireland had been declared a kingdom in 1541, but such a passive policy had little effect on the political realities of the Ulster that James MacDonnell and his brothers knew.[24]

In the early 1540s the fortunes of the Antrim MacDonnells, the O'Neills, and other great Ulster families became increasingly intertwined. The submission of O'Neill and O'Donnell opened Ulster to outside influences from England, Scotland, and Counter-Reformation Europe. Responding, the Antrim Scots and the native Irish moved close together in temporary alliances to face a revitalized English effort in Ulster and to seek a foreign ally. But without an enemy actually in the field to hold their attention, the Gaels of Ulster fell to fighting among themselves. This was not an uncommon occurrence in a society in which the great families saw little benefit in long-term cooperation and, as a result, shifted alliances as situations warranted.[25]

In 1542 the Antrim MacDonnells became involved in a serious quarrel between the O'Donnells and several of the lesser families of the north. Led by Colla MacDonnell, they allied with the MacQuillins, but were severely checked by the O'Cahans near the river Bann. While of little military significance, these skirmishes were important for two reasons: 1) they pointed to the Gaels' inability to overcome petty territorial concerns and concentrate against an outside threat; and 2) they signalled the Antrim MacDonnells' introduction to the fertile lands of the Route.[26]

James V's death in 1542 marked a turning point in the history of the MacDonnells. James MacDonnell at that time lived on his family estates in Antrim, but recently had spent a good deal of time on Islay. Since the lordship's fall in 1493 and the subsequent Dunaverty affair, the family's hold on Islay had been tenuous at best. During James's tenure as lord of Dunyveg, he thus far had concerned himself with Islay and Kintyre while his younger brothers devoted themselves to the family's Irish territories. The quarrels of 1542 demonstrated how eager the younger MacDonnells were to fight to acquire new lands. James's policies toward Islay and Kintyre were shaped more by cautious diplomacy than by impetuous derring-do. So long as James V lived, Dunyveg could count on support in his Scottish claims; but the king's demise opend the way for the powerful earl of Argyll to expand Campbell influence in the southern Hebrides.[27]

The internal politics of the Gaelic heartland increasingly focused on relations between the MacDonnells and the Campbells and their Irish connections. Also, Edinburgh and London had begun to exert external pressure on the region. It was likely that France, too, would interfere in the Hebrides and Ulster, since she now influenced affairs in Lowland Scotland. In September 1542 St. Leger reported to Henry VIII rumors of a planned Franco-Scottish invasion of Ireland.[28] Shortly thereafter an English official advised that "the captain appointed at Knockfergus [Carrickfergus] and Olderfleet may have a galley or bark assigned . . . to keep the seas betwixt Scotland and Ireland, so as the Scots may be driven from further arrival in those parts of the north."[29] St. Leger appeared apprehensive about the pending crisis and asked the king for instructions should war come; however, he discounted rumors of a conspiracy between the major Ulster chiefs and Argyll.[30]

Things remained relatively quiet in Ulster for the rest of 1542 and throughout 1543, except for sporadic quarreling between the MacQuillins and the O'Cahans. The entire region had suffered abnormally cold and wet weather for the past few years, and both grain and livestock were scarce.[31] This further exacerbated the overall political situation in Ulster in 1543, which had steadily deteriorated after the submissions of O'Neill and O'Donnell. At first glance, things appeared calm, and from an English standpoint they were proceeding quite nicely. For the Gaelic subjects of O'Neill and O'Donnell, however, there had been an intolerable shift in the fundamental balance of power. Such proud and warlike people refused to follow a vassal of the Sassenach king, and it took precious little effort to stir them to action. When Argyll's intrigue and the Antrim MacDonnells' ambitions were added to the Ulster brew, it became potent indeed.

The threatening storm finally swept over the Gaelic heartland in 1544–5. Since becoming lord of Dunyveg, James MacDonnell had exerted little influence in Ireland, residing mainly on his Scottish estates. He and Colla now came to Ulster with a powerful redshank army to establish control of the Route. Colla, Sorley Boy, and the others were already familiar with these fertile lands claimed by the MacQuillins. Two years earlier the younger MacDonnells had become involved in the clash along the northern Antrim coast. Now, after the submission of O'Neill and O'Donnell, they were anxious to have James throw in his lot with them. They renewed the MacQuillin alliance and again struck the O'Cahans.[32]

The immediate cause of conflict in the Route stemmed from Manus

O'Donnell's capture of chief Edward MacQuillin's castle at Inishloughan on the Bann, just south of Coleraine. O'Donnell handed over the fortress to the O'Cahans and then moved eastward and took Ballylough Castle, seven miles south of Bunnamairge Friary. According to the Four Masters, O'Donnell "obtained many spoils, consisting of weapons, armour, copper, iron, butter, and provisions. . . . He burned the whole country around, and then returned home safe after victory."[33] As the O'Donnells and the Antrim MacDonnells were supporting the O'Cahans and the MacQuillins, respectively, there loomed the prospects of a bloody struggle in the Route. In contrast to O'Donnell's show of strength, Con O'Neill wrote a pitiful letter to Henry VIII on 1 May 1544, complaining of the former's aggression. For the remainder of the year, resentment smouldered between the various Ulster factions, but their attention was diverted from local affairs by persistent rumors of a Franco-Scottish invasion.[34]

The prospect of a larger conflict in the Gaelic heartland in 1545 involving the kingdoms of England, Scotland, and France overshadowed local conflict in the Route and provided the occasion for an attempted resurrection of the lordship of the Isles. In late February St. Leger expected an invasion of Ireland by a redshank host under Donald Dubh, grandson of John, fourth lord of the Isles. Donald had claimed the title for himself and received support from several West Highland chiefs. If this Gaelic resurgence attracted sufficient French military support, England's position in Ulster could be severely compromised. Dublin and London, therefore, set about to exploit a confused and extremely fluid situation. As soon as the Scottish regent, James Hamilton, earl of Arran, learned of the attempted revival of the lordship, he faced the difficult choice of whether to acknowledge the lordship's existence and use Donald Dubh's force in conjunction with the French to invade Ireland or to proclaim against Donald Dubh and risk a revived English–Highland Scots alliance. The English undoubtedly were aware of Arran's difficulties, though St. Leger remained concerned over a possible Edinburgh-backed redshank descent on Ulster. In early June, however, the picture became clear, thanks to the efforts of Matthew Stewart, fourth earl of Lennox. Lennox, a candidate for the regency upon James V's death, was an enemy not only to Arran but to Argyll as well, and in the previous year had secretly negotiated with the island chiefs on behalf of Henry VIII. Arran certainly knew of Lennox's influence in the Isles, and in June 1545 the regent and council decided that their best bet was to proclaim against Donald Dubh and his supporters.[35]

Of all the major Highland chiefs, only James MacDonnell declined to support Donald Dubh's claim to the lordship. In 1544 James had aligned himself with Argyll, a stand that brought Lennox into Kintyre with fire and sword against the MacDonnell chief. Dunyveg took Argyll's position in defending the interests of the infant Mary, Queen of Scots, because of his (Dunyveg's) betrothal to Lady Agnes Campbell and of his growing ambition. The alliance of Arran, Argyll, and James MacDonnell was countered by Lennox, who in early August arranged for negotiations between Donald Dubh's commissioners and English representatives at Carrickfergus. Two months earlier Dublin had reported that Donald Dubh presumably would serve Henry VIII in exchange for an English pension, but the official agreement did not come until August. By swearing allegiance to the English king in return for English gold, Donald Dubh and the island chiefs immediately handed Lennox 4,000 troops and 180 galleys.[36]

As echoes of the chiefs' oath reverberated through Greyfriars Abbey at Carrickfergus, Donald Dubh's thoughts were on the promise of English gold. A week had not elapsed before he was clamoring for money and munitions from Henry VIII. Within a month of the Carrickfergus meeting, details of aid to the new lord of the Isles had been hammered out. Henry agreed to wage 3,000 Scots and to supplement them with 1,500–2,000 Irish troops under the earl of Ormond. Lennox, acknowledged now as the legitimate Scottish regent, would command the entire expedition.[37]

James MacDonnell refused to support Donald Dubh in 1545, even though Dunyveg's younger brother, Angus Uaibhreach ("the proud"), had thrown in his lot with the lord of the Isles. James withstood with difficulty the pressure to join his brother against Edinburgh. But he could not risk defying Argyll, whose influence over Islay and Kintyre had increased markedly under the regency. James's decision to back the Scottish crown against his own brother in 1545 is evidence of his maturity and grasp of the prevailing political situation. Though leaving himself open to charges of opportunism, James MacDonnell displayed leadership qualities befitting a man of his station. James, rather than submit to pressure from his brother to support Donald Dubh, stood his ground and made Angus appear the disloyal party. When Donald Dubh died not long after the Carrickfergus conference, James's stock rose even higher among his peers.[38]

James MacDonnell's firm position in late 1545 stood in start contrast to the confusion that befell the now leaderless island chiefs. Quarreling over a pittance from England and still awaiting material aid, they disbanded. When imminent danger forced their hand, they looked to Dunyveg for leadership. Though MacDonnell had refused to join the uprising and nominally sided with Arran and Argyll, he actually remained neutral. Both Arran and Lennox had striven to keep the other from exploiting MacDonnell power. When the Hebridean chiefs chose James to succeed the late Donald Dubh, Lennox, on behalf of Henry VIII, again suggested that English aid might be forthcoming to the lordship. Henry VIII, however, was more concerned with continental affairs and the Scottish Lowlands than with supporting a Gaelic rebellion in the Hebrides. His main objective there turned on keeping MacDonnell military strength out of Arran's hands.[39] Arran, too, scurried to retain James's loyalty (or at least his continued neutrality). Earlier in the year

Edinburgh had granted certain lands in Kintyre and Islay to James and his brothers:

> In 1545 Queen Mary, for the good service done in her minority by James MacDonnell of Dunyveg and [the] Glynnes, especially in opposing the English the ancient enemies of the kingdom, granted to him the barony of Bar in North Kintyre, with remainder successively to his brothers Angus, Colla, Charles [i.e. Sorley Boy], Alasdair, and Donnell Gorme MacDonnell, and to his own male heirs whomsoever.[40]

Now, however, Arran and Argyll realized that more was necessary to keep the MacDonnells from moving closer to the English. While Arran had already played his trump card – the grant of lands to James and his brethren in Kintyre – Argyll held out. In order to placate James MacDonnell, Argyll arranged at last for him to wed Lady Agnes, whose dowry included additional lands in Ardnamurchan.[41]

James's flirtation with the lordship of the Isles in 1545–6 impressed upon him the risks of drawing too close to either the English or the Lowland Scots. From Ardnamurchan in January 1546, he informed the Irish Lord Deputy that:

> We, James MacDonnell of Dunyveg and the Glynnes, and apparent heir of the Isles, grants us to send [a] special letter, direct from your Lordship to our kinsmen and allies, touching the effect and form of their promises to the King of England's majesty, to fortify and supply our noble cousin Matthew, Earl of Lennox. Wherefore, we exhort and praise your Lordship, my deputy of Ireland . . . to show in our behalf, and express to the King's majesty, that we are ready, after our extreme power, our kinsman and ally, namely our cousin, Alan MacLean of Gigha, Clanranald, Clancameron, Clancayn, and our surname, both north and south to take any part with the said Earl of Lennox, or any order whatsoever, the King's majesty pleases, to have authorized or constituted by his grace, in Scotland. . . .[42]

In writing to St. Leger, James tried to secure his goodwill by using him as an intermediary to communicate with Lennox and the King. MacDonnell was in the midst of a Scottish political tug-of-war. He could not afford either to alienate Argyll or to cast away the mantle of leadership bestowed on him by his kinsmen. But his most important consideration in contacting St. Leger concerned his family's situation in Ulster. Because Argyll's star was on the rise, James, after having consulted his brothers, undoubtedly saw the Antrim Glynnes and the Route as offering more opportunities for expansion at the moment than did Scotland. In remote Ulster the power of the English king, the Scottish regency, and Clan Campbell would be greatly diminished, and only the native Irish would stand in the way of MacDonnell ambition.

James's letter to St. Leger contained an offer to cooperate with Lennox in the spring of 1546 if England would provide ships and supplies.[43] But English aid never materialized, and James MacDonnell was relieved that it had not. After the trouble in the Isles faded, he affected a reconciliation with Argyll and the Scottish crown that allowed him to secure and enlarge his Scottish possessions. James had lost no favor with the island chiefs, who also were glad that the whole affair had ended. In spring 1546, then, James had come into his own as the chief of Clan Ian Mor. He owed his rise to a combination of political sagacity and good fortune. But all was not well for the MacDonnells. James knew all too well that he was now, at least as a Scottish lord, a *de facto* vassal of the house of Argyll and that his own family henceforth could exert only limited influence in the western Highlands and Isles. As his predecessors had done, James MacDonnell looked to Ulster, where his brothers were carving out claims westward from their base in the Antrim Glynnes.[44]

Donald Dubh's uprising behind them in the mid-1540s, the Antrim MacDonnells began the rise that would make them a formidable power in Ulster for the remainder of the century. They stood openly with the pro-French party in Scotland, a decision that put them at odds with England and almost assured that the two sides would clash in the north of Ireland. They began a rigorous campaign to take the Route and other lands by force of arms or diplomacy. Having Kintyre and Islay nominally in their possession and access to redshank recruiting grounds in the Hebrides, the MacDonnells looked upon Scotland as a relatively stable eastern flank as long as Edinburgh and the earl of Argyll remained friendly. But if Scotland turned cold, the Antrim MacDonnells would face hard times. To guarantee continued support from that quarter, James and his brothers were quick to lend support, when requested, to the prevailing powers in Scotland between 1547 and 1551.[45]

Ulster and western Scotland at mid-century represented a "back door" through which Protestant England's continental enemies might launch a flank attack against the very areas over which the Tudors had yet to exert firm control, including Wales and northern England. The house of Valois, in the person of Francis I (1515–47), though engaged in a long-running contest with the Hapsburg dynasty, kept an opportunistic eye on the Celtic fringe. In the spring of 1545 Francis had set about to recapture the Channel port of Boulogne from Henry VIII. The plan also involved aiding the anti-English factions in Scotland and Ulster. France, though, could spare few troops from her continental commitments, and the attempt in the Gaelic heartland failed. Consequently, when the promise of French material aid was revived after the deaths of Francis I and Henry VIII in 1547, the manpower burden fell squarely upon the Scots islanders in general, and upon the Antrim MacDonnells in particular.[46]

In 1547 Edward Seymour, newly created duke of Somerset, governing in the name of the young English king, Edward VI (1547–53), raised an army to combat the Franco-Scottish problem in the north. Argyll was among the great Scottish lords who countered Protector Somerset's threat, enlisting the support of James MacDonnell. English spies in Edinburgh reported in June that while the earl of Huntly promised to be on the river Forth with 8,000 men in the coming month, Argyll and James were to land a Hebridean army and capture Glasgow. In early July Argyll and MacDonnell landed near Glasgow with 4,000 men and there awaited the arrival of 2,000 more from Ireland. The showdown finally took place at the battle of Pinkie in September, where the Highland archers fled before the combined firepower of English musketeers and warships anchored in the nearby mouth of the river Esk. In desperation, the pro-French Scots appealed to the new Valois king, Henry II (1547–59). A deal resulted whereby young Mary, Queen of Scots, was betrothed to the dauphin, and in June 1548, 6.000 French troops landed at Leith.[47]

The presence of a large body of French troops in Scotland did not bode well for the English in Ulster. Neither did the return of James MacDonnell, who had arrived in the province before the debacle at Pinkie. Rumors abounded that Henry II had decided to support Gerald Fitzgerald by despatching an army to Ireland. According to Dublin, the French were losing their grip on Scotland and would likely shift their efforts to Ireland to maintain a foothold within the Gaelic heartland.[48] Any French blow against the English in Ireland surely would be directed at Ulster.

In early 1549 Ulster provided fertile ground for intrigue against England. London's carefully laid plans for dividing the loyalties of the native Irish, as evidenced by the treatment given O'Neill and O'Donnell in the early 1540s, were coming unraveled. One reason, although not readily apparent at the time, was the emergence of Shane O'Neill, Con's twenty-year-old son, who was destined to be one of Ireland's central figures for the next two decades. For now, however, Shane's role was restricted to local affairs in Tyrone and Clandeboy, while his father and the Antrim MacDonnells made overtures to the French.[49]

England sought to prevent a combination of the MacDonnells and the O'Neills and O'Donnells by aiding the Irish chiefs against the Scots.[50] But Con O'Neill mustered enough courage to meet with Jean de Monluc, the French ambassador, who stopped off in Ulster on his way from Scotland to the continent. Accompanied by Robert Waucop, the blind Scottish bishop, and Angus MacDonnell, de Monluc landed at the mouth of the river Bann, where "we rested [for] . . . three weeks, tarrying upon a . . . Highland bark which James MacDonnell . . . sent from Kintyre with his brother Angus. . . ."[51]

Prospects of a French invasion of Ulster in 1549–50 alarmed the English, especially since de Monluc had the support of the Antrim MacDonnells.

To oppose further Scottish penetration southward from the Glynnes, Dublin sent Andrew Brereton, an English planter and adventure, with a considerable force into Lecale and the Dufferin. Brereton defeated a Scottish contingent in mid-1549, a clear indication that, if pressed, the English would adopt a more militant policy than they had in the early 1540s. In reality, England had little to fear. Though both O'Neill and O'Donnell had listened to de Monluc's proposals, they had no intention of joining the MacDonnells in an alliance with France. By spring 1550 both chiefs were writing to Dublin in great detail of de Monluc's visit and the Antrim MacDonnells' complicity in the affair. Other Irish chiefs, who had hoped for a joint Franco-Scottish invasion, however, did not share O'Neill's and O'Donnell's timorousness.[52]

Decisive French involvement never came to Ulster and the southern Hebrides; thus the Antrim MacDonnells undertook the more practical and rewarding course of expanding their territories in Ireland. During negotiations with France and the Irish chiefs, James MacDonnell had kept mainly to his Scottish estates, allowing Sorley Boy and Colla to run the family's affairs in Ulster. Angus, of course, had been extremely active in de Monluc's enterprise. Little is known of the whereabouts of either Alasdair Oge or Donnell Gorme in the 1540s, though the former received a pardon from Dublin for some unnamed misdeed in the summer of 1550.[53]

At mid-century the MacDonnells at last turned their full attention to the problem of Ulster, and it was then that Sorley Boy began to emerge from the shadow cast by his elder brothers and into the harsh light of Irish history. Sorley and his brothers knew that since James's sons would inherit the Antrim Glynnes, they would have to carve out holdings for themselves and their descendants farther west into the Route and perhaps even into Donegal. But Sorley himself encountered unexpected trouble in 1550. After being apprehended by the English authorities, he was imprisoned in Dublin Castle. Upon his release the following year, Sorley Boy and his brothers began to expand the Antrim MacDonnells' hegemony westward along the coast of northeastern Ireland.[54]

Chapter Three
The Westward Extension of
MacDonnell Hegemony, 1551–9

On aird thuaidh thig an chobhair.
It is from the North assistance comes.

The mid-sixteenth century marked a turning point in the fortunes of the
Antrim MacDonnells in general and of Sorley Boy in particular. Seeing
that the family had turned its full attention to Ulster, the English in
1551–7 sought to drive Clan Ian Mor out of Ireland. But because of
Sorley's and Colla's hard-nosed persistence and James MacDonnell's overall
leadership, the clan stood fast. The MacDonnells' consolidation of the
Glynnes and Sorley's extension of his own authority into the Route began
a fundamental shift in Ulster's balance of power. Clan Ian Mor's hegemony
in the northeast moved the English in 1557–8 to seek its employment as
a counterweight to the native O'Neills and O'Donnells. Thus the 1550s
witnessed the collision of MacDonnell, English, and native Irish interests
in northern Ulster.

Sorley Boy emerged from his year's confinement in Dublin Castle in the
autumn of 1551. The circumstances of his capture are not known,[1] but it
is likely that English authorities recognized the talents of the youngest
MacDonnell brother and the role that he might play in a Franco-Scottish
invasion of Ulster. Sorley's confinement during a period of international
turbulence attending the Habsburg–Valois wars, the Council of Trent, and
the passing of Henry VIII and Francis I suggests that Whitehall feared the
Antrim MacDonnells' ability to foment trouble in the north of Ireland.
Sorley ostensibly was freed in exchange for some important English prisoners; however, he probably was liberated because the Dublin government
feared that to keep him captive too long might provoke the lord of Dunyveg
to undertake military action, a situation that the English were not prepared
to counter at the moment. Ironically, the Antrim MacDonnells' military
potential was the cause of both Sorley's confinement and release.

In late April 1551 Sir James Crofts replaced St. Leger as Irish Lord Deputy. He had been despatched to Ulster in February to hold the main English ports (especially Carrickfergus and Olderfleet) against the expected Franco-Scottish invasion, but was recalled from his field command and made Lord Deputy. Crofts was a moderate reformer who preferred the selective planting of garrisons throughout Ireland to an expensive and bloody campaign of outright military conquest. As long as such a policy was in the ascendancy, the specter of invasion would haunt Dublin and London. The continued infiltration of Scottish redshanks into Ulster under the MacDonnell banner heightened English fears. One of Crofts's first tasks, then, was to close off the northeastern Antrim coasts to these mercenaries. Despite his reservations against field operations, the Lord Deputy decided to use his limited military resources by taking the fight to the enemy before they found him first.[2]

In the first half of 1551 the English sought to penetrate Ulster above an east–west demarcation from Carrickfergus to Lough Erne. Their goal was to secure such strategic points as the outlying environs of Carrickfergus, Armagh, parts of Tyrone, and Rathlin Island. Carrickfergus had been recently resupplied so that it might hold fast on the eastern flank against a Franco-Scottish descent. Armagh received its first English garrison under the command of Sir Nicholas Bagenal, Marshal of the Army in Ireland. Tyrone, seat of the powerful O'Neill family, presented a more complex problem for Crofts. There, old Con Bacagh O'Neill watched helplessly as his sons–Shane and Matthew (the pro-English baron of Dungannon)–fought for position to succeed him. The English pinned their hopes on the illegitimate Dungannon, whom Con was forced to name as his successor. The independent-minded Shane, however, would foil their carefully laid plans before the decade ended.[3]

For England, the key to securing Ulster against further Scottish incursions lay just off the coast near Ballycastle– Rathlin Island. This largely barren rock of nine square miles had been claimed by the MacDonnells in the fifteenth century. It stood in 1551 as a fortified link between Ulster and the southwestern Highlands and Isles of Scotland, as well as a safe haven for the Antrim MacDonnells if things went awry on either mainland. Only the most knowledgeable mariners dared brave Rathlin's treacherous currents.

Crofts invaded Rathlin in the early autumn of 1551 after having done his best to secure the English position on the Ulster mainland. The Lord Deputy and Sir Ralph Bagenal, elder brother of Sir Nicholas and Lieutenant of the Army in Ireland, marched north from Carrickfergus to assault Rathlin on the pretext of revenging the MacDonnells' recent plundering of Clandeboy and the Route. Crofts had about 2,500 men in Ireland (including nearly 500 native Irish), but it is not known how many he commanded on this expedition.[4] Details of the campaign are few and sketchy; it is known that once they reached Ballycastle, the English learned that James MacDonnell had several galleys lying unguarded "at Roode" on Rathlin. Crofts and Bagenal, lacking enough shipping to land more than 200 men at once, hoped to capture the MacDonnell vessels, sail them back to the mainland, and return with 500 men. Several English men-of-war would provide cover for the landing.[5]

Crofts despatched Bagenal and Captain John Cuffe with the first wave of 100 archers and arquebusiers to secure the anchored Scottish vessels. Sir Thomas Cusake described the debacle:

> And as the boat [in which] . . . the lieutenant [Bagenal] and Cuff . . . approached nigh the place where their galleys were, they saw the galleys drawn to dry land. So they could not come by them without danger, and saw a number of Scots towards the same place, which did not yield nor retire for any great gunshot, that was shot out of the ships.[6]

As Bagenal and Cuffe observed the Scots, the unpredictable currents suddenly washed them ashore and into the waiting hands of James and Colla MacDonnell. The two MacDonnell brothers, aware of the impending attack, had joined forces on the isle, James hurrying over from Saddell on the Kintyre peninsula. They slew twenty-five Englishmen and made prisoners of Bagenal, Cuffe, and the others.[7]

When the Lord Deputy began negotiating the release of his lieutenants, he found that James MacDonnell would accept no less than Sorley's release. It is not unlikely that Crofts was looking for just such a face-saving opportunity to be rid of his prisoner before Sorley became the excuse for a MacDonnell attack south of the Carrickfergus–Erne line. Crofts, despite Cusake's glowing report, clearly had been bested by the wily MacDonnells. To save face, he fired a few departing shots at Colla's stronghold of Kinbane Castle, just west of Ballycastle.[8] The episode points up England's military ineptitude in Ulster in the early 1550s. But Cusake, summing up the Rathlin expedition, confidently maintained that "the Scots will no more attempt to inhabit in Ireland."[9]

Upon Sorley Boy's release in 1551 it became clear that the Scots would not only continue to inhabit Ulster but would flourish there as well. Cusake's report indicates that the Antrim colony had grown strong and prosperous under the sons of Alasdair Cahanagh. They supplied the northern Ulster chiefs with redshanks who were "quartered . . . in the Route, Clandeboy, and O'Cahan's country beyond the Bann. . . ." The MacDonnells employed them "when necessary, for their own purposes, but . . . [required] the native population to support them."[10] The situation must have pleased James MacDonnell, for after the Rathlin affair he returned to Kintyre, leaving Colla and Sorley Boy once again to look after the family's Irish estates.[11]

Though the MacDonnells' settlement in Ulster enjoyed a temporary respite from English incursion in the waning days of 1551, events westward in Tyrone threatened to disrupt the uneasy peace. The power struggle between Shane and the baron of Dungannon intensified because of the mistreatment of their father. In May 1551 Andrew Brereton had treacherously murdered two prominent Scots of Lecale–Alasdair and Gillaspick MacRanaldboy MacDonnell–who also were brothers-in-law to Con Bacagh O'Neill. Brereton, acting upon information from the MacQuillins, accused Con of secret dealings with the French. Concurrently, Dungannon, who no doubt saw his father leaning toward Shane, advocated the old O'Neill's imprisonment, an action that Dublin quickly undertook.[12] The fate of the earl of Tyrone moved the impetuous Shane to take up the sword in his defense. Thus he entered upon a stormy career that would last until his tragic death in 1567.

In the early 1550s Shane O'Neill and the Antrim MacDonnells formed a loose alliance to keep the English out of central and northern Ulster. Drawn together by Brereton's example, the Gaels temporarily put aside their problems with each other to face the English. In fact, Crofts had already marched into Ulster in early autumn to counter Shane. The young warrior skillfully avoided a direct confrontation, forcing Crofts to leave troops at Armagh to protect his western flank as he advanced northward. In late October 1551 Sir Nicholas Bagenal noted that a reconnaissance in force into Tyrone revealed that Shane had obstructed the approaches to Con's castle at Dungannon and broken down much of the structure to keep it from being used by the English. Shane's abandonment of Dungannon should not be construed as weak or cowardly behavior reminiscent of his father's in the late 1530s; rather it reflected a sagacious policy that took advantage of the rugged Ulster topography. There certainly were, as Shane knew, more natural obstacles to, rather than avenues for, an English military advance into the north. If conventional troops were drawn into the inhospitable Ulster fastnesses, they could be worn down by guerrilla tactics and finished off by the fearsome Celtic charge. Anglo-Saxon commanders were slow to learn the lessons of Gaelic warfare against both the O'Neills and the Antrim MacDonnells.[13]

While the English remained moderately active against Shane and the Scots in Clandeboy from November 1551 until February 1552, Colla and Sorley Boy advanced their own interests in northern Ulster.[14] During this period Colla and the MacQuillins had moved against the O'Cahans beyond the Bann, venturing all the way into Tyrconnell. Returning, Colla and his men quartered themselves (apparently against MacQuillin's wishes) in the Route and extracted *buannacht* for the winter of 1551–2. To further exacerbate the situation, Colla wooed and won the beautiful Eveleen MacQuillin. The resulting animosity and the tenuous matrimonial "alliance" between these erstwhile partners served as a convenient pretext for a MacDonnell invasion of the Route later in the decade.[15] As Colla stirred up trouble for the MacQuillins in the Route, James MacDonnell and the fourth earl of Argyll were thought to be involved in a plan to solicit aid for the Irish chiefs from Edinburgh. London informed Crofts in late February 1552 that one George Paris had been appointed ambassador to the Scottish court to negotiate on behalf of MacDonnell and Argyll. MacDonnell inroads into the Route and an alliance between the houses of Dunyveg, Argyll, and Stewart boded ill for Crofts's attempts to maintain the Carrickfergus–Erne line.[16]

After Henry VIII's death England had built up her troop strength in Ireland and by 1552 dominated much of the country below the Carrickfergus–Erne line. During Crofts's deputyship London had no intention of reverting to St. Leger's policy of gradual reform.[17] Under St. Leger the influx of rapacious New English adventurers into Ireland had been successfully resisted in favor of promoting Old English interests. But the assumption that Ireland (and Ulster, in particular) could be brought under English control by means other than military conquest and colonization was quickly put aside. The Old English, who were identified with a more conciliatory Irish policy, found themselves out of favor in Dublin by 1552.[18] The New English now controlled policy, and when Sorley Boy stated "plainly that Englishmen had no right to Ireland and said further they [i.e. the Antrim Scots] would never trust Englishmen . . . ," it was to the New English that he spoke.[19]

In the spring of 1552 Cusake wrote a lengthy essay on the state of Ireland, concluding that "Irishmen were never so weak, and the English subjects never so strong, as now."[20] Such optimism might have been justified south of the Carrickfergus–Erne line; farther north, however, things were not going so well for the Sassenach. Their attempts at settlement in Ulster most often had occurred in the southeast. If somehow a colony could be planted on the eastern Antrim coast, it would be a hinge in a frontline defense against the Scots. But at the time of Cusake's report, the Antrim MacDonnells had put together a loose group of alliances that, if its members could overcome their penchant for self-aggrandizement, might drive out the English. The heart of this temporary alliance was the Antrim MacDonnell–Tyrone O'Neill combination, but lesser families such as the MacQuillins and Clandeboy O'Neills also figured prominently. As an example of this cooperation, Colla MacDonnell, fresh off his campaign in the Route, quickly crossed to Scotland, returning with 140 bowmen to aid Hugh MacNeill Oge O'Neill, chief of Clandeboy, in defending his territory against Sir Nicholas Bagenal. Cusake realized only too well England's difficult position relative to the MacDonnell–O'Neill combination. The closest permanent English garrison and supply depot to the Antrim Glynnes lay at Carrickfergus, and it was not long until the Scots attacked the castle there.[21]

Sorley Boy attacked Carrickfergus upon orders from James MacDonnell and thus exposed England's precarious foothold in Ulster. His assault on this principal coastal stronghold and Colla's aid to the Irish in Clandeboy demonstrated the Antrim MacDonnells' determination to protect their southern flank. The Scots did not destroy Carrickfergus as a base of operations, but they did humiliate the English by driving the garrison out of the castle and capturing the constable, Walter Floddy, on whose head they laid a heavy ransom.[22] After such muscle-flexing by Sorley and Colla, James MacDonnell boldly asserted his claim to the Antrim Glynnes, despite London's reference to his "pretended title." In informing Crofts of James's claim, the council had stressed the need to temporize with him: "[W]e have thought meet that you should prolong time with him" in order to "obtain the country wherein the Scots have long resisted the devotion and obedience of his Majesty. . . ."[23] London's policy statement was a frank admission that the MacDonnells, who were cooperating at least for the time being with Shane and other Irish chiefs, posed a problem for which there was no clear-cut solution.

Having struck Carrickfergus, Sorley then withdrew to Ballycastle, probably to plot his next move against the MacQuillins in the Route.[24] While Sorley consolidated his position at Ballycastle, Shane broke loose in Tyrone. In May 1552 Cusake revealed that O'Neill had recently aided the Scots against the English. After meeting Shane, Cusake "perceived nothing in him but pride, stubbornness, and all bent to do what he could to destroy the poor country."[25] Shane's support of the MacDonnells' advance into Clandeboy had won over several Irish chiefs in the area; consequently, later in 1552 Crofts and Dungannon struck Hugh MacNeill Oge and the Scots in Clandeboy. Crofts was repulsed near present-day Belfast, and when Dungannon sought to ride in with reinforcements, Shane gave pursuit and routed his force in a daring night attack.[26]

Shane continued to hound both the English and his rival Dungannon for the balance of 1552 and throughout the next year. Shortly after their night battle near Belfast, Shane and Dungannon met again with much the same result. The almost constant internecine strife and miserable weather during 1552–3 reduced central Ulster to the point of starvation. Grain, when it could be had, quintupled in price. Desperate conditions forced Hugh MacNeill Oge of Clandeboy to leave Shane and submit to the English in December 1552 in return for what proved a meaningless royal grant of the abbey of Carrickfergus and Belfast Castle.[27] Similar logistical problems hampered the English at Armagh, and it was thought that if Con O'Neill were set free perhaps the situation in Tyrone would ease and the Scots then could be "more easily expelled from the northern parts. . . ."[28]

That the English by the mid-1550s recognized the relationship between events in Tyrone and the continued Scottish presence in Antrim suggests that they grasped the potential dangers of any sort of Gaelic alliance, however tenuous. The MacDonnells, who had consistently looked out for their own interests since 1493, were central to any such combination. The Glynnes and the Route lay outside the wide swath of destruction that cut through Tyrone, Clandeboy, and Tyrconnell. So too did the southern Hebrides. The heart of MacDonnell country, therefore, was quiet except for occasional minor disturbances. The Scots' policy of fostering alliances with Shane and other Irish chiefs along the Carrickfergus–Erne line was obviously self-serving, relieving them of a major military responsibility. Thus with a minimum expenditure of men, material, and money, they were able to keep the English at bay. To break the deadlock along this devastated "no man's land," London and Dublin could no longer rely on the relatively inexpensive policy of surrender and regrant. The alternative was a dramatic increase in military expenditures and the commitment of sufficient forces to Ireland to end the stalemate. This course of action would necessarily shift power from Dublin to London and thus into the hands of a new breed of English office-holders and adventurers.[29]

England's Irish policy in the late 1540s and early 1550s had vacillated between reform and conquest, Ulster being the ground on which one or the other would prevail. The ascent of Mary I in 1553 and her subsequent marriage to the future Philip II of Spain (1556–98) gave impetus to a policy of conquest and colonization based on the Spanish model, despite the fact that the target would be fellow Catholics. The arrival in Ireland of Lord Deputy Thomas Radcliffe, Lord Fitzwalter (later earl of Sussex), and his Undertreasurer (and later Lord Justice and Lord Deputy of Ireland) Sir Henry Sidney at mid-decade suggests that London was prepared to implement a vigorous program. Sidney, who had been in Spain in 1554, "began to develop there his undoubted interest in the Spanish empire. . . . We may, therefore, suspect . . . that Sidney was the representative in Ireland of a 'Spanish' policy of treating the Irish harshly and of colonising widely."[30]

When the Ulster Gaels realized that conquest rather than reform would be the prevailing English policy in Ireland, they steeled themselves for the coming conflict. Though the mild-mannered St. Leger had returned as Lord Deputy in late 1553, he found himself forced to look more and more to London for policy directives. But St. Leger did find opportunities–in Clandeboy, for instance–that allowed him to use diplomacy rather than force. Hugh MacNeill Oge died in 1555, and to prevent a family power struggle that surely would bring in other parties, Clandeboy was divided between his nephew Con, who received northern or lower Clandeboy, and his cousin Hugh (son of Felim Bacagh O'Neill), who got southern or upper Clandeboy. But shortly the country became a target for meddling by both the New English and the Antrim MacDonnell–Tyrone O'Neill alliance.[31] The troubles in Clandeboy in 1554–5 had been presaged, so it seemed, by an extremely harsh winter that oppressed Scot, Englishman, and Irishman alike.[32] The MacDonnells, themselves apparently well provisioned, tried to disrupt the English logistical system in eastern Ulster by besieging Carrickfergus, a move they hoped would make desperate an already bad situation and ruin any plans St. Leger might have had for a peaceful solution to the Ulster problem.[33]

London revealed the decision to conquer and colonize Ireland with the despatch of Fitzwalter to replace St. Leger in spring 1556. The Privy Council realized that a man of Fitzwalter's harsh nature was needed to break the siege of Carrickfergus (which was no "siege" at all in the normal sense of the word). After Edward Walshe of Waterford's "Conjectures Concerning the State of Ireland" had been published in 1552, it was clear that the English were moving toward a classical military solution to the Irish problem.[34] But St. Leger's reappointment as Lord Deputy in 1553 had been designed to allay pressing financial problems brought on by increased military spending. Dublin did manage to cut military expenses temporarily, but in the longer run St. Leger's conciliatory policy resulted in even greater hardship for the English in Ireland. England's weakness and a lack of will and direction in her Irish policy had encouraged the MacDonnells and Shane O'Neill to challenge the Carrickfergus–Erne line in 1555.[35] To counter such aggression, Fitzwalter implemented a much more vigorous policy than that pursued by St. Leger. The immediate objective was to safeguard Carrickfergus, for if it fell, England's position in eastern Ulster would be jeopardized. Fitzwalter and Sidney hurriedly marshalled their forces for a campaign into the heart of MacDonnell country.[36]

England's "soft" policy in Ulster before Fitzwalter's arrival had allowed the Scots to entrench themselves in the Glynnes and the Route. An English official opined that "it will be more hard to expel them thence (after they be planted) than to keep them out before they enter."[37] To their credit, some English policy-makers had foreseen the dangers of a MacDonnell–O'Neill combination. In 1555 Whitehall began a concerted effort to disrupt the flow of redshanks to Ireland. Because Irish "rebels" were eager to employ them, Hebridean mercenaries "have of late inhabited in the north parts of this Realm in several places, and have out thereof expelled the very inheritors of the same. . . ."[38] To rid Ulster of this dangerous presence, London undertook in 1555–6 to restrict Scottish access to northern Ireland, warning that it would be a treasonable offense to wage redshanks or to marry, without license, a Scot who was not a denizen of Ireland.[39]

Fitzwalter and Sidney initiated a "hard" policy in Ulster to eradicate the Scottish colony. This demanded that they establish influence in Scotland and control the North Channel and strategic points along the Antrim coast, specifically Carlingford, Strangford, Carrickfergus, Olderfleet, the mouth of the Bann, and Lough Foyle. But the first step was an invasion to destroy the MacDonnells' power base in the north. Until deprived of their foothold in Antrim, Clan Ian Mor would remain impervious to attack on the periphery. The Scots' success in the Carrickfergus area in 1555 drew James MacDonnell back to Ireland early in the following year, where he and his brothers assembled a strong force and several pieces of brass ordnance.[40] Meanwhile, there were reports that the MacDonnell–O'Neill accord was falling apart because of Shane's ambitions. The young O'Neill reportedly "induced Lord Sussex [i.e. Fitzwalter] to proclaim a hosting and march northward against 'the sons of MacDonnell and the Scots, who were working conquests in the Route and Clandeboy.'"[41] As Fitzwalter advanced against the Scots, Shane, according to one contemporary source, submitted to the Lord Deputy at Kilmainham. But according to another, he stood with the Scots during the campaign.[42] Shane, however, likely avoided committing either way in 1556, though he remained a nominal MacDonnell ally.

On 1 July 1556 Fitzwalter and Sidney marched into Ulster to crush the Scottish colony, concurrently despatching four vessels to patrol the North Channel to prevent redshank reinforcements from leaving Scotland. They intended to drive out the MacDonnells and construct a series of fortifications from Dundalk to Lough Foyle, thereby intersecting the Carrickfergus–Erne defenses along a northwestern axis. The drawbacks to such an ambitious plan, besides the obvious expense, involved cutting across the heart of O'Neill territory, a move that would surely raise the ire of the excitable Shane. But O'Neill feigned submission to the Lord Deputy. He knew that the MacDonnells were as much a barrier to his own dominance in Ulster as they were to England's and undoubtedly hoped that both the Scots and the English would weaken their own hands by engaging each other. The two sides met on 18 July in the pass of Ballohe M'Gille Corrough (or Balldromm Clashahe), where the English claimed a victory.[43] Over 200 Scots reportedly fell. But the validity of English battle accounts is called into question by Sidney's fantastic boast:

> In the first journey that the Earl of Sussex [i.e. Fitzwalter] made, which was a long and great and honourable one, against James MacDonnell, a mighty captain of Scots, whom . . . Sussex, after a good fight made with him, defeated and chased him with slaughter of a great number of his best men; I there fought and killed him with my own hand, who thought to have overmatched me. Some more blood I drew, though I cannot brag that I lost any.[44]

Sidney's claim to have slain James MacDonnell, though made more than a quarter-century after the alleged event, was pure braggadocio. James's numerous feats over the next decade certainly were not unknown to Sidney.

Despite English claims of victory, the battle of Ballohe M'Gille Corrough did not diminish the MacDonnell hold on eastern Ulster. The Scots had been bested, as is attested by the departure of James and Colla for Scotland less than a week later. Fitzwalter and Sidney found the approaches to

Glenarm Castle unprotected, "wherein was taken the Scots' keraht [*creaght*] or prey."[45] The loss of some veteran troops, Glenarm Castle, and the all-important livestock thereabout, as well as the hasty flight of James and Colla MacDonnell under cover of darkness and a blowing rainstorm, no doubt humiliated the Scots. But the campaign did not produce the decisive fight for which Fitzwalter and Sidney, or for that matter Shane, had hoped. As 1556 closed, both the MacDonnells and the English prepared for the renewal of the struggle in northern Ireland.[46]

While James and Colla operated in eastern Ulster and the southern Glynnes against Fitzwalter in 1556, Sorley stood guard on the northwestern flank in the Route. His position at Ballycastle was the linch-pin in the MacDonnell defenses that extended along the coast from Glenarm to Dunluce Castle.[47] Because their way south was blocked by the English in North Clandeboy and Carrickfergus, the Antrim MacDonnells looked westward to the Route. And it was to Sorley Boy that they turned to lead them against the MacQuillins, the traditional overlords of that part of Ulster.[48]

Sorley Boy became "Captain of the Route" upon the death of his brother Colla in May 1558, but he had already established himself as *de facto* hegemon there by early 1557. Colla, as described above, had campaigned with James in North Clandeboy in 1556 and had fled with him to Scotland after their defeat. Since Alasdair Oge also was scurrying from one place to another, Sorley remained alone in Ballycastle and the Route for much of 1556–7. In reference to his effectiveness in pushing ahead Clan Ian Mor's interests there and, conversely, to the difficulty which the MacQuillins and their allies had in defending their own, a contemporary manuscript notes:

> When the Scots do come, the most part of Clandeboy, MacQuillin, and O'Cahan, must be at their commandment in finding them in their countries; and hard it is to stay the coming of them, for there be so many landing places between the high land of the Rathlins and Knockfergus, and above [i.e. west of] the Rathlins standeth so far from defence, as it is very hard to have men to be there continually being so far from help.[49]

With favorable winds and tides Scottish galleys could cross between Kintyre or Islay and Ballycastle in two or three hours. Sorley, then, enjoyed a luxury that his elder brothers did not–that of virtually unmolested landing sites, as the passage above reveals, from Rathlin Island to Lough Foyle.

Sorley's affairs in the Route drew little attention from the English, who were preoccupied with James MacDonnell and Shane O'Neill in the Glynnes, Clandeboy, Tyrone, and now in Tyrconnell. In early January 1557 Fitzwalter notified London that James had returned to the Glynnes, ostensibly to aid Hugh MacFelim of Clandeboy, who had recently escaped from Carrickfergus Castle. English officials, however, soon discovered that it was not James MacDonnell, but Shane O'Neill, with whom they had to contend. About the time James returned from Kintyre, Shane invaded Tyrconnell to depose Calvagh O'Donnell, son and successor to Manus O'Donnell. In the 1550s Tyrconnell had been ravaged by constant warfare between Calvagh and his father. Calvagh went to Scotland in 1555 seeking the hand of Argyll's daughter and the strong arms of his redshanks.[50] He returned, according to the Four Masters, "with a great body of Scots, to desolate and ravage Tirconnell," and thereafter imprisoned his father for the rest of his days.[51]

Shane's invasion of Tyrconnell threatened not only the western reaches of the Carrickfergus–Erne line but the balance of power in Ulster as well. If Shane overthrew Calvagh and established himself west of Lough Foyle, it would upset Fitzwalter's plan to build a line of forts from there to Dundalk. As Sorley Boy and the MacDonnells were pushing westward into the Route and Shane was moving into Tyrconnell, the tenuous MacDonnell–O'Neill entente, if it could hang together, might exclude the English from all but a small enclave in southeastern Ulster.

In spring 1557 Shane, accompanied by Hugh O'Donnell (Calvagh's brother), led 4,000 foot and 1,000 horse toward Tyrconnell until he reached Carricklea between the rivers Finn and Mourne (in the parish of Urney, barony of Strabane).[52] According to a contemporary chronicle, "The time was spent very happily in the camp . . . , for they carried on the buying and selling of mead, wine, rich clothing, and all other necessaries." Calvagh O'Donnell, aware of Shane's presence on the Tyrconnell frontier, drove his cattle into the wilds. His army was no match numerically for Shane's; thus he decided to wait for O'Neill to enter his territory in hopes that he could catch him (O'Neill) unawares. As Shane crossed the Finn and encamped near Balleeghan on Lough Swilly, O'Donnell perfected his stratagem.[53]

Calvagh took only thirty horse and several hundred MacSweeney *gallóglaigh* ahead to monitor Shane's progress to Balleeghan. The O'Donnell chief despatched two men, one a kinsman of Argyll, to O'Neill's camp where they "mingled with the troops, without being noticed." The two spies eventually made their way

> to the great central fire, which was at the entrance of [Shane's] . . . tent; and a huge torch, thicker than a man's body, was constantly flaming. . . and sixty grim and redoubtable gallowglasses, with sharp, keen axes, terrible and ready for action, and sixty stern and terrific Scots [i.e. redshanks], with massive, broad, and heavy-striking swords in their hands, [ready] to strike and parry, were watching and guarding the son of [Con] O'Neill.[54]

That evening the two spies returned to O'Donnell with detailed knowledge of Shane's camp. Seeing an opportunity, Calvagh prepared for a night attack. The small contingent of O'Donnell cavalry and MacSweeney heavy infantry advanced "and did not halt until they had reached the central troops that were guarding . . . O'Neill." Calvagh's warriors made "a fierce and furious attack upon the men in the camp, and both armies then proceeded to kill, destroy, slaughter, hack, mangle, and mutilate one another. . . ." Shane, hearing the clash of cold steel and realizing he had been taken by surprise, "passed through the western end of his tent unobserved" and into the rainy darkness. O'Neill traversed the flooded streams and rivers on his flight to Tyrone, but many of his troops drowned. O'Donnell did not pursue, preferring to occupy Shane's camp, where he and his men drank away the remainder of the night.[55]

Shane's repulse by Calvagh, in reality, did no immediate harm to his military or political position in Ulster, just as the Antrim MacDonnells' setback in the previous year had done little to threaten their hold on the southern Glynnes. O'Neill's failure to conquer Tyrconnell and subdue O'Donnell did mean, however, that the resources of that province and its strategic location, which allowed for the turning of the Carrickfergus–Erne line from the west, were denied him. Moreover, the English began to cultivate an alliance with O'Donnell in hopes of using him and Dungannon to destroy Shane. But more importantly, England now undertook to foster discord between Shane and the MacDonnells.

In June 1557 Fitzwalter, the newly created earl of Sussex, received royal approval for another expedition against the Scots in Ulster. Mary I also instructed him to cultivate better relations with the Stewarts in Edinburgh, that they might bring pressure to bear on the MacDonnells' vulnerable eastern flank.[56] In early August Sussex struck northward, accompanied by the earls of Kildare and Ormond. Unlike earlier campaigns against the Ulster Gaels, this one lacked a specific objective, and thus degenerated into little more than a "search and destroy" mission. As Sussex advanced, James MacDonnell and his brothers shadowed him through the rugged fastnesses of northern Clandeboy and the southern Glynnes. But the MacDonnells' refusal to give battle frustrated Sussex's designs. All he accomplished militarily was the capture of some Scottish *creaghts*. Sussex continued on as far north as the Route, where he offered protection to the MacQuillins, who recently had been "banished from house and home" by Sorley Boy.[57]

Sussex's summer campaign of 1557 accomplished little, but it did reveal the untrustworthy character of Shane O'Neill. According to Dublin officials, Shane had made overtures to them during the previous year. But a contemporary recorded that he "did not only refuse to repair to her Majesty's said Lieutenant [i.e. Sussex], but falsely and traitorously did, with all his force and power of men of war, repair to James MacDonnell, conspiring and combining with him against our . . . sovereign . . . Queen Mary." And though James MacDonnell and his brothers were "still reputed as foreign enemies, Shane did contrary to his oath refuse to repair to [Sussex] . . . upon any protection or assurance that [he] . . . could make unto him . . . , [rather] receiving presently into his fostering and keeping the goods and cattle of James MacDonnell and his brethren. . . ."[58] It should have been clear to England by late 1557 that Shane could not be trusted to serve her interests in remote Ulster. Sussex, stinging from O'Neill's "betrayal" during the summer campaign, plundered Armagh twice in October, finding a large store of victuals. There was so much that he could not carry it away, so he burned it instead.[59] A good deal of what went up in smoke doubtless belonged to the MacDonnells, but the loss did not seem to hurt either them or Shane. In November George Dowdall, archbishop of Armagh, informed London that Ulster "is as far out of frame as ever it was before, for the Scots beareth as great rule as they doth wish, not only in such lands as they did lately usurp, but also in Clandeboy."[60]

Dowdall perhaps overstated the gravity of the Ulster situation, especially since the English had not been defeated on the battlefield and the Carrickfergus–Erne line had not been breached. But there is no question that by late 1557 Sussex's Ulster policy was in disarray. Gerald FitzGerald, eleventh earl of Kildare, Gerald FitzJames FitzGerald, fourteenth earl of Desmond, Dowdall, and St. Leger all questioned the deputy's military effectiveness. But Sussex, who loathed the "soft" policies of the Old English, was angered by opposition in the Irish Council. He moved to oust St. Leger's supporters and bring his own into important civil and military positions.[61]

At the beginning of 1558 the Ulster problem was complicated by the outbreak of war between England and France, a part of the wider Habsburg–Valois struggle that had ravaged Europe intermittently since 1494. The Holy Roman Emperor, Charles V (1519–56), had abdicated in 1556, leaving the Habsburg's western domains to his son, Philip II of Spain. Charles had burdened his son with a huge debt of 20 million ducats which forced him to declare bankruptcy shortly after ascending the throne. Philip prevailed upon his wife, Mary I of England, to declare war on France in June 1557, thus giving him a considerable English auxiliary force that was despatched to the continent to serve Spanish Habsburg interests. The French were beaten at St. Quentin in August, but recovered to wrest Calais from the English in January 1558.[62] Because France had tried before to stir up trouble for England in the Gaelic heartland, the outbreak of war in 1557 rekindled the specter of Valois intervention. Sidney feared that James MacDonnell would lead a Franco-Scottish invasion of Ulster, prompting hundreds of disaffected Palesmen to take up arms to further the Gaelic cause. Sussex, too, appeared unnerved, especially by St. Leger's and Dowdall's criticism of his stringent military policies. But the Lord Deputy had enough support on the Privy Council in London, and under these circumstances the government continued to implement an aggressive policy toward the Gaels.[63]

The English were too weak in Ulster to withstand an attack from without, especially one backed by France, while concurrently facing a hostile Sorley Boy in the Route and Shane O'Neill in Tyrone and Clandeboy. To make matters worse, James MacDonnell stood in the good graces of Mary, Queen of Scots, who in May 1558 renewed an earlier grant in Islay and Kintyre to him and his brothers.[64] Because the queen of Scots and her "Auld Alliance" supported them, the Antrim MacDonnells undoubtedly felt fairly secure with their backs toward Scotland. But less than a month later Clan Ian Mor lost Colla, one of its ablest leaders, who died in the vicinity of Bunnamairge Friary.[65] Contemporary sources are silent on the cause of Colla MacDonnell's demise. He had fought at James's side throughout much of his early career, but later earned his reputation with Sorley Boy by taking on the MacQuillins and O'Cahans in the Route. In 1555 he had been made Captain of the Route by brother James. Sussex referred to Colla as "the best of them [i.e. the MacDonnell brothers] . . . that ever continued in Ireland."[66]

Colla MacDonnell's death in May 1558 allowed Sorley Boy to step onto center stage in Ulster at a time when his family needed the continuity of a strong hand there. Sorley's first task was to consolidate MacDonnell gains in the Route and to protect them from encroachment by the English or the native Irish. Sussex noted the changing of the guard after Colla's death,

> since which time James offered the Route to Alysander [Alasdair Oge], who refused it, then he offered it to Eneas [Angus], who also refused it, and lastly he offered it to Sorleboye, who only of all the brothers remaineth in this realm, and hath since that time written letters to me . . . . His meaning is but to win time this summer.[67]

By early summer 1558, then, James had in his youngest brother a leader whom he could trust to handle the clan's affairs in northern Ulster, which shortly were to become extremely complicated. Apparently James was so confident of Sorley's abilities that he felt secure in returning to Scotland with most of his own troops.[68]

While Sorley established himself as the new Captain of the Route, trouble erupted between Shane and the English over the latter's support of the baron of Dungannon. Both sides courted the MacDonnells' favor. It was then, in mid-1558, that England made her first overtures to the MacDonnells in an attempt to use them against Shane. But while Sidney made initial contacts with James MacDonnell and his brothers, he also parleyed with Shane concerning the succession rivalry with Dungannon. Shane insisted that he was Con Bacagh's lawful heir under both English and Irish jurisprudence. Con's agreement with Henry VIII in 1542 had been illegal all along, O'Neill contended, since it was made without proper authority, and because Shane in the meantime had been elected chief by his own people.[69]

By the late 1550s everyone with an interest in Ulster politics knew that Shane's star was on the rise. Consequently, while Sidney negotiated with O'Neill, Sussex despatched an agent to Scotland to solicit Argyll's aid in pressuring Clan Ian Mor to support Dublin's efforts to contain Shane. James, as seen earlier, returned to Kintyre after appointing Sorley Captain of the Route. Sussex hoped that the lord of Dunyveg would persuade Sorley to cooperate with the English against O'Neill.[70] Shane was aware of the pressure Sussex had brought to bear on James and Sorley Boy. O'Neill doubtless put some pressure of his own on Sorley, who realized that Shane could do him more immediate harm than either Sussex or Sidney. At this point, James and Sorley began a series of dangerous diplomatic maneuvers designed to preserve their neutrality. James negotiated with the English and Sorley with Shane. MacDonnell neutrality indeed incensed both the English and Shane. But at the time, it was the family's most advantageous course, as it allowed them to await the outcome of the struggle between Shane and Dungannon before committing one way or the other, or remaining neutral.

Dungannon's death at the hands of Shane's followers in mid-1558 removed the last obstacle to the young firebrand's claim to the O'Neill succession. Edmund Campion, the Jesuit historian and Old English official in Ireland, reported that Shane and his foster brethren, the O'Donnelleys, laid a trap for Dungannon.[71] The Four Masters cited Dungannon's death at the hands of "the people of his brother John [i.e. Shane]; and the cause of his killing was because he was appointed to the dignity of his father, if his father should die before him."[72] According to Sidney, Con Bacagh was not entirely displeased with Dungannon's demise after he had seen "the proof of his lawful son and heir; and thenceforward fancied Shane, put him in trust with all, himself being but a cripple, notwithstanding that Matthew [Dungannon] left issue male which liveth, to whom the inheritance appertained."[73] But Con's opinions mattered little as he neared the end of his days. And because Dungannon was gone, Shane stood alone as the unchallenged leader of the most powerful Irish family in Ulster.

Shane's rise in Ulster created a situation in which three powers–he, the English, and Clan Ian Mor–took center stage for the next decade and introduced a triangular struggle that would climax during the mid-1560s. For now, however, the MacDonnells remained neutral, preferring to strengthen their own hand in the Glynnes and the Route and perhaps to nibble away at territory in northern Clandeboy and west of the Bann. As summer faded to autumn, Sussex undertook another campaign to crush the Scots. Like Crofts's in 1551, his plan called for an attack on the clan's strongholds, especially Rathlin, Islay, and Kintyre. To aid Sussex, Mary I provided enough shipping to transport 1,100 troops. On 14 September Sussex,

Sidney, and the army sailed from Dublin in twelve ships. The elements, though, were against them, and they were forced, with the loss of one vessel, to land at Rathlin and establish a small garrison before sailing for Kintyre and the adjacent isles of Arran, Bute, and the Cumbrays. Unlike Crofts's Rathlin campaign, Sussex's took the Scots by surprise and destroyed all their provisions and supplies on that island. On 29 September Sussex landed at Loch Kilkerran (just south of present-day Campbeltown) and laid waste an eight-mile stretch along Kintyre's east coast, including James MacDonnell's residence at Saddell. Afterwards, Sussex crossed the peninsula and cut a twelve-mile swath which, he claimed, destroyed another residence and the castle at Dunaverty. He burned and plundered the adjacent isles before sailing to Islay, which escaped his wrath because of bad weather and dangerous currents. Sussex returned to Carrickfergus in early November, whence he hoped to mount an expedition to drive the Scots from the Route. But his army was in no shape to conduct a strenuous search-and-destroy mission against the MacDonnells on the Ulster mainland; therefore, after burning a few settlements, Sussex returned to Dublin on 8 November.[74]

The Lord Deputy's expedition against the MacDonnells, though it destroyed a significant amount of property, did not bring the family to obedience. James had displayed a firm understanding of the military situation by refusing to allow his men to join battle with Sussex's superior army. Instead, they harassed him, especially during his three-day stay in Kintyre, preferring to skirmish when circumstances gave them a temporary advantage.[75] This, coupled with Sussex's failure to reach Islay and his vain attempt thereafter to subdue the Route, pointed up the futility of trying to defeat Clan Ian Mor by conventional means in 1558.

Sussex's failure to subdue the Antrim MacDonnells coincided with Elizabeth I's accession to the English throne in November 1558. The realm was in disarray after a decade of financial and foreign policy mismanagement. Moreover, England faced a two-front war with France and Scotland. And with a young, inexperienced female on the throne, the Dublin administration was unlikely to undertake anything too risky, especially in regard to Gaelic Ulster. The beginning of Elizabeth's reign thus portended difficult times in Ireland. Sussex was replaced by Sidney and returned to London shortly after her accession, where he would remain until the following May, receiving instructions on future Irish policy. The upshot of these instructions involved keeping expenditures below IR £1,500 per month and reducing the army to fewer than 1,500 men. Also, membership on the Dublin council was increased and an earldom was to be offered Shane O'Neill. The establishment of a plantation in eastern Ulster to keep out the Scots, however, fell victim to severe spending cuts.[76]

Political retrenchment in London meant that, at least in the near future, the English would negotiate with, rather than fight, Clan Ian Mor. Sorley

Boy certainly was aware of England's weakened position in Ulster, and in 1559 he was left undisturbed to pursue his family's interests in the Route against the MacQuillins. As we have seen, the MacDonnells for long had desired the fertile lands between Ballycastle and the Bann. Since Colla's appointment as Captain of the Route in 1555 and his marriage to Eveleen, the MacQuillins had remained quiet. But after Colla's death in May 1558 Edward MacQuillin began plotting an attempt to banish the new captain. Sorley Boy had no ties to the MacQuillins, and they in turn expected little from their new MacDonnell overlord. By midsummer 1559 the elder MacQuillin and his three sons, Edward Oge, Charles, and Rory, had assembled a sufficient force to meet Sorley Boy in the field.[77]

Sorley's campaign against the MacQuillins in 1559 tested his mettle as a military leader. The initial battle in early July occurred southwest of Bunnamairge at Beal-a-faula. Details of the battle are scarce, but it is known that the MacQuillins attacked Sorley's camp and were repulsed with severe losses. Sorley then pursued them southward up Glenshesk to a point on the eastern bank of the river Shesk. Several days later Sorley attacked the MacQuillin camp. His assault was blunted by a determined resistance, both sides suffering heavy casualties. Edward Oge MacQuillin, leading the army in place of his father, retreated toward Slieve-an-Aura, where he joined Hugh MacFelim O'Neill of Clandeboy, an experienced military man, to whom Edward entrusted command. With Sorley following, the decisive contest for control of the Route drew near.[78]

The battle of Slieve-an-Aura (13 July 1559) was Sorley Boy's first great victory as commander-in-chief of Clan Ian Mor's Irish forces. Having fought beside his elder brothers in numerous encounters, Sorley demonstrated at Slieve-an-Aura the sagacity, decisiveness, and tenacity of a seasoned military leader. During the short summer campaign of less than a fortnight, Sorley and his men exhibited a physical hardiness that allowed them to operate without a complex logistical system. The Scots suffered shortages of food, but, according to local legend, Sorley and his men subsisted on oatmeal which they mixed with water in the heels of their boots. Before giving battle at Slieve-an-Aura, Sorley scraped together a small reinforcement of redshanks, including four Highland pipers. He now stood ready to attack the combined forces of MacQuillin and O'Neill of Clandeboy.[79]

After gathering his forces to attack the enemy on the banks of the Owennaglush, Sorley devised a stratagem to draw the opposing army out of its strong defensive position. On the night before the battle he covered the marshy ground between him and his opponent with rushes. Hearing the MacDonnells at work in the darkness, the MacQuillins obviously thought that the boggy ground was being made passable and that Sorley intended to attack across it at daybreak. But they were mistaken. Apparently an O'Cahan piper deliberately misinformed Edward MacQuillin of the nature of the marshy ground and of Sorley's preparations to make it traversable by

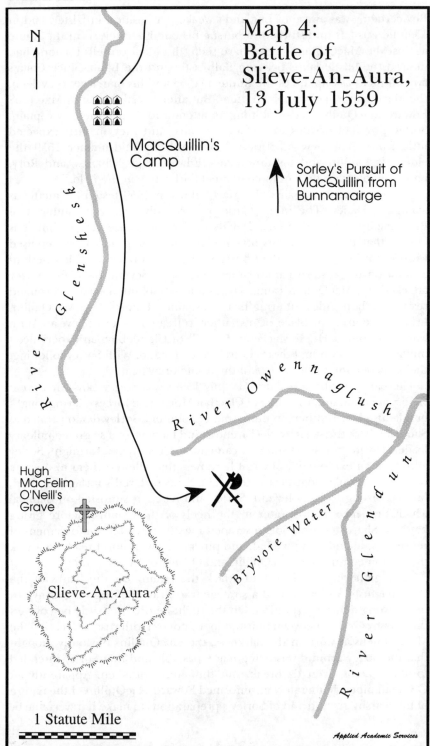

N

Map 4:
Battle of
Slieve-An-Aura,
13 July 1559

MacQuillin's
Camp

Sorley's Pursuit of
MacQuillin from
Bunnamairge

River Glenshesk

River Owennaglush

River Glendun

Bryvore Water

Hugh
MacFelim
O'Neill's
Grave

Slieve-An-Aura

1 Statute Mile

Applied Academic Services

constructing a bridge. For whatever reasons, MacQuillin decided to strike first. But his cavalry and infantry became mired in the bog and fell easy prey to Sorley's archers and swordsmen. In the ensuing rout both Edward MacQuillin and Hugh MacFelim O'Neill were slain.[80]

Slieve-an-Aura assured MacDonnell domination of the Route in 1559, as England was too preoccupied elsewhere in Ulster to be concerned with the MacQuillins' misfortune. Sussex, who had returned at mid-year, was determined to colonize eastern Ulster and to recover Lecale, Newry, and Carlingford from the Scots. But Shane O'Neill continued as Elizabeth's most pressing concern, his power having grown tremendously since the death of Con Bacagh and Dungannon. Shane sought nothing less than complete control of Ulster. This, of course, was unacceptable to the English and Clan Ian Mor. The new queen was willing to offer him an earldom, but she rejected out of hand Shane's claim to the overlordship of Ulster. However, she stopped short of sanctioning Sussex's military plan for his destruction. The Lord Deputy made no attempt to hide his hatred for Shane. Sussex's emotions indeed affected his ability to deal dispassionately, and thus effectively, with O'Neill.[81] It is improbable that O'Neill could have been persuaded, like his father, to accept an English earldom. This hot-blooded warrior simply would not have acquiesced to holding his ancestral lands from an alien prince.

By 1559 Sussex had become a serious problem for Shane. The Lord Deputy's influence in the Privy Council, though not strong enough to allow him a free hand in mounting an expedition against O'Neill, did constitute enough of a threat to the Tyrone chief to force him to seek aid outside Ulster. Disregarding the MacDonnells' preference for neutrality, Shane, with his superior strength, had tried to bully James and Sorley Boy into an alliance in 1558–9. But the brothers had held firm in their neutrality. Now, in mid-1559, the tables were turned, and Shane was forced to seek an accommodation with the MacDonnells. Sorley's success in the Route and James's in Clandeboy in the previous autumn revealed to Shane the family's resiliency. If the Scots allied with England or remained neutral, O'Neill's position would be imperiled. Shane, then, attempted to influence the MacDonnells through Argyll, all the while nervously watching as the English tried to deal directly with James and Sorley Boy.[82]

England's position in Ulster in summer 1559 appeared no better than Shane's. The influence in Scotland of the queen regent, Marie of Guise-Lorraine, mother of Mary, Queen of Scots, portended a possible French invasion of Ireland. Marie was vehemently opposed to the Protestant fifth earl of Argyll, Archibald Campbell, and sought closer ties with the Catholic MacDonnells. Her attempts, though, were frustrated by the enduring marriage alliance between Argyll's sister Agnes and James.[83] Because the Protestant Argyll controlled access to Clan Ian Mor's redshank recruiting grounds in the West Highlands, James and Sorley were not inclined to offer support to the Catholic French party in Scotland. This state of affairs led, curiously enough, to both Shane and the English looking to Argyll to influence the MacDonnells in one direction or the other. Argyll's role as power-broker in the Gaelic heartland certainly made for a confused and intriguing diplomatic process.[84]

For Clan Ian Mor a great deal hung in the balance in the complex negotiations of 1559. In May Sussex received the following report:

> The north parts of our said realm [of Ireland] hath been long time out of good and quiet order, by reason partly of the multiplication of the Scots under the rule of James MacDonnell and his brother Sorliboy, and partly by the disorder of Shane O'Neill. . . . As Sorley Boy has made means to become our orderly subject and to receive his lands of us, he shall have our free pardon.[85]

In June Elizabeth wrote James MacDonnell in hopes of winning his support (or at least his neutrality) in the struggle against Shane. Sussex apparently had spoken well of James's behavior. Indeed, it was obvious that both the English and the Antrim MacDonnells desired a respite from the almost constant conflict of the 1550s. Even with Sorley on the verge of banishing the MacQuillins from the Route, England acknowledged that the MacDonnells were no longer considered "foreign enemies." As reported to Sussex in May, Sorley had intimated his willingness to hold his lands by royal favor. But the prospect of such easy cooperation was not completely warranted. In fact, the English were so anxious to secure a MacDonnell alliance that they deluded themselves concerning its feasibility. It was noted erroneously in mid-1559 that the Scots had already committed to the English against Shane. This report, though, presumably was intended to make the Scots appear culpable should negotiations break down with London. While the English publicly proclaimed good relations with Clan Ian Mor, they also plotted to ultimately exclude them from Ulster. It was clear by July (at the time of Sorley's victory at Slieve-an-Aura) that the MacDonnells, for the time being, could afford to bide their time and enter the contest on their own terms, but only as long as they did not offend Argyll.[86]

More than anything else, the MacDonnells feared an agreement leading to improved relations between Sussex and O'Neill. The groundwork appeared to be in place for such an accommodation when in mid-July Elizabeth instructed the Lord Deputy to allow Shane "to succeed his father as his heir and presently occupieth and possesseth all that Country . . . which his father enjoyed. . . ."[87] To ensure that the recently triumphant Sorley Boy did not interfere by seeking to combine with O'Neill, the queen sought to placate the Captain of the Route:

In likewise where the chief captain of the Scots now remaining in the north parts of [Ireland] . . . named Sorley, brother to James MacDonnell, maketh suit and means to recover our grace, and to become our true liege man and so far the same to submit himself and all that he may rule or govern upon divers good reasons in that behalf well weighed and considered. . . .[88]

Elizabeth and Sussex saw Shane as the greater threat, but they also were alert to the likelihood of Scottish encroachment in the Carrickfergus, Carlingford, and Newry areas.[89] Certainly the MacDonnells would be tempted to descend from the Glynnes and the Route if the English went to war with Shane in the Blackwater valley and Tyrone. The prospect of picking up the pieces following a conflict between the other two powers, after all, was a salient element in the strategies of all involved in the Ulster struggle. In mid-1559 the Antrim MacDonnells, because their neutrality allowed them to play both sides against the middle, were favorably positioned to benefit from the turmoil.

England, though much stronger than either of the Gaelic powers and freed from her continental obligations by the loss of Calais and the Peace of Cateau-Cambrésis (March 1559), was still reluctant to become involved in an Ulster war. Sussex commanded only 300 horse, 900 English foot, and 300 Irish kerne in July.[90] Earlier in the year, Sidney, who temporarily replaced Sussex, had marched to Dundalk and summoned Shane to meet him there for a parley rather than a military engagement. Instead, O'Neill ignored the summons and invited Sidney to his Benburb residence, where one of the chief's children was to be christened. Sidney accepted the invitation and stood "gossip" for the child. Afterwards, O'Neill presented his case to Sidney, who entertained a much more understanding view of Shane's position than did Sussex and pledged to represent it in a favorable light to the queen. Sidney understood that England's best policy was to give Shane a free hand and hope that he could be persuaded to hold his lands and title from Elizabeth. In this way England might avoid a protracted and costly war in remote Ulster and at the same time push Shane closer to a conflict with the MacDonnells. Whether O'Neill would have agreed to Sidney's plan in 1559 cannot be known, for shortly Sussex returned to relieve him. Sussex opposed a conciliatory attitude toward Shane, perhaps because the Lord Deputy knew that O'Neill in some ways represented a Gaelic version of Machiavelli's Renaissance prince and thus understood the use of raw power. Sussex's return to Ireland signalled the beginning of England's "hard" policy toward the MacDonnells and O'Neill. Sussex had been informed immediately upon his arrival in Ulster that the country could not be pacified except by the use "of force upon some stubborn sort, and [by the] . . . peopling of some parts there, and specially the North, now possessed with the Scots. . . ."[91]

At the close of the decade the Antrim MacDonnells had withstood every effort by the English and the native Irish to drive them from Ulster. Between 1551 and 1559 Clan Ian Mor had actually advanced its claims in northeastern Ireland. The rise of Sorley Boy as Captain of the Route in 1558 and James's continued influence in the Glynnes and across the water in Scotland combined to give the family a solid power base from which to extend its interests in Ireland. MacDonnell success in the late 1550s is evidenced by the fervor with which both the English and O'Neill sought to gain their allegiance or to ensure their neutrality. Sorley and James MacDonnell in 1559 understood their strong negotiating position and thus withheld their open support from either side. This non-committal policy infuriated both Sussex and Shane and, in the long run, caused the English and the O'Neills to put aside their differences long enough to combine against the MacDonnells in the coming decade. As the 1550s ended, the complex web of negotiation and intrigue that characterized the first stage of the triangular struggle in Ulster had already begun. And Clan Ian Mor, falling more and more under Sorley's influence, was well positioned to continue its drive for dominance in the Gaelic heartland.

Chapter Four
The Beginnings of the Triangular Struggle in Ulster, 1560–3

> The chiefest caveat and proviso in the reformation of the North must be to keep out the Scots.[1]
>
> Edmund Spenser

From 1560 to 1563 Sorley Boy and James MacDonnell tried to protect their interests in northeastern Ireland by remaining neutral in the conflict between Shane O'Neill and the English, and, if possible, to obtain recognition from Elizabeth I of their claim to the Antrim Glynnes and the Route. England looked to profit from the recent "diplomatic revolution" that ended the long-standing Anglo-Scottish rivalry by employing the Protestant fifth earl of Argyll, Archibald Campbell, against its enemies in Ireland. And Shane simply desired to crush all opposition to his rule in Ulster. The triangular struggle that ravaged the north of Ireland in the 1560s resulted from the interplay of these several forces and led to near disaster for Clan Ian Mor, lost opportunity for the English, and a short-lived dominance of the province for O'Neill.[1]

O'Neill's desire in 1560 to crush all Gaelic opposition in Ulster was stronger than any alliances he might have made. As a result, the Antrim MacDonnells and the English faced a common enemy who possessed the wherewithal to drive them both from the province. Though allied with the Scots in the 1550s, Shane was tempted by his firm hold over Tyrone in 1560 to try to conquer all Ulster. The Scots' colony could be tolerated no more than could England's presence on the Carrickfergus–Erne line. Shane was the key to peace or war in Ulster, but the reactions of Argyll, Sussex, and the Antrim MacDonnells would be instrumental in determining the timing and severity of the impending conflict.

A rapid series of international events, beginning with the loss of Calais in 1558 and followed by the Peace of Cateau-Cambrésis in 1559 and the treaties of Edinburgh and Berwick in 1560, relieved England of considerable foreign threats and obligations and allowed her to concentrate on improving her position in the Celtic fringe. The last two treaties laid the cornerstone for the "diplomatic revolution" and solidified the hold of the Lords of the Congregation and the Scottish Reformation on the Lowlands. They also improved London's relations with Argyll, who, as the most powerful lord in the western Highlands and Isles, wielded considerable authority in Ulster.[2] Argyll's importance in Ulster affairs is pointed up by a February 1560 memorandum concerning the Treaty of Berwick, in which he agreed to intercede on the English queen's behalf in Ulster.[3] By early 1560, then, London was most assuredly moving toward a "British" strategy that included a central role for Argyll and Protestant Lowland Scotland in the subjugation of Ulster.[4]

Argyll, a Protestant, was a Lowland laird and a leader of the Lords of the Congregation, as well as a Highland chief with an army of 5,000 of the most capable fighters in the entire archipelago. He also was an enemy of the Scottish regent, Marie of Guise-Lorraine, and the "Auld Alliance." In early 1560 Argyll pressured his Ulster allies to move against Shane. He despatched 1,000 redshanks to bolster Calvagh O'Donnell's position on Shane's western flank in Tyrconnell.[5] By early April William Cecil, Elizabeth's principal secretary, informed Argyll of London's desire to secure Sorley's goodwill and cooperation,

> who hath under his governance certain people named Scottishmen and of long time hath remained in doubtful terms showing themselves sometime toward subjects, sometime contrary, and nevertheless now of late suit hath been earnestly made by the said Sorleboy in the name of his brother James ... to the earl of Sussex the Queen's Majesty's Deputy in Ireland to receive the same Sorleboy and all his kin, friends, and followers into her Majesty's grace, and hath offered to become and remain faithful and true subjects....[6]

That both the English and Argyll recognized Sorley Boy's importance in arresting O'Neill's power reveals that by early 1560 James MacDonnell, lord of Dunyveg, was only *primus inter pares* in regard to his brothers in Ireland. Though Dunyveg was still rightful head of Clan Ian Mor, Cecil's memorandum clearly stressed Sorley's importance in expediting a successful Ulster policy. As Captain of the Route, Sorley was to "animate his brothers and his followers so to remain and continue [in] ... that which may in this behalf be done by the Earl of Argyll ...."[7] If forged into a military alliance, Argyll, the MacDonnells, and Calvagh O'Donnell would be able to squeeze Shane from the east, north, and west. Indeed, by mid-April both Sorley and James appeared to have taken a pro-English stance.[8]

Sussex, elevated to Lord Lieutenant of Ireland in April, was to bind Sorley

Boy "to contribute to the public service" in Ulster and "to reduce Shane O'Neill by force or otherwise."[9] By spring 1560 the Tudors fully intended to curb the independence of the Ulster chiefs, and if this necessitated a temporary alliance with the Antrim Scots, London was willing to play that game. Upon Sussex's return to Ireland, England implemented a policy that would use the threat of force as a diplomatic tool against Shane. Though the Lord Lieutenant preferred direct employment of the English army, the queen's parsimony called for a policy of cooperation with Argyll, Clan Ian Mor, and the O'Donnells.[10]

Shane kept a keen eye on the negotiations between England and her potential Gaelic allies. Fearing a combination against him, O'Neill approached Argyll concerning an entente. But Argyll reaffirmed his pledge of support for the English in Ireland.[11] Campbell cooperation was a means for the queen to rid herself of the chief Ulster rebel at minimum expense, while concurrently pitting the two power blocs in the Gaelic heartland against each other. If this plan could be pulled off, thus saving England manpower and material, she might emerge as the dominant power in the region. On 4 August Elizabeth wrote Argyll, congratulating him on his "zeal and consistency towards the maintenance" of English policy in Ulster.[12] As of yet, however, the earl had done little to reduce O'Neill. Argyll publicly expressed his unswerving allegiance to the queen, but privately he seemed to be steering an independent course.[13]

While negotiations proceeded apace between London, Edinburgh, and Argyllshire, Dublin hastily tried to pull together a sufficient force to employ against Shane before the onset of bad weather. Gilbert Gerrard, the English Attorney General in Ireland, revealed to Cecil in early September that "O'Reilly, O'Donnell, Sorley Boy, and Maguire ... have promised all to make war against [Shane] ... & to join with my Lord Lieutenant. . . ."[14] The queen had written Sussex in August, instructing him to subdue O'Neill and install young Dungannon, Brian O'Neill (Matthew's eldest son), in his place.[15] But Elizabeth vacillated between making war in Ireland and preserving her treasure to aid the rebellious Huguenots across the Channel. By the time she had decided on an Irish military venture, it was too late. Under such circumstances it was hoped that a bargain could be struck with Shane, thus postponing the Ulster problem until the 1561 campaigning season.[16]

As autumn approached, both Argyll and the MacDonnells anxiously awaited Sussex's summons to the battlefield. Pressured from all sides, O'Neill decided to stall the English through negotiation. By late autumn 1560 it appeared that face-to-face talks in London between O'Neill and the English were becoming more likely. Sussex's plans to solve the Ulster problem militarily were quietly shelved without Argyll, the MacDonnells, or any of England's potential Gaelic allies being informed of the momentous decision.[17]

An air of mistrust had dominated Ulster diplomacy in 1560. None of the major players wanted to be the first to commit to a military solution. The Antrim MacDonnells, more than anyone, realized the importance of continued neutrality and were uniquely positioned to maintain it. Having territories in both Ulster and the remote western Highlands and Isles, Clan Ian Mor could avoid military conflict. Only Argyll seemed genuinely committed to a military expedition against O'Neill. It is surprising, therefore, that Elizabeth never requested his services, which would have been far cheaper than fielding an English force under Sussex. James and Sorley Boy were not forced to make the difficult decision whether to cooperate with Argyll and the English. Rather they were left temporarily undisturbed in their neutrality.[18]

England's attempt in late 1560 to bring Shane to London included an agreement with the MacDonnells. That the queen and James MacDonnell concluded an indenture on 20 January 1561 certainly must have suggested to O'Neill that the MacDonnells were inclined toward intervention on England's side if war should come. The indenture would give James title for a period of twenty-one years to most of the lands that his family already occupied in the Glynnes and the Route. But perhaps more importantly to O'Neill, Sorley Boy agreed to commit his military forces, at MacDonnell expense, to the direction of the Lord Lieutenant, who would use them against all "rebels" dwelling between Carrickfergus and Lough Foyle.[19] At the same time, James

> shall at all and every sundry request of the said Lieutenant for the time being send 200 men out of Scotland into the Queen's Majesty's service in Ulster for the which 200 men the said James shall receive such sufficient bonaghe [i.e. *buannacht*] as they be used commonly to receive.[20]

The MacDonnells' agreement in her pocket and Argyll continuing to assure aid, Elizabeth doubtless believed that she held the upper hand against O'Neill. If negotiations broke down, a military solution could be tried. From Benburb Shane penned a letter to the queen on 8 February, elucidating his past services to England while upholding his claim as the O'Neill. His letter was a curious mixture of submission and boastfulness, perhaps designed to confuse rather than to inform. But Sussex was not fooled, recognizing full well that O'Neill desperately needed a respite. Bringing him to London for an audience with the queen would provide it.[21]

Was Shane O'Neill invited to England as a means of deluding him into a false sense of security and thus catching him unprepared to resist an invasion of Ulster?[22] Lord Lieutenant Sussex saw O'Neill as a determined enemy to be destroyed by force rather than appeased by negotiation. He bluntly noted that "If Shane be overthrown all is settled, if Shane settle all is overthrown."[23] But for now Sussex agreed to diplomacy.[24] Despite Shane's overt aggressiveness along the Carrickfergus–Erne line in winter 1560–1, Sussex and the militarists were held in check by the queen.[25]

In early 1561 England hoped that any threats of military action against Shane would come from James and Sorley Boy MacDonnell. Sorley quickly responded to English inquiries about such a move against O'Neill. Captain William Piers, constable of Carrickfergus and liaison between the English government and Sorley, had found the MacDonnell leader unwilling to abide by the terms of the recent indenture between James and the queen. Piers, therefore, sent Brian MacFelim O'Neill of Clandeboy to James MacDonnell with word of Sorley's obstinacy. But Piers did not get the favorable response for which he had hoped. He reported to Undertreasurer Sir William Fitzwilliam (who would serve as Irish Lord Deputy in 1572–5 and 1588–94), Sussex's temporary replacement, that James apparently favored Mary, Queen of Scots, over Elizabeth. Dunyveg also had set about to complete his residence at Red Bay as a refuge from the vagaries of Scottish politics. According to Piers, James intimated that he had corresponded with the French court, a claim designed no doubt to unnerve the English. Indeed, Piers's letter is characterized by a sense of urgency, if not panic.[26]

The ambiguity of the MacDonnells' policy toward England did not prevent Elizabeth from dealing harshly with Shane. After Sussex returned to Ireland in late May the queen sent notice that Shane was to be branded a rebel. Elizabeth, Cecil, and other officials knew that O'Neill was trying to buy time, but Sussex again was cautioned to "consider the manner of your proceeding against him [i.e. Shane] prudently and substantially."[27] England now reluctantly agreed to a military expedition against Shane, but the Lord Lieutenant was ordered "to foresee that herein our charge be neither further increased nor any longer continued than necessity shall require."[28] The queen suggested that Sussex might

> do well before this your enterprise to solicit and provoke James MacDonnell and his brother Sorleboy to make war upon the said Shane at the same time that you shall determine your attempt and the like you shall seek to be done by O'Donnell . . . and by . . . the friends and followers of the young baron of Dungannon. . . .[29]

But before Sussex could draw together this coalition against O'Neill, Shane outfoxed him by sweeping into Tyrconnell near the end of May and kidnapping Calvagh and his wife, the former Catherine MacLean.[30]

Shane's abduction of Calvagh and Catherine, according to the Four Masters, allowed him to assume "the sovereign command of all Ulster, from Drogheda to the Erne, so that at this time he might have been called with propriety the provincial King of Ulster, were it not for the opposition

61

of the English to him."[31] Because O'Donnell was gone, the pressure on O'Neill from Tyrconnell disappeared as well. And since the prospects of MacDonnell aid were as uncertain as ever, the proposed expedition against Shane stood to accomplish little.[32]

A successful invasion of Ulster in mid-1561 depended on control of Armagh as the major point of troop concentration and supply. By mid-June 1561 Sussex had established a substantial military presence there, but he suffered severe logistical problems. After a month of inactivity, Sussex informed Elizabeth in mid-July that overtures to Shane continued concerning his journey to England, but the Lord Lieutenant also noted a recent skirmish with O'Neill's troops near Armagh. Sussex, though, assured the queen that he soon would begin his drive into Tyrone.[33] London was not so optimistic; Cecil sought confirmation of a rumor that Shane had defeated the English army and taken Carrickfergus.[34] Such was the confidence the Lord Lieutenant inspired in England.

From his headquarters at Armagh Sussex despatched numerous search-and-destroy missions that resulted in only limited success. Such a timid policy was not likely to bring about the liberation of Calvagh O'Donnell, one of Sussex's main objectives. In fact, Sussex complained that O'Neill refused to even discuss O'Donnell's release. Shane, after having defeated a 1,000-man English detachment near Monaghan, was in a strong position in mid-1561 and thus could demand to have his own way. O'Neill's favorable situation perforce made Sussex regroup south of the Blackwater and reassess his military policy in Ulster.[35] Shane, in the aftermath of victory, subjugated the O'Donnells and extended his control into parts of Tyrconnell.[36] The Lord Lieutenant, however, was not deterred. Though forced to abandon his forward position at Armagh, Sussex set about to convince Elizabeth and Cecil that a military solution deserved another try.[37] But following the Monaghan debacle and Sussex's withdrawal south of the Blackwater, London appeared in no mood to risk another confrontation. Thus England's position provided little leverage for bargaining with Shane. Nonetheless, O'Neill was to be assured that if he refrained from attacking the O'Donnells, neighboring Irish chiefs, and Sorley Boy, he need not fear another expedition into Ulster.[38] In truth, Shane had no reason to fear anything from the English in Ireland as long as the MacDonnells remained neutral.

Early August brought rumors to London that several of Shane's kinsmen, including his tanist, Turlough Luineach O'Neill, had come in and were ready to serve the queen. Moreover, James MacDonnell reportedly had raised 1,000 redshanks to be employed for the queen in Ulster. Sussex persuaded London to sanction another Ulster military expedition. Ignoring Dublin's request for 3,000 more troops, Elizabeth undoubtedly hoped that Shane preferred negotiation over war. Sussex was instructed to temper his anger and cooperate fully with Shane if combat gave way to diplomacy.[39] For now, however, the army was to march against O'Neill near the end of August. As Sussex prepared his second invasion, he received a brutally frank letter from Cecil. The secretary warned that Elizabeth thus far was not pleased with the Lord Lieutenant's military efforts, and that she had little confidence in future operations that lacked MacDonnell and Campbell aid:

> Here is some offence taken, that where so manifest an error was upon the suffrance of Shane's charged, yet no example is made thereof. It breedeth in the Queen's . . . head some further judgment of the matter than I would. For God's sake, my good Lord, bestir you, and recover this mishap as you may. I assure you I have, as it becometh me, diverted all the fault upon the faint soldiers, and am sure that the judgment of your Lordship is nowise to you prejudicial. I pray God that I may hear well of James MacDonnell. The Earl of Argyll hath remained in readiness all this year, to harken whom you would send to him for aid; and as I perceive he imagineth that your Lord- ship alloweth not his offer of friendship, it were well done that he should not conceive mistrust.[40]

Only by defeating Shane quickly and inexpensively could Sussex put things right between him and his sovereign. But he did not heed Cecil's advice to seek aid from Argyll and the MacDonnells. Instead, he formulated an elaborate, overly ambitious plan to garner for himself the lion's share of the glory for crushing O'Neill.[41]

Sussex's second military expedition called for marching through Tyrone and linking up with a seaborne expedition at Lough Foyle. The Lord Lieutenant and his army indeed marched unopposed all the way to Lough Foyle, as Shane simply disappeared into the Ulster fastnesses and refused to give battle. The failure of Sussex's campaign caused Elizabeth and Cecil again to take matters into their own hands.[42] In late August the queen informed her Lord Lieutenant that "If Shane O'Neill may be drawn unto any reasonable points to come into this our realm we would not that you should neglect it."[43] The stage thus was set for serious negotiations to bring Shane to England in the following year.

In August 1561 Shane desperately desired to plead his case against Sussex before Elizabeth. He had failed to conclude an alliance with Philip II of Spain and saw an audience with the queen as the only means of protecting himself against further invasion. But he knew it would be risky to depart Ulster. Before agreeing to leave he demanded guaranteed safe conduct from Elizabeth herself. Sussex's word was not to be trusted. Anxious to parley with Shane, Elizabeth wrote Sussex on 25 August that it would be preferable to "recover our subject [i.e. O'Neill] . . . by mercy than by extremity."[44] The queen's haste in summoning Shane to England revealed her lack of faith in Sussex. As it was now apparent that O'Neill could not be forcibly removed from Ulster, he would have to be coaxed from his lair. The queen despatched Gerald, earl of Kildare, to the Great O'Neill with what she hoped were acceptable terms.[45]

James and Sorley Boy had carefully monitored negotiations between Shane and the English while tending their own affairs. Argyll's continued assurances that James would oppose Shane doubtless began to wear thin in London. James reportedly was still enthusiastic about an enterprise against O'Neill, but he doubted that it could be executed before winter. And even if Shane were attacked, both MacDonnell and Argyll believed that only a pincer movement from east and west would defeat him. Since Calvagh O'Donnell was still O'Neill's prisoner, an assault from Tyrconnell was out of the question. After Sussex's defeat in Monaghan the English were more cautious than before. Thomas Randolph, England's diplomatic representative in Edinburgh, complained that he would be delayed in meeting the usually accessible Argyll, who was in Edinburgh in early September. Surely Randolph expected the earl to enlighten him on "the bruit . . . of an overthrow that divers of our men have had in Ireland." Apparently, however, neither Argyll nor James MacDonnell's assurances could calm the normally staid Randolph, who excitedly quizzed Cecil whether all Ireland was lost and the Lord Deputy dead.[46] Thus an inability to understand Edinburgh's political situation and to ascertain Argyll's and the Antrim MacDonnells' next move pushed Whitehall to negotiate with O'Neill in early autumn 1561.

At October's end Shane left for England, thereby temporarily freezing any official negotiations between London and either the MacDonnells or Argyll. Because O'Neill was out of Ulster and therefore no immediate threat to England's position there, London's stance toward Clan Ian Mor changed noticeably in the winter of 1561–2. By the early 1560s Tudor foreign policy had become much more sophisticated than during previous decades. Now that Shane was in London, and the likelihood of a Franco-Scottish alliance had disappeared with the beginning of a Huguenot–Roman Catholic civil war in France (1562–89), England sought to isolate the MacDonnells and prevent them from joining forces with either O'Neill or a continental power.

In early 1562, though desirous of an alliance with the MacDonnells against Shane, Elizabeth and Cecil were piecing together a much more realistic policy toward their Gaelic neighbors. The queen had complained the previous December to Mary, Queen of Scots, that James MacDonnell had recently entered Ireland and committed various unspecified crimes against Englishmen. Though such depredations were not unusual, Elizabeth now suggested that the queen of Scots force the Dunyveg chief to pay reparations and prevent him from taking such actions again. But Sussex warned that the MacDonnells should be placated so that they might still be used to threaten

Shane if negotiations bore no fruit. By now, however, the English council knew that James and Sorley Boy preferred dealing with Edinburgh rather than with London. The queen obviously needed to formulate a new policy for the Gaelic heartland.[47]

In January 1562 the situation in the southwestern Highlands and Isles began to darken for Clan Ian Mor. Since the days of John Cahanagh, they had kept a watchful eye on the earls of Argyll. Other Highland chiefs also were able to challenge the MacDonnells in Scotland by the mid-sixteenth century, especially Hector MacLean of Duart, chief of the MacLeans of Mull, whose family had long desired the Rhinns of Islay. The Rhinns belonged *de jure* to the MacDonnells, but since 1542 they had been held by the MacLeans in return for certain services. As both clans held lands in Islay and Jura, it was almost inevitable that their interests would clash. To head off trouble, several Highland and Island chiefs met at the end of January but reached no conclusive agreement.[48]

Argyll was the only man who could successfully mediate the nascent MacDonnell–MacLean quarrel, and he had reached Glasgow just before the meeting between the rival chiefs soured over an alleged slaying. Since the late 1550s Argyll had been the central figure in bringing together the MacDonnells and the English. Now he was even more important, as his goodwill and favor were sought by all involved in the region's politics. In early 1562 James and Sorley MacDonnell were in the southwestern Highlands and the Antrim Glynnes, respectively, eagerly awaiting news of O'Neill's progress to London. Both depended on Argyll for accurate and timely information from the Sassenach court. Though Elizabeth and Cecil were occupied with O'Neill, Argyll made certain, through Randolph, that they were kept informed of the MacDonnells' precarious relations with the MacLeans. Randolph had informed Cecil in mid-January that Argyll was anxious to use his leverage with James MacDonnell to free one George Butside, a Devonshire gentleman betrayed to the Scots during Crofts's 1551 expedition, who still languished in Kintyre. Argyll appeared so confident of having his way with MacDonnell that he instructed Sir Ralph Bagenal to send forth Butside's ransom money. It is unlikely that Argyll would have intimated to Randolph Dunyveg's weakening diplomatic and political position if he (Argyll) had not intended to undermine the MacDonnells on both sides of the North Channel as soon as circumstances allowed.[49]

While relations soured between Clan Ian Mor and Argyll, Shane's visit to London was marked by terribly inclement weather and even worse English hospitality. It is not necessary to dwell here on the particulars of Shane's journey to England. But it is important to note that contained within the 30 April indenture between Elizabeth and O'Neill was a clause that bound the latter to attack the Antrim MacDonnells' Ulster territories. English duplicity now became clear. At the end of March Cecil learned that Shane, while in London, had corresponded with Argyll. O'Neill doubtless believed himself vulnerable in the hands of his enemies and hoped that good relations with Argyll might prevent some unfortunate incident during his stay. Argyll was moving away from the MacDonnells and closer to Shane, while Shane was moving closer to Elizabeth, at least according to the indenture. And since the MacDonnells were moving away from Argyll and the English by drawing nearer to the queen of Scots, a major shift was underway in the balance of power in the Gaelic heartland in 1562.[50]

Elizabeth invited O'Neill to London because she hoped he might be used against the Scots in Ulster. The queen understood the importance of expelling Clan Ian Mor from its long-established foothold in Ireland. It goes without saying that she never wavered in her opinion that Shane, while a considerable local threat, was not as dangerous as the MacDonnells, especially when they were backed by foreign interests. Now that Elizabeth had established closer relations with Shane and Argyll in early 1562, she looked to form a coalition against Clan Ian Mor.[51]

The MacDonnells understood the severity of their situation now that England was on the brink of an accord with O'Neill and a tacit entente with Argyll. Moreover, they could not ignore the smouldering quarrel with the MacLeans. That James MacDonnell feared the combined power of the English and O'Neill is evinced by his presence in Islay rather than on the mainland in Kintyre in mid-July. From his Islay retreat James penned a letter to Sussex to inquire whether the Lord Lieutenant, who had followed O'Neill to London to protect his own reputation, had news of any progress concerning his (James's) 1561 indenture. For his part, Shane returned triumphantly to Ireland at the end of May, having received more than he gave, including England's recognition of his *de facto* hegemony in Ulster. But the English could not tolerate such a situation for long. What Sussex had professed to know all along had become evident by late summer–that England was unable to handle Shane with diplomacy. Sussex continued to stress the importance of cooperating with James and Sorley in any military solution to the Ulster problem.[52]

Upon Shane's return to Ulster, Sussex recognized that the English, the Scots (including Argyll's Irish interests), and the O'Donnells, unless they formed a cooperative pact, were in danger of being defeated one by one by O'Neill. In late July Sussex reported that Shane was preparing to move against Con O'Donnell, son of the imprisoned Calvagh. Ostensibly to head off conflict over Shane's aggressive behavior, Sussex instructed Terence Daniel, dean of Armagh, to discover O'Neill's intentions toward O'Donnell and neighboring chiefs and to arrange a parley between Shane and the Lord Lieutenant. But in early August Sussex doubted that Shane could be restrained any longer by words. Rumors abounded that serious fighting had already broken out between O'Neill and Con O'Donnell.[53] If someone did not move immediately to aid the O'Donnells, the western theater of operations against Shane would disintegrate, allowing him to turn eastward against both the English and the Antrim MacDonnells.

O'Neill's threat to overrun Ulster made it imperative that the English and Clan Ian Mor reach an understanding or else risk piecemeal destruction. On 12 August Sussex wrote the queen concerning the MacDonnells:

> It may please your majesty I received the Xth of the present letters from James MacDonnell and Sorleboye the copies whereof I send your highness. . . . And as I did not indeed receive instructions from your highness for answer to be unto them neither can I make any (James being a Scottish subject) without your pleasure knowing. So considering all matters which are not yet executed with Shane O'Neill according to the capitulation, I thought best to make such dilatory answer as by the copy enclosed may to your majesty appear and do humbly beseech your highness to direct unto me your pleasure what other answer I shall make unto them.[54]

The next day Sussex wrote James MacDonnell concerning his and Sorley Boy's pending indenture, wherein they were told that, "not having received as yet any final order touching your lordship's causes, we have now written to her majesty to understand her resolution and good pleasure therein, upon knowledge whereof we will advertise the same."[55] Sussex had long proclaimed that the best strategy for dealing with Shane called for pitting the MacDonnells against him. His "dilatory answer" to James and Sorley Boy, then, was intended not to lull them into a false sense of security regarding London but to keep the MacDonnells in the picture as long as possible, in case the queen finally saw fit to employ both them and Argyll against O'Neill.

In August and September Shane caused such distress in Ulster that neither the English, the Scots, nor the native Irish alone could stop him. But London made no attempt to cement an agreement with Clan Ian Mor or to aid Con O'Donnell, Shane Maguire of Fermanagh, or other hard-pressed Irish chiefs. Indeed, upon learning of Shane's overt aggression, the Lord Lieutenant expressed regret to the queen for his having guaranteed O'Neill protection in leaving Ulster in the first place. His frustrations mounting, Sussex pleaded with Cecil to remove him from command in Ireland in late September. For what he undoubtedly hoped would be the last time, the Lord Lieutenant called upon London to crush Shane through open warfare.[56]

Shane's strength in Ulster had much to do with Sussex's desire to resign his post. After receiving letters in late August and early September from James and Sorley Boy, however, the Lord Lieutenant's spirits were bolstered. James was still anxious to know about his indenture, and Sorley further confused the situation by holding out the promise of aid to Sussex, but only after imploring him "to advise me what is your Lordship doing with O'Neill. . . ."[57] Neither Sussex nor the Antrim MacDonnells could formulate a plan without knowing the other's intentions toward O'Neill. From Kintyre in late September 1562 James MacDonnell admitted to Sussex that Sorley Boy had been forced into an alliance with Shane, because "he is unable to resist nor defend the Glynnes from the invasion of O'Neill." James tried to reassure Sussex by telling him that if he and Sorley (the latter now also in Kintyre) received their patents of indenture, they would adhere to the original agreement of "obedience" to the queen.[58] But such assurances rang hollow, as O'Neill's power had finally made the MacDonnells flee Ireland for the safety of their Scottish dominions. Finally, James and Sorley had been forced to lay their cards on the table for the first time since the triangular struggle had begun in the late 1550s.

Sorley Boy's agreement with Shane drastically changed the complexion of Ulster politics in 1562. How would England respond to the apparent forced alliance between Clan Ian Mor and O'Neill? Almost immediately after James MacDonnell informed him of the arrangement, Sussex drafted a letter to the queen revealing that Shane also had come to terms with Con O'Donnell and several other chiefs and that

> three of the MacLeans (kinsmen to the Countess of Argyll) were then with Shane and preferred him great services for the delivering of the countess [i.e. Catherine MacLean] and that he thought they were agreed. He [i.e. Gerot Fleming, O'Neill's secretary] told me also that Shane would have again James MacDonnell's daughter and would marry her openly and that Sorleboye and he were agreed and that Sorleboye should foster with him and should give him 500 kine and eight horsemen's furnitures . . . and serve him with 400 or 500 men in every journey. . . .[59]

The Lord Lieutenant told the queen that Shane had been in contact with Mary, Queen of Scots, and with the Spanish ambassador in London. Sussex further noted that the MacLeans had pledged 4,000 redshanks to O'Neill for six months' service (an agreement to which Argyll must have been a party) and that James MacDonnell, also pledged to this bond, probably would return to Ulster with his men. Sussex concluded by reiterating that Shane, emboldened by these prospects of aid from the Antrim MacDonnells, the MacLeans, and Argyll, would be inclined to make trouble, a course "like[ly] to prove perilous to the whole state [of Ireland]. . . ."[60]

While the MacDonnells apparently drew closer to Shane, Con O'Donnell vacillated between allying with O'Neill and steering an independent course in Tyrconnell. Sussex promoted Con as a nucleus around which an anti-O'Neill coalition might be built. Hoping that O'Donnell might stand firm against O'Neill in the west, Sussex again attempted to convince Elizabeth and Cecil to try to pull Clan Ian Mor out of Shane's orbit. But Sussex was caught between the queen and James MacDonnell. The Lord Lieutenant could do little more than reassure James in mid-October that he and Sorley could expect their letters patent at any moment.[61] Until Sussex actually had those documents in hand to give the MacDonnells, however, he could only hope he was correct in informing Elizabeth and Cecil of the clan's reliability against O'Neill.

Further negotiations with James and Sorley Boy were put aside in order to formulate a plan to counter Shane's forays south of the Carrickfergus–Erne line. In mid-October O'Neill had cut a fiery swath through Fermanagh, prompting Shane Maguire to warn Sussex that if he did not deal immediately with Shane, "you are like to make him the strongest man of Ireland, for every man will take an example by my great losses."[62] Perhaps the accumulation of such dire warnings from the chiefs and Sussex finally convinced England to enlist the O'Donnells as a counterweight to O'Neill in Ulster.

By the end of 1562 events began to wear hard on James and Sorley. Relations with both Argyll and Shane remained difficult.[63] James refused to accept the long-awaited letters patent from England because he believed that they would "prejudice his duty of allegiance to the Queen of Scotland. . . ." Sussex found in the patents no "such matter contained," and informed the MacDonnells that if they accepted the indentures, Elizabeth would continue to look favorably on their affairs. To facilitate Clan Ian Mor's acceptance of the patents, Sussex forwarded them to James with instructions that after reading the documents he might delete any passages that "should prejudice his duty towards the Queen of Scotland. . . ."[64] Elizabeth, once and for all, sought to force James and Sorley Boy either to accept the patents to lands in Antrim and ally with England or to reject the patents and retain their independence and neutrality. But the elusive MacDonnells still refused to take sides.[65] Earlier such calculated deception might have borne fruit; now it only angered Whitehall.

During the waning days of 1562 Clan Ian Mor's Ulster policy was coming unraveled. Above all, now as in 1560, James and Sorley Boy desired neutrality. But neutrality was becoming more difficult to maintain as pressure mounted from all sides for the MacDonnells to join one camp or the other. By the beginning of 1563 tortuous negotiations with James and Sorley began to irritate both the queen and O'Neill.[66] Sussex's belief that the Scots should be tolerated in Ulster as a means of pressuring Shane no longer carried weight with the queen's government. The MacDonnells had paid only lip-service to the numerous attempts to silence O'Neill directly by military action and indirectly by stealth and trickery. James's and Sorley Boy's failure to support the English in Ulster would no longer be ignored by London and Dublin.

The MacDonnells had set a risky, yet potentially profitable, course and steered closely to it. James and Sorley were realistic, tough-minded negotiators. But so were Elizabeth, Cecil, Sussex, O'Neill, and most other successful princes and statesmen in the age of Renaissance power politics. Neutrality, James and Sorley believed, would have allowed them to husband their resources and avoid a costly conflict with either Shane or the English. If those two adversaries went to war, then the MacDonnells rightly reasoned that they might stand aside and afterwards collect most of the spoils. Nothing less than the political and military dominance of the Gaelic heartland hung in the balance.

The frustrations of dealing with Clan Ian Mor had persuaded Elizabeth, Cecil, and even Sussex by early 1563 that the best policy might be simply to go it alone against O'Neill. Though more costly in the short run, over time it would be more effective in pacifying Ulster. There were now two political prerequisites for another military operation against Shane: 1) isolating him from potential Irish allies, especially his tanist, Turlough Luineach, and 2) establishing the rule of English law under lord presidents planted at Armagh and Newry.[67] Sussex had with difficulty maintained a foothold at Armagh, and the Bagenals continued to control Newry.

If England finally decided to move against O'Neill without the Scots, Clan Ian Mor would have virtually a free hand in northeastern Ulster until the conflict was settled. Sussex, who possessed neither the resources nor the confidence of the queen and the colonial community in Ireland, had little hope of success in the impending struggle. For the time being, things boded well for James and Sorley, provided Argyll did not double-cross them. The Campbell earl appeared confident that he could persuade a truculent James to accompany him to Edinburgh, where he might finally agree to commit the MacDonnells to an anti-O'Neill policy. But James MacDonnell did not go to Edinburgh. Rather he remained secure in the rugged Kintyre peninsula, seeking to remain neutral in the coming struggle between Sussex and Shane.[68]

From Kintyre in early 1563 James MacDonnell used Argyll as a conduit to negotiate with Randolph, who passed on information to London. Such tenuous connections did not portend a firm agreement. MacDonnell's ambiguous position being factored in, the sum amounted to even more frustration and confusion for England. In early February James reintroduced the question of the letters patent. He continued to complain that the general terms were unsatisfactory. When Piers arrived in Kintyre from Carrickfergus to represent Sussex's viewpoint, Dunyveg implied that he himself could do nothing without Sorley Boy's cooperation, and that he (James) was no longer able to control his younger brother's actions across the North Channel.[69]

Certainly the elder MacDonnell felt the pressure building, as the climax to the drama quickly approached. The English were so desperate to force James's hand that they sought the aid of two pirates, Thomas Phettiplace and William Johnson, who were questioned about the feasibility of kidnapping Dunyveg and then taking strategic Rathlin Island. Plans for a strike against James MacDonnell came to nothing, but that such a scheme was even considered suggests that the English were prepared to try almost anything to deprive Clan Ian Mor of its independence. James undoubtedly knew something was afoot, for in early spring he moved to Red Bay and assumed a hostile attitude toward whomever dared question his political stance. His correspondence also confirmed that he no longer controlled Sorley Boy, who now was the MacDonnells' acknowledged leader in Ireland.[70]

Sorley Boy, though seemingly a secondary figure beside James in the negotiations, actually controlled Clan Ian Mor's military strength in the Glynnes and the Route. That most of the extant MacDonnell letters and papers were either addressed to or despatched by the literate James should not diminish Sorley's significant role, especially as military commander. Had the family agreed to support England against O'Neill, the military burden would have fallen squarely on the shoulders of the Captain of the Route. In the early 1560s James spoke for and advised Sorley in official matters, and certainly could claim *de jure* leadership of Clan Ian Mor, but Sorley steered an independent course in Ulster. As the triangular struggle moved toward a crisis point, James and his brothers could rest easy knowing that the family's Irish affairs were in Sorley Boy's capable hands.

Sussex had weightier problems in early April than pursuing an alliance with Clan Ian Mor, preparing as he was to mount an immediate campaign into Tyrone to silence O'Neill. The ill-fated expedition arrived at Armagh on 6 April and frittered away several days there. A fortnight later Sussex himself would lodge a scathing complaint with Cecil that he had had no chance of defeating Shane without MacDonnell assistance.[71] But excuses could not hide the fact that Sussex's invasion was poorly planned and executed.

As Sussex sought out O'Neill in the fastnesses of Tyrone, he also looked to negotiate further with the MacDonnells. On 11 April Sussex heard from Piers, who had been shadowing Dunyveg:

> It may please your honour to be advertised of my doings with James MacDonnell the vii day of this month. I met with him at the Red Bay and . . . I found him very far off. Your honour may perceive by the copy of his articles which I have sent to your Lordship by this bearer and for finding any men in any place farther than from Lough Foyle to Newry . . . he utterly refused for that he said he could not do it without special licence of the Queen his mistress [i.e. Mary, Queen of Scots]. I had very much ado to bring him to grant licence that Owen Roe [a captain of Sussex's *gallóglaigh*] or other such captain of Scots as here remain within this realm . . . [may] serve the Queen's majesty . . . .[72]

Reacting to Piers's report, Sussex dashed off a letter from Armagh to James

MacDonnell, in which he reassured Clan Ian Mor that Elizabeth would likely issue revised letters patent. While he waited for the queen's decision, however, James was asked to employ Sorley in harassing Shane from the north and east.[73]

By mid-April Sussex and Clan Ian Mor had reached a tentative agreement. James informed Randolph that the Lord Lieutenant had offered him a commission to act against O'Neill.[74] Surmising that he had broken the long deadlock with the Antrim MacDonnells, Sussex believed that now he could assemble the necessary forces to defeat Shane. On 20 April he wrote Sorley Boy, informing him that he was to prevent O'Neill from crossing east of the Bann. Sorley was also to despatch forces immediately to Sussex at Armagh. Buoyed by this turn of events, Sussex boasted that he would be ready to hammer O'Neill by early May.[75]

While Sussex negotiated with the MacDonnells, his expedition against Shane encountered rough going. The elusive Shane, operating in his own country, refused to join battle with the slow-footed English.[76] By midsummer 1563 a frustrated Sussex admitted that "It is but a Sisyphus labour to expel Shane."[77] Sussex's claim to have secured aid from Clan Ian Mor and several important Ulster chiefs actually undercut his own defense of the failed attempt against O'Neill. Claiming such strength, he should have accomplished more than he did. Until now Elizabeth and Cecil had been overly patient with the Lord Lieutenant. In all fairness, he must be commended for his dogged determination to isolate the Scots from O'Neill and pull them into England's ambit. But a more sagacious captain would have realized that the MacDonnells, like others in the triangular struggle, were playing their own hand. After Sussex's failure, Elizabeth began considering a more conciliatory policy toward O'Neill.

Now that the English had resolved to negotiate again with Shane, they hoped to bring about Clan Ian Mor's destruction. Elizabeth and Sussex knew that the Antrim MacDonnells' presence on Shane's eastern flank certainly rankled him. If these two Gaelic powers could be set at odds, then England might stand aside and profit handsomely from the internecine bloodshed. Shane boasted that he would brook no opposition to his rule in Ulster and believed that the MacDonnells threatened his dominance as much as did the English. And even worse in O'Neill's eyes, James again declared his loyalty to Elizabeth in mid-May 1563. Randolph had met Dunyveg in Edinburgh, whereupon the elder MacDonnell saw "little cause why he [i.e. James] should bear kindness unto Shane O'Neill . . . ."[78]

It is difficult to ascertain whether James and Sorley now knew that their continued promises were no longer being taken seriously in London. Had the MacDonnells themselves been serious about an English alliance, Sussex would have welcomed their cooperation against Shane in the recent campaign. But after the failure to win over Clan Ian Mor and the subsequent move toward a more conciliatory policy with O'Neill, few

Englishmen expected anything from James and Sorley. Sussex believed that Sorley, in particular, would oppose further attempts to quell O'Neill, and he thought it imperative that the MacDonnells be dissuaded from this course by the granting of royal recognition of their territorial claims. The Lord Lieutenant concluded that "It were better in my opinion to collaborate with him [i.e. Sorley] for the time [being] than to hazard a worse matter ... ." A worse matter, however, appeared to be in the offing, as rumor spread that Shane had turned over most of his cattle to James MacDonnell for safekeeping in the Route. O'Neill reportedly had also arranged to introduce several thousand redshanks into Ulster to serve his cause. Sussex's report thus contradicted current orthodoxy that O'Neill would receive no MacDonnell support.[79]

Though London and Dublin policy-makers realized the futility of pursuing an accord with Clan Ian Mor any further, they were unwilling to abandon James and Sorley Boy completely in favor of a possible entente with O'Neill. Accordingly, the queen presented Sussex with two copies of the MacDonnell indenture, one of which was to be sent ahead to James while the other was to be held by Chancellor Cusake. But while James and Sorley Boy continued to swear public allegiance to Elizabeth, James's wife, Lady Agnes Campbell, was in Scotland making overtures to the queen of Scots.[80] Once this news reached Cecil in mid-June 1563, he and his mistress believed that the only course was to strike a deal with Shane and employ him against the Scots' colony in Ireland.

An accord between Clan Ian Mor and the queen of Scots would bring opposition from both England and the Protestant earl of Argyll. O'Neill, of course, was ready to oppose anyone who threatened his hegemony. James and Sorley thus faced three hostile powers in mid-1563. Piers, who was now England's point man in Ulster, suggested several ways of dealing with the MacDonnells. He also chronicled the Scottish queen's recent attempts to bolster James MacDonnell's position in the western Highlands, as well as countermeasures taken by Argyll against Clan Ian Mor. Argyll tried to arrange a coalition of island chiefs headed by Donnell Gorme MacDonald of Sleat, one of James's disgruntled kinsmen, who was reminded of the Dunyveg chief's aversion to him. Only by actively opposing Dunyveg in Scotland could Argyll "stay that there is no further invasion into Ireland by the Scots."[81]

The attempt by Elizabeth, Cecil, and Argyll to sever Clan Ian Mor from the queen of Scots and her pro-French party in Scotland hinged, in part, on exploiting the suspicion between the Highlands and Edinburgh and on reviving the old alliance between the chiefs and England. Donnell Gorme, self-styled lord of the Isles, pledged to serve the English crown by making war on the Antrim MacDonnells, and if provided proper support, "he should so weaken James, as the Scots would be the more easily *expulsed out of Ireland*" (author's italics).[82] There is no doubt that the Argyll–Sleat–English coalition intended great harm to Clan Ian Mor; however, barring the clan's complete destruction, the problem remained as to where the MacDonnells were to be driven. On the one hand, England clearly wished to expel them from Ulster to the western Highlands and Isles where they would be Scotland's problem. On the other, Argyll and the Presbyterians doubtless hoped that Clan Ian Mor could be isolated in northeastern Ireland, thus becoming primarily England's headache.

Despite the lingering problem of where Clan Ian Mor was to be banished, English authorities in Ireland were undoubtedly delighted with the numerous pledges of support against the MacDonnells. Piers boasted that should "the Scots . . . chance hereafter to deal in war with England, we being planted in the North of Ireland, what exploits and destructions we might daily do in Scotland is easily seen, considering how the lands lie one against another." This threat rested on an expanded English naval presence in the Irish Sea and the North Channel, "for if we plant there," wrote Piers, "we mean to build shipping . . . to annoy them both by sea and land. . . ." Mary, Queen of Scots, was to be warned that her subjects, especially the MacDonnells, would encounter hostile action should they continue to bring redshanks into Ulster. Piers's final recommendation in this lengthy and remarkable report was predicated on his opinion that the MacDonnells "had now become their own masters and lords," a situation unacceptable to the English in Ulster:

> We . . . will enter the North part of Ireland in the chief place of the Scots' force and expel them from all possessions in that realm, and plant ourselves where we shall be most near to aid O'Donnell and join with him against O'Neill and the Scots in such wise as within five years or less next coming if any [of] the people either noble or other of the North shall not be ready to serve her highness or her deputy and yield to her laws we shall with continual war so persecute them. . . .[83]

If an independent MacDonnell lordship in Ulster was unacceptable to England, it was also unacceptable to O'Neill. Shane was bent on dominating the province and saw Clan Ian Mor as a threat to his ambitions. Despite overtures toward them, O'Neill never trusted James, Sorley Boy, or their kinsmen. Piers had suggested that it would profit the queen to maneuver Shane and the Scots into war with one another. But he also knew that England eventually must deal with both Gaelic powers. In his opinion, the key to victory was an alliance with the Tyrconnell O'Donnells, who might be used to destroy both O'Neill and the MacDonnells.[84]

But for now London was content to treat with Shane before turning to the MacDonnells. Indeed, Elizabeth hoped that O'Neill could be employed to destroy them as a political and military force, thus alleviating the problem of whether Clan Ian Mor was to have residence in Ireland or Scotland. Heretofore, the conquest of Ulster had not warranted a steady, long-term military commitment by the Tudors. Sussex and his predecessors had been asked to subdue a large territory inhabited by a hostile populace without benefit of a coherent grand strategy.[85] Since Henry VIII's death, the Tudors had accomplished virtually nothing for all the money and manpower expended in Ulster. Thus by late summer 1563 Sir Thomas Cusake and Gerald, earl of Kildare, began negotiations with Shane.

Shane O'Neill and the English signed a treaty on 11 September 1563. The Peace of Drum Cru (or Benburb) ended a long and excruciating series of negotiations. Elizabeth finally recognized, at least temporarily, the Great O'Neill's superiority in Ulster. Shane's traditional Gaelic title was confirmed and he received the right of heritable jurisdiction over his *urraights*. He also was left free to re-establish relations with the Tyrconnell O'Donnells on his own terms. As he distrusted Sussex, Shane was exempted from appearing before him, and all disputes were to be settled immediately before representatives of both sides. The treaty would remain in force until the feast of All Saints Day (1 November), at which time the English garrison at Armagh would be withdrawn and the town restored to Shane.[86]

For all the concessions made to O'Neill, England received only vague assurances that Shane would behave himself until All Saints Day. Only a month after Drum Cru, which superceded all former agreements between the two parties, Elizabeth began to regret signing the treaty. Sussex, however, was instructed to uphold the bargain.[87] Shortly after the deadline Cusake presented Shane with the final draft:[88]

> Her Majesty receives Shane O'Neill to her gracious favour, and pardons all his offences; he shall remain captain and governor of his territory or province of Tirone, and shall have the name and title of O'Neill, and all the jurisdiction and preeminces which his ancestors possessed, with the service and homage of the lords and captains called Urraughts, and other [of] the chieftains of the O'Neill country, and he shall be created Earl of Tyrone.[89]

In return, Shane promised to do some service to show his gratitude. As it turned out, that service was to be an attack on the MacDonnells in the Glynnes and the Route in 1564–5.

England's attempt to destroy Clan Ian Mor stemmed from her desire to keep the MacDonnells from allying with Shane O'Neill and from acting as a conduit for foreign intrigue in, and perhaps even invasion of, Ulster. By 1563 this objective overshadowed the more modest goal of curbing Shane O'Neill's local power in Tyrone. Shane's claim to the overlordship of Ulster through Drum Cru amounted to *imperium in imperio*, a situation that Elizabeth could not permanently sanction. But, as pointed out above, Shane and the other Irish chiefs were local magnates with local ambitions. Clan Ian Mor, however, represented a larger power bloc that might successfully defend the entire region against English encroachment. By the early 1560s northeastern Ulster was marked for colonization; coercion replaced persuasion. But the parsimonious Elizabeth proved unwilling to expend the necessary manpower and material and unable to persuade Argyll to support an Irish enterprise. As a result, English forces despatched to Ireland were too weak by themselves to subjugate either the MacDonnells or O'Neill. Because England alone could defeat neither Gaelic power, and because Clan Ian Mor posed the greatest long-term threat, the queen hoped to persuade O'Neill under the Drum Cru agreement to crush James and Sorley Boy and end their long-standing neutrality.[90]

Chapter Five
Shane O'Neill's Campaign Against Clan Ian Mor, 1564–5

> . . . but time and chance happeneth to them all.
>
> Ecclesiastes 9:11

The peace of Drum Cru had serious consequences for Clan Ian Mor. Once the final version of the treaty was concluded in November 1563 and Shane O'Neill had pledged to serve Elizabeth, it was only a matter of time until the MacDonnells' settlement in northeastern Ulster was attacked by the Tyrone chief. James's and Sorley Boy's stubborn neutrality from 1560 to 1563 had convinced both Shane and the English that the Scots were opportunists who wished to profit from a general Ulster conflict in which they themselves would not participate. Thus in 1564–5 O'Neill and England reached an understanding which would banish the Scots from Ireland. The campaign and its concluding battle of Glentaisie (or Glenshesk) on 2 May 1565 was one of the most momentous internecine conflicts ever witnessed in the Gaelic heartland.

For England the triangular struggle in Ulster from 1560 to 1563 had been characterized by a series of missed opportunities to rid themselves of either O'Neill, or Clan Ian Mor, or both. But by late 1563 they had begun to formulate a coherent policy based on using O'Neill against the Scots and on establishing a strong O'Donnell presence in Tyrconnell.[1] By driving a wedge between two major Gaelic powers–in this case, the Tyrone O'Neills and the Antrim MacDonnells–the English queen continued a practice begun by Edward I (1272–1307) during the Scottish Wars of Independence. Furthermore, prospects of a cooperative pact between the leading Gaelic families of Ulster and the southwestern Highlands and Isles suffered a terrible blow because of the hostility between Shane and Clan Ian Mor in the 1560s. For the remainder of the century, the Gaels were unable to overcome their narrow, selfish concerns and unite against the Sassenach. This is pointed up, for instance, by the refusal of the Antrim MacDonnells to provide significant aid to Hugh O'Neill, second earl of Tyrone, in his war against the English from 1595 to 1603.

Drum Cru was the culmination of a rather inglorious phase of England's Irish policy wherein she had reacted to, rather than initiated, events. This passive strategy could only defend the Pale rather than expand England's influence throughout Ireland. Lord Lieutenant Sussex had lamented in 1560 that Ireland might be "sunk in the Sea" lest it become "a ruin to England as I am afeared to think of."[2] Since the late 1540s the French had threatened to intervene in Ireland, but by the early 1560s that danger had disappeared. Despite the current continental political climate's being unfavorable for Catholic exploitation of the Tudor's geo-political Achilles heel, English policy toward Gaelic Ireland hardened discernibly after 1563. The tougher policy stemmed from a realization that once the Counter-Reformation powers finally put their own houses in order, the specter of foreign intervention in Ulster undoubtedly would appear once again. Now, while things were relatively quiet abroad, Elizabeth and Cecil moved to destroy the most likely magnet for international intrigue in the Gaelic heartland–Clan Ian Mor.[3]

Since the early 1550s the debate in English political circles between the proponents of persuasion and those of coercion undoubtedly had appeared like so much pusillanimous dallying to most Gaelic leaders. But upon Sussex's departure in early 1564, there was no longer any doubt about the course of England's Ulster policy. Colonization, reasoned English policy-makers, was the only viable way of cultivating civilization in the Ulster wilderness. Because O'Neill was now in England's camp, Elizabeth and her council could focus on an aggressive policy to squeeze the MacDonnells out of the Glynnes and the Route and create a second Pale in Antrim. New English adventurers were now executing, if not making, Irish policy; it is not surprising, then, that the subjugation and colonization of eastern Ulster should be given high priority.[4]

The triangular struggle from 1560 to 1563 had yet to break into open warfare despite numerous border raids and skirmishes between the contending parties. But England's determination to rid Ulster of the Scots with O'Neill's assistance meant that a general conflict was likely. Bearing this in mind, it is necessary to examine briefly some important facets of sixteenth-century Gaelic warfare. A contemporary Englishman observed that Gaelic *seanachaidh* (historians)

> make the ignorant men . . . to believe that they be descended of Alexander the Great, or of Darius, or of Caesar, or of some other notable prince. . . . [I]f they see any young man descended of the septs of O or Mac, and have half a dozen about him, then they will make him a rhyme, wherein will commend his father and his ancestors, numbering how many heads they have cut off, how many towns they have burned . . . and in the end they will compare him to Hannibal or Scipio or Hercules. . .

wherewithal the poor fool runs mad, and thinks indeed it is so. Then will he gather a sort of "rackells" [rakehells] to him, and . . . have a bagpipe blowing afore them. . . .[5]

Though exaggerated, this passage contains a kernel of truth in that it conveys the importance of the military ethos in traditional Gaelic society.

Medieval Irish warfare was based on a combination of native light infantry (kerne) and light cavalry. But in the fourteenth and fifteenth centuries large numbers of heavily armed Scottish *gallóglaigh* migrated to Ireland and offered their services to the highest bidder. The introduction of Hebridean heavy infantry dramatically changed the nature of Irish warfare. The melding of mobile Irish guerrilla tactics and Scottish shock tactics had driven the Normans from the Irish countryside. The traditional Celtic charge carried out by fierce heavy infantry usually decided the contest after the nimble kerne and cavalry had harassed and disorganized the enemy. By 1550 the large-scale introduction of firearms into Ireland brought about some important tactical changes; however, the fundamental nature of Gaelic warfare remained the same. It continued to be based on a combination of finesse, mobility, and the primal shock of cold steel at close quarters, preferably under irregular battlefield conditions.[6]

The informal nature of Gaelic warfare made it difficult for conventional armies to stand up to the Scots or Irish except when Gaelic commanders attempted to fight on plain ground with formal, continental tactics. Throughout the Celtic fringe, methods of combat were much less formal than in areas of Europe where strong central governments dominated. Besides the lack of central government, rugged Gaelic Ireland had few roads over which conventional armies burdened by supplies and artillery could effectively move about. It was impractical for a conventional army to fight anything except defensive and static war based on the control of strategically located castles.[7]

Because of their differing styles of warfare, the Gaels and the English met infrequently in major battles. If the English met the Gaels in the wilds of Ulster and sought a decision by close-quarter tactics, the Sassenach likely would lose. But if the Irish or Scots met the English in formal battle on an open plain, or if they besieged an English stronghold, it was the Gaels who probably would suffer defeat. As long as the Gaels stood on the strategic defensive and forced the English to penetrate their rugged and unfamiliar homeland, the former could usually dictate the time, place, and nature of combat. By limiting the extent of their offensive strategy to lightning raids against enemy logistics on the borders of the Pale, the Gaels ran little risk of being cornered and forced to give conventional battle. If they mounted a full-blown strategic offensive to drive the English out of Ireland, however, they would have to fight a type of war at which they did not excel. Conversely, if the English were to drive Clan Ian Mor out of the Glynnes and the Route or O'Neill from Tyrone, they, too, would have to fight under disadvantageous conditions.[8]

Because England found it necessary to take the offensive to conquer and colonize eastern Ulster, she needed O'Neill's assistance in fighting the MacDonnells on their own turf and terms. But Shane was not the typical Celtic military leader as was, say, the great seventeenth-century warrior, Alasdair MacColla. O'Neill's stubborn pride, haughtiness, and boastful claims to sovereignty in Ulster are well known, but questions have been raised about his personal courage and willingness to lead his troops into battle, as did MacColla and other Gaelic commanders before and since.[9] Sir George Carew, the military adventurer and President of Munster (1599–1600), characterized the late Shane as a

> prudent, wise captain, and a good giver of an onset or charge upon his enemies, during the time of his reign, and was given from fourteen years of age, till the day of his death, always in the wars. . . . Proud he was and arrogant, for the thought that no man ought of right to be his superior, or seem his equal. He had great policy in the wars, that he was practiced with, no man more in his time. . . .[10]

Carew credited Shane with formulating "great policy in the wars" and with the ability to "procure his men to do well, for he had many good men according to the wars of his country," but he also revealed that, individually, O'Neill "was the last that would give the charge upon his foes, and the first that would flee. . . ."[11] Thomas Phettiplace confirmed Carew's opinion of the chief's lack of personal courage in battle by noting that the "quality in warlike might indeed is little in him at all. . . ."[12]

Shane O'Neill, by most accounts, was a more modern military leader (as would be his nephew, Hugh O'Neill, second earl of Tyrone) than any of his Irish or Scottish contemporaries. One of his most noteworthy accomplishments was the revolutionary practice of recruiting, training, and arming common Irishmen. But his decision not to command from the front ranks, probably more than anything else, accounts for his martial success. Standing back from the fighting, O'Neill could direct his forces more effectively in either guerrilla or conventional tactics. Phettiplace's account, though obviously intended to belittle Shane's military methods, actually points up one of his principal strengths: the temperament and ability to avoid battle under all but the most favorable circumstances.[13] Again, Shane was content on several occasions to allow Sussex to march virtually unopposed through Ulster. He knew that exhausting marches, punctuated by pinprick guerrilla attacks, demoralized English armies. To fight the MacDonnells, however, demanded that Shane go straight for the throat. Because the Scots could utilize the rugged terrain of Ulster just as effectively as could O'Neill's Irishmen, irregular war that stressed the disruption of logistics and the exhaustion and demoralization of the enemy through hit-and-run tactics would not suffice to defeat Clan Ian Mor's veteran redshanks.

That O'Neill would keep the peace with England and banish the Antrim MacDonnells from Ulster was far from certain in early 1564. Though Terence Daniel informed Cecil of Shane's intention to keep his word, English officials preferred some concrete assurances of loyalty. Robert Fleming, mayor of Drogheda, noted in mid-April that the Scots were venturing dangerously close to Tyrone. In light of these developments, he continued, if Elizabeth approved and then supplied material aid for a counterstroke, O'Neill would drive Clan Ian Mor from Ireland before year's end. But the English government, though slowly carrying out a change of policy from persuasion to coercion, proved unable to respond to Fleming's despatch. Sussex being out of favor (and soon out of Ireland), the Dublin administration's policy had begun to drift. On 2 May Lord Justice Nicholas Arnold replaced Sussex as head of the Irish government. Immediately, the army's strength was reduced and a number of unsavory practices were eliminated in hopes of fielding a more effective force in the near future. Arnold, then, came to Ireland to undo, or at least to smooth out, the disastrous effects of prior policy decisions; consequently, his administration purposefully avoided relations with Gaelic Ulster, hoping that O'Neill would see to English interests there.[14]

O'Neill doubtless perceived that England's temporary weakness and confusion in Ireland gave him an opportunity to further his own political ends while pretending to serve the queen. Drum Cru had given him a free hand in dealing with the O'Donnells. One of the few concessions that Shane made was to agree that Calvagh O'Donnell could return to rule the lordship of Tyrconnell, as old Manus had died the previous February. But as Calvagh and Con O'Donnell made their way from Dublin to Tyrconnell via Fermanagh in May, O'Neill set upon them. He then swept into Tyrconnell and occupied Lifford Castle, which he previously had agreed to return to the O'Donnells. Ostensibly, O'Neill was in O'Donnell country to collect the cattle promised him as ransom for Calvagh. He actually was there to put down any attempt by the English to restore the O'Donnells to power. Shane now counted the O'Donnells among his *urraights,* this privilege having been guaranteed him in the 1563 treaty. But O'Neill's plans for Tyrconnell conflicted with England's desire to re-establish the O'Donnells as a counterweight to his ambitions. For the time being, though, English officials had to hold their tongues and suffer Shane the Proud to have his way in Tyrconnell.[15]

Ulster reportedly was quiet and prosperous in May 1564. Springtime brought relief from a severe winter in the Gaelic heartland, and Terence Daniel informed Cecil that Ulster's bounty overflowed now that Shane had established his peace over the province. But the idyllic Ulster described by Daniel was, according to O'Neill, endangered by Clan Ian Mor's aggressive behavior. Shane probably depicted Ulster as a troubled paradise to obtain substantial aid against the MacDonnells, whom he portrayed as the principal agents of evil in Ireland. O'Neill himself had written Elizabeth on 23 May, detailing the constant acts of aggression perpetrated against him by the Scots. He also complained that he could not get a letter past them to Mary, Queen of Scots, who he hoped might persuade Sorley and James to keep the peace. Shane asked Elizabeth to confer with her Scottish cousin concerning the appointment of commissioners to settle things with Clan Ian Mor.[16]

Shane tried to blame the Antrim MacDonnells for breaking the peace, but any troubles that befell Ulster could be laid squarely upon his broad shoulders. He continued to prey upon the O'Donnells in Tyrconnell, especially Con's followers. The queen of Scots wrote Elizabeth in early June that a ship owned by one of her (Mary's) subjects had been plundered at port in Carlingford by a force of 300–400 men under O'Neill and Fedoracha Magennis. For this and other reasons, the Scottish queen was not likely to support Shane against the MacDonnells. A few days later Sir Thomas Cusake traveled to Tyrone but found that Shane was still away. The chancellor learned, however, that O'Neill remained anxious to strike the Scots.[17] Shane feared that he could no longer conceal his real intentions of self-aggrandizement and the fact that the queen's interests were not necessarily his own.

To smooth things over with England in the summer of 1564, Shane continued to threaten Clan Ian Mor. There is no question that a successful invasion of the Glynnes and the Route would have secured O'Neill's position in Ulster and, in the long run, freed him to drive out the English. For the past three years the Scots had grown so powerful that they endangered Shane's hold over his portion of Ulster. O'Neill realized that Sorley Boy and James must be dealt with before he could turn on the English. He also knew that Elizabeth feared the MacDonnells even more than she feared him. This undoubtedly rankled the mighty O'Neill, but he astutely used England's dread of the Scots as a pretext for breaking the peace in 1564–5. Accordingly, he informed the English on 18 August 1564 that he would be willing to mount a military expedition against the MacDonnells if he received the queen's approval.[18]

English authorities quickly accepted O'Neill's offer to drive the Scots from the Glynnes and the Route. Less than a week after receiving Shane's letter, the Dublin council informed him that the expedition had been approved. But O'Neill wanted more than England's approval; he demanded material assistance, especially from the earl of Kildare and from Piers at Carrickfergus. Shane also requested access to Carrickfergus as a base of operations for his campaign.[19] Terence Daniel informed Lord Justice Arnold that O'Neill believed "his ancestors of old time had freedom there [i.e. Carrickfergus], and he requireth to have the like. . . ."[20] The English, of course, were suspicious of Shane's every turn. Thus they informed him at once that both Kildare and Piers were already occupied and that Carrickfergus could offer no assistance.[21] Dublin's refusal to become involved in the campaign prevented the Lord Justice and council from exerting any control over its direction. O'Neill obviously had been given a free hand to deal with Clan Ian Mor.

Shane stood ready to begin his campaign in early September, having gathered enough supplies for five or six weeks in the field. He believed a *coup de main* was his best chance to defeat the Scots, and in order to preserve the crucial element of surprise he had to avoid any large movement of troops or supplies that might arouse suspicion. Because the traditional redshank campaigning season extended from *Bealtainn* (1 May) to *Samhain* (1 November), it was imperative that nothing be attempted before Clan Ian Mor's mercenaries left to winter in the western Highlands and Isles.[22] Between November and May MacDonnell strength would be significantly diminished. Shane had to subdue Sorley Boy quickly before either the redshank host returned in the spring of 1565 or he could call in reinforcements from James in Kintyre. O'Neill's preparations for war in autumn 1564 were designed to draw Sorley's attention westward toward the Bann and away from the southern approaches to the Glynnes. It was not unusual for O'Neill to operate on the western bank of the river, especially since his authority in the area of Lough Foyle and eastern Tyrconnell was recognized by the Peace of Drum Cru. On 5 September he wrote the Lord Justice that he was rebuilding the old castle at Culrath (Coleraine) just west of the Bann. O'Neill knew all too well that Sorley would not jeopardize control of the Route by allowing a potentially hostile force to assemble on its western flank. To draw the MacDonnell leader's attention, Shane despatched a small force across the river and occupied a friary on the eastern side. Sorley Boy had kept a close watch on O'Neill, but he was taken by surprise at his opponent's sudden crossing of the Bann, which was in spate due to recent heavy rains.[23] Daniel described the river-crossing and the occupation of the friary:

> O'Neill did gather an host to go upon the Scots and came to the water of the Bann, where he found a great flood and could not get over, and then began to make a strong fort in the old castle of Culrath, and had there ii or iii little cots [i.e. small boats or coracles] and sent some of his men over in the same and went over himself, and set some horsemen and harquebussiers ward in the friary of Culrath. And then the Scots was [sic] within two or three miles to the friary and O'Neill came over again and when the Scots heard that he was in the friary . . . they made as much haste as they could to the friary. . . .[24]

O'Neill's operation on the Bann in early September brought the first

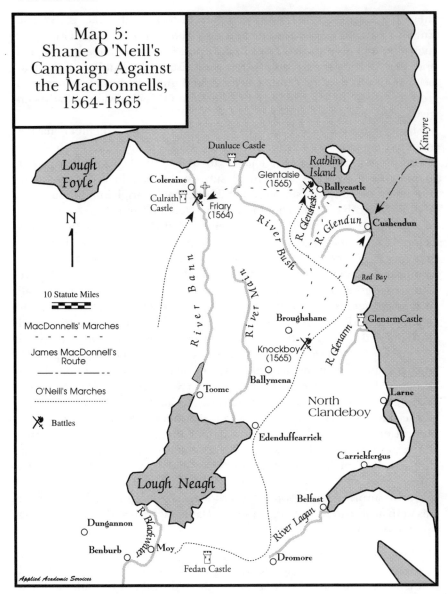

Map 5:
Shane O'Neill's
Campaign Against
the MacDonnells,
1564-1565

Lough
Foyle

Dunluce Castle

Rathlin
Island

Coleraine

Glentaisie
(1565)

Ballycastle

Kintyre

Culrath
Castle

Friary
(1564)

N

River Bush

R. Glenshesk

R. Glendun

Cushendun

River Bann

River Main

Red Bay

10 Statute Miles

MacDonnells' Marches

Broughshane

GlenarmCastle

James MacDonnell's
Route

Knockboy
(1565)

R. Glenarm

O'Neill's Marches

Ballymena

Battles

Toome

Larne

North
Clandeboy

Edenduffcarrick

Carrickfergus

Lough Neagh

Belfast

Dungannon

R. Blackwater

Benburb

Moy

Fedan Castle

River Lagan

Dromore

Applied Academic Services

bloodshed of the campaign. His occupation of the friary at Culrath forced Sorley's hand. The captain of the Route brought forward a detachment from his 600 to 700-man force to wrest control of Culrath from the enemy and drive him back across the Bann. According to Daniel, they

> came to it [i.e. the friary] . . . like mad men and continued all that night bickering, and there was a great number of the best of them killed and . . . they were killed and wounded about the number of iiii^{xx} and x. And in the morning after they came over the sides and the horsemen that was ward within took some faintness and thought to swim over the Bann with their horses, and some of them was drowned, and the best of them came away, and when the Scots saw that being nigh to them they turned again to the friary, and as many as they took of the footmen and harquebussiers that could not swim, they killed them.[25]

Sorley Boy accomplished his objective of pushing Shane's small contingent back to its starting point, but the MacDonnells sustained fairly heavy casualties as a result of O'Neill's spirited defense. On the morning after the battle, wrote Daniel, Sorley, who reportedly had received a minor wound, parleyed with O'Neill on the banks of the Bann. Just what the two men conferred about is unknown; however, it is unlikely that they spoke words of peace, as Daniel noted that "my Lord O'Neill begins to gather another host, and goes next week towards the Bann. . . ."[26] Shane obviously intended to keep Sorley focused on the Bann so that he would neglect preparations in the southern Glynnes.

Geography and topography proved to be among the most important factors in Shane's planning for the campaign. Mountain ranges dominated much of Ulster. They were pierced by the rivers Erne, Foyle, Bann, and Lagan, the only gateways into the heart of Ulster through which sizeable armies could move. The Irish and Antrim Scots were more mobile than the English and could operate effectively in small units over rugged terrain, but the major expedition that O'Neill envisioned called for using a conventional route into MacDonnell territory. The two most practical pathways were across the lower third (or northern sector) of the Bann, which for some fifteen miles threatened the western approaches to the Route, and south of Lough Neagh, up the Lagan valley into northwestern County Down, across North Clandeboy, and through the southern entrance to the Glynnes. Shane had threatened the Route on the lower stretches of the Bann to draw Sorley's attention. The fighting at Culrath Friary would be the only significant military action for the remainder of 1564, but it forced Sorley Boy to be ever vigilant on the Route's western borders. O'Neill would spend the next few months mapping out his plans to strike the MacDonnells from the south and trying to persuade the English to provide assistance.[27]

In his report on the battle at Culrath, Shane continued to push for aid from Piers and Kildare. But Dublin insisted that nothing could be spared for

Shane's Ulster campaign. The government claimed that Kildare and most of the English army in Ireland were employed in the other provinces. Piers offered no help either, as Carrickfergus had to remain strongly garrisoned to anchor the eastern flank of England's defenses. Even if aid could be spared, Arnold argued in mid-September, a general hosting such as O'Neill wanted would take too long to carry out. Thus the English, who were in the midst of changing from a defensive policy under Sussex to an aggressive policy of coercion under Sidney, refused for the moment to sanction another Ulster adventure. But Arnold assured Shane that Elizabeth would be consulted on the matter. The queen and her council, however, were in no mood to commit precious resources when O'Neill already possessed enough to carry out his task.[28]

While Shane was occupied in late 1564 with planning the impending invasion of northeastern Ulster, Sorley Boy and James MacDonnell were ordering their affairs on both sides of the North Channel and pulling together Clan Ian Mor's military strength. In late October James went to Edinburgh with news of the troubles brewing in Ulster and saw fit to leave behind an ambassador to brief Randolph. James complained of Shane's treachery, explaining that the O'Neill chief had ravaged several Scottish settlements in Lecale on the eve of *Samhain*. The Lecale MacDonnells, kinsmen of the dominant Antrim branch, were led by MacGillaspick MacDonnell, son of MacRanaldboy, whom Brereton had slain years earlier. If the Lecale MacDonnells fell to O'Neill, Sorley's and James's first line of defense in Clandeboy would disappear. To prevent the loss of the strategic southern approaches to the Glynnes, James contemplated sending his own forces from Kintyre to Lecale.[29]

Affairs within the MacDonnell camp in late 1564 were centered on James as he traveled between Kintyre and Edinburgh seeking support against O'Neill. According to rumor, Shane had been pressing both Argyll and Mary, Queen of Scots, for an alliance. That O'Neill, who already had an agreement with England, would now seek support from Argyll and the Scottish queen must have unnerved James. Without safe access to the western Highlands and Isles, Clan Ian Mor would lose its redshank recruiting grounds as well as its line of retreat. To cement his good standing with Mary, James asked for confirmation of his title to lands previously granted him in Kintyre. He also pledged to answer for any transgressions committed by Sorley Boy in Ireland. But Randolph, writing Cecil on Christmas Eve, doubted that James could be trusted, though he (James) still expressed a willingness to serve against O'Neill. It is doubtful whether Randolph yet knew of the plan to use Shane to drive the MacDonnells from Ulster. But he was quite correct in believing that James (as well as Argyll) could not be trusted to further English interests in Ireland.[30]

As James continued his efforts to improve Clan Ian Mor's political position in Scotland, Sorley Boy monitored Shane's actions in Ulster. Both MacDonnell leaders sensed that something was afoot; it is not surprising, then, that O'Neill tried to mislead Sorley by reassuring him that all was well between the two Gaelic powers. Sir William Fitzwilliam, now Irish Vice-Treasurer, disclosed to Cecil in early January that "Shane O'Neill hath put over his parlement last appointed [i.e. in the previous autumn] with Sorley Boy until Candlemas [2 February], friendship . . . there is between them two, and all I can do then is to wish that it were the contrary. . . ."[31] Fitzwilliam's report proved erroneous, for there was no friendship between Sorley and Shane, nor would they meet in early February. As on the Bann in the previous autumn, Shane attempted to mask his true intentions.

The MacDonnells realized in early 1565 that the English and O'Neill had isolated them. As a result of his anti-MacDonnell posturing, Shane had drawn closer to the queen. For her part, Elizabeth simply wished to be rid of the Scottish enclave in Ulster so she could then deal with Shane. To accomplish this objective, she decided to forgo Argyll's offer of military assistance (which he likely would not have agreed to use against the MacDonnells anyway) and to employ O'Neill alone against the Scots. Argyll had assured Randolph in January that James MacDonnell would cause no trouble in Ulster. But for the English to have drawn closer to the MacCailein Mor (a title for the earls of Argyll, meaning "son of the great Colin") would have meant sanctioning the entry of more redshanks into Ulster, a situation that well might undo what England hoped to accomplish by driving out Clan Ian Mor in the first place. It appears that Elizabeth and Cecil had convinced themselves that Shane possessed the ability to defeat the MacDonnells without aid and expenditure from either England or Argyll.[32]

The immediate chain of events leading to Clan Ian Mor's defeat at Glentaisie (Glenshesk) in May 1565 began in February when the MacDonnells sensed the seriousness of their plight. They remembered O'Neill's campaign on the Bann and his raids into North Clandeboy in the last months of 1564 and thus prepared for a resumption of his aggressive behavior. The mayor of Drogheda divulged to Cecil that at the beginning of February James MacDonnell sent 300 of his *Luchdtach*, or elite guard, to raid Lecale and the Ardes. That James despatched these troops from Kintyre suggests that he expected O'Neill to attack at any time. Perhaps the arrival of this advance guard was intended to make Shane reveal his hand. The normally impetuous O'Neill, however, stood fast. He preferred to lull the MacDonnells into a false sense of security, patiently awaiting the right moment to unleash his fury. The remainder of the winter passed without serious incident.[33]

Shane had completed his campaign preparations by early April. He enjoyed a two-to-one (2,000 to 1,000) numerical superiority over the combined MacDonnell forces, and Sorley did not expect most of his redshanks to return until after the beginning of May.[34] He was clearly outnumbered, but Sorley Boy appeared unconcerned, even smug, about his situation. In February Robert Fleming had reported that he

> spoke with a man that was at Sorley Boy's house [in Ballycastle] about twelve [in the] evening after supper, there being disposed to talk one gentleman [who] said that there was but 120 miles from Coleraine to Dublin and we [i.e. the Scots] have 100 miles of that under our rule for the most part. . . .[35]

Underestimating an enemy certainly was not characteristic of the victor of Slieve-an-Aura. But for whatever reasons, Sorley had failed to prepare adequately for O'Neill's onslaught.

Shane's march to the borders of Clandeboy in April took Sorley by surprise. Over the past several months O'Neill had made a number of feints specifically designed to mask the actual invasion of the Glynnes. Sorley apparently perceived Shane's advance toward Clandeboy as merely another raid to discipline his unruly *urraights*. But Shane, after spending Easter at Fedan Castle in the Fews, advanced some sixteen miles to Dromore (just south of the Lagan in County Down). The next morning he cleared passes through the forest in order to enter Clandeboy. At this point, Sorley realized that O'Neill's move might be more than just a raid. Consequently, he hurried from his headquarters at Ballycastle to join the Scottish front-line forces in North Clandeboy, where he attempted to orchestrate a defense.[36]

After entering Clandeboy in late April, Shane moved twelve more miles through the rugged forests of Kilwarlin to Edenduffcarrick (also called Shane's castle). O'Neill spent the next four days (27–30 April) reorganizing his army to enter the southern Glynnes and stocking Edenduffcarrick as a base of operations. Gerot (Liam) Fleming, a member of Shane's inner circle, detailed his chief's activities after reaching Edenduffcarrick:

> The morrow after being Thursday [27 April], he rode towards Gallantry, a mile from Edenduffcarrick, where he camped that night, in which place he built and renewed an old fort . . . Friday, Saturday, and till noon Sunday, and from thence (having left certain of his men in the said fort) he removed towards Cloghdonaghy [i.e. Clough, County Antrim] in the Route, and enter[ed] into a pass called Knockboy [near Broughshane]. . . .[37]

The two forces joined battle in the quarter-mile-long pass of Knockboy on Saturday, 29 April. It was at Knockboy, a strategic point that allowed entry into the Glynnes from the southwest or the Route from the southeast, that Sorley had established his first line of defense. By now he knew that Shane had unleashed a full-scale invasion of MacDonnell territory. According to Fleming's campaign report, when Shane entered the pass of Knockboy, "the Scots being ready before him, unawares set upon him, where he killed of them to the number of twenty, and the rest were fain to take the bogs and woods. . . ."[38] O'Neill himself noted that "Somhairle [Sorley] Boy defended a certain pass, with the objective of preventing my further progress. But by divine aid I gave them battle, in which many of his men were slain; and the remnant fled. . . ."[39]

Before Sorley evacuated Knockboy Pass in the late afternoon, his messengers were already on their way to Ballycastle with word to light the signal fires on Fair Head (Benmore), Murlough Bay, and Torr Head that would summon James MacDonnell's galleys from Kintyre. It now appeared that a race would ensue between the MacDonnells in Scotland and O'Neill to see who could intercept Sorley's small band as it retreated toward Ballycastle. But a confident Shane, with the larger army, did not set out immediately to overtake Sorley Boy on that Sunday evening. Rather he rested his men overnight at Sorley's abandoned camp near Clough for the next day's march.[40]

Marching from Clough through Glenballyemon on 30 April, O'Neill reached James MacDonnell's castle at Red Bay, just south of Cushendall. He burned the stronghold and plundered the adjoining district of Glenariff.[41] The destruction of Red Bay drove home to Sorley and James the seriousness of Shane's offensive. The town and adjacent castle not only protected the southern approaches to the Glynnes, but also was a crucial landing-place for incoming redshanks. Since Red Bay was lost, the Scots fell back to the Cushendun–Ballycastle line. At the close of the day on 30 April, the MacDonnells had precious few troops with which to hold that axis. James had not been idle while Shane's troops overran the Red Bay–Glenariff district. From his residence at Saddell, Dunyveg summoned the *Fir Chinntire* (men of Kintyre) to their galleys. Leaving behind younger brother Alasdair Oge, steward of Kintyre, to raise more reinforcements, James sailed that evening for Cushendun, where an anxious Sorley Boy and his small band awaited. They combined forces in the early morning hours of Monday, 1 May. As James and Sorley looked to the south, they saw plumes of smoke rising through the morning mist from the burnt-out ruins of Red Bay Castle and from the fires of Shane's nearby camp. The MacDonnell leaders hastily marched their combined forces northwest over the bleak moors past Loughareema, down the left bank of the river Carey, and then due west to Ballycastle. The town was the most prominent redshank landing-place on the North Antrim coast. Ballycastle occupied a narrow stretch of coastal plain where the northernmost of the Antrim Glynnes met the Route. In the shadow of the hill of Knocklayd (elevation 1695 feet/515 metres), rising two miles south of town and marking the start of rugged, mountainous terrain, Ballycastle commanded the most accessible east-west gateway between the

Glynnes and the Route.[42] It was here, then, that the MacDonnells believed Shane would direct his main effort.

Shane roused his troops on *Bealtainn* morn (1 May) and began the fateful trek to Ballycastle. His own description of the march from Red Bay disclosed that he met no opposition to his entry into the town.[43] It is puzzling why O'Neill was allowed to reach Ballycastle with such ease. As the bay was now the closest entry point for reinforcements from Alasdair Oge in Kintyre, reason suggests, on the one hand, that Sorley and James erred in camping a mile west of town near Dunanynie Castle. This position permitted Shane to occupy the landing-place unopposed. On the other, however, the MacDonnells may have concocted a stratagem designed to draw O'Neill through Ballycastle and into the valley of the river Tow, or Glentaisie, to the southwest of town where the battle was to be fought. Sorley and James knew that even though O'Neill was superior in numbers, he likely would not leave a garrison in Ballycastle. After all, Shane had secured neither Red Bay nor Cushendun, both of which could have been used by Clan Ian Mor to land troops to his rear. If Shane followed Sorley and James down Glentaisie, Alasdair Oge could land at Ballycastle and squeeze O'Neill between two MacDonnell armies that together would equal his own in number.

The answer to why the MacDonnells abandoned Ballycastle hangs, in part, on the route that O'Neill took in reaching the town on 1 May. As Shane's 2,000-man force left Red Bay, it moved west through Glenaan, skirted north of the site of Sorley's victory at Slieve-an-Aura, and then turned sharply northward into the valley of the river Shesk and on to Ballycastle. There has been some historical debate whether the battle took place in Glenshesk or Glentaisie. Circumstances strongly suggest that the contest occurred in Glentaisie. Otherwise, Shane would have encountered Sorley and James on his way to Ballycastle on 1 rather than 2 May, after he had already occupied the town for a night.[44] MacDonnell scouts monitored O'Neill's every move, and once they reported that he was taking the eastern route around Knocklayd down Glenshesk, Sorley and James moved west of Ballycastle and down rugged and picturesque Glentaisie. At this point, they had three tactical options: 1) to cooperate with Alasdair Oge in bottling up O'Neill between Ballycastle and Glentaisie, as explored above; 2) to slip around the northern edge of Knocklayd and strike Shane's left flank as he approached the town; or 3) to fight a rearguard action while falling back to the southwest towards Armoy. Sorley apparently never seriously considered a formal defense of the town. As a Gaelic commander, he knew that his men fought best when attacking, and the defense of Ballycastle probably would not have presented an opportunity to take the tactical offensive.[45]

On the evening of Monday, 1 May, the stage was set for a crucial test of arms between the two strongest Gaelic powers in Ulster. The Scots chose to stay and fight in Glentaisie, but they did not attempt to disrupt Shane's march to Ballycastle. Sorley and James now pinned their hopes on the

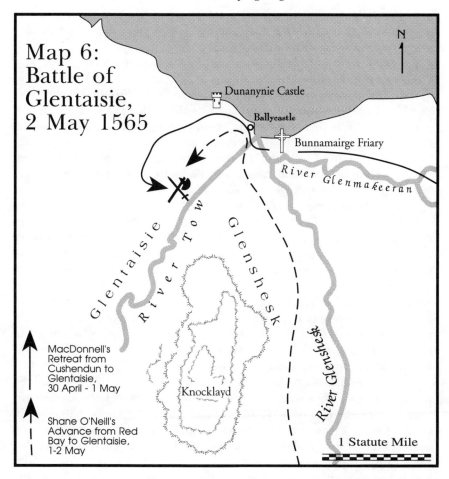

Map 6: Battle of Glentaisie, 2 May 1565

N

Dunanynie Castle

Ballycastle

Bunnamairge Friary

River Glenmakeeran

Glentaisie

River Tow

Glenshesk

River Glenshesk

Knocklayd

MacDonnell's Retreat from Cushendun to Glentaisie, 30 April - 1 May

Shane O'Neill's Advance from Red Bay to Glentaisie, 1-2 May

1 Statute Mile

timely arrival of Alasdair Oge. The MacDonnell leaders paused to rest their men after a whirlwind flight across Antrim, for when the sun rose again battle would be joined.[46]

The battle of Glentaisie began in the early morning of Tuesday, 2 May 1565, and continued intermittently throughout the day. Before setting out toward the Scots Shane "exhorted his men to be true to their prince [i.e. Elizabeth], and of a good courage, showing them what praise should follow unto them if they overcame their enemies. . . ."[47] Shane himself noted that "we advanced upon them drawn up in battle array, and the fight was furiously maintained on both sides. But God . . . gave us the victory against them."[48] Fleming, who also witnessed the contest, revealed that O'Neill "gave [them] the overthrow, and took of their banners and ancients [i.e. ensigns and military insignia] thirteen. . . ."[49]

Unfortunately, O'Neill and Fleming's letters are the only known extant eyewitness accounts of the actual fighting at Glentaisie. Neither reveals much about the tactical nature of the battle, thus lending credence to G. A. Hayes-McCoy's observation (actually concerning Farsetmore in 1567, but equally applicable to Glentaisie) that "Once again, as with so many Irish battles, all detail is lost."[50] By piecing together other contemporaneous accounts, however, it is possible to reconstruct the contest. Both sides presumably arrayed in line-of-battle formation after having advanced to the field in column. On this occasion, though, according to the Book of Howth, Shane "did set upon them [i.e. the Scots] in the morning, before . . . which time the Scots did think to set upon O'Neill, which O'Neill did prevent by his early rising. . . ."[51] Thus Sorley Boy and James apparently were surprised and formed only a hasty and incomplete battleline in front of their encampment. Dioness Campbell, dean of Limerick, also insinuated that the MacDonnells were taken unawares when he wrote that they "camped without watch or regard of . . . [themselves]."[52] Why Sorley and James committed such an elementary blunder is difficult to ascertain, but it appears, from all accounts, that they were not fully prepared for battle when O'Neill arrived.

Both sides at Glentaisie made use of heavy infantry–*gallóglaigh* and redshanks–clad in iron helmets and medieval shirts of mail and armed with both single-handed and two-handed claymores (*claidheamh mor*), Lochaber axes, and spears. Light infantry, or kerne, also appeared on the battlefield, unprotected by armor and armed with light bows, javelins, and short swords and targets. There were few cavalry troops on either side. Some of the light infantry on both sides were armed with arquebuses or matchlock muskets, but firearms were used by the Gaels to harass and disorganize an enemy rather than to administer a crushing blow. Consequently, it is likely that gunpowder weapons had only a secondary effect on the fighting at Glentaisie. When opposing the English in the sixteenth century, Irishmen and Scots usually employed guerrilla tactics in which firearms played a salient role. But when fighting among themselves, the Gaels squared off and decided the contest with brute strength and cold steel.[53]

At Glentaisie the performance of the heavy infantry, arrayed on open ground with blade weapons, decided the day. Both armies evidently fought hard, as the initiative swung back and forth throughout much of the day. O'Neill finally prevailed, and the remnant of the MacDonnell army scattered to the winds. The pursuit was furious, as one of Sorley's best captains, John Roe MacDonnell, was chased down and butchered at the head of Glenshesk on the opposite side of Knocklayd.[54] First reports of the engagement estimated that 600–700 out of about 1,000 MacDonnell troops were killed, including Angus Uaibhreach ("the proud" or "contentious"), brother of James and Sorley. Many of the rest were taken prisoner. Initial reports put Shane's losses at only about sixty men, a ridiculously low figure.[55] A fortnight later Fitzwilliam informed Cecil that "The slaughter of the Scots which Shane wrote of is not so many by 300 or 400, as they say, who were the soldiers with him. . . ."[56] MacDonnell losses, therefore, probably stood somewhere between 300 and 500.

Not only did Clan Ian Mor suffer heavy casualties, but Sorley Boy, James, and a score of important leaders from the western Highlands and Isles were captured as well.[57] Moreover, James had been "very sore wounded."[58] He, Sorley, and the other captives were taken to Ballycastle on the night of 2 May, where, according to Fleming, the Dunyveg chief offered to buy their release from O'Neill. James also reportedly affirmed "by oath that he would never seek . . . revenge. . . ."[59] Shane claimed that he could not act on so weighty a matter without Elizabeth's approval, but, in truth, he never intended to free his distinguished prisoners, especially Dunyveg, his greatest rival in Ulster. Thus began a period of cruel confinement and humiliation for the proud leaders of Clan Ian Mor. The only remaining MacDonnell brother, Alasdair Oge, had come with 900 men to aid his kinsmen. But upon learning of the battle's outcome he returned to Kintyre, the family's future resting in his hands.[60]

Now that the MacDonnells' military strength in Ulster had been almost completely destroyed, O'Neill truly was master of northern Ireland. Several thousand Clan Ian Mor redshanks stood ready in Scotland to cross the North Channel, but Shane's power, for the moment, went unchallenged. He had attacked the Scots in the Glynnes and the Route to further his own interests and not those of the English queen. It would not take long for London and Dublin policy-makers to see through O'Neill's self-aggrandizement. Now, however, they rejoiced in Sorley's and James's severe defeat. But the more perceptive among them were secretly delighted that the ever-dangerous O'Neill seemed to have made an implacable enemy in the Antrim MacDonnells.

The O'Neill–MacDonnell quarrel destroyed any hopes of ending the political fragmentation and the almost continuous Gaelic infighting in

Ulster and the Hebrides since the fall of the lordship of the Isles in 1493. That relations between the O'Neills and Clan Ian Mor remained cool for the balance of the century indeed can be seen in the ultimate failure of Sorley and Turlough Luineach O'Neill (Shane's successor) to pull together an "Ulster League," and in the failure of Sorley's heirs to fully support Hugh O'Neill in the 1590s. In fact, it would not be until the alliance of Alasdair MacColla and James Graham, marquis of Montrose, in the 1640s that an effective accord between the Gaelic Scots and Irish could be refashioned from the debris left by Glentaisie and its aftermath.[61]

On the day after Glentaisie Shane marched his army westward into the Route and occupied the strategic castles of Dunseverick and Dunluce. He garrisoned Dunseverick, an ancient structure standing eight miles west of Ballycastle, and then with Sorley Boy and James in tow, crossed the river Bush to besiege Dunluce. This grim and foreboding redoubt proved a tough nut to crack. Fleming wrote that O'Neill

> could not win [Dunluce] in the space of three days after [the fall of Dunseverick] . . . till at last, partly through fear of Sanhirly Boy's death, who was kept without meat or drink to this end the castle might be sooner yielded, and partly for safeguarding of their own lives, seeing the manifold and cruel skirmishes and assaults on every side, the ward were faine to yield the castle into his hands, which also he [i.e. Shane] committed to the safe keeping of such of his men as were most able to defend the same, and most true to him [i.e. the O'Donnelleys]. . . .[62]

The timely surrender of Dunluce Castle most assuredly saved Sorley Boy's life, as Shane would not have hesitated to starve his celebrated prisoner had the garrison been more resolute.[63]

The Scots defeated and the North Antrim coast from Ballycastle to Dunluce in his hands, O'Neill began to consolidate his position. After garrisoning the castles, he decided the fate of his distinguished captives. Shane would take Sorley Boy and the main army and march southeast through the Route into Clandeboy, while a smaller force escorted James and the other prisoners to Castle Corcra in Tyrone (near Strabane).[64] When the prisoners arrived at Castle Corcra, Fitzwilliam informed Cecil that "some say James [MacDonnell] is dead of a wound he received, but for truth I know it not. . . ." Throughout the summer rumors would abound concerning James's fate. While Dunyveg languished in captivity for the remaining two months of his life, a relatively healthy Sorley Boy settled down to spend the next two years accompanying Shane throughout Ulster. The two MacDonnell brothers were never to meet again.[65]

Even as Shane disposed of his prisoners and returned to Clandeboy, ostensibly to "restore the [rightful] captains and gentlemen [there] to their own lands and tenants," the English and Clan Ian Mor were already seeking ways to counteract the effects of his victory. News of Glentaisie had quickly reached Scotland, as Lady Agnes briefed Randolph on 11 May of the disaster.[66] Doubtless, James's wife hoped that there might be some response forthcoming in her husband's favor from either the queen of Scots or Argyll. For their part, the English immediately began to doubt Shane's loyalty. Though O'Neill continued to speak well of Elizabeth, reports from the likes of Hugh Brady, bishop of Meath, belied a contrary attitude:

> he giveth fair words, attributing the glory thereof [i.e. Glentaisie] to her Majesty. Of my part I can say little, but I pray God he may prove so faithful as he saith of himself; surely he hath done good services, if he employ all to the furtherance of her highness' service, and if he do not, he will never so much be looked unto [again]. . . .[67]

Shane's occupation of Clandeboy in the early summer of 1565 unnerved some English officials. But others seemed still to dread the wrath of the Scots. O'Neill was in Clandeboy, he told Cecil, to guard against an imminent Scottish invasion by Alasdair Oge, with support from the queen of Scots and Argyll.[68] Fitzwilliam, too, feared a Scottish descent upon Ulster. In mid-May he informed Cecil that he regretted the imprisonment of Sorley Boy and James MacDonnell, for if they had perished, his "own enterprise" would have been easier to execute.[69] Fitzwilliam's "own enterprise," on which he elaborated in a letter to Cecil in late August, involved keeping the Scots from re-entering Ireland–either as opponents or as allies of O'Neill–to free the MacDonnell leaders. Fitzwilliam observed that

> chiefly for James MacDonnell hath the Scottish queen written unto O'Neill and overcometh one [i.e. a letter] from the earl of Argyll . . . and certain other[s] of the out isles, which being true, I fear it will prove that it had been good that the subtle Scot had never fallen into . . . [O'Neill's] hands, for surely Sir, if these men come . . . then is treason the greater to be expected. . . . [I]t will be good . . . to have some careful ear towards these matters. . . .[70]

After Glentaisie England tried to gain control of Shane's prisoners to prevent a Scottish attempt to free them by force or diplomacy. The latter course, Elizabeth feared, might result in another attempt at a temporary MacDonnell–O'Neill entente. On 3 June Cecil suggested that "If now the Queen's Majesty may have the possession of these prisoners, it shall be profitable, otherwise Shane's victory will be dangerous for Ireland."[71] Cecil and Fitzwilliam, among others, expected only the worst from the continued imprisonment of James and Sorley Boy. Thus from June until they learned of James's death in late August, the English tried desperately to get possession of him. Shane informed Elizabeth in late June of the overtures from Scotland concerning the release of his captives. He told how he had put off Argyll and the queen of Scots by insisting that he could not act without first learning the desires of the English queen. Buoyed by O'Neill's assurances, the London council instructed Dublin to send an agent to negotiate with him for the MacDonnells' release. At the same time, the council also wrote Shane directly to ascertain the identities of the rest of his captives and their condition and location.[72]

The English were very much aware of O'Neill's power in Ulster as a result of Glentaisie. Sir Thomas Cusake intimated to the dean of Armagh that he hoped Shane would remember his pledges of peace made to the queen. The dean reported that O'Neill indeed appeared to be so inclined. Daniel went on to describe Ulster "as one of the quietest counties of Ireland and best ordered. . . ."[73] But Ulster was quiet only because O'Neill ruled supreme. This situation pleased neither the queen nor her Irish lieutenants, some of whom saw through Shane's feigned submission and pledges of support. In early July Elizabeth warned Sidney, who would receive his patent as the new Lord Deputy in the coming autumn, not to provoke Shane for fear that "he forget his natural duty and seek help out of Scotland, or any other way contrary to her Majesty's liking."[74] Neither Elizabeth, Sidney, nor any Irish official yet knew, however, that four days earlier (5 July) James MacDonnell had died at Castle Corcra.[75] With James went the likelihood of a Scottish invasion of Ulster backed by the queen of Scots or Argyll. But O'Neill, as noted below, did not inform England of James's demise until 25 August. In the meantime, Whitehall remained virtually in the dark regarding MacDonnell–O'Neill relations in Ulster.[76]

Elizabeth and her council had two viable means of countering O'Neill in mid-1565. The first was Calvagh O'Donnell and his supporters in Tyrconnell, whose animosity toward Shane England had been quick to exploit earlier in the decade. The second was Clan Ian Mor. The circumstances of James's death suggested that his surviving kinsmen would be out for revenge. Consequently, after the English were informed of James's fate, they moved closer to both the MacDonnells and the O'Donnells in hopes that those families might be persuaded to challenge O'Neill's hegemony.

The O'Donnells had been humiliated by Shane, Calvagh having spent nearly three years in close confinement in Tyrone and Con recently being imprisoned by O'Neill. Both men were free in the summer of 1565, but Calvagh had complained to the queen in the previous autumn that about 4,500 of his people had perished by Shane's hand since the late 1550s. He also pleaded with Elizabeth to send aid so that he might defend himself.[77] The queen presently informed Sidney that O'Donnell would be restored in Tyrconnell. Elizabeth cautioned, however, "that the proceeding therein dependeth much upon Shane O'Neill's conformity."[78] It must be remembered that Shane, in the Drum Cru agreement, had been given virtually a free hand in dealing with the O'Donnells. As a result, he harassed them unmercifully and tried to reduce them to vassals. England meanwhile realized that she needed a strong and dependable Gaelic ally in Tyrconnell if Shane was to be defeated without a corresponding and dangerous increase in the power of Clan Ian Mor in Antrim. O'Donnell, then, should be restored to his country, if necessary through war with O'Neill.[79] To cement what proved to be a very fruitful alliance, a treaty was concluded between the Lord Deputy and Calvagh O'Donnell, by which the Tyrconnell chief promised to aid the English "against the rebel O'Neill and his adherents."[80] Thus England finally had put together a western strategy in Ulster.

The second means of countering O'Neill was to persuade the MacDonnells that he, rather than England, represented the greatest threat to their continuation in Ulster. After James's death was confirmed in late August, it was not difficult to play on his kinsmen's desire for revenge. The English doubtless hoped that the MacDonnells' rage would make them forget London's recent entente with O'Neill that had permitted him to attack James and Sorley Boy in the first place. Finally in possession of the Glynnes and the Route, Shane was reluctant to give them up to either the Scots or the English. Elizabeth desired that Shane banish the Scots from Ulster, but at the same time she feared that by doing so he would increase his own authority there to an unacceptable degree.[81] She proposed that the Glynnes and Rathlin Island "be brought to the possession and use of some English subjects, or some trusty person of the birth of Ireland . . . ."[82] But in lieu of outright English colonization, the Antrim MacDonnells were the only Irish family capable of holding eastern Ulster against O'Neill. The queen again had to suffer an unwanted presence–and for now the lesser of two evils–in the north of Ireland.

If Shane controlled the Antrim coastline from the southern Glynnes to Rathlin, not only could he summon redshanks from friendly Hebridean chiefs (especially if he were on good terms with Argyll), but he also could threaten Carrickfergus and ports farther south. Elizabeth knew "that for the readying of Ulster into obedience, nothing is more necessary than that the castles upon the havens and seaside were at her Majesty's commandment."[83] Only two days before he received word of James MacDonnell's death, Cecil learned from Fitzwilliam that a Scottish invasion of Ulster was imminent. The invasion did not come, however, as Alasdair Oge was not prepared to challenge the victorious O'Neill. In all likelihood Alasdair saw Shane's presence on his family's lands as proof that the Dublin administration had sanctioned the recent aggression against Clan Ian Mor. Three weeks earlier a forged letter from Justice Arnold and the council to Argyll had fueled a rumor that the earl and James MacDonnell's widow were raising a force to descend upon Shane and punish him for Dunyveg's death. Yet it should have been clear that in the wake of Glentaisie the Scots were still incapable of recouping their losses in Ulster.[84] If Elizabeth wished to win over the MacDonnells and use them against Shane, she would have to be patient.

O'Neill's words toward the English were agreeable, even conciliatory; his actions, however, betrayed a growing contempt. On 23 August it was learned that he had despatched Daniel to the Pale with gifts for the queen. In response, Cusake suggested that a letter be written to O'Neill congratulating him for his service against Clan Ian Mor.[85] The London council had requested in late June that Shane provide details of his "service" in Ulster, which he finally gave on 25 August. Besides revealing James MacDonnell's fate, Shane assured Elizabeth and Cecil that the Scots' castles were now safely under English control and that the MacDonnells had been driven completely from Ulster. But less than a week later, Arnold notified the council that O'Neill had installed his own warders in Dundrum and Newry castles and probably would garrison the others.[86]

As Shane openly defied the English government, Lord Deputy designate Sidney informed Cecil that "Ireland would be no small loss to the English crown, and it was never so like to be lost as now."[87] Even before returning to Ireland, therefore, Sidney had determined that O'Neill must be destroyed. Because the English were still reforming their military establishment in Ireland, a process that, according to Fitzwilliam, would take upwards of two years, they were forced to approach the Scots for aid.[88] Shane indeed feared (and perhaps expected) an Anglo-Scottish entente because of his recent success. According to Randolph, the counterfeit letter of early August, supposedly written by Arnold and intended for Argyll, in all probability came from O'Neill to ascertain the earl's military strength and his intentions of using it.[89] Whether the forgery came from Shane's hand, it is certain that by late 1565 he was concerned with having made enemies among his fellow Gaels.

The death of James MacDonnell, lord of Dunyveg, at the hands of Shane O'Neill in 1565 marked a watershed in the history of Clan Ian Mor. Though he was succeeded by his eldest son Archibald, James's position as *de facto* leader of the Clan Donald South temporarily fell to his younger brother, Alasdair Oge. Dunyveg's tragic death deeply saddened the Gaelic world. According to the Four Masters:

> The death of this gentleman was generally bewailed; he was a paragon of hospitality and prowess, a festive man of many troops, and a bountiful and munificent man. And his peer was not at that time among the clann-Donnell in Ireland or in Scotland; and his own people would not have deemed it too much to give his weight in gold for his ransom, if he could have been ransomed.[90]

James's ransom, however, had proved impossible, Shane's objective being the destruction of MacDonnell power in Ireland. But when Dunyveg died at Castle Corcra, reportedly from complications of a head wound received at Glentaisie,[91] the way had been opened for Sorley Boy to emerge as the greatest leader ever to spring from this illustrious branch of Clan Donald. Yet for the next two years the man destined to leave such a deep impression upon Ulster's troubled history would remain a captive at the hands of the Great O'Neill.

Chapter Six
From Glentaisie to Cushendun, 1565–7

And the stern joy which warriors feel
In foemen worthy of their steel.

Sir Walter Scott

Sorley Boy remained O'Neill's prisoner from Glentaisie until the Tyrone chief was hacked to death by Alasdair Oge and his Clan Donald kinsmen at Cushendun in 1567. During these two years England attempted to reverse its policy of 1564–5 by employing Clan Ian Mor against O'Neill. Since James was dead and Sorley captive, the English looked to Alasdair Oge as the instrument of Shane's destruction. Though he was partly responsible for O'Neill's death at Cushendun, Alasdair Oge was not motivated primarily by revenge. Rather he was concerned with maintaining the MacDonnells' power base in the Gaelic heartland by whatever means necessary, including negotiations with Shane. O'Neill's death in 1567 certainly removed a major MacDonnell rival, but it also further damaged the chances of any sort of effective Gaelic combination that might have checked English ambitions in Ulster. O'Neill's departure thus cleared the way for a twenty-year struggle between Clan Ian Mor and England for control in northeastern Ireland.

After Drum Cru O'Neill's star rose rapidly, and at Glentaisie he reached the zenith of his career. He could muster an army of 4,000 foot and 1,000 horse, not including his personal retinue of 700 elite troops, but Shane was prudent enough not to further antagonize the vanquished MacDonnells.[1] For the remainder of 1565 he paid lip-service to the queen. But O'Neill's actions did not equal his fair words. It was as if he had suddenly realized that England and her Gaelic allies–and not the MacDonnells–were his real enemies. Shane's relatively easy treatment of the Antrim Scots, an appeal for support to Argyll, and an invasion of Connacht suggest that he wished to solidify his position before the English and their O'Donnell allies moved against him.[2] There is no question that certain elements of

Clan Ian Mor–namely the widow and sons of James MacDonnell–desired revenge against Shane. Sorley Boy and Alasdair Oge, however, appeared ambivalent toward O'Neill. The two MacDonnell leaders certainly were experienced enough in the power politics and shifting diplomacy of the late-Renaissance Gaelic world to understand that yesterday's deadly adversary might well be tomorrow's ally. The desire for revenge, then, gave way to a more balanced, pragmatic view of the post-Glentaisie era based on the ethos of Machiavellianism.

Because of the advantages afforded by his unique position in Ulster politics, Argyll was the most important factor in O'Neill's strategy in the winter of 1565–6. In his dual role as earl of Argyll and MacCailein Mor, Archibald Campbell enjoyed a measure of independence rare in a sixteenth-century subject within the British Isles. As a result, he was able to hold out the promise of assistance to several parties at the same time.[3] Elizabeth recognized Argyll's importance, seeing his presence in the Celtic fringe as a potential Protestant bulwark against the unruly Catholic clans to the north and west.[4] Mary, Queen of Scots, saw him as a rank opportunist who could, by controlling several thousand redshanks, tie down Protestant English armies in Ulster. That both monarchs in the archipelago desired Argyll's friendship, and that he was kinsman to both the MacDonnells and the O'Donnells, attests to his powerful position in the mid-1560s. Far from stabilizing the Gaelic heartland, the Campbell chief was prepared to use the threat of sending aid to O'Neill or, conversely, the promise of good behavior, to wring concessions from both queens.[5] For now, however, Argyll sought to control the house of Dunyveg, which he saw as the most effective tool for influencing Irish affairs.

O'Neill's concern over the future course of England's Irish policy allowed Alasdair Oge to re-establish a secure foothold in Ulster sooner than he otherwise might have after Glentaisie. If London actively opposed Shane's dominance of the north, he knew that the Scots, especially with Argyll's support, could be either a valuable ally or a formidable opponent. The new Lord Deputy Sidney doubted that England could establish a colony as far north as Carlingford without Shane's acquiescence. Not long after Sidney assumed the deputyship, Cecil penned an insightful and prophetic letter to Sir Thomas Smith, the wealthy Essex statesman, scholar, and author, noting that the Lord Deputy

> hath found all out of joint there [i.e. in Ireland]. The good subjects in all parts oppressed, the Irish bearing rule, but in all no peril, saving in Shane, who will (he sayeth in his drunkenness) be Lord or King of Ulster; but I trust *his head shall be from his shoulders before any crown can be made ready to make him either King or Earl* [author's italics]. . . . We have cause to fear that O'Neill's boldness is fed out of Scotland.[6]

One of Sidney's first acts as Lord Deputy was to despatch representatives

101

to parley with O'Neill, who had refused to come to Dublin for fear of treachery. Sidney himself had declined to meet with Shane on the latter's terms, and O'Neill retorted by informing Sidney that he intended to keep what he had won with his sword. But beyond the boasting, posturing, and casting of verbal threats, both Sidney and O'Neill would have been foolish not to have respected and feared each other's power.[7] Along with Cecil, the Lord Deputy was concerned over O'Neill's Scottish connections. Sidney believed Shane to have agents at the Scottish court, and was quick to point out that the Tyrone chief had become emboldened enough to threaten the countryside from Carrickfergus to Dundalk. "Attila nor . . . no Vandal nor Goth . . . ever was more to be doubted for overrunning any part of Christendom than this man."[8] Sidney warned further:

> If it be an angel of heaven that will say that ever O'Neill will be [a] good subject till he be thoroughly chastised, believe him not, but think him a sprite of the error, and sure if the Queen do not chastise him in Ulster he will chase all hers out of Ireland.[9]

Clearly such colorful prose was intended to paint a desperate picture of England's position in the Pale and in Ulster. But the English had ample reason to be concerned about Shane's occupation of the MacDonnell strongholds in the far north and of Newry, Dundrum, and others farther south, and his continued intercourse with Scotland. After Sidney's arrival, England's Ulster policy took a more aggressive turn.[10]

Sir Henry Sidney's coming to Ireland in January 1566 began the New English ascendancy in Ulster politics. The Old English in Dublin were quickly supplanted. Sidney had served previously in Ireland under Sussex and then as Lord President of the Welsh Marches, but he had yet to face a determined challenge in the Celtic fringe. Because Shane was on the loose, a peaceful political solution seemed unlikely. Also, by the mid-1560s the uncompromising zeal of evangelical Protestantism, pent up in the previous reign but since unleashed by the Elizabethan religious settlement, accompanied many New English adventurers to Ireland. Frustrations brought on by ineffectual government and inconclusive military campaigns were to be swept away by Sidney's policies. The Lord Deputy demanded unqualified financial and logistical support from a united London government, something that had eluded Sussex. The real departure of Sidney's program, however, lay not so much in its structure, which was basically an adaptation of Sussex's 1562 strategy, but in its execution. Both men wished to overthrow O'Neill and banish Clan Ian Mor from Ulster as a prerequisite to colonizing the Antrim coasts. But Sidney's methods of achieving these objectives were more ingenious than Sussex's.[11]

Sidney's demands of pecuniary support for the establishment of *pacata Hibernica* conflicted with Elizabeth's celebrated parsimony. Despite pledges of financial support, Sidney, like Sussex, soon learned that little would be forthcoming. Elizabeth also reminded Sidney that she preferred her subjects in Ireland to provide for their own defense whenever possible. The queen, though, still expected Sidney to destroy Shane through an aggressive policy. Both she and her council "earnestly require you to employ your whole care, consideration and wisdom, how such a cankered, dangerous rebel may be utterly extirpated."[12] Sidney knew that a favorable settlement in Ulster would require an unprecedented English effort. The Lord Deputy complained to Cecil of his sovereign's stringent policies, but the young queen subordinated long-term strategic goals to short-term, highly visible tactical gains in Ireland. When Sidney complained of a lack of men, money, and material, Whitehall suggested that he seek aid among the province's native inhabitants. Elizabeth, in fact, began to question whether it was prudent to employ the O'Donnells against O'Neill unless they agreed to help pay their own way.[13]

Sidney cast about for ways to drive a wedge between Shane and the Scots and to draw the latter into a deadly scheme against him. The eventual execution of this stratagem separated Sidney's success from Sussex's failure. Sussex had attempted on numerous occasions to bring Clan Ian Mor into the field against O'Neill. But James and Sorley had insisted on steering a neutral course, much to the chagrin of both Shane and the English. When the Scots refused once and for all to be drawn into an Ulster-wide conflict on either side, Sussex was already on the way out and O'Neill and Elizabeth, for different reasons, had affected an unnatural "alliance" (Drum Cru) that resulted in the MacDonnells' defeat at Glentaisie. But Glentaisie did not end Clan Ian Mor's presence in Ireland; thus when Sidney arrived in early 1566 the English were virtually where they had been from 1560 to 1563. Once again, they had to persuade one side, now the MacDonnells, that it was in their best interests to help destroy the other–Shane O'Neill.

Shane's contemptuous behavior convinced Sidney that war was the only solution to the Ulster problem. Sussex, too, had favored military operations. Both men believed that an alliance with the Scots was the key to Shane's destruction because of limited English resources in Ulster. Sussex's failure to deal effectively with the MacDonnells had ended his Irish tenure and forced the humiliating Drum Cru agreement. Sidney was determined not to repeat his predecessor's mistakes and insisted on London's full cooperation in pacifying Ireland's most troubled province.

In mid-April Sidney informed the London council that though O'Neill had agreed to talk, he was also hastily preparing for war. Sidney could muster fewer than 1,000 English effectives and 300 undependable Irish kerne. Yet more disturbing was a report that O'Neill had abandoned Catherine MacLean (O'Donnell's wife) and was about to marry Lady Agnes Campbell. As a result of the presumed match with Dunyveg's widow, it was bruited that Shane, with Argyll's consent, "will possess Sorleboy in the

Route and the Glynnes and others of his assured followers in Clandeboy and Tyrconnell." Besieged by bad tidings, Sidney desired to know the queen's mind regarding war or peace with O'Neill.[14]

Nothing came of the proposed match between Shane and Lady Agnes, thus preventing the English from facing an O'Neill–MacDonnell–Campbell combination; but London's prospects in Ulster in early 1566 were none too promising. Sidney had no Gaelic ally, and without one any attempt to check Shane could not succeed. By the same token, Sidney realized that the Gaels alone could not (or would not) harness O'Neill. Rather a strong English army must be the nucleus of any endeavor to bring Shane to his knees. The Lord Deputy recommended to Cecil in mid-April that war against O'Neill should begin by mid-September and continue, if necessary, until the following summer.[15] According to the bishop of Meath, Shane's "tyranny joined with his pride is intolerable, daily increasing in strength and credit, with admiration and fear of the Irishry."[16]

As O'Neill's prestige and power were rising within Ulster itself, Sidney and the queen were aware of the danger should he extend his influence to Scotland or to the continent. Though Shane is generally seen as an aspiring local dynast, his family's reputation and connections abroad were greater than might have been expected of a sixteenth-century Gaelic lordship. To bolster his position with the Counter-Reformation powers, he played upon his Catholicism, but neither Spain nor France was able to provide aid. Tension hampered relations between Elizabeth and Philip II, but neither monarch was willing in the mid-1560s to risk war over Ireland. As for France, she would be mired in bloody civil war between Catholics and Huguenots until the accession of the Bourbons in 1589. O'Neill nonetheless penned a letter to Charles IX (1560–74) in mid-April, promising him the crown of Ireland in return for 5,000 to 6,000 French troops.[17] Nothing came of Shane's offer, but his correspondence with the house of Valois must have caused considerable consternation in London and Dublin.

While Shane failed in his overtures to the continental powers, his relations with Scotland were a more serious matter for English policy-makers. Clan Ian Mor, Argyll, and the queen of Scots all had tried unsuccessfully to obtain Sorley Boy's release, but they were not openly hostile to O'Neill. Since the previous autumn, Shane had sought an agreement with Argyll. Randolph reported in early May that O'Neill had sent a representative to Scotland to confer with Argyll and the Scottish queen, and by mid-month the Campbell earl had despatched an agent to Ireland to ascertain Shane's strength and the likelihood of his using it to attack the Pale.[18] Because her Irish lieutenants were determined to make war on the intractable O'Neill, Elizabeth anxiously inquired about "the disposition of Argyll towards us. . . ." Argyll was to be kept from joining Shane, and the queen made it known that when Sidney thought the time was right, the Scots would be paid to move against O'Neill. But for now the English were more concerned with forestalling a Scottish invasion of Ulster in support of O'Neill.[19] To counter the apparent warming of relations between Gaelic Ulster and Scotland, Elizabeth desired Argyll's promise that he would not assist O'Neill. But according to Randolph, Argyll was prepared to send redshanks to Ireland. In fact, in early summer 1566 he sent 1,500 to 2,000 men under Alasdair Oge to Ulster. But Alasdair was to maintain an independent command, which suggests Argyll's desire to hold out the prospect of aid to the highest bidder–Shane or the English. Neither side yet suspected the game that the Scots were playing.[20] Because both Elizabeth and O'Neill were counting heavily on Scottish support, Argyll and the MacDonnells enjoyed a strong bargaining position in June 1566.

Events in early June portended a bad summer for the English in Ulster. Fearing that Shane "will be tyrant of all Ireland," Sidney determined to drive a wedge between O'Neill and his potential Scottish allies.[21] First, through Sir Francis Knollys, Vice-Chancellor and special commissioner to Ireland, he requested an English naval presence in the North Channel in the form of two brigantines–the sixty-ton *Saker* and the forty-ton *Hare*. Next, and again with Knollys's support, he pushed for a diplomatic offensive to persuade Argyll and Clan Ian Mor to withhold aid from Shane, and, if possible, to bring them into the field against O'Neill at the appropriate time.[22] But on 9 June Sidney confessed to Cecil his having received word from an agent in Scotland that Argyll "hath confessed himself to be much beholding to Shane. . . . All this confirmeth my opinion of some great confederacy and combination of the Scot and Shane."[23]

The presence in Ireland of Alasdair Oge's redshanks coupled with news of Argyll's sympathetic attitude toward O'Neill prompted Sidney to call for military action in the winter of 1566–7. Knollys supported Sidney's plans to blockade the Antrim coast, to undertake an amphibious landing at Lough Foyle, and to bolster the O'Donnells in Tyrconnell while the main force advanced from the Pale into Ulster. But Sidney, Knollys, and the Privy Council knew that two brigantines could not prevent Campbell and MacDonnell galleys from crossing the North Channel. Thus the English continued their attempts to woo Argyll away from O'Neill. A special agent sent to Scotland, Henry Killigrew, was to ascertain once and for all the true state of affairs between the Gaelic Scots and Shane. But Killigrew's instructions belied the anxiety within English inner circles. Ordered to avoid the appearance of desperation in his appeals to Argyll, Killigrew played down English fears of a new Gaelic entente. In reality, though, the Scots were much more important to Ulster's future than Elizabeth cared to admit publicly.[24]

Argyll remained the wild card in the diplomatic intrigue between the English, O'Neill, and Clan Ian Mor in the summer of 1566. England was under no illusions that Argyll alone possessed the wherewithal to control the flow of redshanks to Ireland. But the MacDonnells, as the second greatest power in the Hebrides, could not be discounted. For now, however, Sorley Boy remained a prisoner, and Angus MacDonnell, the most dynamic of the late Dunyveg's sons and his presumed successor, reportedly was coming more and more under Argyll's influence. Cecil learned that the queen of Scots had given Argyll *carte blanche*, allowing him to send as many troops to Ulster as would be needed to accomplish whatever purpose he had in mind. The earl did not wish to become directly involved against either Shane or the English with large numbers of his own troops. Rather in mid-June he proposed that if Elizabeth would agree to overtly back the Presbyterians in Scotland he would use his power (excluding his own military forces) and influence to defeat O'Neill at no expense to the queen's exchequer.[25]

Elizabeth doubtless welcomed the news that Argyll had begun to distance himself from O'Neill. Hoping that the Campbell earl and Clan Ian Mor would do the task for her, the queen instructed Sidney in mid-June not to undertake a winter campaign against O'Neill. Just in case (and to her credit), however, she approved the military plan drawn up by Sidney and Knollys and initially consented to everything but an actual full-scale Ulster invasion. Elizabeth resolved that

> we cannot prescribe but generally to have O'Donnell surely placed in his country . . . and to have the coasts towards Scotland so possessed as the Scots may be impeached from coming to succour the rebel, and thirdly to have the earl of Kildare to enter into Lecale and recover it from Shane and so to keep war upon him and to attempt all the means that can be to withdraw from Shane his gallowglass [i.e. *gallóglaigh*] and other that now accompany him. . . .[26]

The queen wished to keep pressure on O'Neill, and after further consideration she grudgingly acquiesced to the implementation of most of Sidney's invasion plan for winter 1566–7. Elizabeth probably saw in Argyll's ambivalent behavior toward Shane a viable opportunity to crush the Ulster chief before he pulled together any sort of combination. But near the end of June, Killigrew thought it likely that O'Neill would receive assistance from Argyll. This presumably confirmed London's decision to make a move in Ulster as soon as preparations were complete.[27]

When he learned that England had began to prepare for an Ulster offensive, Shane characteristically beat his opponent to the punch by making ready to take the field.[28] But O'Neill's eagerness to invoke the gods of war in 1566 resulted not from confidence, but from desperation. His impetuosity played squarely into English hands. In a dispatch to Sidney in early July Elizabeth revealed her stratagem against Shane. English preparations for an Ulster war, she believed, would cause him to "break his brittle peace" by carrying out a pre-emptive strike against the borders of the Pale.[29] O'Neill, then, was to be lured into committing an act of aggression that would allow the English to tag him as a rebel once again. If the Tyrone chief could be made to commit to an aggressive policy in either Lecale or farther south toward the Pale, Argyll and Alasdair Oge likely would not treat with him. When Shane realized that his overtures to the Gaelic Scots would not bear fruit, he desperately appealed to Edinburgh, whence he received 200 crowns to purchase aqua vitae.[30] Such was not the sort of Scottish succor for which he had worked so hard since Glentaisie.

O'Neill could not meet with Argyll and would not meet with Sidney in July 1566; thus he decided to besiege Dundalk at month's end. The Irish were quickly driven away, and on 3 August Shane again was branded a rebel and a traitor.[31] At this point, Sidney claimed, O'Neill

> departed with speed to the furtherest part of Ulster, to treat with the Scots to have assistance of them. I am certainly informed, that he offered to them of Kintyre all Clandeboy, all the geld kine of his country; to deliver Sorelboye, and to give them pledge and assurance for his fidelity towards them. But I, fearing this beforehand, have so temporized with the Captain of Kintyre, Sorley's brother [i.e. Alasdair Oge], that they have utterly refused his requests, as I am certainly advertised, and without hope of aid and relief from thence, he is now returned again to the borders [of the Pale].[32]

Sidney had done a masterful job of isolating O'Neill in Tyrone and surrounding him with hostile forces. O'Donnell of Tyrconnell already stood as a counterweight, and in mid-September Sidney informed the Privy Council that Alasdair Oge had offered his services to the English queen. Sidney asked the council "to direct me in what sort I shall compound with them [i.e. the Scots] either to have them in actual service or to keep them with some promises from combining with the rebel."[33] It is clear from Sidney's tone that England was determined at all costs to keep Shane and the Scots apart.

The Lord Deputy still believed that O'Neill might be held in check by hostile neighbors but that he could be defeated in the field only by English troops. Consequently, throughout the summer Sidney had tried to marshal a powerful and well-supplied army to use against Shane.[34] He seems to have been the first to grasp the geo-political importance of planting a garrison and accompanying storehouse at Derry on Lough Foyle. The position easily could be maintained by sea and would "open the gap for . . . entry with many numbers into the bowels of the northern territories. . . ."[35] In Derry, England would have a permanent base of operations from which she could draw sustenance and to which English troops could retreat in time of need. A strong presence on Shane's northern flank would also allow for better cooperation with the O'Donnells. These factors caused Sidney and his lieutenants to believe that O'Neill might soon be brought to battle and defeated.

The English landing at Lough Foyle with 600–700 troops in September 1566–the first amphibious operation of Elizabeth's reign–began Sidney's assault on Ulster.[36] The expedition was launched amid complaints that the queen controlled nothing in Ulster besides Carrickfergus. Though such pessimism was unwarranted, O'Neill, indeed, appeared a formidable opponent. He reportedly could field 7,000 Irish and redshanks compared with Sidney's 2,000 troops. Though in all likelihood the odds were not quite this long against him, the Lord Deputy, with Kildare and O'Donnell, advanced northward from Armagh with a relatively small contingent on 22 September to link up with Colonel Edward Randolph at Derry and cut Ulster in two.[37]

Sidney had envisioned a long campaign against Shane lasting from autumn 1566 until the following summer. The mid-point of the campaign, therefore, would fall in the winter, the season best suited for fighting the elusive Irish. Shane would be unable to use the deciduous forests for cover, and the barren mountains and drumlins would offer no pasturage for his *creaghts*. Sidney's plan to deprive the Irish of these natural advantages and to strike a blow against their rather primitive, but efficient, logistical system anticipated Mountjoy's policies a generation later against Hugh O'Neill. To counter Sidney's strategy, O'Neill employed evasive tactics, using his superior mobility to simply avoid the enemy. Thus, all that the Lord Deputy could hope to gain was the destruction of property and the prestige of marching across the mighty O'Neill's country. Shane had been bloodied by the English at Dundalk the previous July. Now he wisely backed off to allow the rugged terrain and harsh weather of his native Ulster to ravage the raw and poorly provisioned English troops.[38]

Though England was incapable of bringing O'Neill to battle without Gaelic military support, Sidney was aware of the logistical advantages that would accrue from having Randolph at Derry. As Shane clearly was determined to avoid combat, Sidney could only destroy the tangible property encountered on his march through Tyrone. At the conclusion of his trek, Sidney claimed to have deprived O'Neill of all his castles. Moreover, the Lord Deputy entered Tyrconnell and installed old Calvagh O'Donnell in Donegal Castle in opposition to his brother Hugh, a vacillating ally of Shane.[39] Tyrone littered by a trail of destruction, most of Shane's *urraights* unwilling to support him any longer, Randolph entrenched at Derry with six weeks' provisions, and Calvagh O'Donnell re-established in Tyrconnell, Sidney appeared to have put O'Neill in an untenable position. Only Clan Ian Mor remained aloof from the combination that England hoped would bring down this "monstrous . . . tyrant of all Ulster. . . ."[40]

All except the Scots seemed to be in place to carry out O'Neill's destruction in early autumn 1566. Argyll had told Shane that he would send no aid, but neither the earl nor his MacDonnell kinsmen could forget that O'Neill remained Sorley Boy's captor. Alasdair Oge was back in Scotland in October and apparently became involved in a scheme to free Sorley. The Scottish court and Argyll presumably discussed the scheme, but declined to implement it for fear of offending Elizabeth.[41] At this juncture, Alasdair Oge's actions take an interesting twist, as he made a discernible break with both Argyll and Edinburgh and set about on his own to free his brother. And he cared not one whit whether he had to cross England or O'Neill to attain his objective.

Alasdair Oge returned from Scotland to the Antrim Glynnes in early November and linked up with Alexander Carragh MacDonnell of Lecale. Bypassing Carrickfergus, their army of 1,200 Scots crossed the Lagan west of Belfast and preyed on Con MacNeill Oge, the O'Neill chief of southern Clandeboy. Apparently satisfied with the impression he had made, Alasdair returned to the safety of the Glynnes. On the way, however, he called at Carrickfergus Castle, where Captain Thomas Browne commanded while Piers was away in the Ardes. Browne wasted no time in telling Alasdair that the English would welcome his assistance against O'Neill. Alasdair Oge revealed that though he had ample cause for revenge against Shane, he had come back to Ulster to serve the queen. Moreover, he intimated that Argyll could not be trusted, especially where O'Neill was concerned.[42] The MacDonnell leader requested English aid against the MacLeans, a sure sign that he no longer believed help would be forthcoming from Scotland for his own cause.

Alasdair Oge's strange behavior upon his return to Ireland was confirmed by Alexander Carragh, who told the inexperienced Browne that after the two Gaelic leaders had parted company, "he [i.e. Alexander Carragh] knew not what these Scots meant. . . ." Browne admitted that he "neither . . . could tell what he meant in saying so to me, nor what to judge of it because I am yet a stranger to them [i.e. the Scots]. . . ."[43] That Browne and Alexander Carragh were unable to deduce Alasdair Oge's real intentions points up the latter's delicate predicament. If he made a clean break with Scotland, he risked reprisals from Argyll or the widow and sons of James MacDonnell; if he pressed ahead with MacDonnell claims in Ireland, he chanced the wrath of both Shane and England. By first asserting his independence in returning to Ulster and then by carrying out a daring foray so close to the borders of the Pale, Alasdair seemed anxious to show that he was no longer beholden to anyone. He knew that Argyll, England, or O'Neill alone might crush him or at least make life miserable for his family. But Alasdair finally realized what Sorley Boy had seen in the previous decade: that for Alasdair Cahanagh's younger sons, Ulster was a land both of danger and of opportunity where *de jure* succession to the lordship of Dunyveg counted for little when compared with *de facto* military and political power.

Alasdair Oge's attempt to reorganize an independent MacDonnell presence in Antrim and the untimely death of Calvagh O'Donnell threw

Ulster into utter confusion in late 1566. Alasdair now would be able either to favor or to oppose O'Neill with what amounted to an open-ended policy. The English certainly understood that winning over Alasdair Oge would not be easy. And because Hugh O'Donnell, Calvagh's successor, was unable to decide whether to support England or Shane, Sidney could not afford to lose Clan Ian Mor. The results of the Lord Deputy's recent campaign in Tyrone, which had forced O'Neill into hiding near Armagh, were now jeopardized by Colonel Randolph's accidental death at Derry and Hugh O'Donnell's equivocation. Though Shane reportedly still possessed a large army, his all-important reputation had suffered irreversible harm. The decision to forgo battle after his abortive attack on Dundalk earlier in the autumn had raised some doubt about O'Neill's military abilities. But perhaps more damaging was Shane's failure to dislodge the English from Derry, which pointed up the inability of his Irish troops to fight a campaign of positional warfare. When Hugh O'Donnell crossed the Finn in strength in late November to prey on Tyrone, another plank in O'Neill's gallows was put in place. Shane now felt pressure from the south by Sidney's presence on the borders of the Pale, from the north by the Derry garrison, and from the west by an openly hostile O'Donnell.[44] His only hope of avoiding encirclement and sure defeat lay in an accord with Clan Ian Mor, however risky that might be.

Shane's precarious position gave the Antrim Scots greater diplomatic leverage as the new wild card in Ulster politics. Alasdair Oge had the unenviable task of negotiating with Sidney, but he stood to benefit from being in a position to threaten the Lord Deputy with the possibility of conducting separate talks with O'Neill. Thus the Scots' decision turned on which man–Sidney or Shane–could offer them the best deal. Sidney remained cool toward a MacDonnell alliance. Writing the Privy Council on 12 December, the Lord Deputy wished to ascertain

> the Queen's Majesty's pleasure touching the Scots, of whom . . . there is a great number already entered, and no doubt a great confluence will shortly resort. These men are yet in all appearance enemies to him [i.e. O'Neill], but undoubtedly as well these already arrived, as the rest that will come after if the Queen either entertain them not with the gift of some part of her country here [i.e. the Glynnes] (which I counsel not) or prevent their arrival, or resist them with force, being arrived. If the rebel be able to hold up [his] head they will become his.[45]

Sidney still thought it unwise to grant the Scots a legitimate foothold in northeastern Ulster in return for support against Shane, even though this might have been the only way to forestall a temporary MacDonnell–O'Neill combination. For now, the Lord Deputy undoubtedly believed that the English and the O'Donnells together could check, if not defeat, O'Neill, as a combined presence had been established on his vulnerable northwestern flank.

Sidney preferred that the Antrim MacDonnells remain neutral if in exchange for their support England had to agree to their continuation in Ulster. But if Alasdair Oge could be maneuvered into war with O'Neill, then Sidney might realistically hope for a Glentaisie in reverse. Should an English colony be planted on the Antrim coast while Clan Ian Mor and O'Neill clashed, then even if the MacDonnells prevailed, they would be in no position to make the type of demands Shane had made after his victory in 1565. Sidney must have been elated when Piers informed him of Alasdair's thrust across the Bann in early December. But Piers's letter also brought disturbing news that Argyll might still assist Shane. As constable of Carrickfergus, Piers had monitored Alasdair Oge's movements closely since his return from Scotland in early November.[46] Realizing the importance of binding the Scots to England's cause, Piers arranged for Argyll's representative in Ulster, Thomas Stevenson, to advance him (Piers) a moderate sum which he used to induce Clan Ian Mor to move against O'Neill. Thus when Shane "proffered them to serve him, . . . [the Scots] utterly refused . . . , and I [Piers] hearing of it sent to Alasdair . . . and willed if he . . . would now do somewhat upon Shane and thereupon he went over the Bann and did his exploit. . . ."[47]

Piers's presence of mind in moving quickly, and apparently independently, forestalled a possible accord between the Scots and O'Neill, the feasibility of which Argyll's representative undoubtedly had been instructed to explore. Moreover, because Alasdair Oge was on the Bannside, it now appeared that the Scots might make war against O'Neill without official recognition of their claim to the Glynnes. The MacDonnells, though, were much too sagacious to commit themselves to a course that, if successful, would enhance England's position in Ulster. Rather they continued to weigh their alternatives. Alasdair's crossing of the Bann did not change Clan Ian Mor's fundamental stance towards Shane, but it did visibly disturb the Tyrone chief. Sidney learned on Christmas Day 1566 that O'Neill had destroyed Armagh Cathedral, a traditional response of the O'Neills when they considered an invasion imminent. But it was not only the Scots and O'Neill who had to consider unpleasant alternatives. At year's end the Lord Deputy was acutely aware of the sorry state of the Derry garrison; therefore, he hoped to move against Shane while Clan Ian Mor still threatened him (O'Neill) and while England was able to maintain a military presence on Lough Foyle.[48]

The English did not want to cut a deal with the Antrim MacDonnells, but at the beginning of 1567 London concluded that such an unnatural alliance was necessary to defeat O'Neill. After the humiliation of Drum Cru, the English now were in no mood to negotiate with Shane.[49] On 16 January Elizabeth wrote Sidney that Clan Ian Mor ideally should not be allowed to remain in Ireland. However, because of the trouble brewing with O'Neill and England's lack of military strength in Ulster, the Scots had to be tolerated for now.[50] But Elizabeth clearly saw the danger of a revitalized Clan Donald settlement in the Glynnes and the Route as a threat to her plans to colonize Ulster. If O'Neill was removed, there would be no way of dislodging the MacDonnells except through a Scottish alliance, which surely would involve the unpredictable Argyll, or by the sacrifice of much English blood and money in a prolonged military campaign. Consequently, she instructed Sidney:

> we think it good that . . . all policy be continued to suffer as few Scots to come into those parts as may be and to keep those which be there from the serving of Shane. And to this end we think it good that you use Alexander Oge with good words and reasonable entertainment, by allowing unto him . . . some convenient wages. . . . And as concerning his request to have habitation granted him, to the intent time may be won therein, you may cause him to be dealt withal, so he may remain in hope of obtaining his desire. . . .[51]

Elizabeth and Sidney were willing to keep alive negotiations with Alasdair Oge, but, as the queen had emphasized, nothing significant was to be granted to the Scots. London was concerned not only about the size of Alasdair Oge's army already in Ulster, but also that more redshanks would arrive from the Highlands and Isles.[52] Nonetheless, the Scots were to be wooed as the lesser of two evils. Alasdair thought no better of dealing with England. It is implausible that he had no idea of the queen's real intentions toward him. Rather Alasdair Oge, who was making no progress in negotiations with Dublin, must have seen little harm in resuming relations with Shane. O'Neill, aware of the MacDonnell leader's failure to establish an agreement with Sidney, sought to open communications with Alasdair through Sorley Boy. Any accord with the Scots certainly would be risky for Shane, but his deteriorating position *vis-à-vis* England and the O'Donnells forced him to undertake a desperate course in early 1567.[53]

O'Neill's situation indeed was dangerous in January 1567, "these winter wars [having] . . . daunted his courage. . . ."[54] There can be no doubt that Shane the Proud had been reduced to skulking from place to place in a land that only a short time before he had traversed with impunity. Neither his cattle, his personal property, nor his people were safe from the Sassenach or their allies. Sidney observed in mid-month that Alasdair Oge again was preying on O'Neill from the Bann to Carrickfergus. At this point, however, it was unlikely that the Scots were openly hostile toward Shane. Nonetheless, his plight had become so frightful that he again appealed unsuccessfully to the continent in hopes of soliciting aid from the Valois dynasty. It now appeared that Shane, if he was to be saved, must save himself. True to his character, he marshalled his forces for a last desperate throw of the black dice of his Geraldine kinsmen to crush his enemies and break their stranglehold on Tyrone.[55]

For the next three months Shane tried to rebuild his once almost unassailable position in Ulster. The Derry garrison continued to annoy him, but, in truth, it was deteriorating rapidly. Rumors abounded that Hugh O'Donnell would betray the English.[56] The winds of fortune now seemed to have shifted against England. If Shane was to be prevented from regaining his former strength, the heretofore impenetrable ring that constricted his every move had to be shored up, especially to the northwest. Thus in early 1567, London shifted its immediate diplomatic efforts away from the Scots in the east and toward the O'Donnells in Tyrconnell. This move hampered serious negotiations with Alasdair Oge; it did not mean, however, that Sidney had given up on keeping Clan Ian Mor from moving closer to O'Neill or from strengthening its own position along the Antrim coast while the English were busy elsewhere. The Lord Deputy's attention suddenly was diverted from the O'Donnells in late February when Cecil informed him that the queen of Scots had agreed to prohibit the passage of her subjects to Ireland. But it was reported from Derry that Shane had hired 5,000 redshanks who were expected to land on the Antrim coast at any moment. Fact and rumor becoming more intertwined every day, Sidney again called for an English colony to be planted in eastern Ulster to prevent the alleged influx of Scots.[57] He apparently had little faith in the assurances of Mary, Queen of Scots, and preferred to depend on military power rather than promises to keep Clan Ian Mor at bay.

In early April the Privy Council reassured Sidney that the proposed English colony would be planted, but only after Shane was dealt with properly. Thus the Scots who already dwelt in the Glynnes and the Route were to be suffered to remain there undisturbed in hopes that they might be used against O'Neill. There continued to be mixed signals, however, concerning the movements of redshanks from Scotland to Ireland. But shortly the English learned that Argyll, without whose assistance further redshank units could not be recruited and transported to Ulster, had become involved in a controversy with the MacLeans over the isle of Gigha. Thus the MacCailein Mor would be able to spare few troops from Scotland for either side in the Ulster struggle.[58]

England's Ulster policy appeared to be jelling in late April, but subsequent dealings with her temperamental Gaelic allies were unsettling. Events in the western Highlands and Isles prevented a steady stream of redshanks to Ulster, thus the forces under Alasdair Oge likely would be the only Scots directly involved in the O'Neill affair. One of England's crucial concerns–further encroachment by Clan Ian Mor along the Antrim coast–had therefore been temporarily eliminated. The ruin of the Derry garrison had reduced pressure on Shane's northwestern flank, but the

English looked to Hugh O'Donnell to shore up that area. O'Donnell intimated to Sidney that he was considering a marriage arrangement with Lady Agnes so that the two of them might avenge James MacDonnell's death. But far from being comforted by O'Donnell's plan, the English looked on this proposed marriage with considerable trepidation. O'Donnell, though, was not finished yet, making known his desire to join Alasdair Oge against O'Neill. This combination might prove fortunate for Sidney in the short run by bringing together enough military power to defeat Shane. In the longer run, however, a possible combination brought about by the O'Donnell–Lady Agnes marriage threatened England's domination of Ulster by throwing open the door for hordes of redshanks to pour into Ireland.[59]

While England grappled with her unpredictable Gaelic allies, O'Neill, who was "now driven to the woods," stood at a crossroads. There was no hiding his desperation, as erstwhile allies reportedly deserted in droves, including his tanist, Turlough Luineach. O'Donnell raiding parties continued to prey upon his dwindling herds of cattle.[60] One of Shane's most intimate English acquaintances, the condemned pirate Thomas Phettiplace, believed that the O'Neill chief's strength was not in large numbers of troops, but in "his crafty slights." Shane apparently had settled on a war of movement, having reportedly razed his strongest castles. Indeed, it appeared that the once-mighty Shane had been reduced to a mere wood-kerne, commanding only a handful of "rascals" and hiding out in the most remote, inaccessible fastnesses of Tyrone. Reality, however, was quite different. O'Neill faced serious threats, both internal and external, and Gaelic and non-Gaelic, but he remained a formidable foe with an efficient spy network, an army of almost 5,000 men, and ready access to powder, shot, and other materials of war.[61]

O'Neill realized in the spring of 1567 that he must act while still strong enough to strike a decisive blow. If he waited, flying from place to place and avoiding battle with the English, his military power would evaporate. Thereafter he could only await his sorry fate at the hands of the English and the O'Donnells or the Scots. This was not the style of Shane *an diomas*; he resolved, therefore, to attack the most vulnerable and immediate target, the Tyrconnell O'Donnells, a decision that resulted in the battle of Farsetmore (8 May 1567). The battle was brought on by O'Neill's reckless invasion of Tyrconnell. Hugh O'Donnell's determined counter-attack drove Shane's troops off the field and into the river Swilly, where many of those not hewn down by cold steel were swept away in the current of the tidal estuary. Overall, Shane lost about 1,300 men, though some estimates run as high as 3,000, including many notables. He also was forced to abandon his camp, thereby losing valuable equipment and provisions.[62] Shane himself barely escaped, but the crippling blow to his military power and prestige reportedly caused "his reason and senses [to become] . . . deranged after it."[63]

After his rough handling at Farsetmore, O'Neill limped back to Tyrone with the remnant of his army, having failed in his calculated gamble to destroy the English–O'Donnell alliance. His options were now severely limited: either he could take refuge in the more remote parts of his territories and wait for the inevitable and humiliating end or he could strike a deal with Clan Ian Mor. A third course–submission to the Lord Deputy–was never seriously considered, though a contemporary chronicler noted that Shane was "cast in such despair, that he consulted with his secretary ... [whether] to present himself unknown and disguised to the Deputy, with an halter about his neck, begging his pardon."[64] As he pondered his fate, O'Neill realized that a rapprochement with the Scots was his only viable option; thus he prepared to meet Alasdair Oge MacDonnell, hoping, no doubt, that his [Shane's] possession–and lenient treatment–of Sorley Boy would be the catalyst for an anti-English accord.

Shane's tragic death at the hands of the Antrim MacDonnells a short time after Farsetmore is one of the most important, yet misunderstood and misrepresented, episodes in the history of sixteenth-century Ireland.[65] Alasdair Oge returned from Scotland to Ulster on 18 May, less than a fortnight after Farsetmore. Two days later he wrote Sidney from the Glynnes, apologetically explaining why he had not returned to Ireland sooner. He assured the Lord Deputy that he fully intended to pursue O'Neill in Tyrone.[66] But did Alasdair return to Ulster with a burning desire to avenge O'Neill's humiliation of Clan Ian Mor? He most likely did not. Certainly negotiations concerning O'Neill's overthrow had occurred between Alasdair Oge and the English at some point since Glentaisie. Sidney's notation in his memoirs that his detractors within the government believed "that the Scots stumbled on him [i.e. O'Neill] by chance"[67] suggests that the Lord Deputy might have been defending himself as the author of some sort of plot involving the Scots against Shane. Too, that Alasdair had wasted no time before contacting Sidney upon returning to Ulster seems to lend credence to the Anglo-Scottish conspiracy theory. But in Sidney's own recollections, written in defense of his actions against Shane, he made no mention of ever having actually concluded a formal agreement with Clan Ian Mor to bring about O'Neill's demise.[68]

Before leaving Kintyre for Ireland in May 1567, Alasdair Oge, according to Sidney, had been contacted by the Lord Deputy's man, John Douglas, "by whom the Scots that killed O'Neill were brought over."[69] Alasdair undoubtedly negotiated with Sidney through both Douglas and William Piers at Carrickfergus, especially after Farsetmore, but his desire for revenge should not be overemphasized. The MacDonnells and O'Neill had quarreled and fought on numerous occasions during the past decade; neither side, however, behaved as if it wished to destroy the other. On the contrary, Shane had been generous after Glentaisie and, by all accounts, had treated Sorley Boy well during his extended captivity. The Antrim MacDonnells, barring Lady Agnes and her sons, were not unwilling to consider an entente with O'Neill if it suited their purposes. But in truth, the MacDonnells probably desired no more than Sorley's freedom and to be left undisturbed for the moment to consolidate their territories in the Glynnes and the Route. The most important question for Alasdair and Sorley in the weeks immediately preceding O'Neill's death was which man–Shane or Sidney–could offer them the best deal? A similar dilemma faced O'Neill. He had to choose between bowing to Sidney or approaching Clan Ian Mor. It is not surprising, then, that the two Gaelic powers decided to try one more time to strike a deal to exclude the Sassenach from northern Ireland.

In late May Shane, accompanied by Sorley Boy and a small entourage, made his way across the Bann and on toward Cushendun, one of Clan Ian Mor's most important landing-places on the Antrim coast. Alasdair Oge and 600 redshanks waited there. Had Shane expected trouble, he certainly would have brought a much stronger force than he did.[70] It appears that Shane and Alasdair Oge and the soon-to-be-freed Sorley Boy were prepared to spend several days in intense negotiations. In fact, the captive Sorley had actually arranged the meeting at Cushendun:

> Sorleyboy, remaining prisoner this two years, was very desirous to be at liberty if by any means he might. O'Neill, lacking men to defend his country, told Sorleyboy that if he would procure his brother Alasdair to aid him with a thousand men, he would set him at liberty. Sorleyboy, desirous to be out of thralldom, wrote very earnestly to his brother for so many men as O'Neill did desire. . . .[71]

The prospect of receiving MacDonnell troops in return for Sorley Boy's release undoubtedly loomed large in O'Neill's decision to meet the Scots at Cushendun. And though, as it turned out, Shane made a tragic miscalculation, he did not act in the irrational manner of which he was accused by the Four Masters after Farsetmore. On the contrary, O'Neill ventured into a potential enemy's lair with the appearence of utmost confidence. The grueling negotiations at Cushendun during the two or three days preceding the fatal 2nd of June make for an unfamiliar tale to most students of Irish history; rather they have been schooled in the "banquet story," which asserts that Shane's death was the result of a drunken brawl between impetuous Celts. The roots of the original version of Shane's death can be traced to the historical preamble to the Act of Attainder passed against him in the Irish parliament of 1569–71. The English most assuredly concocted this tale as a way of absolving themselves from any blame for O'Neill's violent death. Instead, they preferred to emphasize the traditional hostility between O'Neill and MacDonnell.[72]

The traditional tale of Shane's death varies somewhat from one reporter to another, but most agree that excessive drink and hot words caused the deadly quarrel. It is unnecessary here to present the numerous accounts of the "banquet story." But because its origins grew out of the preamble contained in the Irish Statutes, a brief excerpt from that dubious "historical" document is in order. O'Neill

> took his journey towards the Scots, who were . . . under the leading of Alexander Oge, brother to James MacDonnell, and one MacGillaspick his nephew, son to Angus . . . , brother also to the said James, which [sic] was slain in the late overthrow given by . . . O'Neill to the Scots, and so entered the tent of the said Alexander, accompanied with . . . Swarley Boye, brother to the said Alexander . . . and . . . fifty horsemen, where after a few dissembling gratulatory words . . . betwixt them, they fell to quaffing and drinking wine.

At this point, MacGillaspick,

> all inflamed with malice and desire of revenge for the death of his father and uncle, began to minister quarrelling talk to O'Neill, who took the same very hot, and after some reproachful words passed betwixt them the said MacGillaspick demanded of . . . [O'Neill's] secretary, whether he had bruited abroad, that . . . his aunt [Lady Agnes Campbell] . . . did offer to come out of Scotland . . . to marry with O'Neill, the secretary affirmed himself to be the author of that report, . . . [whereupon MacGillaspick] said withal, that . . . the lady . . . was a woman of . . . [such] honesty and reputation, as would not take him that was the betrayer and murderer of her worthy husband.

Shane overheard the taunts from MacGillaspick and

> began to maintain his secreatry's quarrel, and thereupon MacGillaspick withdrew himself out of the tent, and came . . . amongst his men, who forthwith raised a fray, and fell to killing of O'Neill's men; and the Scots, as people thirsty of O'Neill's blood, . . . thrust into the tent, . . . and there with their slaughter swords hewed him [O'Neill] to pieces. . . .[73]

One thing is certain about O'Neill's death: the Antrim MacDonnells were directly responsible. The crucial question is, however, why did they kill Shane? There was no doubt in late spring 1567 that both Clan Ian Mor and O'Neill saw some benefit in negotiating with each other. The MacDonnells, unlike Shane, were not desperate to strike a deal. If Shane had an advantage, it was his possession of Sorley Boy. And this, perhaps as much as anything else, persuaded Alasdair to treat with him at Cushendun. According to a contemporary source, Alasdair Oge had come to Ireland "only to redeem his brother Sourlyboy."[74] But upon entering the Scots' camp with only a small force, Shane forfeited his trump card. At that moment he no longer controlled Sorley's destiny, thus the MacDonnells

117

actually had to give up nothing to gain his freedom. In effect, they now became masters of Shane's fate, though this did not mean that his death was premeditated or inevitable.

Credible evidence suggests that the killing of Shane O'Neill resulted from the breakdown of serious negotiations with Clan Ian Mor. While there is certainly no way of knowing what spark ignited the hot-blooded Gaelic passions that led to the deadly blows being struck, it is unlikely that either Alasdair Oge or his subordinates, including MacGillaspick, the supposed instigator of the affair, and the nephew rather than the son of Angus MacDonnell, intended the *raison d'être* of the Cushendun meeting to be O'Neill's murder.[75] It is not unreasonable to suggest that Alasdair might have considered slaying O'Neill in the absence of some sort of agreement, as Shane's demise would greatly simplify Ulster politics. Therefore, perhaps Clan Ian Mor had considered his murder beforehand as a last resort. But that the two sides initially agreed to meet and hammer out an agreement based, in part, on Sorley's release and subsequent aid to O'Neill is beyond question. The quarrel probably resulted from the frustrations built up during several days of stressful negotiations.

The dismissal of the "banquet story" in favor of one based on a series of hard-headed negotiations over several days is corroborated by most contemporary sources. Among Irish sources, neither the Four Masters nor the authors of the Loch Cé annals suggest anything similar to the traditional version of O'Neill's death. The Four Masters noted that Shane went to Cushendun "under the protection of" the MacDonnells to seek an alliance against the O'Donnells. He was killed only "after having been for some time in their company. . . ."[76] As for contemporary English accounts, Sidney revealed that O'Neill and his entourage were entertained for two days in "great cheer," the deadly quarrel breaking out sometime between the second and third day.[77] Sir William Fitzwilliam, writing Cecil a week after the incident, made no mention of a drunken altercation. He supports Sidney's claim that the Scots and O'Neill had spent the better part of two days in serious negotiations. On the last day of Shane's life the MacDonnells "thought to have ended a full conclusion . . . binding [the two sides] in friendship, . . . [but] God so disposed his pleasure as he suffered that traitor to receive his end amongst those Scots. . . ."[78]

What role did Sorley Boy MacDonnell play in the death of Shane O'Neill? The captive Sorley has been conspicuously absent from the present chapter, but he probably exerted a good deal of influence over O'Neill, especially after Shane began to feel pressure from the English–O'Donnell alliance in 1566. After Farsetmore, Sorley Boy became Shane's crucial link to Alasdair Oge. When O'Neill entered the Scots' camp at Cushendun, Sorley's role became even greater. The following letter describes what appears to be the actual scenario that culminated in Shane's death on 2 June 1567. On the fatal Monday the Scots and O'Neill parleyed and could not agree, but broke off for an hour or two. O'Neill said he would once again go talk to the Scots and see if he could bring them to any better end. But Sourlyboy willed O'Neill that he should not trust the Scots too far. Shane O'Neill swore . . . he would once again go talk with them. . . . And O'Neill coming to the Scots separated himself with five men with him a little from his strength and Alasdair Oge with five men in like sort from his strength, and talked of the matter. But God blinded the eyes of O'Neill that he doubted not the mischief the Scots meant to him.[79]

The Rev. George Hill, the foremost nineteenth-century authority on the Antrim MacDonnells, believes that Shane had taken Sorley into his confidence and that all along the captive MacDonnell had plotted his captor's murder. Hill thinks that Sorley, with only a word or a wave of his hand, could have called off Alasdair Oge and the others and saved Shane's life.[80] But the letter quoted above presents a very different picture.

Sorley's role in bringing about O'Neill's fall probably can never be known; neither can we ascertain why the Scots decided that Shane must die. It is highly probable, however, that the English were involved in the MacDonnells' decision. Alasdair Oge abandoned the prospects of an alliance with O'Neill perhaps because he was no longer a serious military factor after Farsetmore. Sidney, operating through Piers at Carrickfergus, might have hinted that England was finally willing to negotiate with Clan Ian Mor concerning title to the Glynnes and the Route.[81] It probably became clear to the MacDonnells at this point that Sidney could offer them the best deal. There is no concrete evidence that a firm bargain was struck between the Lord Deputy and the Scots; it is not unlikely, however, that the MacDonnells had been led to expect a reward for ridding Ulster of O'Neill. That Piers lurked close enough to rush in and claim the arch-traitor's head, spirit it off to Dublin, and collect a handsome reward suggests that he (if not other Englishmen) was involved in some way in O'Neill's death.

Shane O'Neill's dramatic and tragic death has occasioned the spilling of much ink by those who seek either to praise or to vilify him. The Four Masters described Shane as the O'Neills' "Conchobhar in provincial dignity, their Lugh Longhanded in heroism, and their champion in danger and prowess."[82] Another contemporary observer, though pro-English, admitted that he "was of such policy and strength as his like was not a long time afore in his room."[83] O'Neill has been depicted by others as a blood-thirsty, adulterous drunkard; however, he was never defeated in battle by the English. If he were barbarous, it was partly in response to English barbarity in Gaelic Ulster. His defiance of Elizabeth and his obvious popularity among his own people should have secured for him a more respected place in Irish history. Blame for this misrepresentation rests with both Irish and English historians. The former curiously have had little to say in defense of a man who arguably laid the foundation for a proto-nationalism fostered a generation later by Hugh O'Neill. The latter, understandably, have continued to build on the story begun by the pro-Sussex faction immediately after O'Neill's death. According to Sidney, they dismissed Shane as "a beggar, an outlaw, and one of no force. . . ."[84] This characterization of a man whom the English could not suppress on their own is not, of course, to be taken seriously. A more realistic depiction of this impetuous Gael was provided much later in a verse by poet John Savage, entitled "Address to the Head of Shane O'Neill":

> Thy ghastly head grins scorn upon old Dublin's Castle tower,
> Thy shaggy hair is wind-tossed, and thy brow seems rough with power.
> He was "turbulent" with traitors; he was "haughty" with the foe;
> He was "cruel" say ye Saxons! Aye, he dealt ye blow for blow!
> He was "rough" and "wild"; and who's not wild, to see his hearthstone razed?
> He was "merciless as fire". Ah, ye kindled him–he blazed!
> He was "proud"–yes, proud of birthright, and because he flung away
> Your Saxon stars of princedom, as the rock does mocking spray.
> He was wild, insane for vengeance–aye, and preached it till Tyrone
> Was ruddy, ready, wild too, with "red hands" to clutch their own.[85]

O'Neill's departure from Ulster politics greatly simplified the struggle by reducing it to one between the English and Clan Ian Mor, the latter now under Sorley Boy's strong hand. The new O'Neill, Turlough Luineach, though it was not known at the time, would be only the shell of the man his cousin Shane had been. After all, it was estimated that the late O'Neill had cost Elizabeth nearly £150,000 and the lives of 3,500 soldiers, in addition to incalculable lost revenues and shattered reputations. Shane's mangled remains being consigned to the lonely graveyard of Croise-Scrine ("the shrine of the cross") in the townland of Ballyteerim outside Cushendun, and his head adorning a pike outside Dublin Castle, a new era had dawned in the Gaelic heartland.[86] Only a few days after O'Neill's death, Sir William Fitzwilliam recommended that the Scots be rewarded for their services and then summarily dismissed from Ulster.[87] The way would then be cleared for the plantation of Englishmen along the eastern Antrim coast. While the queen was not averse to compensating Turlough Luineach and Hugh O'Neill, the young baron of Dungannon, for territories surrendered to make way for the plantation, she had not yet "considered how the Scots . . . shall be ordered . . . [or] whether any or no part of those countries shall be allowed unto them." But Elizabeth, caught up in the whirl surrounding Shane's death, believed that "the whole [of Ulster] may come to us now by conquest."[88]

Sorley and the MacDonnells were under no illusions as to where they stood with England. Their affairs had been disrupted by Glentaisie, and though Alasdair Oge had performed courageously in the absence of James and Sorley Boy, his work represented little more than a holding action until Sorley returned. But even with Sorley Boy at liberty, the Scots still needed time to regroup before re-evaluating their position in Ireland. It was obvious that any reassertion of MacDonnell power in Ulster would depend on Sorley's success in establishing good relations in Scotland. For their part, the English sought to secure and expand their foothold in northern Ireland throughout the remainder of the summer. The O'Donnells remained nominal allies, but their value to Dublin had decreased rapidly after O'Neill's demise. They were unable to exert any influence outside Tyrconnell, and England presently needed a strong ally operating in eastern Ulster to counter Clan Ian Mor's resurgence. Captains William Piers and Nicholas Malby were virtually isolated at Carrickfergus. They depended on the goodwill of Brian Carragh MacDonnell, the sole pro-English Ulster chief, for their very survival.[89]

Shane's death found neither the Antrim Scots nor the English prepared to seize the initiative in Ulster. Both had general, if not somewhat vague, objectives that called for the domination of certain areas and the expulsion of the other's forces as a prerequisite for such territorial aggrandizement. London desired simply to expel Clan Ian Mor and colonize the eastern Antrim coast. Meanwhile, they supported Dungannon, who had been raised by the Sidneys in England, as a counterweight to Turlough Luineach in central Ulster.[90] If Turlough could be isolated and neutralized by Dungannon and the troublesome Scots driven from Antrim, then the queen's plantation scheme could begin. Elizabeth wrote Sidney on 6 July, setting forth her rationale and plans for banishing the Antrim MacDonnells. They were to be "well rewarded according to such promises as you [Sidney] made" them, whereupon they should "be expelled speedily by force. Wherein the sooner you employ yourself, the better it is, in respect of the inward troubles in Scotland [i.e. with the MacLeans] from whence otherwise it is to be feared that they may have support."[91]

Elizabeth and her officials knew that Clan Ian Mor was a much more formidable enemy than Shane had been, if for no other reason than its ability freely to cross back and forth between Scotland and Ulster. Driving Sorley and Alasdair away temporarily, then, would not solve the problem. In her letter to Sidney, the queen thought it "fit to consider how the [Scots] . . . shall be hereafter kept from returning out of Scotland thither. . . ." The only way to accomplish this policy would be "either by keeping . . . garrisons there [i.e. along the Antrim coast] to our own continual charge, or else by planting the sea coasts . . . with English subjects. . . ."[92] Elizabeth and Sidney knew what they wanted in the north of Ireland; to bring about the desired changes, however, demanded that England commit quickly and decisively to carving a new Pale out of the wilderness of Gaelic Ulster.

Before the struggle began, both Clan Ian Mor and Sidney withdrew in late 1567 to Scotland and London, respectively. The leaders of each side were seeking support in formulating a viable Ulster policy and in raising troops and supplies before returning to Ireland. As for Sidney, he wished to implement a strategy of conquest as a prerequisite to colonization.[93] By doing so, therefore, he could justify his policy recommendation based on the queen's twin desires of banishing the Scots and of planting eastern Ulster. The Gaels could expect little mercy from the Lord Deputy.[94] As for the MacDonnells, they looked to accomplish three things before returning to Ulster to face Sidney: 1) they hoped to quickly raise a large redshank army and transfer it to the Glynnes and the Route; 2) they wished to secure their Scottish recruiting grounds by reaching an accord with Argyll, whose support was a prerequisite to the unimpeded flow of redshanks to Ireland; and 3) Sorley and Alasdair desired to develop good relations with Turlough Luineach and other important Irish chiefs.[95]

The two years between Clan Ian Mor's defeat at Glentaisie and O'Neill's death at Cushendun were a crucible for the Antrim MacDonnells. The family survived James's death and Sorley's captivity mainly because of the cool-headed leadership of Alasdair Oge and the continuation of the bitter rivalry between Shane and the English. Had either Elizabeth or O'Neill considered the destruction of the Scots' enclave in Antrim to have been in their best interest, Clan Ian Mor would have been hard pressed to have retained its independence. Consequently, the MacDonnells perhaps would have been reduced to vassalage by the earl of Argyll. But because of skill, perseverance, and good fortune, Clan Ian Mor held tenaciously to a foothold in the Glynnes and the Route until it once again became a major player in the struggle for the Gaelic heartland in 1567. And the newly freed Sorley Boy was the key factor in the family's resurgence.

Chapter Seven
The New Power Balance in the North, 1567–72

> Blessed be the Lord my strength, which teacheth my hands to war, and my fingers to fight.
>
> Psalm 144: 1

Upon his release in 1567 Sorley Boy became the acknowledged leader of Clan Ian Mor. The death of James, lord of Dunyveg, had left Sorley and Alasdair Oge to carry on against England, the native Irish, and the earl of Argyll. Since Shane O'Neill was gone, the English turned their attention to ousting the MacDonnells from Ulster; thus from the moment he drew his first breath again as a free man, Sorley steeled himself to the task of resisting the extension of English power into the Glynnes and the Route. The struggle upon which he embarked in 1567 lasted nearly twenty years. The first quarter of that tumultuous era is the subject at hand.

Elizabeth believed that if the Scots were allowed to remain in Antrim, it would prove difficult, if not impossible, to plant eastern Ulster with "obedient" Englishmen.[1] But she knew that it would be costly to subjugate or banish Clan Ian Mor. Indeed, it was unlikely that Sorley would agree to any diminution of his own power, especially since so much of his family's blood had been spilled in extending MacDonnell influence in northern Ireland. Both Sorley and the queen preferred to maintain their Irish territories as cheaply as possible, which meant, of course, avoiding further military conflict. After securing his freedom Sorley renewed his quest for a royal charter to his Irish lands. But he found himself in a disadvantageous negotiating position in mid-summer 1567, because nearly all MacDonnell strongholds from Red Bay to Dunluce either had been destroyed or were in English hands. Too, Clan Ian Mor's hold over its traditional Scottish lands was tenuous at best, and Sorley's hasty departure for the Highlands and Isles after O'Neill's death pointed up his concern. Before long, Alasdair Oge took over the MacDonnells' Scottish interests, thereby allowing Sorley to concentrate on Irish affairs. Sorley Boy undoubtedly now saw himself as Clan Ian Mor's leader in Ulster; therefore, he understood the urgency of making an agreement with England as soon as possible.[2]

Sorley realized that it would improve his position in Ulster to come to terms with Turlough Luineach O'Neill and Argyll. Certain English officials were already at work in July trying to poison relations between the MacDonnells and the new O'Neill. Sir Francis Knollys advised that Turlough's lands be granted to the Scots on the condition that they drive him out.[3] Elizabeth, though, preferred a different tack, as she informed Sidney of her desire to mollify O'Neill "to the end that his government may not grow . . . out of order. . . ."[4] If the new O'Neill, unlike the old, was willing to live quietly as the queen's vassal, then Ulster might have peace. Otherwise, it would explode again. The key, at least as the English saw it, was to keep Sorley Boy and Turlough apart and to prevent the unpredictable Argyll from meddling in Ulster.[5]

The English understood that Clan Ian Mor had yet to recover fully from Glentaisie and that Sorley Boy would be forced to rebuild the family's strength in Ulster by recruiting heavily in the southern Hebrides and Argyllshire. Thus for most of the summer he was in Scotland arranging an agreement with Argyll. Though Sorley did not wish to settle the issue with England by force, he realized the probability of war. The *ultima ratio* for Sorley's accord with Argyll, then, was obvious–unfettered access to redshanks. In response, the queen told Sidney in late July that she would provide a bark, two frigates, and 100 men to keep the Scots from enjoying free passage of the North Channel.[6] When the declining state of the English army in Ulster is compared with Sorley's and Alasdair's recruiting success in western Scotland, it is obvious why the queen desired to avoid hostilities with Clan Ian Mor. An early November message from Piers and Malby revealed that the MacDonnells had 1,200 redshanks ready to sail to Ulster.[7]

Sorley Boy arrived at Ballycastle on 17 November 1567 with about 400 MacDonnell and Campbell redshanks. More were set to follow shortly. Sorley's return signaled his determination to regain, through force if necessary, the lands his family had lost after Glentaisie. The arrival of these veteran Scottish troops brought the number of redshanks in Antrim to 1,500. Many of these men were not directly under Sorley's command, but they were a potential reserve from which he might draw support.[8] After having been briefed by Piers and Malby on Sorley's landing, Lord Justice Fitzwilliam passed the information on to Elizabeth in late November. One of her chief concerns was the prospect of Turlough's taking a

Scottish wife, especially Lady Agnes Campbell, James MacDonnell's widow, thus creating an O'Neill–MacDonnell–Campbell combination. While the new O'Neill by himself was only a nuisance, there is no question that his alliance with either Sorley Boy or Argyll would give the Scots a firmer hold in Ulster. To pressure Turlough Luineach, Fitzwilliam set about to find out all he could about the new Tyrone chief. What he discovered was O'Neill's adeptness at playing both sides against the middle. Turlough had already begun negotiations with both Clan Ian Mor and the English, but when pressed by Fitzwilliam, he denied charges of disloyalty to the queen, and to prove his goodwill he offered to raise an army against the Scots. It was evident that Sorley's landing had complicated the situation in Ulster, especially for Turlough, a tragi-comic figure who was being swept along by forces beyond his control.[9]

English authorities hurriedly marshaled forces to combat Sorley Boy's Scots. Even though he had returned to Ireland with the means to re-establish MacDonnell hegemony by force, if necessary, Sorley was not belligerent. His goal, again, was peaceful possession of the Glynnes, the Route, and the baronies of Monery and Cary through a royal grant. Dublin, however, viewed his unexpected arrival and firm determination as a threat. Consequently, Piers despatched his few available troops against Clan Ian Mor on 1 December. Fitzwilliam complained to Cecil of the poor state of the army and pleaded for a restoration of funding to the level that Sidney (who was temporarily away from the Irish service) had enjoyed.[10] Sorley preyed on the MacQuillins and then called for the "rest of the Irish Scots" to come to him on the North Antrim coast, swearing "that he would never depart Ireland with his good-will."[11]

English attempts to banish, or simply to contain, Clan Ian Mor failed miserably. Their forces suffering from the Irish winter, Piers and Malby excused the postponement of a December campaign, saying that Turlough Luineach intended to entrap them.[12] Daniel informed Fitzwilliam in early December that though MacDonnell messengers were with O'Neill, he "said openly, he would never take part with them. . . ." Daniel, however, was doubtful of Turlough's good intentions toward England. As events shortly proved, his fears were justified. All parties concerned realized by mid-December that England had lost the opportunity to invade Ulster and banish Clan Ian Mor. Turlough, as yet an unknown political factor, moved closer to Sorley Boy.[13] Sorley's next move–a letter to Piers and Malby requesting a truce until 1 May 1568–presumably was designed to persuade them that he was unreceptive to O'Neill's overtures. Sorley suspected, however, that England was not convinced of his sincerity. He informed Piers and Malby on 16 December 1567:

we thought needful . . . that rest, peace, and assurance be affixed betwixt you and us to the next May day, whereof if you be content with the advice of the rest of the captains you shall send the letter of assurance to us thereupon with this bearer. Sure that peace and tranquility may be had . . . both by land and sea betwixt you and us. . . . I have thought necessary to send my obligation to you thereupon as follows. I, Somarlie MacDonnell, on name and behalf of Angus MacDonnell of Dunyveg, [son of the late James MacDonnell] the space and term of May day next immediately following the day and date hereof, and that I shall in no ways molest, hurt nor pursue any of the queen's majesty's servants . . . by sea or land . . . during the said space. . . ."[14]

England was willing to accept an agreement with Sorley Boy as a temporary alternative to a military solution in Ulster. Sorley had agreed to the truce only under condition that Piers and Malby "take in hand to do . . . such business as I have written to you at the queen's . . . hands."[15] But in their response on 20 December, the two Englishmen brought up Sorley's alleged promise "to return immediately without delay unto his own country . . . and there to remain . . . until the return of me, captain William Piers, or till the first day of May."[16] Sorley had made no such promise, despite Malby's report to the Lords Justice on the previous day after having received Sorley's letter of 16 December. Malby informed Dublin that the expedition against the Scots had been postponed, in effect, because Sorley Boy had promised to depart Ulster for Scotland.[17] The first Sorley learned of his supposed obligation to depart Ireland came in the letter he received from Piers and Malby on 20 December. Despite his oath never again to leave Ireland against his will, the MacDonnell chief realized that for now it was in his family's best interest to cooperate with England. Replying on 23 December, Sorley offered to reward Piers and Malby for presenting his case to the queen. He also calmly addressed the issue of his departure from Ulster:

[A]nd further where you desire me to advertise you in all haste of my departing of this country, I thought needful (concerning the variance as standeth betwixt you and us at our first coming over to these parts) for fair keeping of our galleys and boats to send thence home, and have sent my men fourteen days since to bring in the said vessels again as soon as the wind serveth, and therefore seeing the weather is so inconstant, I know not when I may pass over. Notwithstanding I shall not fail, God willing, to return home on the first fair day after the coming of our galleys. . . .[18]

Sorley Boy's willingness to return to Scotland in exchange for a royal patent to his lands was neither an admission of weakness nor a ruse to mislead the English. Rather, on the one hand, Sorley hoped that his goodwill would bring reciprocity from the queen. On the other, he had dealt with the English for much of the decade on this matter and by now had little faith in their promises. To bolster his position in Antrim, Sorley engineered a covert deal with Turlough Luineach whereby the O'Neill chief would provide employment for most of the MacDonnell redshanks, thus allowing them to stay in Ulster while he [Sorley] recruited in the western Highlands and Isles.[19] The agreement to return to Scotland, then, was a means for Sorley to finally ascertain how serious England was about negotiations.

Throughout December Elizabeth had instructed Fitzwilliam to keep pressure on the Scots and to prevent them from allying with O'Neill. But neither Fitzwilliam nor Piers at Carrickfergus had the wherewithal to challenge Sorley Boy. Under such circumstances, the queen's Irish officials probably were none too disappointed to see Sorley leave for Scotland in January 1568.[20] But more circumspect English policy-makers, including Elizabeth herself, realized that Sorley's departure meant he would further strengthen his military forces by additional recruitment. Though she wished to avoid a costly conflict, the queen would have preferred to strike Sorley before he consolidated his hold on the Antrim shores.

As the new year opened, Piers reassured Fitzwilliam that Sorley Boy thus far had been granted peace only "upon condition that he should depart the realm with all his men of war which he hath promised to perform, and without doubt is upon the point of departing, if he be not already gone. . . ."[21] But Piers's confident words obscured the true state of affairs in Ulster, for Sorley clearly was cultivating a series of loose alliances. His negotiations with Turlough Luineach had apparently so emboldened the O'Neill chief that, according to Sir Nicholas Bagenal, he (O'Neill) finally reached a firm agreement with Clan Ian Mor. To christen the alliance, Turlough attacked Armagh and destroyed much of the settlement. He also betrothed his daughter to Rory Oge MacQuillin, who himself recently had come to an agreement with Sorley. And as the chief of the Clandeboy O'Neills, Sir Brian MacFelim, was now among his allies, Sorley indeed posed a considerable danger to the English in Ulster.[22]

The English stood on shaky ground in eastern Ulster in early 1568 mainly because several lesser Scottish and Irish chiefs in the area had pledged to support Sorley or Turlough. England, therefore, had been forced to remove most of her garrisons from the Antrim coast to protect the vital port of Carrickfergus.[23] Less than a week after Sorley left for Scotland, Fitzwilliam had informed Cecil that the MacDonnell chief was going to Scotland to bring over even more redshanks.[24] Though the Scots did not return to Ireland as quickly as he expected, Fitzwilliam ultimately was proven correct in his assessment of the Scottish danger.

Fitzwilliam detected an emerging crisis in mid-January, intimating to Cecil his suspicion that Sorley Boy "hath deeply desembled with Piers and

Malby. . . ." He continued: "If Piers and Malby had at any time before their finishing of their peace made . . . me privy thereto, as I know not what reason leads them to mistrust us, or what authority to work such a matter without our consents and advices, we would presently have advertised the same unto you. . . ."[25] Piers and Malby unquestionably had taken liberties in conducting policy in this sensitive and important region. They had, after all, misrepresented Sorley's position in the previous December. They also had neglected to mention the truce or their agreement to present Sorley's case for a royal grant to Fitzwilliam.

Piers was the architect of the entente with Sorley Boy, an agreement that allowed the captain to disguise England's inability to expel Clan Ian Mor from Ulster. That Piers was able to circumvent Fitzwilliam in dealing with the Scots suggests that he enjoyed the queen's support. It was well known that Piers was a long-standing favorite of Elizabeth and had helped protect her from harm at the hands of Mary I. But for whatever reasons they may have arisen, strained relations between Fitzwilliam in Dublin and Piers in Carrickfergus did not bode well for England. Fitzwilliam believed that had Piers and Malby "dealt within one month after the Lord Deputy's departure [mid-October 1567] in such sort with those Scots in the north as his lord appointed them to do, Sorley Boy . . . [might not have] found so many Scots at his landing to join with him. . . ."[26] But because Piers and Malby had been willing neither to acknowledge nor to shoulder responsibility for England's military unpreparedness in eastern Antrim, their situation there was critical in early 1568.

After departing Ulster for Scotland, Sorley landed first on Rathlin Island, causing Fitzwilliam to be concerned about his close proximity to the Glynnes. Terence Daniel believed that Sorley never intended to vacate the Glynnes and the Route, because he left behind several thriving agricultural settlements. Daniel also saw Argyll's crafty hand behind attempts to arrange a marriage alliance with Turlough Luineach and to keep O'Neill supplied with Campbell redshanks. But in all fairness to Sorley, pestilence had already ravaged parts of Scotland in the winter of 1567–8, a situation further complicated by bad weather and scarce provisions. The country, then, was not ripe for recruiting. This, perhaps, was why Sorley, well provisioned with 600 cattle, remained on Rathlin for the time being.[27]

Sorley Boy's decision to leave most of his redshanks in Ulster, and the fact that he himself had gone no farther than Rathlin by late January, caused Dublin to accuse the Scots of double-dealing. As Sorley had distributed his men among several Ulster chieftains, including Turlough Luineach, England had to keep watch throughout eastern Antrim and northern Down. Fitzwilliam, however, refused to sanction open war on Sorley's redshanks who remained in Ulster, insisting that the truce be observed. The Lord Justice well understood England's vulnerability in northern Ireland.[28] O'Neill was leaning closer to the Scots, despite his assurances to the contrary. The English would have liked to establish the baron of Dungannon as a counterweight to Turlough, but the task was deemed too perilous for one so inexperienced. To make matters worse, Munster verged on open rebellion. There is no question that England's hold on the island was precarious in early 1568. Pending Sidney's return, Fitzwilliam planned to proceed to Carrickfergus to maintain the delicate balance between peace and war.[29]

Sorley reportedly fortifying Rathlin, his allies involved in running skirmishes with English troops in the Glynnes, and Turlough Luineach practicing with Clan Ian Mor and Argyll, England expected a redshank invasion of Ulster at any moment. In early February Sorley landed in Kintyre, which gave rise to rumors that 1,000 Scots were being readied to invade the north of Ireland. Piers and Malby believed that Turlough's overtures to the Scots "argueth great mischief. . . ."[30] Indeed, Bagenal confirmed Piers's and Malby's fears when he revealed that O'Neill's messenger had returned with Argyll's promise of aid in the form of Lady Agnes Campbell's hand in marriage. There was little doubt that her dowry would occasion a flood of redshanks into Ulster.[31]

Negotiations between Sorley Boy, Turlough Luineach, and various other Irish and Scottish chiefs led to the formation in 1568 of a cooperative pact. Realizing the potential danger of a Gaelic entente in Ulster and the difficulty of further negotiations with Sorley, England sought to prevent Turlough from joining Clan Ian Mor. Until now, O'Neill's only breach of his agreement with the English had been the hiring of Sorley Boy's redshanks. Fitzwilliam had few means at hand to counter a serious Ulster combination. He recommended moving reinforcements to Carrickfergus, which was in a miserable state, desperately short of meal and malt. Even worse, several pro-MacDonnell chieftains had begun to plunder the countryside in Antrim and Down. Amid these disturbances, both Fitzwilliam and Malby were anxious for Sidney to return and put things right. To strike Sorley and his allies at the source of their strength–the redshank recruiting grounds in western Scotland–Elizabeth considered making an agreement with the Scottish regent, James Stewart, earl of Moray, who presumably would pressure Argyll to stop the flow of mercenaries to Ulster.[32]

The English no longer trusted Sorley Boy nor, for that matter, any chieftain within his political ambit. Fitzwilliam continued to expect an imminent invasion, "considering how Sorley boye hath already broken with you, he and the rest are the less to be trusted and mean only as we take it to win further time for . . . their future malicious enterprises. . . ."[33] Consequently, Fitzwilliam attempted to secure the most important redshank landing-sites along the eastern Antrim coast. But despite the movement of troops and supplies to Ulster, England could not overcome the most damning weakness of all–a lack of will to use military force.[34]

The possibility of an Ulster alliance in spring 1568 can be attributed to a combination of the ubiquitous Sorley Boy's firm leadership and England's irresolution. Despite Piers's and Malby's report to the contrary, the MacDonnell chief was fashioning political links in Scotland that he hoped would ensure his success in Ireland.[35] His letter of 16 March to Malby exuded a burgeoning confidence:

> I have received Captain William Piers's writing whereby I do understand that (as he says) he will do his diligence about the performing of my nephew's business and mine at the queen's hands, which if he do it shall be not only to our profit but also to her majesty's commissioners' utility and honour in your part and herewith where he has desired us not to enter the coast of Ireland till his returning according to our promises . . . I shall not do any wrong or hurt to any of the queen's subjects there, neither in person or [sic] goods. . . .[36]

But Sorley cautioned Malby that if Elizabeth did not refrain from harassing his Ulster allies and abide by her end of the bargain, then "no man will listen in your sayings or writings."[37] These, indeed, were the words of a man who believed himself to be in possession of the political high ground.

Sorley's business in Scotland centered on the marriage alliance between Lady Agnes and Turlough Luineach O'Neill. Turlough indeed was invigorated by the prospect of marrying such an important woman. But as the Tyrone chief awaited Sorley's and Lady Agnes's arrival, he again wavered between open defiance and feigned humility. In mid-March he penned a letter to Fitzwilliam in which he blathered about his inability to dismiss Sorley Boy's redshanks because their contracts had yet to expire. It is difficult, of course, to ascertain whether Turlough simply wished to put off the English with such pusillanimous pleadings or whether he sincerely feared that they would harm him unless he feigned submission.[38]

Sorley wished to cement an alliance between his erstwhile sister-in-law and O'Neill to facilitate his own dominance of Clan Ian Mor's Irish territories. As the sixth (and youngest) son of Alasdair Cahanagh MacDonnell, Sorley had virtually no chance of becoming lord of Dunyveg and the Glynnes. James MacDonnell's eldest surviving son and heir had inherited that title and the right to hold the accompanying lands, including the Glynnes. Lady Agnes would be quick to protect and advance her sons' interests. Thus it might be asked why Sorley brought Lady Agnes back to Ireland? He apparently had carefully weighed the alternatives and decided that what she could provide justified the political risks to his own position. Her provision, of course, was redshanks in sufficient numbers to overrun Ulster. Lady Agnes's Campbell kinsmen, the source of most of these mercenaries, figured prominently in Sorley's decision, as they could be either valuable allies or dangerous enemies. He preferred that they stay out of Ulster politics, at least directly, and be content to provide the manpower with which he might expand his own Irish holdings. An Ulster entente was central to Sorley's strategy of conquering the Route. But if this band was to be effective, Lady Agnes Campbell and her MacDonnell sons must be brought under his guiding hand.

According to various English reports, the marriage between Turlough Luineach and Lady Agnes was to occur in late April or early May 1568. Her daughter, Ineen Dubh ("the dark-haired"), had been paired with young Hugh O'Donnell of Tyrconnell. The marriage of mother and daughter to these two powerful Ulster Irish chiefs would draw together the O'Neills and O'Donnells. Sorley Boy hoped to use this native Irish coalition to keep England at bay while he extended his influence westward from Ballycastle. As the date for the wedding was set, preparations went on apace both in Scotland and Ireland. Plans were set in motion, too, by the English to prevent this dangerous union. In mid-March Malby had instructed the English naval squadron in the North Channel to be ready to intercept the ladies on their passage to Ulster. London saw the pending marriage as a threat to English authority not only in the northeast, but in all of Ireland. Because Argyll had approved the marriage and was becoming increasingly hostile to the Protestant regime of the regent Moray in Edinburgh, the conflict took on overtones of the wider European religious struggle in the wake of the Council of Trent. Argyll himself was Protestant, but he was not one to let religious sensibilities interfere with political aggrandizement.[39]

The marriage between O'Neill and Lady Agnes was postponed from April 1568 to August 1569. Perhaps the most important reason for the delay was England's quick and decisive action. In late March Fitzwilliam reinforced the English presence on the Antrim coast to prevent a Scottish landing. Sorley Boy was moving supplies to Turlough's castle at Dunnalong, and as the wedding day approached it appeared that the bridegroom-to-be had persuaded Sir Brian MacFelim of Clandeboy to join a Gaelic combination. Thus by mid April Fitzwilliam and Bagenal had ample reason to be troubled. The Lord Justice was suspicious of Sir Brian's pledge of loyalty, but assured the queen and Cecil that he (Fitzwilliam) and Bagenal would hold their ground in the Glynnes.[40]

Sorley had upheld the May Day truce which he made with Piers the previous December. The truce was about to expire, though, and Dublin officials feared the renewal of hostilities by an enemy who obviously had used the lull to prepare for war. When Sorley began to position himself to strike in April, England knew that to dally further could prove disastrous. Fitzwilliam immediately tried to entice Sir Brian MacFelim and other wayward Irish chiefs back into the English camp. But Fitzwilliam's thoughts were mainly on Sorley Boy, having received a report via Turlough Luineach that the MacDonnell leader "intendeth on Tuesday the 27 of this month to land at the Markettown [i.e. Ballycastle] bay with the rest of the Scots that are with him to the number of . . . twelve hundred or rather more. . . ." Once they had landed at Ballycastle, Fitzwilliam continued, the Scots would join O'Neill, giving them together

> nigh about two thousand five hundred Scots. And therefore we have devised to draw ourselves by Monday next [i.e. 26 April] at noon, nigh to Markettown bay, there to hold ourselves close and to expect if Turlough Luineach shall so observe that appointment, or the Scots theirs. . . .[41]

The English objective, then, was to prevent the two Gaelic leaders from joining forces. If he succeeded, Fitzwilliam might first defeat Sorley before he could consolidate his position in the Glynnes and thereafter destroy O'Neill. But if the Gaelic forces combined, the numerically inferior English army would "not be able to countervail them. . . ."[42]

Sorley Boy had kept his pledge not to make war in Ulster, but his comrades had not; thus the English scurried about putting out various "brushfires." Circumstances forced them to maintain constant vigilance. No effort could be spared to retain Sir Brian MacFelim's loyalty. Barring Turlough Luineach, Sir Brian was the most important Irish chief in Ulster, and Sorley desperately wanted him as an ally. England continued to suspect him of treason, but the Clandeboy chief's refusal to forswear his allegiance to the queen must have troubled Sorley Boy, even though he and Turlough together could field 3,400 troops. An attack on the MacQuillins by Malby and Sir Brian pointed up the weakness of the Ulster allies on the upper Bannside and the North Antrim coast. Because a large hostile force was ranging in the area, conditions were less than ideal for the proposed marriage and an Ulster offensive.[43]

At the beginning of May 1568 the English were taking precautions to prevent Sorley Boy from descending on the northeastern Ulster coast, sweeping across the Bann, and delivering to O'Neill his bride-to-be and her redshank host. Sorley being away in Scotland, his Ulster cohorts were unable to combat the English and Sir Brian MacFelim. But the immediate, and perhaps most important, reason for the postponement of Turlough's marriage was a series of developments in Scotland. Argyll, according to Piers, had notified O'Neill that no redshanks would be forthcoming until details of the Scottish-Irish band had been worked out to the Campbell chief's satisfaction. Argyll's reluctance to commit himself to an Ulster invasion in support of his kinswoman's marriage likely resulted from the crisis caused by the escape of Mary, Queen of Scots, from Lochleven Castle in early May. It was not until her subsequent defeat at Langside on 13 May that Argyll could again turn his attention to Ireland.[44]

Sorley arrived in the Antrim Glynnes on or about 24 May 1568 and hastily conferred with Turlough on the Bannside. O'Neill, who had broken his promise to parley with the English at Dundalk, must have been disappointed following his brief meeting with Sorley. MacDonnell, who shortly returned to Scotland, had come only to inform Turlough that the nascent Ulster alliance would remain inactive at Argyll's insistence. O'Neill withdrew to Benburb to ponder his next move now that the union with Lady Agnes had been postponed, and as trouble brewed with the O'Donnells, Turlough's situation became critical.[45]

Sorley's short stay in Ulster left O'Neill to shore up as best he could a moribund system of local alliances. As no new redshanks would be coming to Ireland, Turlough had to rely on his *gallóglaigh*. Piers believed that Argyll and Clan Ian Mor were too busy with their Scottish affairs in the early summer to pursue an active policy in northern Ireland. Indeed, so absorbed were the Scots, including Sorley Boy, in the affairs of the western Highlands and Isles that Thomas Lancaster, archbishop of Armagh, informed Elizabeth in mid-June that none in Ulster of any standing dared to draw "the sword against Her Highness. . . ."[46] Fitzwilliam, seeing that Sorley had not intended to remain in Ulster and that his own supplies were dangerously low, had shifted his forces from their exposed position at Ballycastle to Carrickfergus. Despite Fitzwilliam's assurances to Elizabeth that his troops would have given a good account of themselves on the battlefield, it was not the English army that deterred a Scottish invasion of Ulster.[47] Rather the Gaels were unable to mount an offensive in summer 1568, at least as a unified force, because they succumbed once again to their old nemesis: political disunification.

That Sorley Boy was unwilling in mid-1568 to stake his future in Ireland on any sort of Ulster combination that did not have Argyll's backing pointed up his realistic appraisal of the situation in the Gaelic heartland. By now Sorley despaired that England would ever give him a royal grant to the Glynnes and the Route. Furthermore, he doubted that Turlough Luineach or any combination of Gaelic Ulster lords–Scottish or Irish–could provide the assistance needed to defeat the queen's army. At this point, Sorley probably gave up on the idea of an effective alliance in Ulster. Centrifugal forces in the Gaelic political world simply discouraged such a combination. Not surprisingly, then, Sorley threw in his lot with Argyll and Donald Gorme MacDonald of Sleat. In the earl of Argyll, Sorley clearly had sided with the most powerful man in Scotland, despite opposition to the Campbell chief from the regent Moray and the Edinburgh regime.[48]

In attempting to cement an accord with Argyll and the Sleat MacDonalds, Sorley faced the same problem of Gaelic political disunity he had encountered in Ulster. In early July Piers and Malby informed Elizabeth of the reported discord among the Scots, who were "so busied one against another at home, as they can not intend hither, but have broken off their enterprise." However, they continued, if the Scots should come, "we have provided to be in readiness to set upon them at their landing. . . ."[49] The infighting among the Scots included an alleged quarrel between Sorley and Alasdair Oge. Alasdair had returned to Kintyre after Shane's death, apparently content to inhabit a rather modest estate while busying himself raising redshanks to serve Sorley in Ireland. Why the MacDonnell brothers disagreed cannot be ascertained. It is likely, however, that Alasdair, considering himself caretaker of the late James's sons, did not approve of Sorley's close ties with Donald Gorme of Sleat, the self-proclaimed "Lord of the Out Isles."[50] But, unfortunately, the row between Sorley and Alasdair was not the only bad blood between Scottish leaders.

Argyll brought together the disgruntled clan chiefs–Sorley and Alasdair Oge, Donald Gorme, MacLean of Duart, and Tormod MacLeod of Dunvegan–in hopes that they might iron out their differences and present a unified front in favor of the captive queen of Scots and against Moray. Despite MacCailein Mor's best efforts, the convention broke up amidst great acrimony. The only positive accomplishment was the MacDonnell–MacLean agreement to temporarily put aside their differences over the Rhinns of Islay.[51] Otherwise, in light of their fragmentation, Argyll and the Scottish chiefs found it sound policy to mend their political fences with both Moray and the English queen.

Both the Protestant-controlled Edinburgh and London governments feared that Argyll's involvement in Ulster would turn the province into a Catholic enclave, thus drawing the Counter-Reformation powers into Irish politics. Ambitious, duplicitous, and acutely aware of his own weakening position, Argyll sensed England's determination to oppose a Scottish foray into northern Ireland. Therefore, he moved quickly to ingratiate himself with Elizabeth and Moray.[52] Sidney, yet to resume his Irish duties, believed that the queen should "write to . . . Argyll . . . that he keep at home those idle Scots; for he may do it if he will."[53] Indeed, in mid-August Elizabeth praised Argyll's wisdom in deciding not to despatch redshanks to Ireland:

> We have thought good thus plainly to write unto you, that if these reports shall prove true, and that any numbers shall resort into our said realm, being in this sort aided and relieved under your rule, we doubt not but they shall find small advantage of their coming, or intentions to annoy our realm. And for your part, we shall make less account of such goodwill, as in appearance you have pretended, both heretofore and lately towards us. . . . And in this sort we have thought best to write as plainly as we mean, which in all causes proveth best.[54]

Because of the English queen's resoluteness and Argyll's opportunism, it was clear by the beginning of autumn 1568 that Sorley's attempt at an Ulster alliance was a dead letter. The nebulous state of affairs in Scotland since the flight into England of Mary, Queen of Scots, undoubtedly had unnerved the Campbell earl.[55] His Scottish strategy in disarray, all Sorley could do was patiently fashion a new policy to resurrect some sort of Ulster agreement.

While Sorley Boy remained in Scotland formulating a new strategy for re-entering Irish affairs, the unpredictable Turlough Luineach plunged into open rebellion. O'Neill had made peace with the O'Donnells (both Hugh and Con) on his western flank and Fitzwilliam believed that he intended to enlist the aid of some of the minor chieftains formerly in league with Sorley. In early September the Lord Justice informed Cecil that O'Neill had torched over a dozen towns in Ulster. Lacking men, money, and supplies, the Dublin administration notified London of Ulster's peril. Lord Deputy Sidney returned to Ireland in late October, whereupon he devoted himself to rebuilding Ulster's defenses and negotiating with Turlough O'Neill. Sidney quickly saw that Fitzwilliam had not exaggerated England's weakness. Only days after the Lord Deputy's return, Argyll dropped a bombshell when he agreed to cooperate with the English in Ulster if Elizabeth openly supported Mary, Queen of Scots, and threatened to invade Ireland at the head of 5,000 redshanks if she refused. Argyll also informed Sidney that Lady Agnes would be willing to marry an Irish lord of the English queen's choosing if in return Elizabeth would grant the Glynnes to her and her MacDonnell sons. Obviously, then, Argyll was attempting to cast himself as power-broker in the Gaelic heartland, controlling not only Lady Agnes and the young lord of Dunyveg, but most of the redshank recruiting grounds as well. Sidney thus suggested to Cecil that a 2,000-man force be sent to Ulster to garrison eight redoubts from Dunluce to Olderfleet. Central also to the Lord Deputy's plan was the division of Tyrone between various Irish chiefs so that Turlough's authority might be diminished accordingly.[56]

Fortunately for Sidney, neither Argyll nor O'Neill proved capable of mounting military actions commensurate with their verbal threats. Though Lady Agnes was dependent upon her Campbell kinsman, her eldest surviving son Angus, as lord of Dunyveg, brooked no interference from Argyll in MacDonnell affairs. Sorley Boy, too, remained a free agent, and not for one moment did Sidney underestimate his continuing threat to Ulster. As for Turlough, Cecil learned in mid-November that he had only about 1,000 redshanks and they served mainly to consume his cattle as *buannacht*. Thus for the remainder of 1568 and well into 1569, an uneasy, unofficial truce descended on Ulster and the southern Hebrides. Sorley and his Scots continued to cross the North Channel in small numbers virtually at will. For now, Sidney simply ignored them.[57]

Calm settled over much of Ulster in early 1569, while preparations for war went on apace in London, Tyrone, and the western Highlands and Isles of Scotland. Taking full advantage of the respite, the English government formulated a plan for dividing Ireland into shires and for granting letters patent to those who were to be shire "captains."[58] This amounted to a resumption of something similar to Henry VIII's policy of surrender and regrant; however, some Englishmen, among them one John Smith, understood that such an ambitious undertaking must be predicated on bringing the Scots under control:

the question of Ulster and Connacht is to take away the isle of . . . Rathlin from the Scots and there to place 25 soldiers in that castle that one Soyrle booy [Sorley Boy] doth now keep, for . . . Rathlin is the greatest enemy that Ireland hath, it is the only succour of the Scots for thither they bring their spoils out of Ireland, and they keep them until they can well convey them into Scotland.[59]

Smith's opinion that Rathlin was Ireland's "greatest enemy" obviously stemmed from Sorley Boy's having spent much of his time there since departing Ireland in late 1567.

Unless London policy-makers were prepared to mount a major effort similar to that of 1560–7 to drive out Clan Ian Mor, they would have been wise to consider Smith's recommendation to implement a plan to keep redshanks from ever returning to Ulster in force. He advocated that the queen

have there a pinnace or galley well-furnished to scour the Scots' galleys as well about the Isles of Scotland as Olderfleet, the . . . Bann, Lough Foyle, [and] Lough Swilly . . . so shall the said pinnace . . . do the Scots much mischief on their own coast and also keep them from fishing of the Bann and other places of the country where they have such commodity as they cannot well live without.[60]

Elizabeth, parsimonious as always, decided in June that it would be less costly to fortify strategic areas of Ulster than to provide funds to populate the north with English colonists. But this policy, while not without merit, would have taken far too long to carry out, especially since rumors surfaced that the long-awaited wedding of Turlough Luineach and Lady Agnes was about to occur. Significant numbers of Scots had already begun to filter into Ireland.[61] It appeared, then, that the dam finally was about to break, sending a flood of redshanks into the Antrim Glynnes.

Before England could settle on a firm policy in Ulster, Turlough and Lady Agnes were married. From Carrickfergus Piers reported in early August that she had arrived with 1,000 to 1,200 of Argyll's redshanks. Piers had not commanded a large enough force to stop the landing. Though few particulars of the marriage are known, including the exact date, the ceremony probably had already taken place when Piers penned his letter on 5 August. For such an important union there must have been elaborate festivities. Fitzwilliam informed Cecil that O'Neill had remained on Rathlin for a fortnight.[62] By early August Turlough and his new bride most certainly had departed Rathlin for the Irish mainland.

The marriage of Turlough Luineach O'Neill and Lady Agnes Campbell ushered in a new and more complex era in Ulster's history. Lady Agnes, with Sorley and Argyll providing her redshank dowry, gave the vacillatory

O'Neill a backbone. The landing reported by Piers in early August was only the first wave of a large influx of redshanks whose tramp was to echo across the bleak Ulster landscape for a generation. A Bristol merchant, Leonard Sumpter, reported a week later that Sorley Boy had assembled thirty-two galleys and 4,000 Scots (surely an exaggerated number) at Islay and stood ready to sail for Lough Foyle. Before his marriage, Turlough had estimated his own strength at 4,200 troops. The 1,000 to 1,200 redshanks that accompanied Lady Agnes pushed that total well over 5,000. Possessing a reinforced army, O'Neill and his fellow Ulster confederates, according to English informants, advanced south toward Omagh to launch an attack on the Pale.[63]

Believing himself in command of a powerful army, Turlough pressured other Irish chiefs, especially O'Donnell, to join his planned invasion of the Pale. As the O'Donnells had already provided a substantial number of recruits, Turlough apparently succeeded where his late cousin Shane had failed. But the O'Donnells, their Scottish allies–especially the Campbells and MacLeans–and many lesser Ulster chieftains suspected O'Neill of self-aggrandizement. Thus Turlough did not command the respect necessary to rally Ulster as had Shane at his zenith. Much of his strength was illusory, as O'Donnell's and other Irish forces were subject to recall. Lady Agnes seemed to be more loyal to her MacDonnell sons and Campbell kinsmen than to poor Turlough, and it was rumored shortly after the honeymoon that the marriage might end in divorce. The union lasted, but Sorley Boy and Argyll, acting through Lady Agnes, succeeded in casting Turlough in the role of point man in order to ascertain England's intentions and capabilities.[64]

There is little question but that Sorley desired Turlough to inflict as much injury as possible on the English in Ireland. But he understood that if O'Neill was too successful, it would increase the Tyrone chief's standing. There was, therefore, a narrow path that Sorley Boy must tread if he were to control Gaelic Ulster. On the one hand, he found it necessary to tempt Turlough with promises of military aid so O'Neill might be emboldened to take the field. To that effect, it was rumored "that Alasdair Oge and Sorle meaneth to come with an army of Scots about Michaelmas [29 September] to Clandeboy and to land about Knockfergus."[65] For his part, O'Neill knew the futility of launching an enterprise without support from Sorley and Argyll.[66] On the other, Sorley, who had plans of his own, realized that it would be unwise to relinquish control over too many of his own redshanks, even for Turlough's invasion of the Pale.

Sorley Boy's immediate objective–extending his own influence south into Clandeboy–might be masked if Turlough could be induced to invade the Pale. Connacht and Munster were in disorder, and the time seemed right for an Ulster rising as well. In late August a large number of Scots landed at Lough Foyle and were quickly employed by O'Neill and Con

O'Donnell. These redshanks probably came from Sorley and the MacLeans, representing their sole contribution to O'Neill's campaign. Nonetheless, Turlough, buoyed by a fresh supply of mercenaries, plundered the borders of the Pale. He also forced agreements on most of the Ulster chieftains except Sir Brian MacFelim O'Neill, who, unknown to O'Neill, had allied with Sorley. Because Turlough Luineach was at Newry in early September, Fitzwilliam warned Cecil that all available English forces must be concentrated against the Ulster threat. Already Turlough reportedly fielded more troops than had any of his O'Neill predecessors. At minimal cost to himself, then, Sorley had arranged for Turlough to carry the attack to the English while he laid plans to slip unnoticed through the back door on the eastern Antrim coast.[67]

Sorley Boy had high hopes in the autumn of 1569; however, his strategy went awry from the start for several reasons: Turlough's timorousness, his lack of organization and ability to handle large numbers of troops in the field, his failure to rally sufficient support among the Ulster chieftains, and England's decision to stand on the strategic defensive. Ironically, it was Sorley's attempt to join with Sir Brian MacFelim and march through Clandeboy that persuaded Sidney to retreat into the Pale all along the Carrickfergus–Erne line. Had Turlough been a less capricious leader, he could have taken advantage of the confusion in the English ranks caused by the retreat. But he frittered away his chance, and Sidney and Fitzwilliam, consequently, were able to consolidate their position. G. A. Hayes-McCoy believes that "the incipient rebellion broke down for want of a leader."[68] His assessment, however, is too simple. Hayes-McCoy assumes that a lack of leadership on the part of Turlough Luineach caused the uprising to falter. But Sorley Boy, the mastermind behind the military maneuvers against the Pale, had never expected O'Neill to engage the English in a major operation; he simply wished to mask a MacDonnell move into Clandeboy. The "incipient rebellion," then, did not break down for want of a leader; the rebellion, if indeed it properly can be called such, miscarried when the English finally realized that they would have to face Sorley rather than Turlough. Sidney's decision to retreat into the Pale was undertaken in response to MacDonnell's strong leadership and his overzealous advance into Clandeboy. Turlough actually had little to do with the English response and hence with the breakdown of the whole affair.

Since Sussex's lieutenantcy in the early 1560s, English policy in Ulster, and throughout Ireland, had increasingly depended on coercion rather than conciliation. The proponents of coercion–generally the Protestant New English–had committed themselves to a military solution in a remote, unknown region that they viewed as a colony rather than as a separate kingdom. Their policy of military conquest had not succeeded by 1570, mainly because of a dearth of resources committed to the task. Elizabeth proved extremely reluctant to consider Ireland as more than a sideshow. Even after her excommunication in early 1570 by Pope Pius V, the English queen showed little concern that Catholic Europe might use the island as a base of operations on her western flank. Because Philip II's attention was riveted on the Turkish menace in the Mediterranean and the French were still beset by internal religious conflict, no Counter-Reformation power appeared able to threaten Protestant England from any direction. Thus Elizabeth's New English advisors found it difficult to persuade her to sanction a large-scale, government-sponsored military build-up in Ireland. To conquer Ulster would require more men, material, and money than the queen was willing to commit. Since little had been accomplished by force of arms in the 1560s, she thought further direct military action futile in early 1570. The key to changing from an expensive military solution to one based on the permanent settlement of English colonists lay in bringing the proper type of organizers into Ulster. In the queen's mind, one of the most important qualifications for the new leaders was their ability to finance private ventures. Heretofore, Irish warfare had been a matter mainly for military men; however, the advent of New English colonizers looking to undertake a profitable enterprise changed the nature of the conflict.

Internecine warfare within the Gaelic world was not always characterized by the wholesale destruction of human life, either of combatants or non-combatants, but rather by the capture and subsequent exploitation of scarce human resources by the victor.[69] After all, sixteenth-century Ireland had a population of no more than three-quarters of a million. The Old English had been quick to accept this concept of war, and were able initially to exercise a moderating influence over New English officials who joined the Dublin administration. This is not to say that Irish warfare before the 1570s, whether between fellow Gaels or Gael and Englishman, had not been a bloody affair for combatants who had exhausted other means of settling their differences. After all, such is the nature of war as an agent of civilization. But with the coming of the self-financed New English colonial enterpriser, and the subsequent replacement of the Old English governing class, a buffer was thus removed that intensified the cultural clash between Anglo-Saxon and Celt.

Rather than continue costly and ineffective military forays against her Ulster enemies in 1570, Elizabeth preferred a policy that would restrict the flow of redshanks to Ireland. This had been tried unsuccessfully by Mary I in the 1550s. Now, though, Elizabeth believed she could pressure Argyll through the captive Mary, Queen of Scots. As the queen of Scots's freedom ostensibly hung in the balance, she was amenable to a proposed treaty with England wherein all Scots would be prevented from entering Ireland without a license from the Irish Lord Deputy. But Mary had no way of enforcing the treaty articles except through the force of her personality, and Elizabeth and Argyll knew as much. It is no wonder, then, that England continued naval patrols in the waters of the Gaelic heartland in early 1570.[70]

A proposal was introduced by Sir Thomas Gerrard, a Lancashire gentleman, to plant a private colony in Clandeboy and the Glynnes to aid in cutting the Ulster Gaels' access to the western Highlands and Isles of Scotland. Sir Brian MacFelim would be driven from Clandeboy and in his stead Gerrard's colony would be established with the queen's support for three years. The only obstacle to Gerrard's plan was Sir Brian's royal grant to Belfast Castle and his relations with Sorley and Clan Ian Mor. Gerrard also looked to colonize the Glynnes, which, of course, would bring him into conflict with the MacDonnells.[71] Elizabeth, despite her usual fiscal misgivings, supported the proposed settlement of eastern Ulster and instructed Sidney in mid-May to

> use all the best means . . . to reduce such captains that serve there . . . to settle themselves upon some parts of the frontiers, specially upon the sea coast towards Scotland. . . . We . . . understand . . . your opinion for the keeping of the seas betwixt Ireland and Scotland for the impeaching of the frequent resort of the Scots into Ireland and of your opinion for fortifying at Rathlin. . . .[72]

Though Elizabeth intimated to Sidney her willingness to assume part of the necessary expenditures, Gerrard's plan for planting a privately sponsored settlement in Clandeboy and the Glynnes undoubtedly struck a favorable chord with the queen. It is no surprise, therefore, that Sidney came under fire from London for his inability to run an economical administration. He protested, and with some justification, that the queen had expected him to work miracles with limited resources.

Sidney's fall from grace in midsummer 1570 and London's support of the scheme for a private venture in eastern Ulster gave the province's Gaelic allies an opportunity to pursue their own individual interests. Aware that the English were in the midst of a fundamental change in Irish policy, Sorley, Lady Agnes and her sons, and Turlough Luineach all sought to strengthen their hands. Sidney warned Cecil in November that the Dublin administration, which would be handed over to Fitzwilliam upon Sidney's departure, was perilously short of troops and supplies. In fact, the entire English military establishment in Ireland numbered only about 2,000 men. In March 1571 Sorley Boy, who had been in the Glynnes awaiting developments in London and Dublin, left for Scotland, ostensibly because of poor health. But Scotland was in the grip of a severely cold winter, and according to Sir Brian MacFelim, Clandeboy and the Glynnes were flourishing; thus Sorley's excuse is unconvincing. It is more likely that he had journeyed to Scotland to confer with Lady Agnes. Since her arrival there in early April, she was to have arranged to bring more redshanks to Ulster, but according to Captain Malby, young Angus of Dunyveg had prevented her return to Ireland.[73]

Sorley Boy had returned to Scotland in spring 1571 to prevent Lady Agnes from despatching more redshanks to Turlough, a deprivation that would surely weaken O'Neill. In a revealing letter to Sidney on 19 March, Sir Brian explained his temporary alliance with Sorley, which was designed to drive a wedge between Clan Ian Mor and O'Neill so that "Turlough should be weakened and her highness double strengthened. . . ."[74] But like most MacDonnell leaders since 1493, Sorley Boy was playing his own hand. That he had made an alliance with Brian MacFelim at all simply meant that Sorley saw an advantage in moving away from Turlough and in persuading Lady Agnes and her sons, especially Angus, to do likewise. Turlough had become skittish in January, concluding a ceasefire with the queen's commissioners.[75] Sorley Boy quickly seized the opportunity to reduce O'Neill to a mere local power in Tyrone.

That Angus MacDonnell forbade his mother from returning to Ireland in spring 1571 emphasizes Sorley Boy's influence over his young nephew. Angus and his mother hoped that by appearing to restrain Turlough from open rebellion they might persuade Elizabeth to give Dunyveg a royal grant to his Irish patrimony.[76] Sorley Boy, in *de facto* possession of the Glynnes, was not averse to promising to aid his nephew in securing title to that territory, and likely would pay lip-service to Angus's claim. In return, Sorley expected assistance from Angus and Lady Agnes in pushing his own claim to the swordlands of the Route. Thus the two sides of Clan Ian Mor were in the process of striking a *quid pro quo* agreement in early 1571. The pusillanimous Turlough could offer nothing of substance to either side; thus he found himself isolated in Tyrone, to be supplied with redshanks and called into the field only when it benefited the MacDonnells. Because he saw little benefit in trying to deal with Clan Ian Mor, O'Neill, at the behest of Lady Agnes, made an humiliating accord with the English.[77]

Despite Turlough's submission, London was aware of the continued danger posed by the MacDonnells in Ulster. Rumor was rife in 1571 that a Catholic French- or Spanish-sponsored enterprise would be directed against the north of Ireland. French or Spanish intervention in the Gaelic heartland would be a signal for the Scots to descend on the Irish coast in force. Piers believed that a significant danger already existed because of the Scots presently in Ulster. In mid-April Fitzwilliam, who had recently taken over the Dublin government from Sidney, echoed Piers's concern about the MacDonnells, whom he believed to be so thoroughly entrenched in the Glynnes and the Route that they might never be driven out. He also reported the disturbing news that the Scots had moved farther south into Lecale, the Dufferin, and the Ardes, where several Irish chiefs had allied with Sir Brian MacFelim.[78]

Now that Turlough had been brought to heel by the English and Clan Ian Mor, Elizabeth and Fitzwilliam turned their attention to the wooing of Sir Brian. In early July Piers passed on to Elizabeth the results of a conference with O'Neill of Clandeboy, who "hath at all times continued a loyal and true subject and is confirmable to do anything where unto he is or shall be advised for your grace's service."[79] But as with most Ulster chiefs, Sir Brian considered his own interests first. In the previous spring he had informed then Lord Deputy Sidney that Clandeboy could not support a large influx of English colonists.[80] He undoubtedly hoped that his assessment of Clandeboy would be well received (and heeded) by English policy-makers. Sir Brian must have hoped as well that his frankness would be taken as proof of loyalty to the queen. In truth, however, he wished to dissuade the English from planting a settlement near his lands for fear that he eventually would be forced to conform to English ways or be driven out completely.

Sir Brian desired to be confirmed in his lands on both sides of the Bann in return for past service to the queen. Like Sorley, Sir Brian knew that to avoid perpetual conflict with English officials and adventurers, he would need secure title to his lands. Though a royal grant did not guarantee security of tenure, the absence of one almost always meant trouble. But in Brian MacFelim's case, such legal niceties mattered not one whit, because his lands lay directly in the projected path of New English expansion as advocated by Gerrard and others. Sir Brian could expect little aid from Turlough or Sorley Boy. The Tyrone chief had not the nerve or the redshanks to mount a major campaign to assist his junior kinsman, especially since Lady Agnes had returned to Scotland with most of Turlough's mercenaries in November 1571. Sorley wished simply to bide his time and ascertain the nature and effectiveness of England's revised Ulster policy, based as it was on a partnership between the queen and private enterprisers. By December Elizabeth had decided to put that policy to the test, the new Lord Deputy Fitzwilliam being instructed to keep the government's expenditures in Ireland to a minimum.[81] As the new year approached, it remained to be seen just how much interest Irish colonization would generate among New English adventurers.

In 1572 England addressed the sticky problem of Sir Brian MacFelim O'Neill's lands in Clandeboy. Sir Thomas Smith, Elizabeth's Secretary of State, had received a royal grant to the Ardes and Clandeboy in the previous November. This was to be the beginning of an aggressive policy of English colonization in eastern Ulster. Gaelic Ulster was gravely concerned over Smith's claim to Sir Brian's lands, and even the normally cool-headed Sorley Boy was so shaken by such a blatantly provocative act that he marshalled his forces, struck toward Carrickfergus, and reportedly received a slight battle wound.[82] Since gaining his freedom from Shane O'Neill in 1567, Sorley had managed to steer a firm but cautious course in regard to the English in Ulster. But the arrival of the first wave of adventurer-colonists led by Smith and his bastard namesake ended the period of relative tranquility in the Gaelic heartland.

The grandiose scheme for colonizing eastern Ulster obviously hinged on keeping Clan Ian Mor at bay. Piers had submitted a plan to the queen in the previous summer:

> if it might seem good to your highness to grant a commission and to send hither one small ship and a galley to remain here but for one year, I dare take upon me in a short time to enforce the . . . Scots not only to leave these parts, but also to crave for quiet in their own country. . . . Also for that this town of Knockfergus is the only key and stay of the north and the walling of the same would greatly molest your majesty's enemies. . . .[83]

Smith's son also supported a plan to keep the Scots out of Ulster by garrisoning Rathlin Island and out of Connacht by occupying Ballyshannon and Belleek. So determined were the English to finally solve the redshank problem in northern Ireland that they instructed their Edinburgh agents to do whatever was necessary to prevent the recruitment of mercenaries in western Scotland.[84]

Despite measures to stem the influx of Scots mercenaries into Ulster, England faced the more immediate problem of an aggrieved Sir Brian MacFelim O'Neill in Clandeboy. Sir Brian fired off a series of emotional letters to the queen and her advisors, enumerating once again his past services and insisting that Smith's grant be revoked.[85] But London had no intention of intervening on the Irishman's behalf. Sir Thomas tried to calm the Clandeboy chief's fears by pledging to be a good neighbor and to live on good terms with the local inhabitants. Sir Brian, however, was lit with passion; consequently, when the younger Smith landed at Strangford in August and began constructing a castle in the Ardes, he encountered the open hostility of Brian MacFelim and his followers.[86]

Fitzwilliam, strapped for funds, yet still expected to advance the government's interests, predicted in mid-March that Smith's grant in the Ardes would provoke the Ulster Gaels to action. And unless the Smiths could field a substantial army, Sir Brian surely would destroy the Ardes colony. Thus Elizabeth would have to decide whether to shore up the enterprise at government expense or to suffer the humiliation of losing the colony. And if the enterprise were lost, potential colonists surely would be reluctant to settle in Ulster. Piers could inform Fitzwilliam with some assurance that Turlough Luineach would not break his peace agreement, but he dared not "answer against the Scots." The only way O'Neill would take the field, Piers believed, was if Sorley finally cemented an Ulster alliance by coming to terms with Sir Brian. But O'Neill had already dismissed most of his redshanks, and despite persistent rumors of either a French or Spanish descent on the Gaelic heartland, the irresolute Tyrone chief refused to move.[87] By the end of May the English knew that unless Sorley Boy vigorously supported an Ulster enterprise, Sir Brian MacFelim would be virtually isolated in Clandeboy.

The political situation in Northern Ireland had reached crisis-level in mid-1572, precipitated by England's change of policy and the Ulster chiefs' subsequent response. Turlough's vacillation and Sorley's caution finally drove Sir Brian to cooperate with the English. But in June Piers revealed

> that Turlough Luineach with all his power and the aid of the Scots are presently coming upon Sir Brian, [therefore] I thought good to crave your help, for Sir Brian hath driven all his kine to this town [i.e. Carrickfergus] and here we lie in camp to defend them. And therefore as you know of number, and further for that the Scots, namely Sorley Boy, who is at defiance with Sir Brian, and others are in the aid of Turlough Luineach, I do earnestly desire you [i.e. Malby] with all speed possible to be here with so many horsemen as well you may, for the overthrow of this gentleman [i.e. Sir Brian] would be the way to the overthrow of the whole north. . . .[88]

Turlough indeed seemed to have summoned up his courage. If O'Neill proved genuinely determined to resist English colonization in Ulster, Smith and his followers would be hard pressed to succeed in the Ardes enterprise.

The proposed plantation of eastern Ulster precipitated rumors that England would invade Ulster in the summer of 1572. These rumors were directly responsible for Gaelic attempts to re-establish some sort of military combination. The expected invasion was to be led by Walter Devereux, earl of Essex, one of an increasing number of New Englishmen interested in exploiting Ireland's natural resources for their own profit. Thus they were unlikely to become model colonists who would put down roots and turn Ulster into a cultural appendage of England. To carry out the sort of "colonization" scheme proposed by Essex or the Smiths would take an effort that only the English state could muster. Essex soon became Lord President of Ulster with a royal grant of £10,000 to outfit an expedition into the north. He also received a grant from Elizabeth to the Antrim Glynnes, an act guaranteed to provoke Sorley Boy and Clan Ian Mor.[89]

The intractable Scottish and Irish elements in Ulster first had to be dealt with before any plantation could succeed in Clandeboy and the Glynnes. But by the beginning of autumn 1572, a potent combination of Sorley, Turlough Luineach, and Sir Brian MacFelim stood ready to oppose Essex and Smith. Sir Brian quickly proved to be something less than the good neighbor for which Smith had hoped. As Fitzwilliam revealed to Burghley in early October, "Sir Brian MacFelim hath discovered his Irish nature."[90] While O'Neill of Clandeboy refused to submit to Smith's aggrandizement in the Ardes without a fight, he realized that he was not strong enough to oppose both Sir Thomas and Essex at once. Sir Brian bowed to reality when upon Essex's arrival he acknowledged the earl's rights in the Glynnes.[91] But neither Sir Brian nor Sorley Boy could be expected to remain passive with danger so close at hand.

The re-establishment of an Ulster accord in September meant that redshanks would flow once again into Ireland. And to make matters worse for England, the Gaelic allies made peace with the O'Donnells, which permitted their troops to land at Lough Foyle. By mid-October O'Neill of Clandeboy was in the field. Turlough informed Fitzwilliam that he had despatched messengers to the queen to treat for Sorley Boy's request for title to the Glynnes and the Route. By this late date, however, O'Neill hoped only to buy time for his allies to steal a march on the English.[92] Finally, it seemed that Turlough had resolved to strike the Sassenach with all his power.

Turlough briefly assumed the leadership of the Ulster alliance in October 1572 because of his hiring of recently arrived redshanks, his agreement with the O'Donnells, and Sorley Boy's incapacitation from his wound. O'Neill vehemently protested Smith's and Essex's claims to the Ardes and the Glynnes, respectively. Turlough demanded that peace be observed until his messengers had returned from the queen and that he be henceforth addressed respectfully as the O'Neill. He could not have stepped forward at a better time, since Sorley and most of his Scots had moved west of the Bann to avoid a confrontation with Essex. Also, while O'Neill negotiated with Fitzwilliam, Sir Brian plundered and burned in northern and eastern Down. Several weeks earlier the Lord Deputy and council had requested 800 more troops for Ireland, as Smith commanded only about 100 of his own men in the Ardes. Now, facing an arrogant O'Neill, Fitzwilliam requested an additional 2,000 soldiers.[93]

The bright flame of rebellion that had flared in Turlough and Sir Brian quickly diminished as autumn gave way to winter's damp chill. Both Fitzwilliam and Sir Thomas Smith reported to Burghley that Sir Brian desired to repent of his transgressions and to sue for peace. As for the poltroonish Turlough, he lost his taste for fighting when trouble resurfaced with Lady Agnes, who returned hastily to Scotland with her redshanks. After a period of relative inactivity, Argyll apparently had rekindled his interest in Ulster affairs. Thus as 1572 closed amidst dreary weather, disappointment must have prevailed among the Ulster allies. It was obvious that both Turlough and Sir Brian were spent forces. Sorley had wisely avoided committing himself fully to the enterprise until he saw its direction. And as it turned out, Argyll and Lady Agnes continued to control the flow of redshanks to Ireland. For some reason, however, they had shut it off at a critical moment. But England's plight looked no better. The elder Smith, writing from the dry comfort of Windsor, admitted that to destroy the Gaels in the north would be virtually impossible. Rather he desired that they be brought to civility by other means.[94] While Smith advocated a return to a policy of reconciliation reminiscent of the pre-1550s, Essex looked beyond the cold, dark waters of the Bann with the intent of carrying fire and sword to the most important leader of Gaelic Ulster–Sorley Boy MacDonnell.

Chapter Eight
Sorley Boy and Essex:
Fire and Sword in Ulster, 1573–5

The land of Ireland is swordland. . . .

Tadhg Dall O hUiginn

From 1573 to 1575 Sorley Boy fought to prevent Walter Devereux, earl of Essex, from driving a wedge between Clan Ian Mor and the native Irish and colonizing eastern Ulster. Essex ultimately failed to separate the Scots and Irish in Ulster through diplomatic means; consequently, he embarked on a savage military campaign to destroy Sorley and the Antrim MacDonnells. During the two years that Essex dominated English policy in Ulster, Sorley was forced to marshal his family's military strength, which he had carefully rebuilt since Glentaisie. The MacDonnell leader realized that Essex, Sir Thomas Smith, and other New English proponents of Irish colonization were a less capable but more dangerous breed than Sir Henry Sidney and others who had preceded them. Facing such adversaries, Gaelic Ireland indeed became "swordland."

Sorley Boy had moved westward across the Bann and into the Route in 1572 to buy time against Essex, especially as Turlough Luineach and Sir Brian MacFelim O'Neill no longer dared challenge England. Both Sorley and Sir Thomas Smith were of a mind to proceed cautiously, unlike Essex who was willing, if necessary, to risk war to gain the Glynnes and the Route.[1] Smith revealed to Burghley in early 1573 the results of recent communications between his son and Sorley Boy:

> I have received this day letters from my son out of Ireland. Still he proceedeth with his communication with Sarleboy to make those two nations [i.e. the Ardes colony and the Glynnes] all one, and, as it appeareth, the Scot is the more earnest . . . considering indeed that if the English and Scottish should strive together, when the one hath weakened the other, the wild Irish . . . might drive them out, or carry both away. In my opinion, the Queen's Majesty can lose nothing if Sarleboy be made denizen. . . .[2]

Smith's desperate tone seems to acknowledge the fact that outside of Piers's and Malby's forces at Carrickfergus, the English had nothing with which to oppose Sorley. Smith, therefore, recommended that MacDonnell be granted a patent of denization and be allowed to occupy his lands in Ulster.

Smith's emphasis on Sorley's strength and Essex's weakness probably bewildered the English authorities. Terence Daniel informed Lord Deputy Fitzwilliam near the end of March of an impending meeting between Sorley, Turlough Luineach, Sir Brian, and Turlough Braselagh O'Neill. This suggests that Turlough Luineach was again about to assume a more belligerent stance. In fact, in early April he reportedly hired a contingent of redshanks recently landed at Lough Foyle and plundered the baron of Dungannon in southern Tyrone. Sir Brian was said to be negotiating with Turlough Luineach for 400 redshanks.[3] Smith presumably was aware of the native Irish chiefs' preparations to resume hostilities when he recommended granting the denization patent to Sorley. He hoped that any sort of nascent Gaelic combination would be broken by such diplomacy.

If Sorley Boy could be placated with the long-sought royal patent, then he might become a loyal subject and serve the crown's interests against the native Irish. This must have been the logic behind the decision to grant him denizen status in mid-April 1573. But the wording of the agreement bound Sorley to uphold the crown's claim to sovereignty over those Irish, including Sir Brian MacFelim, who inhabited the lands granted to the Smiths in the Ardes and Clandeboy. Because Turlough was threatening to occupy all of Tyrone and was already procuring redshanks for Sir Brian, it seemed as if England at last had isolated Sorley from the two most important Ulster chiefs.[4]

While Smith's policy of dividing Sorley Boy from the Irish chiefs was seemingly furthered by the denization patent, Elizabeth and Essex were engaged in some double-dealing to negate the agreement.[5] Clearly, then, the queen saw in Essex's plans a vigor and determination absent from Smith's more conciliatory policy. In May Essex received a grant to Clandeboy, the Glynnes, the Route, and Rathlin Island, the latter already promised to Sorley. The earl's patent contained twenty-five additional articles which, if implemented, would give him nearly unlimited political, economic, and military authority in Ulster. Elizabeth also agreed to bear some of Essex's expenses if no part of his territories "be assigned or conveyed to any Irish or Scots Irish or mere Scots. . . ."[6] Both Essex and the queen knew that this would result in the dispossession of Sorley Boy, his nephew Angus, and Sir Brian MacFelim, all of whom had legitimate territorial claims in Ulster.

Essex's hard-line Ulster policy undermined Smith's conciliatory gesture of granting a denization patent to Sorley Boy. The Ulster allies now saw London's duplicity in the clear light of day. In consequence, a despondent Sir Brian went on a frenzied rampage, burning part of the town of Carrickfergus and harassing the borders of the Pale from Newry to Dundalk. Dungannon, fearing the spread of rebellion into his lands, threatened to destroy his own residence and depart Ireland.[7] Fitzwilliam's observation that "the North is apparently ill . . ." could not have been more correct.[8] Marshal Bagenal revealed that Turlough Luineach had advanced from Dunnalong to Benburb, and that he, Hugh O'Donnell, Sir Brian, and Sorley could field 4,000 troops between them. With Dungannon about to cut and run, Piers and Malby hard-pressed to defend Carrickfergus, the borders of the Pale virtually undefended, and the O'Donnells negotiating for redshanks with Argyll, things indeed appeared serious for the English.[9]

England's Ulster policy in spring 1573 turned on the recent grant made to Essex. Elizabeth seemed unconcerned that some of the territory promised Essex was already assigned to Smith. Sir Thomas, however, agreed that the earl might have certain lands in North Clandeboy, including Belfast, if Essex would keep his hands off Smith's enterprise in the Ardes. The elder Smith received word in England from his son that the Ardes colony had encountered rough going and needed a fresh infusion of money and supplies. Young Colonel Smith also despatched to London an account of his interview with Sorley Boy, who insisted that his patent be honored and that he be given the liberty of marriage and the right of avoiding wardship. Smith recommended that Sorley's patent be upheld, but only in return for the MacDonnell chief's conversion to Protestantism. About the same time, however, the Ulster allies received word from Anthony de Guaras, the Spanish commissioner in London, that the queen would despatch Essex to Ulster with 3,000 troops in July. The Spaniard held out the prospect of aid from Philip II; thus it was unlikely that the Roman Catholic Sorley would abandon his faith and the possibility of foreign assistance for a mere scrap of paper from an untrustworthy London government.[10]

By summer 1573 Sorley Boy considered his patent of denization worthless in light of Essex's aggressive posturing. The earl demanded from the government £10,000 over three years and a diplomatic effort to neutralize Argyll in Scotland. But Piers reported to Burghley on 28 June that redshanks continued to arrive daily in Ulster. Two days later, Fitzwilliam relayed news of a running, day-long skirmish at Newry between forces of the Ulster allies and Bagenal. The Lord Deputy and others believed that the government must hold Clandeboy at all cost as an advanced base of operations against incoming redshanks. It was clear, though, that many of the inexperienced English troops in Ulster could not be expected to hold the field against the Gaelic veterans of Sorley Boy, Turlough Luineach, or Sir Brian MacFelim.[11] Nonetheless, Fitzwilliam received instructions from London in June to support Essex's plan to plant a colony not only in strategic Clandeboy, but farther north into the Glynnes and the Route as well. Two thousand English colonists would settle these areas, whereupon it was expected that "the rebels and other evil disposed persons in Ulster

. . . will show their discontention by some attempts of disorders. . . ." As a precaution, Fitzwilliam was instructed to put the Pale's defenses in good order "to withstand the incursions of the Scots. . . ."[12]

Essex landed at Carrickfergus in August 1573 and assembled about 1,100 troops to drive the Scots from Clandeboy and then destroy their colonies in the Glynnes, the Route, and Rathlin. London had earlier instructed Fitzwilliam to protect the grain harvest in Clandeboy so Essex would enjoy sufficient provisions for a campaign.[13] The earl, before departing England, had intimated to Burghley the queen's desire that the native Irish be left in peace, as "she thought [they] had become her disobedient subjects . . . because they have not been defended from the force of the Scots. . . ."[14] Thus Essex was to try to separate Sorley's Scots and Turlough and Sir Brian. According to Bagenal, there was good reason to implement such a policy at once, as the enemy reportedly had mustered an army with two weeks' provisions and were set to march on Newry.[15]

England's policy of dividing Clan Ian Mor from the other Gaelic Ulster families sparked controversy on both sides. Sir Brian, who stood directly in Essex's way, not surprisingly attempted to walk a tightrope between his fellow Gaels and the English. Turlough Luineach, though encouraged by the heady atmosphere of rebellion, likely would back away at the first sign of trouble. Taking no chances, however, Fitzwilliam was to keep O'Neill in the dark regarding English intentions. The Lord Deputy also was to prevent the O'Donnells and lesser Irish chiefs from joining Sorley Boy.[16] But in early September Essex apparently had not persuaded Turlough Luineach to abandon the MacDonnells, despite the threat of laying waste Tyrone with fire and sword. He noted to Burghley "that Turlough Luineach and the Scots under Sorley Boy had combined together and bound themselves with an oath to maintain the war. . . ." Certainly Essex had scored what appeared to be a major victory in isolating Sir Brian and forcing him to hand over large stores of provisions in Clandeboy belonging to the Scots. By the end of September, though, he learned that Sir Brian had gone back over to the side of the Ulster Gaels. Despite Turlough's refusal to cooperate fully and Sir Brian's "disloyalty," Essex's letters otherwise were optimistic. He boasted to Burghley that eastern Ulster was at his command, Sorley and his followers again seeking safety west of the Bann.[17]

Essex's claim to have pacified most of Ulster notwithstanding, there were those in both camps who understood that the struggle had just begun in autumn 1573. The earl had been able to induce only about 400 colonists to follow him into southern Antrim, few of whom had the necessary military training and discipline to establish a settlement in hostile surroundings. Shortly after his arrival, young Thomas Smith had been murdered by the Irish. In a frank admission to Robert Dudley, earl of Leicester, Essex set forth his fears of the imminent resurrection of a viable Gaelic combination. Less than a fortnight later, he indeed faced a rebellious Sir Brian, whose initial submission had been feigned. Bagenal reported that Angus of Dunyveg had landed with 500 redshanks. By the beginning of October, the Ulster allies appeared as strong as ever, but Sorley and the others emphasized that their quarrel was with Essex and not with the queen. That Essex recently had been granted further powers as Governor of Ulster and Earl Marshal of Ireland suggests, however, that Elizabeth favored his policy of fire and sword.[18]

Despite (or perhaps because of) the English army's poor condition, Essex hoped that his Ulster adversaries could be brought to fight a conventional, set-piece battle that would quickly decide the issue before the onset of winter. At the end of September, the English army consisted of only 600 regular foot, 200 Irish kerne, 100 sappers, and 200 horse. Besides these, there were about 400 private troops belonging to Essex and Sir Thomas Smith. Against this combined force of 1,500 men, the Ulster allies reportedly could field 3,000–4,000 redshanks and kerne. Promises of Spanish aid were still forthcoming, and English Catholics, though few in number, reportedly opposed an aggressive Irish policy. Since the Great Northern Rebellion of 1569 and the Ridolfi Plot of 1571, Elizabeth and her council were all too aware of the "fifth-column" threat posed by English Catholics in support of Mary, Queen of Scots. Naturally, such "papist" machinations had implications for Ireland. When Essex wrote the Privy Council in early October 1573 of a lengthy skirmish, Elizabeth and Burghley must have held their breath in hopes that the Gaels were not on the point of launching a full-scale assault on Clandeboy, the Ardes, and, eventually, the Pale.[19]

Sorley remained the heart and soul of the Ulster combination, and now Essex believed it worth another attempt to isolate him with enticements of denization and lands in the Glynnes and the Route.[20] In early November the earl penned a letter to Burghley and the council that went as far as suggesting Sorley's being made a "Captain of Her Majesty's kerne, which he being a mercenary man and a soldier, will easily consent unto. . . ."[21] Essex had every reason to be desirous of an accord with Sorley Boy, especially since hostilities continued with the Irish chiefs. In late October the earl had informed London of an encounter near Belfast between his reconnaissance forces and the confederates, who

> were gathered on the other side of the ford, to stop their passage; whereof having knowledge by . . . Malby, I marched thither with three hundred footmen and one hundred horse and the next low water after my coming I passed over the ford with no great resistance, and then with my company I departed. . . . On my return . . . [Sir] Brian [MacFelim O'Neill] and all his power were gathered near the ford to stop my passage . . . into the Pale. On sight of them we entered into

skirmish, which they maintained after their manner [i.e. guerrilla tactics] reasonably well by the space of two hours. . . .

Essex bemoaned the fact that "upon the hard [i.e. open] ground they would not come."[22] If Sir Brian alone could give English regulars such fits, it is no wonder that Essex remained concerned about the MacDonnell chief's military capabilities.

Essex knew that Sorley Boy could be drawn to serve English interests in Ulster only with great difficulty, if at all. But the earl had few other options. He opined (rather optimistically) that if Sorley could be won over, "time, hereafter, and law, shall keep him within bounds, and a stronger force than his own shall ever master him. . . ." Essex continued: "You may enlarge this matter as you think good; which, though it threaten peril, yet a continual eye being had upon him, time may disarm him, and make him a plague in the mean season to the obstinate Irish."[23] But Sorley had no intention of becoming Essex's tool against the Ulster chiefs. Essex apparently understood nothing of the MacDonnell leader's character or intentions.[24] What the earl did understand was that those Irish and Scottish chiefs in the north who heretofore had prevaricated were now sending forces to the Ulster allies. Even Hugh O'Donnell, who had sworn loyalty, secretly conspired "never to annoy them of the confederacy. . . ."[25]

Sorley Boy stood as the most formidable figure in the so-called Ulster "confederacy," but the focus in late 1573 was on Sir Brian MacFelim O'Neill. He had engaged the English in several hot skirmishes and correctly assessed Essex's inability to enforce the queen's writ above the Lagan. The earl confessed to Elizabeth that the rebellion likely would spread, because most of his troops "have not forgotten the delicacies of England. . . ."[26] Essex did note that the Gaels considered their fight to be with him and not with the queen. He doubtless hoped that such a revelation would irk Elizabeth and persuade her to take full financial responsibility for crushing the uprising. Indeed, Burghley received a similar report predicting Essex's ruin if he attempted to defeat the confederates in the fastnesses of Ulster with the troops then at his command. For Sir Brian, however, Essex had a trump card yet to fall–Hugh MacFelim O'Neill (Sir Brian's brother) and Con MacNeill Oge, who, having recently been released from confinement in Dublin Castle, eventually would be set against their kinsman in Clandeboy.[27]

By the end of 1573 Essex seemed enthusiastic about the prospects of a successful northern campaign in conjunction with the Dublin administration. He was anxious to remove himself as an agent of the crown in Ulster and to undertake a private venture with royal support channeled through Dublin, despite his dislike of Fitzwilliam. His private troops were less than reliable, but the earl concluded articles with them in early 1574 concerning the expulsion of the confederates and the subsequent disbursement of confiscated lands in Clandeboy, the Glynnes, and the Route. The queen acquiesced, at least in part, in Essex's plan, though she commanded him to accept a renewal of his royal commission as Governor of Ulster. She continued to view the Scots as the principal obstacle to English expansion in eastern Ulster, and thus desired to employ the entire strength of her Irish establishment against them.[28] Having Elizabeth's blessing, Burghley informed Fitzwilliam and Essex that they should coordinate their actions to protect the frontiers of the Pale by enlisting the aid of the baron of Dungannon and of Clandeboy by transferring forces there from Newry or Lecale.[29] Since Sir Brian had taken up arms, Carrickfergus had been directly threatened. Its loss would be catastrophic; thus Essex's and Elizabeth's first concern was to secure the area thereabouts before Turlough or Sorley came to the aid of their Clandeboy ally.

Essex's preparations for an Ulster campaign caused Sorley Boy and his allies to fear the arrival of English regular troops and money in early 1574. Almost as quickly as he had taken up arms, Sir Brian quit the field. Argyll proved instrumental in the Ulster confederates' decision to avoid military action. Elizabeth requested that he keep Sorley from annoying her loyal subjects in Ulster. But things were not as rosy as Essex had made them appear. Naturally, he might wish to make the situation seem less propitious in order to justify the despatch of men and money from London, but, in truth, England faced serious trouble in Ulster. Essex admitted to Burghley in early February that if more troops did not arrive by May he would with difficulty withstand an Irish rebellion. His colonists were unable to leave Carrickfergus for lack of supplies, and little aid could be expected from the troops at Dundalk and Newry, who themselves were poorly provisioned. Under such circumstances, it is no wonder that the English sought to establish better relations with the Ulster Irish. If Turlough Luineach and Sir Brian were neutralized or brought over to England's side and Argyll was temporarily placated, then Sorley and Clan Ian Mor might be isolated and banished or destroyed. Essex knew that all hinged on operating from a position of perceived strength, for if the Irish chiefs learned of England's actual weakness, successful negotiations would be difficult.[30]

Sorley's utmost concern was to keep an Ulster combination together to prevent Essex from overrunning Clandeboy and then the Glynnes and the Route. This would be a difficult task. Essex informed Fitzwilliam in early March of his intention to conclude an honorable agreement with Turlough. Despite Essex's momentary misgivings about maintaining the Ulster enterprise without Fitzwilliam's full support, the earl set about to divide O'Neill and Sorley Boy. He informed Whitehall of a parley between Sorley, Turlough, and Sir Brian at Castle Toome, at which the Gaelic confederates reportedly agreed to bring in 1,600 redshanks. Responding, Essex promised that his adventurers would persevere in Clandeboy, a territory he believed might be made to yield £6,000 per annum for its own defense. The decision to maintain Essex in Ulster was most assuredly based on his resolve to oppose the influx of more redshanks into the north.[31]

In English eyes Turlough Luineach represented a chink in the Ulster confederates' armor. Toward the end of March 1574 it seemed that he might be persuaded to make a separate peace with Essex and Fitzwilliam that would involve his opposition to Clan Ian Mor. A similar agreement, of course, had led to the MacDonnells' defeat by Shane O'Neill at Glentaisie nearly a decade earlier; the same, however, could not be expected of Turlough. The English had little they were willing to offer O'Neill, despite the latter's having given over his son Arthur as a hostage. But neither Essex nor Fitzwilliam could afford to take Turlough too lightly, because England's military strength in Ireland, though it had increased by one-third (from 1,500 to 2,000) during the previous six months, still stood at only about half that of the Ulster allies. Despite Turlough's sweet words to Essex and the queen, Fitzwilliam was far from convinced of his sincerity. In fact, he and Sir Edward Fitton in Connacht warned of the Ulster confederacy's possible expansion to include the earl of Clanrickard. Large numbers of redshanks reportedly were moving into Connacht, and with the troubles in Munster yet to be extinguished, the situation demanded quick action.[32]

English policy in Ulster presently turned on whether to bring the unreliable Turlough Luineach into an alliance or simply to marshal all available forces and crush the Ulster confederates before their influence spread beyond the province. Elizabeth and her lieutenants knew that May began the redshank campaigning season, and Sorley Boy's virtual absence from recent Irish affairs likely meant that he was busy recruiting for the allies. Turlough was to be strung along with promises that his petitions were being seriously considered by the queen. Meanwhile, Fitzwilliam received a sharp rebuke for remaining inactive in Dublin. He was ordered to prepare to take the field against Turlough Luineach while Essex readied his forces for battle with Sorley and Sir Brian MacFelim. For her part, Elizabeth threatened to revoke Essex's commission and recall him from Ulster while at the same time promising to provide pay for 600 foot and 100 horse. In addition, Sir Thomas Smith was to send men from the Ardes. Having a combined force of about 2,500 men, Essex and Fitzwilliam hoped to catch the Ulster confederates unawares before redshank-laden Hebridean galleys began plowing the tempestuous waters of the North Channel.[33]

It is a tribute to Sorley Boy's success in raising redshank recruits that the queen of England seriously considered abandoning Essex's enterprise in spring 1574. On 30 March several influential members of the Privy Council informed Essex that Elizabeth was extremely disappointed that the project in Clandeboy had not gone according to plan. Uppermost in the queen's mind, of course, was the cost involved. As she ordered Fitzwilliam to take the field against Turlough, she berated Essex for having failed to secure the support of O'Neill and Sir Brian. But Elizabeth's wrath quickly abated, and she revealed to Fitzwilliam her decision to maintain Essex as Governor of Ulster. At this point, Elizabeth finally settled on an offensive in the north, expensive though it might be, as a means of staying further trouble from Sorley and the Antrim Scots.[34]

Elizabeth's decision to proceed against the Ulster confederates was not clearly conveyed to her Irish lieutenants. Fitzwilliam was told to reveal nothing of the proposed expedition to anyone but Essex "until such time as you shall be ready to come to the execution of that which we think necessary to be done for the matter of Ulster."[35] The queen reiterated that the initial order of business was the banishment of the Scots. She believed the first step in weakening Sorley Boy lay in reducing the power of his allies. To this end, she desired Fitzwilliam to apply his talents. Anticipating Mountjoy's targeting of Irish logistics a generation later, Fitzwilliam was to move against Turlough "to the end you may destroy his cattle while they are weak [from the previous winter], and before he shall have certain aid of the Scots, which he looketh for out of Scotland. . . ."[36] Turlough's *urraights* were to be lured away by promises of letters patent which would guarantee their protection from his arbitrary rule. Once ready, Fitzwilliam was to coordinate the start of the campaign with Essex. But first Elizabeth expected her Lord Deputy to subdue the upstart earl of Desmond in Munster, thus postponing the Ulster invasion and the composition with Turlough Luineach.[37]

In early April Essex informed Elizabeth and Burghley of Turlough's desire for peace and the consequent truce. Since the Ulster enterprise had gone awry, in part, because of poor troop performance and improper logistical support, Essex feared yet another uprising from Sir Brian and further disruptions in Connacht if the Scots continued to aid Clanrickard. Such irruptions, Essex believed, were inevitable unless he received the proper backing from London and Dublin. The Ulster enterprise was hemorrhaging badly, as waves of settlers returned to the comforts of England. But difficulties in the north of Ireland steeled the Devereux earl, though he was by no means a first-rate general. He could not expect the capricious Turlough to behave himself much longer, especially if he were emboldened by England's weakness and his own comrades' rising strength. The redshank campaigning season loomed large, and Essex's own troops had suffered a terrible Irish winter. To make matters worse, he complained of poor relations with Fitzwilliam, a situation he believed must be put right lest English interests suffer accordingly. The only positive developments Essex could report concerned the arrival of Sir John Norris and 100 infantrymen, the prospects that Sir Brian might sign a treaty, and the willingness of certain Palesmen to settle in Clandeboy.[38] The good news, however, was short-lived.

Reports of Turlough's treachery reached London only a fortnight after Essex had informed the queen and Burghley of O'Neill's peace overtures. Poised to descend defiantly over the Blackwater against Dungannon, Turlough undoubtedly encouraged Sir Brian, who blocked the passes into Clandeboy. Burghley demanded that both Essex and Fitzwilliam coordinate their efforts and move against Sir Brian and Turlough, respectively. But Essex complained to the London council that without proper funding a summer campaign in Ulster would be ineffectual. The earl's plans for erecting a town at Coleraine and bridging the Bann would be nothing if not costly. Essex's optimism about penetrating into the heart of Gaelic Ulster and establishing a permanent English presence there was echoed in a directive of 26 April in which the council insisted that the adventurers begin pushing settlers to the north and west.[39] Such a plan, if carried out, would require either O'Neill's complete submission or a full-scale military campaign into the bowels of Ulster.

As May approached, English officials puzzled over the proper course of action against the Ulster confederates. Elizabeth preferred an economical (i.e. a non-military) solution to the problem. But as long as Turlough and Sir Brian enjoyed the support of Sorley and Clan Ian Mor, and, in turn, as long as Sorley retained Argyll's favor, it was unlikely that a peaceful solution based on submission could be expected. The month of May promised the return of the redshank hordes to Ireland and a consequent shift in the military balance of power unless Elizabeth was willing to place significant resources at Essex's and Fitzwilliam's disposal. The council urged both men to act before the campaigning season arrived. In lieu of an actual attack upon Turlough (and by implication, on his Ulster allies), the queen's advisors suggested offering O'Neill two choices. The first involved his acknowledgment of Dungannon's right to lands in Tyrone and an agreement to hold his own lands through the policy of surrender and regrant. If Turlough refused, he was to be offered all of Tyrone under surrender and regrant on condition that he renounce his Gaelic title and *urraights* and agree to bring in no more redshanks. Nothing was mentioned specifically about his continued involvement with the Ulster confederates. It goes without saying, though, that the Gaelic allies would suffer a hard blow if O'Neill withdrew his support, evanescent though it had been. Turlough's value to Sorley Boy lay more in his unpredictable potential rather than in his actual accomplishment. Certainly he stood as a major threat to English aspirations in the north. If he could finally be neutralized by Essex and Fitzwilliam, any sort of Ulster confederacy would fall apart. As London saw it, success depended on bringing a credible threat against Turlough before he was encouraged by the arrival of more redshanks.[40]

The English government understood that a military solution against

Turlough Luineach was out of the question in late spring 1574. For one thing, there had been virtually no cooperation between Essex and Fitzwilliam in establishing the logistics for a campaign, and the beginning of May was no time to undertake such preparations. For another, the base at Carrickfergus, on which any successful invasion of the north must depend, stood in dire need of repair and provisions. The humble submission of Sir Brian removed an important obstacle in Clandeboy, but Essex complained that the overall quality of English troops was insufficient for a major invasion. Moreover, in a reported skirmish just before Sir Brian's submission in early May, Essex noted the presence of a number of Scots in the enemy's ranks who showed no inclination to surrender. Nominally in possession of the Down coast from Belfast to Olderfleet and having Sir Brian's promise of military support, the English vacillated once more and switched their focus from Turlough to Sorley Boy.[41]

Essex, always candid with Burghley, made known his desire to face the miseries of Ireland rather than to suffer removal from his post. To commence a successful expedition against Clan Ian Mor, Essex needed not only better troops but a steady stream of replacements as well. The earl was encamped near the village of Belfast in mid-May, but there was no indication that Fitzwilliam would be able to turn his attention from the festering problems in Connacht and Munster long enough to provide any serious aid to Essex. Thus the thankless task of subjugating Ireland's most untamed province fell exclusively to the earl. To make matters still worse, word spread that Sir Brian was only biding his time until the inhospitable climate and terrain wore down the English. As Fitzwilliam was engaged elsewhere, Essex could expect to accomplish little by an offensive against the Ulster Gaels. Rather, he returned to Dublin from Belfast in June, where he attempted to cajole Turlough to keep the peace. Forced to depend upon the financial largesse of Fitzwilliam, it was all the proud Devereux earl could do to defend the Belfast–Newry line.[42]

Essex refused to allow a minor fiscal and logistical setback to divert him from his goal of mounting a full-scale military campaign into the heart of Ulster. Heretofore, England had had difficulty in determining whom to single out for attack within the Ulster confederacy, alternating between Turlough, Sir Brian, and Sorley. Essex now confidently informed the Privy Council on 14 June that the time seemed right for a move against any of the three principal members. Malby reported a breach between Sir Brian and Sorley's Scots, and Essex thought Turlough once again vulnerable to pressure from the O'Donnells, who appeared close to an agreement with Dublin.[43] Writing privately to Burghley, the earl expounded on how best England might proceed in further weakening Turlough Luineach and the Irish chiefs:

At this present there is never a one of the Captains of Ulster, but doth make means unto me to procure his lands by Her Majesty's Letters Patents to them and their heirs, and to yield for the same such rent as their countries shall be able to bear, to alter their Irish customs, and to be bound to such conditions as Her Majesty can almost require; and divers of them say that they have offered this in times past, and it hath been refused. . . . Your Lordship may here see a great fault . . . which Her Majesty may easily remedy, if she will bear but a reasonable charge for a small time.[44]

If Essex can be believed, the "Captains of Ulster," including Turlough Luineach, would have preferred the policy of surrender and regrant in lieu of continued hostilities against England. In this he may have been partly correct; however, it is likely that Essex tried to persuade Elizabeth to pour more royal funds into an enterprise that obviously was going nowhere.

Essex's Ulster strategy in mid-1574 continued to depend in large part on the actions of the unpredictable Sorley Boy. Even after a late spring's journey to the Bann, Essex could not ascertain his adversary's intentions. Sorley's past actions suggest that he still sought title to the Glynnes and the Route through the queen's favor rather than through military conquest. But Sorley's desire for peaceful possession of his family's lands should not be interpreted as an unwillingness to fight. Quite the contrary. He must have known by this time that Turlough was a slender reed upon which to lean and that Sir Brian MacFelim's position was much too vulnerable to withstand a determined English military effort. In reality, both the English and the Ulster chiefs labored under extreme hardship that summer. Cool, rainy weather throughout Scotland and Ireland presaged critical food shortages and high prices in the coming autumn and winter. Besides more troops, Essex also needed provisions to feed the existing Ulster garrisons. Even the resourceful Smith was unable to provide for more than a fraction of the settlers in the Ardes. Under such circumstances, it is difficult to tell whether Essex's calls for assistance were genuine or calculated to take advantage of the perilous situation in Ulster, which he expected to result in open rebellion.[45] Sorley continued to hold the key to the whole affair.

By midsummer 1574 it was much too late to undertake a major military expedition into Ulster. The Privy Council in early July instructed Essex that while a campaign could not go forward until the coming spring, pressure was to be continually applied to Turlough. Furthermore, the English adventurers in Clandeboy were to consolidate their positions so that they might move against Sir Brian at the appropriate time. Essex was to conduct operations for the duration of the summer with no more than 550–600 foot and 100–200 horse, most of whom were to be levied in

Ireland to cut recruiting and transport costs. To further pare expenses, it was hoped that Sir Brian could be induced to fortify Belfast, which, along with Carrickfergus, was to be the principal staging point for operations in the coming spring. Thus London appears to have had no intention of terminating the Ulster enterprise, even though the moment had been lost for a summer offensive. As seen before, England's greatest concern continued to be Sorley Boy and Clan Ian Mor, with whom the earl was instructed to temporize until further notice.[46]

That her Irish officials were being instructed to temporize with Sorley and to bring the Irish chiefs to heel through surrender and regrant reveals Elizabeth's desire to minimize her financial outlay for Ulster while holding the line militarily until the coming spring. Thus far there had been no indication that large numbers of redshanks would be crossing the North Channel. Nor had Argyll recently been active in Ulster affairs. In mid-July the picture began to change. On the 18th, Fitzwilliam requested the despatch of 2,500 troops from England, ostensibly to counter a possible Scoto-Spanish invasion. Fears of such a descent were heightened at month's end when Essex reported the arrival of ten redshank war galleys at Lough Foyle. Furthermore, Argyll was in the midst of a "progress" in July and apparently had stirred up troubles in the Hebrides between Clan Ian Mor and the MacLeans.[47] The situation in the Highlands and Isles, then, looked anything but promising for Essex and Fitzwilliam. It appeared that the queen would escape only with great difficulty a major financial commitment in Ulster for the remainder of 1574.

Essex's powers as Governor of Ulster were increased in early August, and a month later Burghley made it clear that the government expected that the wayward province be brought under English rule. With the small force at his disposal (including Dungannon), Essex, buoyed by support from Whitehall, moved through Turlough's territory toward Lough Foyle. There he and Dungannon were to join Hugh O'Donnell and ravage O'Neill's lands if he proved unwilling to parley. If Fitzwilliam could advance a separate force as far north as the Blackwater, the pusillanimous Turlough might be cowed into submission and his redshanks disbanded and sent home. But on 8 October Essex informed London of his failure to overawe O'Neill. Turlough had shadowed and harassed the English columns, all the while looking for assistance from his stepson, Angus MacDonnell. In a private note to Burghley written on the same date, the earl expressed concern that he had earned the queen's enmity for his inability to subdue Turlough and thus to break up the Ulster confederacy.[48]

Essex refused to accept personal responsibility for the failed operation against Turlough Luineach. Rather, he cited insufficient resources. To remedy the situation, Fitzwilliam, the Munster troubles behind him, agreed to throw the resources of the Dublin administration behind Essex's enterprise. Troops were to be levied from the Pale and supplies gathered for the coming expedition. But Essex seemed less than confident. He confessed doubts to Sir Francis Walsingham that Fitzwilliam would persevere in the Ulster enterprise. He also complained to the entire council of Bagenal's refusal to allow him to quarter troops at Newry during the coming winter and of his inability to procure the services of a victualler to supply his army in the field. While Essex complained of the conduct of others, Burghley learned of the earl's alleged careless behavior and disregard for precious supplies and provisions. It is no wonder that Ulster veterans Piers and Malby were less than enthusiastic about Essex's chances of success.[49]

Essex's personal failures must have been a heavy burden, and he sought to redeem himself with an expedition against Sorley Boy. As Essex had predicted, Fitzwilliam would not commit himself to accompanying the expedition into Ulster. The Lord Deputy did promise to provide men, provisions, and carriages for a twenty-day campaign. Essex's plan hinged on enlisting the aid of Malby and a contingent of regular troops and Sir Brian's Irishmen for a journey into the Glynnes. Essex strained at the bit to take the field and redeem himself, but reined in his passions, and by late October he informed Burghley that his troops would make winter quarters in Carrickfergus, Belfast, and Lecale. Complaints of his conduct and lack of ability notwithstanding, the earl had convinced the government to take a look at a "plat" for the subjugation and reformation of Ulster. In early November he was asked to come to London both to explain his plans and to defend himself against the charges of his detractors.[50] Circumstances did not allow for his return to England, but Essex nonetheless convinced the government that if his plan was followed "the rebel shall be utterly extirpated within two years. . . ."[51] The rather unimaginative plan centered on driving apart the principal Ulster confederates, winning the allegiance of Turlough Luineach and Sir Brian's *urraights*, and implementing the policy of surrender and regrant as widely as possible.[52] Essex, like most English policy-makers, was no longer serious about granting the Glynnes and the Route to Sorley in return for good behavior. In fact, MacDonnell was now Essex's primary target. And he could have made no more dangerous an enemy.

That Sorley Boy was targeted by the English in 1574–5 meant that Essex would need to maintain the strength of his garrisons while concurrently raising a field army to invade the Glynnes. If Turlough could be neutralized by truce or by an O'Donnell threat to the west, then Essex and Fitzwilliam might shift troops eastward away from the Armagh–Blackwater line. In early November it was still uncertain whether Essex would take ship for England; accordingly, the Privy Council instructed Fitzwilliam to be prepared to despatch sufficient forces from the Pale to the Tyrone border to keep Turlough in line should the earl depart Ulster. Either way, more troops would be available for action in Clandeboy and the Glynnes should need arise. The total number of regular English soldiers in the Irish service stood at about 400 horse and 2,000 foot, a considerable increase over the 200 horse and 600 foot of the previous summer.[53]

The first step in any reformation of Gaelic Ulster was to dismantle the Clan Ian Mor–O'Neill–Clandeboy confederation. Sorley Boy obviously stood at the center of the alliance; but if either Turlough or Sir Brian could be separated from the band, then more English resources might be freed to face the MacDonnell threat. Turlough remained an enigma in Ulster politics and, as such, could not be ignored. Sir Brian had proven less difficult to fathom. When he was weak he submitted; when strong he lashed out at his tormentors. In November he anxiously awaited developments in the camps of Sorley Boy and Turlough. There is no question that Sir Brian had suffered one injustice after another since Smith and then Essex had appropriated his lands with royal approval. As a result, on several occasions, he had risen in "rebellion" and taken English lives and property. In November 1574 Sir Brian was accused of treason by Essex, in part for the alleged brutal murder of one Mr. Moore at a parley. He also was accused of plotting to kidnap and murder Captain Nicholas Malby. But his greatest crime had been to ally himself with Sorley Boy.[54] He was kidnapped by Essex, who had been given *carte blanche* in the matter, and later slain. The Four Masters give a credible account of the episode:

> Peace ... [was] established between Brian ... and the Earl of Essex; and a feast was afterwards prepared by Brian [near Belfast], to which the Lord Justice and the chiefs of his people were invited; and they passed three nights and days together pleasantly and cheerfully. At the expiration of this time, however, as they were agreeable drinking and making merry, Brian, his [half] brother [Rory Oge MacQuillin], and his wife, were seized upon by the Earl, and all his people put unsparingly to the sword [115 in all] ... in Brian's own presence. Brian was afterwards sent to Dublin, together with his wife and brother, where they were cut in quarters.[55]

The death of Sir Brian MacFelim O'Neill was a damaging, though not fatal, blow to the Ulster confederates. Far from being an act of desperation, Essex's decision to double-cross Sir Brian appears to have been a calculated move designed to break up the Ulster allies and strike fear into the hearts of those minor Irish chieftains who had not yet taken sides. Treachery proved a bargain when compared to the cost of mounting an expedition into Clandeboy. English military forces in Ireland still suffered from acute shortages. Essex justified his brutal actions by pointing out that Sir Brian had been secretly plotting with both Turlough and Sorley. Now that Sir Brian was gone, the task remained to draw O'Neill away from the Scots.[56]

By late November the situation in Ulster appeared somewhat clearer, though no less dangerous, to England than before Sir Brian's death. Clandeboy was divided into several smaller captaincies to be held by lesser chieftains of the junior branch of the O'Neills, only one of whom–Con MacNeill Oge–was a potential threat to the English.[57] In Tyrone the English hoped to reconcile Turlough Luineach and Dungannon, the latter being cast in the role of the O'Neill's tanist. Piers reported that Turlough "sworc to me that, if he might be sure of the Baron, he would not keep a Scot." Such assurances from O'Neill had to be carefully measured in light of Piers's observation that his wife, Lady Agnes, remained "a great practiser for the bringing of that part of the realm to be Scottish. . . ."[58] Piers also believed that an English garrison should be placed in Clandeboy, echoing Essex's request for a fort near Belfast. It was suggested as well, in a move reminiscent of the campaign against Shane O'Neill, that the O'Donnells be cultivated as a counterweight to Turlough.[59] One thing was particularly clear in the wake of Sir Brian's death: England still sought to isolate O'Neill and MacDonnell and deal with each in her own good time.

At the beginning of 1575 the situation in the Gaelic heartland began to shift in Sorley Boy's favor. While England planned to settle Clandeboy, the Glynnes, and the Route, across the North Channel Angus MacDonnell rallied support for an invasion of Ulster from the MacLeods of Lewis and Harris, the Clanranald MacDonnells, the MacKenzies, the MacKays, and even his erstwhile nemesis, MacLean of Duart. Fortunately for the English, Argyll opposed this combination. Essex learned that the Campbell chief intended to ravage the Kintyre peninsula, a Dunyveg MacDonnell stronghold. Conversely, however, Elizabeth announced toward the end of February that she intended to leave the direction (and presumably the financing and logistics) of the entire Ulster enterprise to Essex and Fitzwilliam. She considered reducing the Irish garrisons from 2,500 to 2,000 troops.[60]

As the campaigning season approached, Essex tried to pressure Turlough to keep his distance from Sorley Boy. In early March the earl employed 600 men to cut passes along the borders of the Pale into southern Ulster. His immediate objective was to destroy O'Neill's grain supply and set Shane's surviving sons against him. Essex indeed had cause for concern. Despite the existing truce, Turlough reportedly had sent to Scotland for 3,000 mercenaries. If this proved true, it meant that he intended to take the field beside his Clan Ian Mor allies. But it also could mean that Turlough was fast losing support among his *urraights*, thus hiring redshanks to bolster his thinning ranks.[61]

The queen had reversed her position by mid-March and reluctantly agreed to support a joint Ulster venture by Essex and Fitzwilliam.[62] Elizabeth laid out strict instructions for the enterprise that reflected her concerns over risking precious money and manpower without a reasonable prospect of success. She insisted that "1,300 . . . of the said number of 2,000, ought and may be employed in Ulster; and the rest of the realm stayed in quietness wherein it is, only with the rest of the numbers, being about 700. . . ."[63] Neither Essex nor Fitzwilliam could be expected to accomplish anything with so few men. The queen knew as much, and thus instructed the Lord Deputy not to provoke the native Irish. English commanders understood that the rigors of the Ulster service wore hard on their troops, and Fitzwilliam began rotating units regularly from Ulster to the Pale. But this policy ignored the likelihood of trouble in the other provinces. Not surprisingly, Elizabeth was doubtful of success in Ulster or elsewhere. By leaving the campaign to Essex and Fitzwilliam, she obviously wished to wash her hands of a difficult situation.[64]

In retrospect, Elizabeth doubtless realized by spring 1575 that the attempt to establish a private-enterprise colony in Ulster had failed. Essex continued to send encouraging reports–for instance, Hugh O'Donnell's alleged declaration of war against Turlough–but the truth could no longer be ignored: the Scots were further entrenching themselves in the Glynnes and the Route and threatening to absorb Clandeboy.[65] Essex believed he could still win the game if only the queen would continue her support. He warned that if she pulled out of Ulster now, she would later "subdue rebellion [only] with intolerable charge."[66] The earl believed that 2,000 troops could hold all of Ireland, but only if they were of sufficiently high caliber and received proper leadership and support. Essex tempered his optimism by maintaining that time was of the essence, and that the queen would only be throwing good money after bad if she dallied any longer in pursuit of the Ulster confederates' destruction.[67]

In early April Elizabeth decided to go ahead with the Ulster enterprise. Essex would move to destroy Turlough Luineach's cattle so that he could not pay *buannacht* to his redshanks. In case Essex failed, Burghley and the council advised that a defensive force be arrayed along the northern borders of the Pale to forestall a Gaelic counter-attack. Strained relations between Essex and Fitzwilliam bred fears that the absence of a unified command might bring military disaster. Supplies and food were at a premium, and the extremely dry weather of spring predicted a barren summer. Late April witnessed Essex hurriedly preparing for a summer campaign, perhaps spurred on by Malby's astute observation that Ulster appeared primed for rebellion.[68]

Essex's objective in April 1575 was the strategic Blackwater valley. Fitzwilliam was ordered to assist the earl with at least part of the 700 troops under his command in the Pale. The Ulster chiefs who lived between the Blackwater and the borders of the Pale could muster 400 horse, 300 *gallóglaigh*, and 2,000 kerne. Turlough, who could not depend on unqualified support from these minor chiefs, commanded 200 horse, 400 galloglaigh, 400 redshanks, and 1,000 kerne. Counting Hugh O'Donnell's troops, the Ulster Irish could raise 8,300 soldiers of all types. But even with such superior numbers behind him, Turlough desired peace.[69]

May brought a temporary reconciliation between Essex and Fitzwilliam and the arrival of much-needed supplies for the Ulster garrisons. The month also brought two unwanted visitors: the Scots and the plague, the former expected, the latter not. Both served to make a demanding task even more difficult. Amid the turmoil, Essex expressed private concerns to Walsingham that the queen would withdraw support and leave him in the lurch. O'Donnell had already backed out of an agreement to oppose Turlough, and by mid-month it seemed as if the entire Ulster plan was coming unravelled. Indeed, on 22 May Elizabeth informed both Essex and Fitzwilliam of her intentions to give up the enterprise altogether.[70] The earl was expressly instructed to

> direct the course of your proceedings in such sort as the enterprise may yet be so given over as our honour may best be saved, the safety of such as depend upon us in some good sort provided for, and the province left in that state as there may follow no such alteration as may disquiet the rest of that our realm.[71]

The queen's decision thus postponed the enterprise and placed the burden of negotiating the best possible terms with the Ulster Irish on the shoulders of Essex and Fitzwilliam.[72]

Elizabeth left the details of an Ulster strategy to Essex and Fitzwilliam, but she insisted that one general policy be followed: a firm opposition to Sorley and Clan Ian Mor. The best means of opposing them hinged on reaching an accord with Turlough and his *urraights* in which they and their 6,000 troops could be used against Sorley.[73] But all depended upon the English moving quickly, as food supplies were running perilously short. In early June Turlough sent Lady Agnes to a parley at Newry from which she emerged with an agreement that after ten days Turlough would relinquish his Gaelic title in return for peace with England. Fitzwilliam, though in failing health, was so optimistic that a fortnight later he reported that the mighty O'Neill could be held in check without a military campaign across the Blackwater. The Lord Deputy's observations proved correct, for even though Turlough misbehaved, he was disciplined with little trouble or expense.[74] On 27 June articles of peace were agreed upon between Essex and O'Neill at the newly constructed English fort on the Blackwater. For renouncing his *urraights*, pledging to hold his lands of the queen, and promising to assist her against the Scots, Turlough was allowed to retain his Gaelic title and was granted much of the Route, the latter provision surely designed to bring conflict with Sorley Boy.[75]

Elizabeth's continued insistence that Clan Ian Mor be expelled from Ulster reflected Sorley Boy's success in holding on to the Glynnes and the Route. The Ulster confederation was rent by dissension between Sorley and Turlough Luineach, but the military power of the Antrim MacDonnells remained intact. Turlough had been forbidden by the recent articles from hiring MacDonnell redshanks, thus freeing a large contingent of mercenary troops that most likely would find employment in Sorley's ranks. Essex realized that Clan Ian Mor's position grew stronger along the Antrim coast with each passing day, and in July the earl finally launched the long-awaited campaign into eastern Ulster. Sorley understood Essex's desperate situation, the earl having been virtually abandoned by London. Both men knew that a high stakes game had begun for control of the north of Ireland.[76]

Before marching into the Ulster wilderness, Essex had secured his left flank on the Blackwater by putting the finishing touches to the fort and bridge there. Not uncharacteristically, Turlough began to make threatening noises, keenly aware that Essex's attention was focused elsewhere. The earl also faced a difficult situation in Clandeboy with Sir Brian's successors.[77] Marching from Dromore on 6 July, Essex soon brought the Clandeboy Irish into his camp. This accomplished, he

> marched through the woods to Massareen, where I was by my espials advertised that the Scot had left the Glynnes, and carried all his cattle to a strong fastness near to the Bann, to which place I removed presently. Sorley was there, accompanied with Brian Carrogh. . . . They showed themselves upon a hill, and were viewed and judged to be to the number of 900 and upwards; they put out a skirmish with my vaward [i.e. vanguard], wherein I was. . . .[78]

Sorley's skirmishers crossed a dry bog and leveled a volley at the English cavalry, whereupon Essex sent forward fifty troopers to "cut betwixt them and their battle [i.e. main body], which Sorley perceiving, came down in great haste to rescue his men with all his force. . . ." Having thus extracted his light skirmishers after suffering about twenty casualties, Sorley fell back toward the Bann. On the following day Essex reported another action in which the Scots "fought a while very valiantly," but were dispersed with the loss of over 100 men. Afterwards, Sorley crossed to the left bank of the Bann, where, according to Essex's account, he "doth send to me in a daily manner for peace. . . ."[79]

Essex's excursion into Ulster accomplished very little. Though he claimed to have inflicted over 120 casualties on Sorley's redshank force and to have sustained fewer than ten himself, the earl had not been able to strike a decisive blow and banish the Scots from either the Glynnes or the Route. As Essex made his way south to Drogheda, where his lengthy campaign report was prepared, Sorley Boy had but to recross the Bann and resume his work in drawing together his allies. To Sorley, an Ulster confederacy had always been an instrument with which to attain his long-standing goal of securing

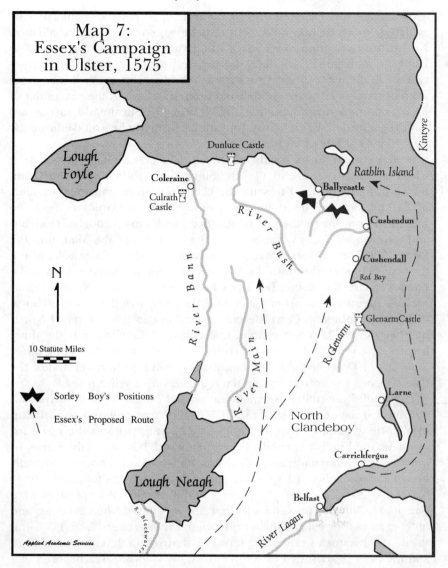

Map 7:
Essex's Campaign
in Ulster, 1575

Lough
Foyle

Dunluce Castle

Coleraine

Culrath
Castle

River Bann

River Bush

Kintyre

Rathlin Island

Ballycastle

Cushendun

Cushendall

Red Bay

N

10 Statute Miles

Sorley Boy's Positions

Essex's Proposed Route

GlenarmCastle

R. Glenarm

River Main

Larne

North
Clandeboy

Carrickfergus

Lough Neagh

R. Blackwater

Belfast

River Lagan

Applied Academic Services

a royal grant for the territories he controlled. If that goal could now be achieved, there is little doubt but that he would abandon the alliance. Not surprisingly, then, after Essex's departure southward, he turned to Dungannon, Bagenal, and Malby for help in procuring title to the Glynnes and the Route before Essex struck again.[80] Sorley most assuredly was weary from decades of constant conflict and desired to live out the remainder of his days laying a firm foundation for his progeny. But the old warrior was not to be afforded such a luxury, for within a fortnight he would endure the most tragic episode of his life.

In desperation, Essex sought to redeem a failed campaign by attacking Clan Ian Mor at the end of July. Since the fighting near the Bann, Sorley Boy had decided to send the clan's non-combatants to the safety of Rathlin Island. This done, the Antrim Scots prepared to meet the English, whom they expected to advance northward through Clandeboy and into the southern Glynnes or up the left bank of the Main into the Route. MacDonnell forces were concentrated south of Ballycastle, where they could move either into the Glynnes or along the upper banks of the Bann to guard the Route. But Essex had pitched camp at Newry to draw Sorley's attention away from the main strike force of 300 foot and 80 horse that was assembled at Carrickfergus under Captain John Norris.[81] Norris had been given "a secret charge, that having at Carrickfergus the three frigates, and wind and weather serving, . . . to set out for the taking of . . . Rathlin. . . ."[82] To disguise his plan, Essex began a withdrawal toward the Pale. The Scots thus were caught flat-footed by the English ruse.[83]

The English amphibious expedition set sail on 20 July and arrived off Rathlin two days later. Clan Ian Mor's women and children took shelter in a castle garrisoned by fifty troops. After laying siege to the castle for two days, the English opened a breach, attacked, but were driven away by a fierce redshank charge. But English numbers and firepower eventually overwhelmed the Scottish garrison, and the massacre that followed forever blackened Essex's name. According to his report, 200 persons were slaughtered in the castle and a further 300 to 400 were hunted down and butchered as they sought shelter elsewhere on the rugged island. Various stores and livestock were either taken or destroyed, eleven galleys burnt, and the island garrisoned by a force of eighty troops. Essex believed that "100 men left there . . . shall do your Majesty more service, both against the Scots and Irish, than 300 can do in any place within the north parts. . . ."[84]

Sorley's decision to remain on the mainland rather than to attempt a rescue mission to Rathlin might be interpreted by some as cowardice. But his actions stemmed from a tough-minded realization that to commit his forces to an attack on Rathlin would have endangered the entire Scottish colony in Antrim. Indeed, had Sorley made a mad dash for the isle he would have left his rear uncovered or severely weakened and vulnerable to attack by Essex. The MacDonnell leader's greatest blunder in the entire campaign had been to neglect posting watch parties along the Antrim headlands to signal the enemy's approach by water. Otherwise, Sorley, though forced to watch what surely was a gut-wrenching spectacle, acted prudently in maintaining his strong position on the mainland. His most pressing strategic concern now was to dislodge the English from Rathlin and thus reopen the way for redshank reinforcements. But unknown to Sorley, he would be rid of Essex in short order, as the Rathlin massacre was to be the last act in the earl's inglorious Irish tenure. In early August Sir Henry Sidney returned to Ireland as Lord Deputy, and both Essex and Fitzwilliam were out.[85] Sidney's task was to be a formidable one, for Essex's atrocities vexed Sorley and the Scots and ushered in a new savagery in Irish warfare. The new Lord Deputy, though certainly not an impartial observer, accurately summed up Essex's administration:

> And surely, sir, so it [i.e. the peace] might have been kept, if the violent and intempestine proceeding of the Earl of Essex and his followers had not been; for undoubtedly treasure, horses, victuals, and other furniture, as well as for the war as husbandry, was spent and spoiled in that his enterprise, whereof came no good.[86]

In fine, Essex's policy of fire and sword had failed miserably.

Chapter Nine
"A New Scotland of Ulster":
Sorley at the Zenith, 1575–83

... the north is far out of order.

Sir Henry Sidney

The Rathlin massacre alerted Sorley Boy to the dangerous task of preserving his family's territories in northeastern Ireland. Its aftermath also brought Sir Henry Sidney and the government to respect Sorley as a warrior-statesman. From 1575 to 1583 he gradually strengthened his hold over the Glynnes and the Route, despite the disintegration of the Ulster confederacy. The ultimate failure to establish a stable Gaelic Ulster combination opened northern Ireland to various outside influences, especially from the earl of Argyll and Counter-Reformation Europe. Moreover, Sorley became deeply involved in the affairs–both Scottish and Irish–of his nephew Angus of Dunyveg. Thus the period saw the aging chief at his zenith in Clan Ian Mor's fight for political and military dominance in the north of Ireland.

Essex was recalled from Ireland in late summer 1575 for reasons of political expediency rather than for his role in the brutal Rathlin affair. Only days after the slaughter, Essex audaciously requested that the government recognize his troops' important service to the crown. This request, however, could not be honored, at least not immediately nor publicly. Had Elizabeth overly praised Essex and Norris, she would have pushed an outraged Sorley Boy, and perhaps even Turlough Luineach, into an all-out military confrontation. To manage a dangerous situation, the queen looked to an old Irish hand, Sir Henry Sidney.[1]

Possession of Rathlin Island was a crucial issue in early August 1575. In the 1560s Sussex had acknowledged Sorley's right to the island. Elizabeth, though now in *de facto* possession, intimated to Essex her reluctance to assert *de jure* claim to Rathlin. But Essex believed it might be secured, as Sorley "desireth to fall to composition." In congratulating Essex for his success against the Scots, Elizabeth appointed him custodian of the isle until Sidney's arrival in Ireland.[2]

Between Essex's and Fitzwilliam's departure and Sidney's arrival in mid-September, Sorley marshaled his forces to attack Carrickfergus. Before moving, he apparently solicited aid from Argyll. Despite Essex's boast that the Scots would flee into Connacht after the bloody Rathlin affair, he advocated keeping a force of 300–400 regular troops in Ulster until the situation became clear. Essex instructed Captain Malby to meet Sorley in Lecale and again offer letters patent for the Glynnes and the Route (presumably including Rathlin). The MacDonnell chief, however, was in no mood to negotiate. The story goes that he burned the patent on the point of his sword, swearing thereafter to hold his lands by force and not by the queen's favor.[3] Such was Sorley's profound distrust of the government after the Rathlin massacre.

Having waged sufficient redshanks, Sorley attacked Carrickfergus in mid-September. His objective was twofold: 1) to prey upon the town and its environs, thus replacing provisions lost at Rathlin, while at the same time depriving the English garrison; and 2) to lure the English out of Carrickfergus Castle and into an ambush. They played squarely into Sorley's hands, as a large force of English infantry pressed northward, only to be surprised and routed by the Scots. That official reports admitted English losses at over 100 suggests a major victory for Sorley Boy. The English consoled themselves by pointing out that Carrickfergus had been spared capture or destruction.[4] But the Scots' victory "gave . . . [them] such reputation, that the Lord Deputy [i.e. Sidney] found it necessary to . . . march . . . into Ulster."[5]

Sorley's victory near Carrickfergus posed an immediate problem for Sidney when he landed in Ireland on 18 September. The new Lord Deputy's strategic goal–the pacification of Gaelic Ulster–differed little from his predecessor's. Sidney, however, realized that this might be better accomplished through less heavy-handed methods, and he suggested that Sorley, Turlough, and other chiefs be offered peerages and an opportunity to hold their lands through surrender and regrant. But more importantly, at least from Sorley's perspective, Sidney agreed to withdraw the Rathlin garrison and to revoke the English adventurers' land grants in Down and Antrim, except for the Bagenals' claim to Newry. Removing these points of friction, Sidney believed, would defuse a troublesome situation.[6]

Sidney probably saw Sorley's strike against Carrickfergus as a response to Essex's savagery. The Lord Deputy immediately journeyed north with 600 troops to evaluate the situation. Sidney understood Sorley's motivation for revenge and attempted to act in an even-handed manner, but he also recognized the Scottish danger. The Lord Deputy's task demanded a measure of

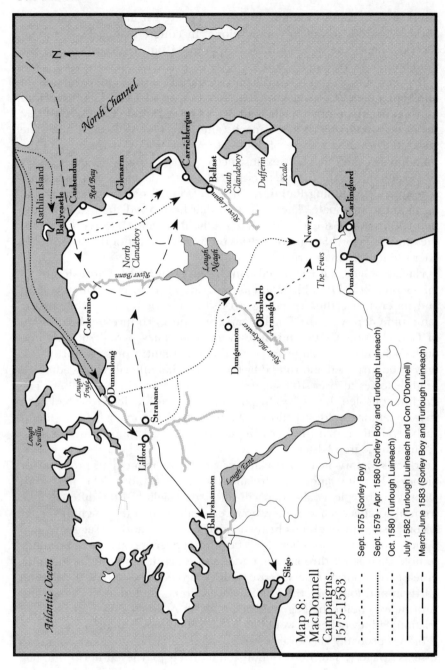

Map 8:
MacDonnell
Campaigns,
1575-1583

– ·· – ·· –   Sept. 1575 (Sorley Boy)

· · · · · · · ·   Sept. 1579 - Apr. 1580 (Sorley Boy and Turlough Luineach)

· · · · · · · ·   Oct. 1580 (Turlough Luineach)

————   July 1582 (Turlough Luineach and Con O'Donnell)

– – – – –   March-June 1583 (Sorley Boy and Turlough Luineach) political sagacity beyond the limits of Sussex, Essex, or Fitzwilliam. But even Sidney could not settle the turbulent north.[7] Indeed, he had warned the Privy Council of "how proud the Scot is grown, so that either to daunt them, or banish them totally, for annoying those parts, that force is too little, that I am able to maintain. . . ."[8] Sidney, then, found it necessary to negotiate. A meeting in the Route between him and Sorley Boy in autumn 1575 brought a temporary cessation of hostilities. Sorley demanded the return of Rathlin. Sidney agreed and put in motion plans to evacuate the island garrison.[9] But not for the reasons he gave the government: "I caused [Rathlin] to be abandoned, for that I saw little purpose, for the present, to keep it; and [its being] . . . so great a charge to Her Majesty, being a place so difficult to be victualled, they within . . . having no fresh water to relieve them. . . ."[10] In truth, Rathlin had several fresh-water springs, thus Sidney's explanation for its abandonment is unconvincing. Rather, he probably knew Clan Ian Mor's strength and wished to avoid conflict. As further proof of his goodwill, the Lord Deputy agreed to Sorley's having the Glynnes, even though James MacDonnell's sons had a rightful claim. Sidney thought that the Route should be restored to the MacQuillins; but because Sorley's domination of the area was so complete the Lord Deputy knew that only an herculean effort could dislodge him.[11]

Sidney entered into a truce and composition with Sorley on 19 October, wherein the MacDonnell leader pledged peace in exchange for recognition of his right to the Glynnes and Rathlin.[12] Sorley presumably did not expect English promises to be more valid now than before. Nonetheless, Sidney wrote:

> I was content for the time to temporize with the Scot [i.e. Sorley], and made as sure covenants as I could with him for observation of the peace, which in truth he observed as long as I was there, suffering anything that was bred or made under his rule to come and be sold at Carrickfergus, (God knoweth at easy prices,) and would buy such things as he needed in the same town, and pay truly for it.[13]

Sidney's description of Sorley is indeed rare, for he cast him in a more humane light than did other Englishmen. Sorley Boy was concerned with obtaining secure title, preferably by means short of war, to the traditional MacDonnell-Bisset lands in northeastern Ulster. He was characterized as a lawless freebooter, but Sorley, in truth, was an honorable man who sought redress outside English law only when forced to do so by Elizabeth's Irish lieutenants. He could be hard and merciless when dealing, say, with the MacQuillins of the Route, Shane O'Neill, or Essex. But for the most part, Sorley only reacted to aggressive policies designed to thwart his very reasonable goal of holding the Glynnes and the Route by royal patent. After meeting Sidney in late 1575, Sorley must have hoped that the prolonged struggle was about to end.

The composition between Sorley Boy and Sidney was a major obstacle to any attempt to renew an Ulster confederacy, as the MacDonnell chief began to distance himself from Turlough Luineach. Sidney, on his way back to the Pale, learned that Turlough and Lady Agnes wished to meet him at Armagh. O'Neill desired to submit in return for an earldom and the patent to his lands promised by Essex. Lady Agnes wanted confirmation of her sons' hereditary claim to the Glynnes.[14] There is no doubt that Sidney saw in her request an exploitable breach between James MacDonnell's sons and Sorley Boy. The Lord Deputy wrote to the Privy Council on 15 November:

> Sorley Boy now enjoyeth the occupation of the Glynnes, which rather of right seemeth should descend to James MacDonnell's son. . . . The Lady O'Neill desireth to have it by grant from her Majesty for her second son [Donnell Gorme], who will . . . dwell upon it himself, and yield rent and service . . . and defend the same against Sorley and his.[15]

Sidney indeed held Lady Agnes in high regard. He described her as "one very well spoken, of great modesty, good nature, parentage, and disposition. . . ." Another Englishman called her a "noble, wise woman. . . ."[16] Sidney respected this kinswoman of the earl of Argyll mainly for her ability to command hundreds of redshanks. But the agreement between Turlough and Sidney did not result in fewer mercenaries coming from Scotland to Ulster, at least for the time being.

Throughout the winter of 1575–6 trouble brewed between Sorley and Turlough. The situation was further complicated by the succession as sixth earl of Argyll of Archibald Campbell's brother Colin and by Lady Agnes's decision to actively support the claims of her sons in Antrim. The new earl of Argyll hinted that he might be willing to loosen his connections with the O'Neills, but Lady Agnes's commitment to her sons' claim in the Glynnes meant that large numbers of redshanks would still cross the North Channel. Argyll might stick to the letter of his agreement by refusing to supply Turlough directly, but there was little chance of completely halting the flow of mercenaries through Lady Agnes. Competition between Clan Ian Mor and the O'Neills for access to the large reservoir of fighting men in the western Highlands and Isles was certain. Thus the nascent troubles between Sorley and Turlough threatened to unleash a Gaelic civil war, especially if Argyll and Lady Agnes pursued self-aggrandizing policies in Ulster.[17]

Turlough delivered the first blow in the conflict. After reaching separate agreements with both O'Neill and Sorley, Sidney departed, leaving "such a pick between [them] . . . as within one month after, Turlough (with the aid of some Englishmen whom I suffered him to hire) killed a great number of the best of Sorley's men. . . ." Sidney, then, by his own admission, had double-crossed Sorley Boy. The Lord Deputy believed that it was "too dangerous a course to grant them [i.e. the Scots] plantation in Ireland;

but yet I thank God I satisfied them, and kept that country in quiet as long as I tarried there."[18] Sidney had never intended to honor the composition with Sorley. The Privy Council favored diminishing the power of Sorley, Turlough, and Lady Agnes's sons by fostering discord among them. In this way, Argyll's influence could be diffused through internecine quarreling, and the pro-English Dungannon might finally be established in Tyrone.[19]

After aiding Turlough against Sorley Boy, the English withdrew to observe the expected bloodletting. But it never came. Elizabeth, with good reason, had intimated her fears of Sidney's Ulster enterprise to Sir Thomas Smith.[20] Sorley's forbearance after Turlough's attack indicated a profound understanding of the complexities of Ulster politics. Had the MacDonnell chief unleashed his forces on O'Neill, it would have benefited no one but England. A decade earlier, a more impetuous Sorley would not have hesitated to avenge Turlough's affront. Now, however, there would be no repeat of Glentaisie or Cushendun. Sorley played on Turlough's natural timidity and allowed the feud to die, wisely using much of 1576 to strengthen his hand for the real foe–England.

The prospects of a major Scottish invasion of Ulster loomed large in 1576–7. Sorley Boy had bolstered his position in eastern Ulster by winning the allegiance of Con MacNeill Oge of Clandeboy and apparently persuading Argyll to allow the unimpeded flow of redshanks to Ireland. The Privy Council queried Sidney at length in July about Sorley's actions in Clandeboy and the Glynnes, and though the Lord Deputy stressed the province's tranquility, the calm was unsettling. In mid-August he informed the council of having received intelligence reports that large numbers of redshanks were about to depart the Hebrides for an invasion of Ulster. "[T]his devil," he wrote, "has been long in hatching. . . ."[21] Only Argyll could supply the necessary galleys to transport a large redshank army to Ulster. His promise to Elizabeth not to aid the O'Neills still allowed him to freely supply Clan Ian Mor. Moreover, that the earl of Clanrickard was providing *buannachta* for Scots mercenaries in Connacht did not bode well for the English. In January 1577 Sidney parleyed with Turlough and Lady Agnes at Newry. At this meeting it became clear that Lady Agnes saw Sorley as the main threat to the establishment of her younger sons in the Glynnes. She forbade her husband from negotiating with Sidney until Turlough had promised the Lord Deputy that he would agree "to repel the Scots, whom she [Lady Agnes] hoped would in . . . time effect a firm settlement in Antrim; and of whom she expected that her younger sons . . . would become the established chiefs, and, as she phrased it, 'stark in Ireland'."[22]

To oppose the Scots, Sidney looked to Turlough Luineach, who used his seemingly strong position to demand the right to maintain 2,000 to 3,000 redshanks as well as his Gaelic title. After meeting with O'Neill, Sidney informed London that there had been little hostile activity by either the Scots or the Irish. Indeed, Turlough, Lady Agnes, and Sorley all sought to

173

position themselves favorably during the first months of 1577. Turlough, though having struck at Sorley, was "sick and weak" and fell more and more under the influence of his wife. She sought to keep her husband independent of either Sorley or Sidney so that they might be set against one another just as Sidney had hoped that Turlough might be set against Sorley. A weakened Turlough, however, no longer counted for much in the struggle.[23] In mid-March he promised to "put away his wife, and do his best ... to chase and expulse all the Scots out of Ireland. ..." But Turlough's promises were empty. Lacking the respect of his own people, he leaned heavily on Scots mercenaries, without whom "he is very weak, and easy to be dealt with."[24]

As Turlough's influence waned, Lady Agnes's machinations on behalf of her sons and Sorley's ominous preparations for invasion drew England's attention. Sidney believed that the Scots should not be permitted to cross over to Ireland, as "it would make the north easier to be governed, the people more quiet and obedient ... than without they can be brought unto."[25] By summer 1577 Sidney apparently had no Ulster allies on whom he could depend to oppose either Sorley or his nephews. But as it turned out, the aging Turlough screwed up his courage and once again offered Sidney his services against Sorley. "And for better proof of his loyalty and fidelity," wrote Sidney, "he hath, since his departing from me, made a journey upon the Scots, and killed Sorley Boy's son [Donnell]. ..."[26] Suddenly, since Turlough's rejuvenation, the situation seemed to have turned in England's favor. It looked as if O'Neill had finally shaken off the influence of Lady Agnes. As a result, the Irish council informed Elizabeth in mid-September that the "state of the North ... is such, as of longtime hath not been better. ..." Turlough Luineach "hath come in [to Sidney] ... without pledge, protection, or hostage, showed such tokens ... of duty and obedience, as the troubles of those parts are not to be feared as before. ..." If trouble "should burst out by means of the insolency, and pride of the Scots, Turlough is to be framed, as an instrument and scourge for them, to continue them in the bonds of obedience."[27]

At the beginning of 1578 troubles in the Hebrides turned Clan Ian Mor's attention temporarily away from Ulster. A dispute arose between Angus MacDonnell of Dunyveg and Lachlan MacLean of Duart over the Rhinns of Islay. Argyll was asked by the Edinburgh government to mediate the quarrel. Young James VI and his regent subsequently were approached by Thomas Randolph, Elizabeth's ambassador in Scotland, with a request that they persuade Argyll not only to keep the peace in the Isles, but to prevent the islanders from passing over to Ireland. Argyll's interest broke with this policy. Despite receiving little cooperation from Scotland, Sidney was quick to point to Ulster's tranquility in February 1578: "The state of the country ... is in good quiet. Ulster at no time quieter... ; [n]either [O'Neill nor O'Donnell] seeketh to entertain

Scots. . . ."[28] Thus Sorley's invasion, at least for now, appeared to be a dead issue.

Sidney continued to claim that Ulster was "universally in peace," but London recalled him in March 1578.[29] His departure the following September can be seen as a reaction to the government's failed Irish policies over the previous two decades.[30] Now perhaps the Ulster problem might be handled by more traditional Tudor methods of first securing the Pale and only then exerting influence elsewhere. In effect, this policy would put an end to the offensive strategies of Sussex, Essex, and Sidney. Winning support from a sufficient number of Ulster chiefs, including Turlough Luineach, and, if possible, persuading Argyll to halt the flow of redshanks, were central to the program's success.

For the remainder of 1578, England sought the cooperation of both Turlough and Argyll in order that Sorley, still perceived as the main threat in Ulster, might be neutralized. Turlough presumably would be "dutiful and conformable to anything he shall be directed and commanded. . . ."[31] Despite Sidney's replacement by Justice William Drury, Turlough remained willing to serve against the Scots. O'Neill's poor health in the winter of 1578–9 (from which he shortly would recover) prompted him to seek good terms with the government for the time being.[32] It was reported to London that Argyll had refused a pension from O'Neill in return for a steady flow of redshanks. Furthermore, he refused to "deal with the Irish in prejudice of any of her Majesty's subjects or service."[33] But Argyll finally had taken sides in the MacDonnell–MacLean feud by supporting Angus of Dunyveg. Edinburgh, however, prevented him from stirring up further troubles that most assuredly would have spilled over into Ireland. Thus by early 1579 an uneasy peace held between Angus and Lachlan MacLean.[34]

Scotland hampered England's Ulster policy, but alone she did not control enough resources to pose a serious challenge. Catholic France and Spain, however, did. By the late 1570s Philip II was free of his dependency on Elizabeth and moved closer to the Catholic Guise party in France, which already exerted a good deal of influence in Scotland. There was little question that the Spanish Habsburg–Guise alliance, with Rome's support and approval, would now look upon Ireland as a possible base of operations against England's western flank. Turlough Luineach, as the most important Ulster Irish chief, would be a key player in any foreign intrigue. In January 1579 his delicate health continued to be a central political issue. To Justice Drury, the most pressing question was: should Turlough die, who would succeed him? The most viable candidates were Dungannon, to whom the English proposed to offer the earldom of Tyrone, and Henry MacShane, one of Shane O'Neill's surviving sons.[35] Dungannon had been groomed as Turlough's heir, and his succession, at least to England, could not come at a better time, as there was a pending threat of foreign invasion. Turlough simply could not be trusted as an ally.

Amidst invasion rumors, Drury met Lady Agnes at Armagh in late January, where he learned of Turlough's request for a parley on the Blackwater. Drury gave Turlough safe passage, but the two could not reach an agreement. It now appeared that reports of O'Neill's ill-health had been greatly exaggerated. Turlough faced a crisis nonetheless, as Drury reported that a proposed "league of friendship" between O'Neill and Dungannon had fallen through, and that the baron was "readier than ever to do any service against Turlough. . . ."[36] The O'Neill chief's desperate position can be illustrated by his efforts to arrange marriage alliances in spring 1579 between two of his daughters and Dungannon and one of Sorley's sons.[37] Drury mistakenly believed that a marriage alliance between Turlough and the MacDonnells would mean that "the Scots now are wholly at his [i.e. O'Neill's] commandment and devotion."[38]

To safeguard her interests in Ulster, England had to prevent Turlough Luineach from bringing in more redshanks. Suspicious moves by Argyll and Lady Agnes in early 1579 threatened to undermine that objective. In February Argyll reportedly had assembled a contingent of "Highland Irish" at Glasgow, and it was bruited about that Lady Agnes would meet him there to "advance the errands of her husband. . . ." She also desired to further the interests of her younger sons in the Glynnes. It is not surprising that her kinsman Argyll had already despatched a force there at Sorley Boy's behest. Sorley's request that Argyll send redshanks to aid his nephews in the Glynnes could have meant only one thing: that the MacDonnell leader was confident of his ability to control their employment. Lady Agnes may have won Argyll's consent for Turlough to import more mercenaries, but there was no doubt that Sorley would control them once they arrived.[39]

Turlough became more aggressive in 1579 because England's attention had been diverted from Ulster to Munster, where the Fitzmaurice rebellion gathered momentum. To complicate matters, Catholic Europe threatened to intervene on behalf of the Irish. James Fitzmaurice FitzGerald, the earl of Desmond's cousin and captain-general, also sought aid from Clan Ian Mor, as he penned letters in July to several chiefs, summoning them to form an alliance. Drury fully understood the situation when he informed the Privy Council on 22 July that Fitzmaurice had made an agreement with the Ulster Gaels. The Lord Justice had planned to launch an attack against the Scots in Clandeboy earlier in the month, but postponed it for fear of an invasion from the south. The climax of the uprising came with Fitzmaurice himself landing at Dingle in mid-July at the head of a small force of Spaniards and Italians. They were butchered forthwith at Smerwick in August.[40]

The Munster troubles sparked further problems in Ulster. Encouraged by England's continuing worries in the south, Turlough threatened to ally with Dungannon and Sorley Boy. Justice James Dowdall reported in early August that Turlough, who was becoming increasingly suspicious of Drury's intentions, stood six miles south of Armagh with Dungannon, 2,500 troops, and six weeks' provisions. Some English officials doubted Turlough's audacity, but the Irish council took no chances and ordered all able-bodied Palesmen between ages sixteen and sixty to muster for service. That Sorley had arrived near Carrickfergus with a large force and ten days' provision undoubtedly prompted Dublin to take the Ulster threat more seriously than it otherwise would have.[41]

Because Sidney was absent and Drury's attention was drawn to other parts of Ireland, the Ulster Gaels seemingly had little to dread from the English. In early September 1,800 regular troops were raised and despatched to Kells to bolster a weakened border defense. The Dundalk garrison consisted of only 180 horse and 60 foot, and a force at Drogheda that had fallen back from Newry lacked adequate provisions. Word circulated that Turlough and Dungannon intended to invade MacMahon's country. But O'Neill's threats were primarily designed to pressure Dublin to withdraw the Blackwater garrison. Turlough hinted that he might be able to preserve the peace if he was not the target of a proposed English invasion. Only days before Drury's departure, the Irish council informed Turlough that the newly raised forces meant him no harm. There were two more important factors, however, that served to keep Turlough in check: 1) his deteriorating relations with Lady Agnes and 2) news of Fitzmaurice's defeat and death. The first meant that he no longer had a reliable source of redshanks and the second that England could now focus her full attention on the north. Fortunately for the English, Turlough perceived the weakness of his own position and by mid-September had agreed, apparently at Lady Agnes's behest, not to put his army into the field.[42] As Turlough was once more at bay, Dublin could turn its attention to the Scottish problem.

During autumn 1579 the threat of a Scottish invasion dominated the affairs of Ulster. As soon as Dublin had come to an agreement with Turlough in September, new fears arose concerning the influx of redshanks into Connacht. In addition, O'Neill had barely reached Strabane before he began issuing threats to the English. The cause of Turlough's reversal is not difficult to ascertain. Sorley Boy would provide redshanks, but only if O'Neill agreed to march south and threaten the borders of the Pale. The combination of Sorley Boy, extremely inclement weather, and England's declining strength along the Ulster frontier so emboldened Turlough that he even demanded possession of the Blackwater fort.[43]

By using Turlough to occupy English forces along the Newry–Dundalk–Kells line, Sorley hoped to open up Down and southern Antrim to a Scottish invasion. On 25 September the Irish council learned from an informant, Thomas Stevenson, that in the Hebrides and western Highlands there were divers of the Island men buying . . . powder, skulls [helmets], and swords with divers other things incident for the wars, who amongst such as were his friends he enquired what should be the meaning of this preparation for the war. Some told him that Angus MacDonnell was levying 2000 men to make a journey upon the Isle of Man; but the chiefest friends . . . told him that it was only for Ireland, and withal said unto him that the wars in Ireland was [sic] not yet begun, and counselled him to leave his house in Knockfergus. . . .[44]

Stevenson's letter makes clear two points: 1) that Carrickfergus was the Scots' target and 2) that Sorley Boy was the driving force behind the impending expedition. The redshank army that his nephew Angus was raising (with Argyll's approval) would be under Sorley's complete control once across the North Channel. Sorley would command the army, but he persuaded Turlough to help fund the invasion. Stevenson revealed that a Captain Crawford "is waged by Turlough and Sorley with a ship and a pinnace to keep the seas off the north of Ireland, and his chief abode to be in . . . Rathlin Island, which . . . shall be the storehouse of his gettings."[45] It was suggested to Elizabeth in October that she might implore thirteen-year-old James VI of Scotland to countenance the despatch of a force of pro-English Scots to Ireland to forestall a MacDonnell–Campbell power play. But the reliability of the so-called "inland Scots," especially those in the southwest, was questionable, as Argyll earlier had toyed with the idea of raising a contingent for Turlough's employment.[46]

England's attempts to prevent Clan Ian Mor's further entrenchment in Antrim seemed to falter at year's end. Angus MacDonnell and Argyll were raising redshanks, and Turlough appeared rejuvenated by the recent flurry of activity. From Newry, Bagenal reported that Turlough "goeth to [the] Bannside, and calls for all his Scots to [come to] him; and as he saith openly he goeth thither to agree between Sorley Boy and MacWilliam [i.e. the earl of Clanrickard]. . . ."[47] Dungannon, no longer trusted by either side, informed the new Lord Justice, William Pelham, of Turlough's attempt to draw large numbers of redshanks to Lough Foyle and the Bannside.[48] In turn, Pelham wrote Elizabeth with word of a possible foreign invasion and the restoration of an Ulster confederacy. He charged that Sorley, Turlough, and O'Donnell have "sworn to assemble all their forces against the next moonlight, although since that oath the Marshal hath by good policy dealt with O'Donnell and deferred the matter. Dungannon also [has been] secretly sworn unto them and accepted into Tyrone as tanist. . . ."[49] Despite Bagenal's success, however, most Dublin policy-makers agreed that most of the Irish favored rebellion. Pelham attempted to combat the impending Ulster troubles by separating Turlough from his *urraights* in hopes that he might be dissuaded from taking the field with Sorley Boy. Scots mercenaries continued to land from Ballycastle to Lough Foyle in late 1579. Nor had the problem of the Scots spilling over into Connacht and western Munster abated. But in late December Pelham and Bagenal brought together Dungannon and several prominent Ulster chieftains against Turlough. Pelham himself would be away in Munster; nonetheless, he sanctioned an Ulster campaign for early 1580.[50]

To defend her Ulster interests, England had to make it more difficult for Clan Ian Mor to bring redshanks across the North Channel. London despatched two vessels–the *Handmaid* and the *Achates*–to patrol the northern seas in January 1580. Pelham reported that Turlough, despite another illness, was prepared to cross the Blackwater. Once more, O'Neill's hostility was revived by the prospect of aid from Scotland. Sorley Boy, who frequently moved back and forth across the North Channel, had landed in the Glynnes with the apparent support of James VI. Pelham quickly contacted the MacDonnell leader, reminding him of his promise to Sidney in October 1575 to keep the peace. Lady Agnes, too, remained active. Plans were afoot for her to sail to western Scotland where Argyll was convening a meeting of the Hebridean chiefs. These various peregrinations convinced England that the long-awaited invasion was imminent. At last, a formidable combination seemingly was being forged between Clan Ian Mor, the O'Neills, the Campbells, and the Scottish crown. But as Argyll and Lady Agnes made plans to journey to Edinburgh in February, the young Scottish king disavowed any complicity in the Gaelic combination.[51]

Despite the tenuous links between Edinburgh, Inverary, Ballycastle, and Strabane, the English remained wary of Scottish support for Turlough Luineach. Real power in Lowland Scotland lay in the hands of James Stewart, future earl of Arran; O'Neill, however, still found advantage in exploiting his connections with young James VI. In fact, an observer noted that Turlough

> hath all his forces together giving out many proud speeches after drinking of his aquavitie. He doth greatly extol the young Scottish king . . . to whom he hath not long ago sent horses and hawks, and seeks to take him for his foster son, when he shall be sure to be well brought up.[52]

O'Neill's drunken foray toward Newry in April with 1,900 redshanks and 4,000 Irish troops certainly threatened the borders of the Pale, the supposed pact with the Scottish king notwithstanding. London's proper concern, however, should have been the very real prospect of Turlough's being supported and directed by Sorley Boy. In the previous month, MacDonnell and his nephew, Donnell Gorme, had brought 500 Scots to eastern Ulster. Bagenal responded to the threat, but when Turlough approached Newry in April, there was little he could do but shift his defenses back there. Because Sorley was loose near Carrickfergus, Bagenal and Pelham could only pray that the unpredictable Turlough wearied "of his own madness . . . as he knoweth not whom to trust."[53]

The English expected Lady Agnes to return to Ireland in May with an agreement that would provide Turlough with a multitude of redshanks. She and Argyll finally met with representatives of the Edinburgh regime at Stirling, where they both assured Elizabeth's ambassador that all Turlough desired was to hold his lands (including the Blackwater fort) in peace. The English believed that O'Neill would take no hostile action until he knew the outcome of Lady Agnes's negotiations. She insisted that the sole reason for her coming to Scotland was to secure Angus MacDonnell's tenure to his lands in the western Highlands and Isles. Upon hearing both Lady Agnes and Argyll disavowing hostile intent, officials in London and Dublin must have been relieved. But to the queen's lieutenants in the field, there remained the omnipresent problem of confronting Sorley Boy.[54]

In mid-1580 England faced actual or potential trouble in all four of Ireland's provinces; however, Ulster posed the most serious threat. Malby believed that Sorley's Scots "be the only hope that any evil-disposed Irishry have to sustain them in their enterprises. . . ."[55] Indeed, there were more Scottish mercenaries in Ireland than at any time during the previous decade. If England was to prevent the situation from deteriorating further, she had to approach Sorley Boy, who, along with Lady Agnes, now exercised tremendous influence over Turlough Luineach.[56] Arthur, Lord Grey de Wilton, replacing Sidney as Lord Deputy in late summer 1580, wrote Elizabeth that O'Neill

> seems yet to stand well devoted, and in good obedience to your Majesty, howbeit that certain Scots be arrived in those parts, whom he yet represseth from doing any outrage upon your subjects. . . . For all this, his assuredness goeth not undoubted by reason of his wife, known to be a pestilent instrument, altogether Scottish, and applying all that is in her to direct him from your loyalty.[57]

Lady Agnes and her sons had cast their lot with Sorley Boy, and any major action would require his sanction. Sorley demonstrated his influence in southeastern Ulster by despatching Angus to prey upon certain uncommitted Irish chieftains.[58] Malby passed on a rumor to the earl of Leicester in mid-August that 2,000 redshanks had landed in Clandeboy. He believed that "Turlough Luineach's marriage with the Scot is cause of all this, and if her Majesty do not provide against her devices, this Scottish woman will make a new Scotland of Ulster." Malby also noted that Lady Agnes "hath already planted a good foundation, for she in Tyrone, her daughter in Tyrconnell (being O'Donnell's wife), and Sorley Boy in Clandeboy, do carry all the way in the north. . . ."[59] If this were not enough, James VI was still suspected of harboring sympathies for the Scots in Ireland, and Sorley threatened to spread Clan Ian Mor's influence into Connacht.[60] Under these rather disquieting circumstances, the English, especially Bagenal and Piers, spared no effort to bring Turlough to oppose the Scots.

As things worsened for England in Ulster, Turlough, not uncharacteristically, became more intractable. He continued to hold out the possibility of moving against the Scots, but this would have isolated him from Lady Agnes and the roots of his military strength. The English could have used his assistance, since the Scots were plundering as far south as the Ardes, thus threatening overland access to Carrickfergus. The Desmond rebellion in the south was another factor that pulled Turlough away from England. In late August 1580 Dublin learned that John of Desmond had made overtures not only to O'Neill but to O'Donnell and Sorley Boy as well. Bagenal and Dungannon informed Grey that Turlough continued at the head of 5,000 men and recently had begun to win back his *urraights*. As autumn approached, Malby warned London that a military campaign was the only solution to the Ulster problem.[61]

England remained alert for a combined Scottish–Continental invasion of Ulster in September. Philip II had recently signed a truce with the Ottoman Turks, freeing Spanish forces from the Mediterranean theater, and had annexed Portugal. Of more immediate concern, however, was evidence that Sorley continued to supply Turlough with redshanks. On 7 September Malby reported O'Neill's approach toward Dundalk with 2,500 Scots and 3,500 Irish troops. To ascertain the severity of the threat, Grey, Pelham, and Dungannon proceeded to Drogheda, whence the Lord Deputy despatched representatives to Turlough. Over the next fortnight Turlough and the English reached an agreement whereby O'Neill would keep the peace in return for an extension of his lands east of the Bann, control of his *urraights*, command of 100 English troops, and possession of the Blackwater fort. No mention was made of Turlough opposing the Scots, though England probably expected the land grant east of the Bann to lead to conflict with Sorley. Afterwards, however, Bagenal was concerned that "[t]his peace can be of no better assurance than other ratifications have been."[62]

After the agreement with Turlough, Grey turned his attention to Munster and a possible Spanish landing, while Sorley Boy continued to prepare to invade Ulster. In mid-October London received word of a Spanish descent on the south coast of Ireland. Grey would defeat the small force handily in November, but word of the Spaniards' arrival prompted the queen and her council to approach Argyll about checking the flow of redshanks to Ulster.[63] The Campbell earl apparently was amenable, as one of Elizabeth's men in Edinburgh noted on 24 October "that none have gone over of late out of Scotland into Ireland, neither is there any number prepared or ready to pass, notwithstanding the bruit given further to the contrary."[64] That the report mentioned rumors of continued preparations for a Scottish invasion of Ulster suggests that Argyll's control over the flow of mercenaries was incomplete. This indeed was true, Sorley having emerged as the principal power-broker between the western Highlands and Isles and northeastern Ireland.

It should have been no surprise to England that Turlough would threaten the borders of the Pale as soon as the Lord Deputy departed Ulster. O'Neill assembled 1,000 troops on the Blackwater in late October, and only a resolute stand by Bagenal and Dungannon (who rushed back from Munster) prevented him from sweeping past Newry.[65] But as the year closed, the possible resurrection of an Ulster confederacy must have elicited great concern in Dublin and London. In January 1581 Walsingham received a warning from the bishop of Ross that unless the redshank hosts were kept from Ireland, "her Majesty otherwise shall be at great charges and loss of men. . . ." Elizabeth had received such advice before; this piece, however, originating from an inside source, further cautioned that if the North Channel were not sealed off, the south of Ireland could not be maintained and the "west seas" would be open to the French.[66]

Early 1581 saw the beginning of a new English policy directed toward Sorley and Clan Ian Mor which hinged on an alliance between Elizabeth, James VI, Argyll, and the MacLeans of Duart. Their first objective would be to banish Angus MacDonnell from Islay and Kintyre, thus cutting off the family's main source of redshanks. James VI was suspected of having assisted the Highland Scots in Ireland, but he had backed away from a major commitment to them. It was James's hesitation that led Walsingham and the Privy Council to believe that he might be pulled into an alliance against the MacDonnells. England needed such an alliance because of her own weak Irish military establishment. Despite increases in troop strength under Grey, many of the units still suffered from illness and desertion, and wheat was scarce and expensive. English soldiers simply did not relish duty in Ireland. The bishop of Ross suggested to Walsingham that the queen would do well "to have some footmen of the Scottish Irish" in her service, an indication of the superiority of the redshank fighting man.[67] The pending alliance perhaps was a way to employ such troops against Clan Ian Mor.

An Anglo-Scottish alliance against Sorley Boy would be greatly enhanced if Turlough Luineach could be persuaded to take the field against him. Piers recommended that the government seize the moment and push O'Neill to attack Sorley. Walsingham learned in late January, however, that Argyll was responsible for a large number of Scots recently landed at Lough Foyle. Undertreasurer Sir Henry Wallop instructed Leicester that those same Scots likely would be sent by Turlough into Connacht, where they would threaten the border's western flank when O'Neill broke into open rebellion.[68] Most disturbing of all was Wallop's report that Turlough "is . . . now in a parley with Sarleboy. . . ."[69] Grey himself feared open rebellion by Turlough and had not yet dismissed the possibility that James VI would aid the Irishman. Clearly, then, London was much more optimistic than Dublin about the prospect of an Anglo-Scottish alliance or of pitting Turlough against Sorley. Facing a hostile redshank host in the north, the Desmond rebellion in the south, and a possible Scottish-sponsored uprising in Connacht, Dublin favored a return to the intensive methods of Sussex and Sidney. If Turlough could not be employed as an ally, the first order of business was to increase the strength of the English military establishment in Ireland.[70]

In spring 1581 Elizabeth again committed to suppressing the Gaels in Ulster as a means of discouraging foreign invasion. Because of Bagenal's prior success in dealing with O'Neill, he was appointed Governor of Ulster in early March.[71] At month's end, however, Malby observed that "we look for nothing but all ill at Turlough Luineach's hands."[72] But in the meantime, Walsingham learned that Philip II had called off an invasion of Ireland. Nonetheless, the problem of the Scots remained. London's agents above the Tweed were instructed to redouble their efforts to ensure that Edinburgh stopped the flow of mercenaries to Ireland. In reality, there was little the Edinburgh regime could do. Walsingham received word in mid-April that a large redshank army had been readied, most probably by Sorley and Angus MacDonnell, to descend on Lecale within a month. The presence of these veteran troops would allow the Antrim Scots to expand an already growing presence in County Down between Carrickfergus and Newry. Turlough would be more likely to cause trouble south of the Blackwater with Dublin's attention focused on the Scots. To oppose this new threat, Grey requested an additional 1,000 regulars from England, that he might overawe Turlough before the Scots arrived.[73]

England's despatch of more regular troops to Ireland and her continued naval presence in the North Channel reflected a grim determination to quell the Ulster troubles. Heretofore, England had strengthened her army units with Irish levies, but Grey was now instructed to employ only regulars. Such would be the price of settling that unruly province. Grey emphasized that Ulster, and by implication all Ireland, would be lost unless stern measures were employed and adequate funds allocated by London. Sorley remained the primary concern, but it was thought politic to offer O'Neill a pardon to keep him quiet for the moment.[74]

An ill wind blew for England at the beginning of the redshank campaigning season in May 1581. Grey reported that Turlough had already preyed on the Carrickfergus area. The Dublin government, still short of troops, again requested 1,000 levies for Ulster. There were those, including future Lord Deputy Sir John Perrott, who advocated the outright "reconquest" and subsequent destruction of Gaelic Ireland. But with Turlough and 4,500 men in the field, James VI and Argyll still wavering, and Sorley and Angus MacDonnell feverishly recruiting in the Hebrides, the English were well advised simply to hang on in the north.[75]

The Byzantine nature of Gaelic politics provided a reprieve for the hard-pressed English. It was not long until Turlough took to quarreling with Hugh O'Donnell of Tyrconnell. The row led to O'Neill's victory over the O'Donnells at Raphoe in early July and to England's provision of aid to the distressed Tyrconnell. Malby was appointed to leave Connacht and survey the situation in Tyrconnell while Grey crossed the Blackwater and moved toward Lifford. The Lord Deputy began formulating plans for a late August expedition into Ulster. But Grey had not deluded himself about English military strength in Ulster and Connacht. He was clearly outnumbered by O'Neill alone, and if more redshanks entered the north under Sorley and Angus MacDonnell, the odds might prove overwhelming.[76] Sir William Stanley, one of the queen's more capable Irish lieutenants, candidly confessed to Walsingham: "We have no advantage over them in fight but discipline. . . ."[77] Besides numbers, England also lacked adequate provisions and money. Under these tenuous circumstances, Grey had no choice but to temporize with Turlough.[78]

A conference between Turlough Luineach and Grey on 2 August near Benburb resulted in a peace treaty favorable to England. At the same time, O'Neill pledged to refrain from further attacks on O'Donnell, who, Turlough claimed, had brought about his own troubles by refusing to wage redshanks for service in Connacht. O'Neill was still puffed up with pride, but he seemed relieved to have come to terms with Grey. Once again the craven chief had thrown away a golden opportunity to combine with Sorley and drive the English from Ulster and, perhaps, from Connacht. The Lord Deputy, however, did not believe peace would last. On 12 August he complained that "I have, against my will, concluded, or rather patched up, a peace with Turlough, being such indeed as I can neither repose any assurance in for a continuation of it, nor . . . justly commend it."[79]

Grey's journey into Ulster doubtless relieved the pressure on O'Donnell and brought Turlough to parley, but Sorley Boy's increasing strength threatened to upset the delicate balance of power. Reports reached London in September that Turlough "at this instant is able to make above 6000 men. . . . And whereas, in time past, they had no weapons but darts and gallowglasses [i.e. axes], they are now furnished with all kind of munition, and as well practised therein as Englishmen."[80] O'Neill could field such a large, well-supplied, and properly trained army in 1581 because of Sorley's support and military sagacity. Not a warrior himself, O'Neill had neither the inclination nor the experience to raise, equip, and train such an army as described above. Only Sorley could have provided it for him. Indeed, MacDonnell's bold presence in Ulster persuaded Turlough time and again to eschew a lasting peace agreement or alliance with the Sassenach.

From autumn 1581 to mid-1582 Sorley and Angus MacDonnell recruited redshanks for an invasion of Connacht by Turlough Luineach and the

O'Donnells. The MacDonnells' strategy involved drawing England's attention away from Clandeboy, the Glynnes, and the Route. In October Argyll
tried to halt the flow of mercenaries to Ulster, undoubtedly at London's
bidding. By then Sorley and Angus were able to operate independently of
the MacCailein Mor in the southern Hebrides, at least where recruiting was
concerned. Angus had become extremely active in Ulster affairs in 1581–2,
crossing the North Channel on numerous occasions. There is no evidence
to suggest hostility between him and Sorley, though both desired to control
the Glynnes. Angus apparently had distanced himself from his mother and
stepfather, Turlough Luineach, and cast his lot with his uncle Sorley.[81]

By July 1582 Sorley and Angus had raised a large enough force of
redshanks for O'Neill and O'Donnell to launch an invasion of Connacht.
Over 2,000 Scots plundered and burned Sligo, but were repulsed with heavy
losses when they stormed O'Conor Sligo's castle. Nonetheless, the redshank
army remained intact and continued to threaten the province. Malby, who
had fallen back to Roscommon, was too weak to stop the invaders, but, contrary to Sorley's expectations, Dublin refused to transfer troops away from
the Carrickfergus–Newry line to the west. By mid-month O'Donnell was
in command of the army, Turlough having already withdrawn into Ulster.
Finally, less than a fortnight after the invasion had begun, Con O'Donnell
withdrew the army into Fermanagh and eastward across Tyrone. Turlough,
despite his obvious role in the Connacht campaign, had meanwhile peti-
tioned Elizabeth for lands in the Pale and for the earldom of Clanconnell.[82]

As the Scots-Irish invasion of Connacht failed to divert England's
attention from Ulster, Sorley hastened to pour more redshanks into
the latter province. In late August Malby advised Walsingham that 2,000
Scots had already arrived and a further 2,000 were preparing to depart
Scotland for Ulster. Malby requested additional troops and supplies to
counter Sorley Boy and advised London that the invasion must be repelled
by both land and sea, otherwise the Scots would establish a permanent hold
on the northeast coast. It was also suggested that Turlough be approached
again about an alliance against Clan Ian Mor. The situation became acute,
Sorley and Angus ignoring the traditional end of the campaigning season
at *Samhain* and continuing to send mercenaries to Ulster. On 5 November,
for instance, the Privy Council learned of the arrival of several companies of
redshanks near the Bann under Angus and Donnell Gorme MacDonnell. In
early December Piers observed that Angus had summoned from Scotland
all the troops under his command. By year's end Sorley clearly was intent on
holding the Glynnes and the Route and possibly extending Angus's claims
into Clandeboy. Through it all the aging O'Neill remained quiet, his Scots
mercenaries having already departed to join their fellow MacDonnells in
Clandeboy.[83]

During the first half of 1583 England again attempted to stop the flow
of redshanks to Ireland by striking at its Scottish source. Walsingham

instructed his Edinburgh agents "That order may be taken that the inhabitants in the Isles and north parts of Scotland be not suffered to pass into Ireland and to serve the rebels there. . . ." The queen herself wrote James VI in May, insisting that "good order . . . be taken for subduing of the disobedient people in the isles and elsewhere in Scotland. . . ."[84] Wallop and the other Lords Justice (Grey had departed the previous August) also insisted that the storehouses at Carrickfergus must be held at all costs, for if lost, there would be no way of adequately supplying a field army operating in Ulster.[85]

Sorley landed on the Antrim coast in early spring and was immediately attacked as he moved into the Route by Hugh MacFelim O'Neill, lord of Killultagh, the MacQuillins, and a band of about 200 English troops led by captains Nicholas Dawtrey, seneschal of Clandeboy, and William Chatterton.[86] The English had been "appointed to lie in MacQuillin's country . . . for the defence against the Scots, on the requisition of . . . MacQuillin."[87] The Four Masters wrote that "Great depredations were committed on Sorley Boy," but he and "his kinsmen went in pursuit of the preys . . . [and] defeated those who were before them. . . ."[88] Not only did Sorley rout the enemy and slay Hugh MacFelim, but he summoned Turlough Luineach, who had moved into the Route, to offer him assistance. The two men then, according to Malby, agreed to combine their forces to the number of 4,000 and march on the Pale. Angus MacDonnell's men had been busy preying on cattle in Clandeboy, and he himself was on his way from Islay with more troops. Indeed, Carrickfergus now seemed in grave danger from the MacDonnell–O'Neill combination. News of the gravid situation prompted Elizabeth to write James VI in early May. There is no question that the queen and council were relieved to hear that the Scottish king would do all he could to prevent further recruitment of redshanks for the Irish service.[89]

In the early 1580s Clan Ian Mor's power in Scotland was beginning to wane, yet until the end of the century James VI still found it difficult to exert authority in the southwestern Highlands and Isles. Thus for the next twenty years the region was politically unstable, large numbers of "leaderless men" enlisting with the highest bidder for service in Ulster. Here, then, is one reason why Sorley and Angus MacDonnell were consistently able to raise large numbers of redshanks. But the diminution of the MacDonnells' political influence in Scotland accounts, in part, for their decision in 1582–3 to bring all available Scots mercenaries to Ireland and keep them there outside of the traditional campaigning season. At the beginning of a new season in May 1583, therefore, Clan Ian Mor, allied with Turlough Luineach, commanded a large and formidable fighting force that was in place and ready to take the field.

Now that Clan Ian Mor had shifted its power base to northeastern Ireland, Turlough might have been expected for once in his fifteen-year tenure as O'Neill to throw himself resolutely into a Gaelic military alliance. But he did not. Instead, he wrote the Lords Justice on 1 May, requesting a truce until the end of the month. A week later his request was granted. Turlough's double-crossing of Sorley and Angus at such a critical (and promising) moment threatened to wreck the entire enterprise. Malby learned on 2 May that Angus was ready to bring in 3,000 additional redshanks who probably would be marched into Connacht.[90] An invasion of Connacht by Angus (or by one of Sorley's other nephews or sons) would have stretched England's forces perilously thin from Carrickfergus to Sligo. The opportunity was missed, though, because of Turlough's vacillation.

An aging Turlough O'Neill was rumored first to be quite ill and then to have died in spring 1583. These reports ultimately proved false, but they caused all parties concerned to prepare for an impending power struggle over a vacant O'Neillship. While all eyes focused on Turlough, Sorley sent out a force to plunder around Carrickfergus. Walsingham kept his attention riveted to the task at hand: negotiating an end to the flow of mercenaries from Scotland. In early July he learned that Argyll, who had been quiet for some time, had agreed to use his influence with the island chiefs. For his efforts, the Campbell earl was awarded an English pension.[91] Though Turlough and Argyll had been separated from the MacDonnell camp, England still could not be sure of the sympathies of James VI. In light of recent disappointments, Sorley wrote Sir Henry Bagenal, eldest son of Sir Nicholas and future Marshal of Ireland, and the other commissioners at Carrickfergus, promising to restore the livestock recently taken in the area and to refrain from harassing the MacQuillins in the Route. Offered a breathing space, the English quickly shored up their weakened defenses from Carrickfergus to Newry. For Sorley, this was a bitter turn of events, preventing what might have been a crushing blow to England's presence in Ulster and Connacht.[92]

Sorley's inability to form an alliance with Turlough in 1583 pointed up the futility of trying to resurrect an Ulster confederacy. Thereafter, the MacDonnell leader marshalled his nephews and sons to aid him in furthering the family's interests in northern Ireland. In October England arranged a truce until March 1584 between O'Neill, O'Donnell, and Dungannon, thereby freeing forces that could, if necessary, be employed against Clan Ian Mor. Also, Elizabeth sought an agreement with the imprisoned Mary, Queen of Scots, through which the latter would urge her son to curb Scotland's redshank traffic. In November Lady Agnes, who no longer wielded much influence over her sons, swore fealty to the English queen and promised the same of her husband.[93] Despite being forsaken by his former allies, Sorley Boy reached his zenith at the end of 1583 and, without question, became the greatest Clan Donald leader of the age. But the rugged, battle-scarred old warrior had yet to attain his ultimate goal of a royal patent to his Antrim lands.

Chapter Ten
The Resilient Warrior, 1584–6

Is treise tuath na tighearna.
A people is stronger than a lord.

From 1584 to 1586 Sorley Boy made his final push to secure royal recognition of the Antrim MacDonnells' claim to the Glynnes and the Route. No longer willing or able to depend on erstwhile Scottish or Irish allies, old Sorley rallied his sons and nephews for the struggle. During these two years the MacDonnells contested an invasion of Ulster under the new Lord Deputy, Sir John Perrott, and defended their interests in the southern Hebrides against the resurgent MacLeans of Duart. But by 1586 the fight had ended, and Sorley, after a ceremonial "submission" in Dublin, received his long-awaited patent. This done, the MacDonnell leader consolidated his gains and laid a firm foundation for his progeny. Because of his success in 1586, Sorley's accomplishments did not perish with him. And as the Antrim MacDonnells' fortunes would demonstrate after his death, a people indeed proved stronger than a lord.

The appointment of Sir John Perrott as Lord Deputy in January 1584 boded ill for Sorley and his kinsmen. Described as an ambitious eccentric with a terrible temper, this supposed bastard son of Henry VIII was determined to drive the Scots from Ulster. But Elizabeth had instructed him merely to hold the line in Ireland while the English army supported the Protestant cause in the Netherlands. This timorous policy, however, was quite out of character for Perrott. Though it would be half a year before he assumed his Irish post, the new deputy monitored the continuing threat of a Spanish invasion. To add to his worries, a report to the queen described the Pale as "destitute of all martial furniture" and revealed that the Irish "do daily store themselves with shot and other warlike necessaries, by means whereof we grow weak and they strong. . . ."[1]

Clan Ian Mor's influence had waned considerably in the western Highlands and Isles since mid-century. In early 1584 Angus MacDonnell returned to Scotland to petition James VI for a renewal of his lease to Kintyre, Islay, and other of the isles. Concurrently, Sorley's third son James, who had emerged as "a principal leader of the Irish Scots," was in Edinburgh seeking assistance. These actions stemmed from the MacDonnells' decision to stand alone against England in Ulster. The unpredictable Turlough Luineach reportedly had allied with Dungannon in March, thus posing a potential threat to the MacDonnells' western flank.[2] Hence a secure eastern flank across the North Channel in Scotland was of paramount importance to Sorley and his kinsmen.

Perrott took his post as Lord Deputy in June and received congratulatory letters from O'Neill, O'Donnell, and MacQuillin, among others. Deteriorating relations between Turlough and his former Gaelic allies, while appearing advantageous to England, actually presented the new deputy with a serious problem. Word spread that James VI was behind the recent arrival in Tyrconnell of 1,500–2,000 MacLean redshanks, whose presence bolstered the claims of Shane O'Neill's sons against Turlough and Dungannon. Moreover, James was said to be gathering a further 5,000 troops, including many "inland Scots," as reinforcements. True to character, Turlough quickly retracted his commendations to Perrott and waged many of these mercenaries. Hugh O'Donnell, who stood to lose by Turlough's *volte-face*, informed Perrott that O'Neill "was never true, but practising with fair words, by the advice of his privy friends."[3] In August Perrott revealed to Walsingham the presence of over 100 Scottish galleys being readied in the isles to ferry more redshanks to Ulster.[4] As summer waned, then, the Lord Deputy faced a potential crisis. Sorley Boy remained the wild card. If the MacDonnell leader supported the MacLeans, Shane's sons, and Turlough, Perrott would be hard-pressed to expel the Scots from the north. But if Sorley stood by while the two sides fought it out, the MacDonnells would emerge as the strongest power in Ulster. Circumstances dictated that Perrott act decisively, regardless of the queen's instructions to the contrary and without waiting to determine Sorley's response.

The MacLeans who landed at Lough Swilly in August 1584 appeared capable of challenging Perrott in western Ulster and Connacht without MacDonnell assistance. Captain Joshua Mince described the redshank army:

> They are of a great force. . . . The number of men is more than I am able of certainty to verify . . . ; of certainty they mean no goodness for they are very well appointed of artillery and cast pieces of great and small size. Further, the bruit is here that there is in Lough Foyle come in three great ships full of ordnance, and do mean to join with the others.[5]

Besides MacLean redshanks in Tyrconnell, England faced a possible MacDonnell–MacLean combination in Scotland. This alliance would hold the incapacitated Argyll's attention while Scots continued to pour into

Ulster. Perrott feared the effects of a MacDonnell–MacLean alliance in Ireland, but he was even more concerned about Turlough joining his fellow Gaels. O'Neill believed that support for an invasion of Connacht and Munster would be forthcoming from not only the MacDonnells and MacLeans but also James VI and Philip II. Perrott complained to Elizabeth that his forces–fewer than 1,000 foot and horse together–were inadequate to face this combination. And he was certainly right. For now, though, the Lord Deputy had to make do with the troops on hand.[6]

Perrott responded to the mounting threat with preparations for an invasion of the north to banish the Antrim MacDonnells and their MacLean allies. In mid-August the Privy Council informed him that troops, money, and supplies were being hastily gathered for the campaign. On the 19th, Geoffrey Fenton, Irish Secretary of State, reported the arrival of 4,000 more Scots. But Fenton did have some heartening news for Burghley: Turlough reportedly had been persuaded to join forces with Perrott's 2,000 troops. This suggests that Turlough probably was at odds with the MacLeans and MacDonnells over the claim of Shane's sons to the chiefship of the O'Neills of Tyrone. The bluff Perrott, despite royal instructions to the contrary, wrote the English council that his "intentions to look through his fingers at Ulster, as a fit receptacle for all the savage beasts of the land, has been altered by the arrival of MacLean's sons and many Scots." Angus MacDonnell had just come with 1,600 redshanks to join Sorley's 300–400 veterans already in the Route. At the same time, Perrott heard disquieting rumors from the south. James VI was said to be considering a Spanish marriage, and Philip II's vessels were now frequently plying the waters off the southern Irish coast. The Desmond rebellion had been quelled, but some of the Fitzgerald survivors fled Munster for the Route, where Sorley aided their escape to Scotland and thence to Spain.[7] Perrott now had to give serious consideration to the possibility of a two-front war in Ulster and Munster.

Perrott's invasion of Ulster began on 25 August 1584. His army marched northward, accompanied by the earls of Ormond, Thomond, and Clanrickard, Dungannon, and Sir John Norris, among other notables. Several of Turlough's *urraights*, including the O'Donnelleys, who had gone over to the Scots, were lost to the English cause. To oppose the MacLean redshanks in Tyrconnell, Perrott had moved Sir Richard Bingham, governor of Connacht since Malby's recent death, north to the banks of the Erne in June. The Lord Deputy also had several English vessels patrol the north coast from Lough Swilly to Ballycastle. Elizabeth had allotted the modest sum of £11,500 to finance these varied operations.[8]

The behavior of Turlough, Dungannon, and James VI was crucial to Perrott's success. The day before the campaign began, Bagenal brought together the two O'Neill leaders in a tenuous peace. As the English campaign unfolded, Walsingham tried to ascertain whether the Scottish

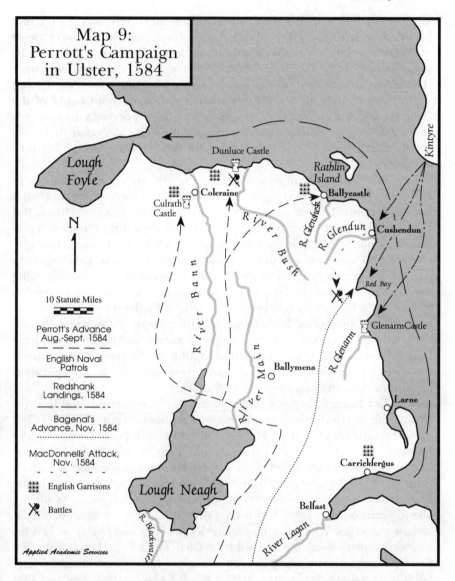

Map 9:
Perrott's Campaign
in Ulster, 1584

Lough
Foyle

Kintyre

Dunluce Castle

*Rathlin
Island*

N

Culrath
Castle

Coleraine

Ballycastle

R. Glenshesk

River Bush

R. Glendun

Cushendun

Red Bay

River Bann

GlenarmCastle

R. Glenarm

10 Statute Miles

Perrott's Advance
Aug.-Sept. 1584

River Main

English Naval
Patrols

Ballymena

Redshank
Landings, 1584

Larne

Bagenal's
Advance, Nov. 1584

MacDonnells' Attack,
Nov. 1584

Carrickfergus

English Garrisons

Lough Neagh

Battles

Belfast

Applied Academic Services

R. Blackwater

River Lagan

king would follow a pro-MacDonnell policy. But there was no attempt by Edinburgh to assist the MacDonnells, for a Scottish invasion never materialized. The redshanks' peregrinations in 1584 were virtually the same as occurred every year between *Beatainn* and *Samhain*. Nor were the persistent rumors of complicity by James VI, Philip II, or the Papacy anything new. Indeed, as Perrott's army marched up both banks of the Bann in late August, many of the Scots in Ulster reportedly had already sailed back to Scotland.[9] Had Sorley and his allies intended to invade the north, they would not have withdrawn forces in the face of Perrott's advance.

The Privy Council informed Perrott on 31 August that sources in Edinburgh had reported little activity in the western Highlands and Isles that pointed to an impending MacDonnell invasion of Ulster. But the council sympathized with the Lord Deputy regarding Elizabeth's parsimony: "Your Lordship is not ignorant how loath we are to be carried into charges, and how we would rather spend a pound, forced by necessity, than a penny for prevention."[10] Here was the main stumbling-block to expelling the Scots from the north. Despite her years, Elizabeth seemed unaware that money (or a lack of it) was the key to solving England's problem in the Gaelic heartland. Sorley Boy's threat to Ulster was no greater now than in the past, but calling off Perrott's campaign after it had begun would have been a blow to morale and a logistical nightmare. The queen and council acted wisely in allowing the Lord Deputy to proceed in the largest operation against the Antrim Scots since the mid-1560s.

A lack of Scottish hostility notwithstanding, Perrott continued to drive toward the North Antrim coast in early September. Meanwhile, he called up 400 reinforcements from Munster. At mid-month Perrott stood on the Bann near Coleraine with Turlough and Lady Agnes. From there the MacDonnells' *bête noire* directed the siege of Dunluce Castle, one of Sorley's principal strongholds in the Route. After landing artillery at Portrush, the English pounded the castle into submission within two days. As during Shane's campaign in 1564–5, the MacDonnell leader once again had been caught unawares. While Dunluce struggled to hold out, Sorley moved his followers and *creaghts* into the wilds of Glenconkine (in Loughinshollin, County Derry), thus evading Perrott's stronger force in traditional Gaelic fashion. This done, Sorley arranged for reinforcements from Scotland. Old Argyll's recent death had not altered the situation in the western Isles, and Sorley and Angus continued to recruit large numbers of redshanks. The MacDonnells were so successful in their recruitment that England, already mistrustful of James VI, feared "a breach between the courts of London and Edinburgh. . . ."[11] As it turned out, James was not actively involved in Ulster affairs, but Perrott had enough to worry about with the MacDonnells themselves.

Perrott campaigned in the Route for but ten days, leaving behind a garrison in Dunluce and a further thirteen companies of regulars under Sir John Norris scattered in the north. The Lord Deputy himself returned to Dublin and drafted a plan for the further subjugation of Ulster. Meanwhile, for much of October Norris tried to root out and destroy Sorley's estimated 50,000 head of cattle. Perrott revealed to the Privy Council in mid-September that the MacLeans had departed Tyrconnell in great haste, barely avoiding the English vessels that landed Perrott's artillery at Portrush. The Lord Deputy believed that the Scottish threat had disappeared after the fall of Dunluce. Impressed by Perrott's expedition, several important Irish chiefs submitted at Newry. But had the Lord Deputy's letter relayed the truth, London would have been alarmed at the likelihood of further Scottish resistance. Sorley's forty-man garrison had been his only force engaged in combat against Perrott. His followers safe in Glenconkine, his *creaghts* still numerous, and his recruiting efforts in Kintyre and Islay paying quick dividends, Sorley still threatened the English in Ulster. Perrott's boast that the north was quiet and that he would shortly invade the southern Hebrides obscured the true situation in autumn 1584.[12]

After returning to Dublin, Perrott sowed discord within the Dunyveg branch of Clan Ian Mor by setting up Donnell Gorme, Angus's younger brother and Sorley's nephew, in the Glynnes. The Lord Deputy correctly assumed that there had been bad blood between Donnell Gorme and Angus. Immediately after the fall of Dunluce, therefore, Perrott granted Donnell Gorme the Glynnes in return for his agreement to supply eighty foot at Dublin's request, to pay an annual rent of sixty cattle, and to serve loyally against Sorley and other Scots in Ireland.[13] Donnell Gorme's pledge and the subsequent submission of several Ulster Irish chiefs appeared to bolster England's position against the MacDonnells. But Perrott had deceived himself concerning the present situation in Ulster. Indeed, his all-important plans to divide the house of Dunyveg developed very differently from what he had intended.[14]

Donnell Gorme did not take the pact with Perrott seriously, for it came to nothing. Sorley Boy, who used the respite to recruit in the western Highlands and Isles, was the sole beneficiary of the negotiations. By now English officials knew that talk would not prevent Sorley from returning in strength to the Glynnes and the Route. Because Perrott's invasion had failed to dislodge the Antrim MacDonnells, Sorley's task was simple. He would bide his time until the right moment for a counter-invasion of the north coast. The Lord Deputy's arrangements for the governance of Ulster through Donnell Gorme in the Glynnes, Turlough Luineach and Dungannon in Tyrone, and Sir Henry Bagenal at Newry fell apart at the first signs of Sorley's opposition.[15]

Sorley Boy had been caught off-guard in September and October 1584. But from November through February 1585, the wily old warrior displayed a master's touch in marshaling and directing his forces against Perrott. Sorley was wise to retreat into Glenconkine, because the English dared not follow into such a remote fastness. Norris and Dungannon crossed west of the Bann in October, but they could only harass the local populace. Nonetheless, Perrott boasted that the elusive Sorley Boy would be forced to flee to Scotland if indeed he could escape from Ulster. Perrott dispersed troops in various garrisons along the North Antrim coast but failed to contain his chief adversary.[16]

Perrott committed a cardinal military blunder: he underestimated the enemy. The Lord Deputy's report in late October that his subordinates had successfully assaulted Sorley in Glenconkine was pure fabrication. It is curious that after such "success" Perrott would find it necessary to petition London for a huge funding increase to establish a permanent garrison of 2,500 regulars. He also requested a continued naval presence in the North Channel. These safeguards seem a bit much considering Perrott's boast that Sorley had been for ever banished from Ulster. Norris, much closer to the action, displayed a keener judgment when he confessed to Burghley in mid-October that war with Sorley Boy had only just begun.[17]

England's Ulster policy began deteriorating in late October when Sorley, who actually had had little trouble in leaving Ireland, returned from Scotland. Perrott's northern garrisons were in grave danger. Captain Christopher Carlyle at Coleraine informed his father-in-law Walsingham that the garrison there could not hold out once Sorley returned in strength to the Route. Perrott learned that Donnell Gorme was not only disloyal but actively hostile to England. After he joined his uncle Sorley, the two Scots began to reclaim the Glynnes and the Route.[18] Perrott refused to admit the obvious–that Sorley, far from being suppressed, was preparing a full-scale invasion of Ulster. Instead, he continued his prattle:

> I have so abated the courage of the Scot, that I believe well he will have small list to return again awhile, I have put such a pique between him and the natives of that country, as they will not willingly bear his yoke any more, and in respect thereof the rather have excepted the defence of Englishmen. . . . [T]he next summer, if I may have maintenance, pinnaces . . . and a warrant to visit the Out Isles (if I see cause), I hope with God's assistance to establish this that is begun with the paring off of some Scots' heads.[19]

Perrott's optimism was unfounded and probably arose from the heady experience of sacking Dunluce and from the need to justify the expenditure of the queen's monies on an expedition that lacked firm support. The Lord Deputy made quite a show of forwarding to London some of the Scot's personal belongings, including "Holy Columkill's cross, a god of great veneration with Surle Boy. . . ."[20] But Perrott's words and deeds were mere theatrics. His subterfuge was revealed in a letter from an

English field officer to Burghley in late October that contradicted the Lord Deputy's assertion that most of the native Irish opposed Sorley. Sir Edward Waterhouse, an experienced hand at Irish affairs and an enthusiastic promoter of colonization, advocated the deployment of 1,100 regular troops in Ulster and the establishment of a naval presence on the inland waters of loughs Neagh and Erne to keep the Scots already in Ulster at bay. Obviously, then, Perrott's subordinates did not share his rosy view of the situation.[21]

The destruction of the MacDonnell redshank army was the only thing that could have justified Perrott's optimism, but that had not been accomplished. The scattered English garrisons–Coleraine, Dunluce, and Dunanynie, among others–were numerically weak and incapable of mutual support. The same strategy–a war of isolated wilderness posts–would plague Elizabeth's lieutenants in the war against Hugh O'Neill in the 1590s. Then, only Mountjoy's policy of destroying enemy armies and their logistical bases saved the queen from inglorious defeat in Ulster.[22] But neither Perrott nor his lieutenants were of Mountjoy's caliber. Despite his superficial accomplishments, mainly wresting Dunluce from its forty-man garrison and haphazardly destroying some MacDonnell cattle, the Lord Deputy received the queen's congratulations for a job well done.[23]

Perrott was not a skilled military leader, but he did possess a dogged determination, several capable subordinates, and a formidable army. Even after considering the Lord Deputy's strengths, it is difficult to understand why Sorley Boy allowed himself to be caught unawares. But for all their advantages at the opening of the campaign, the English were unable to determine Sorley's whereabouts. He easily eluded Perrott's ground forces and her majesty's naval vessels patrolling the North Channel. Thus MacDonnell could choose the time and place of his counter-attack, a blow that almost everyone, English and Irish alike, expected at any moment.

Sorley's return to Ulster in mid-November raised several salient questions for the English. First, to what degree did Argyll's recent death change the *loci* of power in the western Highlands and Isles? Rumor circulated that the southern Hebrides had fallen under control of Angus MacDonnell and the MacLeans of Duart. Second, would Donnell Gorme oppose Sorley's possession of the northern third of the Antrim Glynnes? He did not, rather subordinating himself to his uncle's direction. And third, what role had James VI of Scotland played in Sorley's invasion? James denied complicity and later seemed anxious to demonstrate his loyalty to Elizabeth by impeding the flow of redshanks to Ireland.[24] For now, however, Sorley enjoyed a secure eastern flank and virtually free access to Kintyre and Islay.

Realizing that Sorley Boy, Angus, and Donnell Gorme stood poised for an offensive in mid-November, Sir Henry Bagenal tried to seize the initiative by attacking first. At Newry, Bagenal combined 500 foot and 100 horse drawn from the Coleraine and Carrickfergus garrisons with a comparable number of his own troops and marched into the Glynnes toward Red Bay. There his column was attacked by a band of Donnell Gorme's Scots.[25] The ensuing combat was described to Walsingham by an English observer, Martin Couche:

> as soon as we entered the said Glynnes the enemy being some 260 bow-men . . . charged the rearward of our battle very hotly, whereupon the skirmish was very sharp. The . . . skirmish continued for . . . one half hour . . . wherein was slain of our company of English five or six and wounded besides one hundred and upward insomuch we were enforced . . . to retire shamefully, and the said Scots pursuing us very desperately [to] . . . within one . . . mile of Red Bay.[26]

Captain Nicholas Dawtrey described the encounter as "a very sharp conflict as ever I was in for so short a time, although I have been in some." The English claimed to have killed forty Scots and wounded about twenty-five others. That the English were forced to "retire shamefully" could only have meant that Donnell Gorme won this initial skirmish.[27]

Perrott's problems were further compounded after Bagenal's setback by news that Sorley Boy and Angus were on their way from Kintyre with more redshanks. There apparently had been plans afoot to assassinate Sorley, but, according to Dawtrey, he was untouchable. MacDonnell being on the warpath, Elizabeth sent Perrott one of England's best field officers, Sir William Stanley. Bagenal and Stanley joined at Glenarm on 30 December to oppose the MacDonnell redshank army headed for the northern Glynnes and the Route. After Stanley's supplies were shipped off to Dunanynie, he and Bagenal marched under cover of darkness up the banks of the Bann and into the Route. This stratagem had not fooled Donnell Gorme, who shadowed the English columns. Stanley and Bagenal engaged him in a sharp but inconclusive skirmish in early January near Bunnamairge Friary. Thereafter, Bagenal returned to Dunanynie, while Stanley reconnoitered toward Cushendun, drawn there by reports of Scottish galleys on the horizon.[28]

Sorley's and Angus's sudden landing at Cushendun with 2,000 troops on 5 January split Bagenal from Stanley. Sensing danger, Bagenal headed south for Carrickfergus, which he feared would be Sorley's main objective. Abandonment of the Route was a bitter pill for Bagenal to swallow. He believed the Scots "came . . . in high time, for I would have had no doubt but (by our plot) in one month we had banished them from their glens, but now I hear that many horsemen of the Route and O'Cahan's country are come to Sorley."[29] Meanwhile, Stanley, who had fallen back from Cushendun to near Ballycastle, bore the full brunt of Sorley's wrath. The Scots wasted no time in moving directly from the coast to attack Stanley's camp.[30] The English waited at Bunnamairge Friary with two companies of

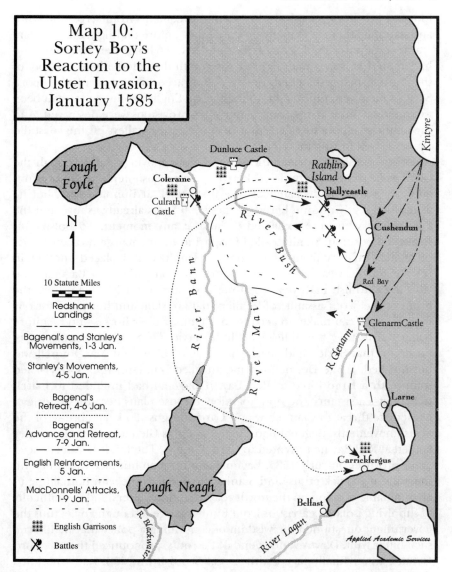

Map 10:
Sorley Boy's
Reaction to the
Ulster Invasion,
January 1585

Lough
Foyle

N

10 Statute Miles

Redshank
Landings

Bagenal's and Stanley's
Movements, 1-3 Jan.

Stanley's Movements,
4-5 Jan.

Bagenal's
Retreat, 4-6 Jan.

Bagenal's
Advance and Retreat,
7-9 Jan.

English Reinforcements,
5 Jan.

MacDonnells' Attacks,
1-9 Jan.

English Garrisons

Battles

Dunluce Castle

Coleraine

Culrath
Castle

River Bann

River Bush

River Main

Lough Neagh

R. Blackwater

Rathlin
Island

Ballycastle

Cushendun

Red Bay

R. Glenarm

GlenarmCastle

Larne

Carrickfergus

Belfast

River Lagan

Kintyre

Applied Academic Services

foot and fifty horse. Stanley called in reinforcements from across the Bann and stationed them at Dunanynie Castle. Just before midnight on 5 January "came certain troops of Scots on foot, and about 6 horsemen with them who had upon their staves wads lighted, wherewith they suddenly set the roof of the church, being thatched, on fire." But, according to Stanley's report, Sorley's men were quickly put to flight. The English commander had been wounded by three arrows, and many of his provisions were destroyed. And the ominous silhouette of another fleet of Scottish galleys off the coast did not bode well for the morrow.[31]

Sorley's decision to clear the Route before moving south through the Glynnes threatened to undo all Perrott's accomplishments of the previous autumn. Stanley had beaten off the first attack at Bunnamairge, but he would be greatly outnumbered by the 2,000 Scots already ashore and the 2,500 more who were expected to land at any moment. To bolster his weakened position, Stanley called forward to Bunnamairge two companies of regular infantry from Coleraine and Dunluce and placed another in reserve on the west bank of the Bann. He complained to Bagenal that "this last skirmish hath weakened me and captain Carlyle [who bore the brunt of the Scots' assault] of 24 men that are slain and hurt; and for our horsemen we can make no account of them for their horses and furniture being burnt, they are able to do little service."[32] Stanley's report leaves no doubt that Sorley had struck him a hard blow. But MacDonnell was not finished. While Donnell Gorme attacked Bunnamairge, Sorley sailed south with a large force to Red Bay. If Bagenal had intended to march to Stanley's assistance, he now abandoned those plans because of Sorley's immediate threat to Clandeboy and Carrickfergus. To keep abreast of the Scots' movements, Bagenal had ranged as far as Glenarm, but once Sorley landed at Red Bay he retreated to Carrickfergus. The English indeed faced grave prospects in early 1585. Bagenal and his men huddled safely behind the walls of Carrickfergus, and Stanley, unable to unite with him, clung to an untenable position on the north coast. London understood the difficulty of supplying isolated garrisons from Bunnamairge to Lough Foyle; thus the government questioned the wisdom of continuing a policy that had borne such bitter fruit. Dawtrey, no friend of Perrott's, pronounced that the Lord Deputy, when finally faced with a real Scottish invasion, had "muddled the war."[33]

The cause of England's misery in Ulster in 1584–5 was twofold: 1) Sorley Boy's superb generalship and 2) Perrott's inexcusable lack of planning and foresight. After quickly recovering from the shock of Perrott's September assault, Sorley commenced a large-scale invasion in the dead of winter. Perrott himself had been caught unawares by this bold stroke. When Bagenal and Stanley were on the verge of linking their forces and sweeping across the north in early January, Sorley foiled their plan by landing between them at Cushendun. Thereupon, he charged Donnell

Gorme with driving Stanley from Ballycastle, while he himself landed at Red Bay and pushed Bagenal into Carrickfergus. This brilliant stratagem had been concluded in less than a week. Perrott and his lieutenants were left impotent, able only to complain to each other or to London in hopes that the queen could be persuaded to throw good money after bad. One thing was certain, however: Sorley had regained the initiative and was well placed to continue his offensive with support from both Donnell Gorme and Angus MacDonnell.[34]

His enemies scotched at every turn, and most of the Route and the Glynnes in his *de facto* control, Sorley Boy now offered to negotiate for *de jure* possession of his territories. On 5 February he wrote Perrott, offering to take peaceful possession of the Route and the northern third of the Glynnes (the southern two-thirds going to Donnell Gorme) in return for his humble submission to the queen. Sorley also pledged to provide a yearly rent and eighty foot and twenty horse at his own expense for the queen's service in Ulster. Writing on the same day from his camp in the Route, Sorley asked Captain Carlyle to inform Perrott of his desire to regain possession of the castles, residences, and towns taken from him. But Sorley warned that he would brook no interference from any native Irish chief employed against him by England. To show his goodwill, MacDonnell promised the English and his MacQuillin adversaries safe passage through his lands and offered one of his sons as a pledge to be held by Dungannon or a trustworthy English official.[35]

Sorley doubtless believed himself in an advantageous position to negotiate with Elizabeth's government. He had solidified his position as the leader of Clan Ian Mor and was acknowledged by both Angus and Donnell Gorme. Both nephews played indispensable roles, Angus recruiting in Kintyre and Islay and Donnell Gorme holding the front-line position in the southern Glynnes, but Sorley was the undisputed focus of power within the family. This was not lost on the English. Her options limited, the queen was forced to turn again to James VI for a solution to the redshank problem. Perrott, anxious to deflect attention from his own poor performance, assured Walsingham that James might easily stop the flow of Scots mercenaries to Ireland if only London would pressure him. Responding, Walsingham wrote Perrott of the queen's intention to approach James about the matter. The Scottish king had for some time been suspect either of supporting or of turning a blind eye to MacDonnell actions in Ulster. James finally agreed in mid-February to demand that the Scots, especially Angus of Dunyveg, behave themselves. As a friendly gesture to Elizabeth, James despatched Sir Lewis Bellenden to London as his ambassador. But Bellenden was instructed to stop short of guaranteeing London that the MacDonnells would become obedient subjects, as the Stewarts' writ did not yet run in the Gaelic west.[36]

The year 1585 proved a strange one indeed for MacDonnell fortunes in both Ireland and Scotland. By mid-February Sorley and his nephews appeared to have England on the brink of defeat in Ulster; suddenly, however, things changed dramatically. Rumors abounded that the Scots would quit their offensive and retreat into the southern Isles. Angus began withdrawing his troops toward the Antrim coast late in the month, and by early March he had sailed for Scotland. Meanwhile, Sorley and Donnell Gorme found themselves on the defensive. Turlough Luineach strung out his troops along the western bank of the Bann to keep the Scots out of Tyrone. Because their western flank was secure, the English sent a force under Captain Edward Barkley into the southern Glynnes. Sorley and his *creaghts* retreated to Castle Toome, only to find passage over the Bann blocked by Turlough. Pressing his advantage, Barkley moved north and preyed on Donnell Gorme, who also was taken by surprise. On the following day, Bagenal joined Barkley, and the two continued to harass the retreating Scots. Barkley learned from a woman among the stragglers that Sorley "means not to fight with us. . . ." As the English pursued toward the north coast, Barkley was convinced that 300 foot and 50 horse stationed in Ulster would force Sorley to "yield unto any thing that your Lordship [i.e. Perrott] will set down. . . ."[37]

Angus already in Scotland and Sorley and Donnell Gorme in full retreat, the MacDonnells' hold on the Glynnes and the Route suddenly was in jeopardy. On 7 March Sir Geoffrey Fenton relayed the news to Walsingham that the Scots "are now so scattered, that the most part are returned to Kintyre with Angus MacDonnell, and the residue that remain with Sorley Boy and Donnell Gorme, are so curbed and weakened by the garrisons, as the power to do further harm is taken from them. . . ." Fenton, however, cautioned against complacency. He believed that a renewed Scottish invasion could be best prevented by distributing

> by way of pension some few crowns amongst the chieftains of Kintyre, who being now in faction amongst themselves, the opportunity serveth aptly for one side to be assured to Her Majesty. If they might . . . be continued in division . . . I see not how the disturbance of Ulster should receive further life or spirit from the Scots. . . .[38]

On 22 March Perrott learned that Sorley and Donnell Gorme had taken ship for Scotland. Bagenal, Barkley, and Stanley (who had recovered from his wounds) installed a garrison on Rathlin. England's position at Dunanynie was strengthened and the remaining Scottish possessions in the Route were laid waste. Only Sorley's son Alexander and 120 redshanks stayed behind to oversee the family's lands and monitor English activities.[39]

Why this dramatic turn of events in Ulster in spring 1585? The MacDonnells were worried about James VI's entente with London, and it is reasonable to assume that their departure, in part, reflected that concern. Sorley, moreover, knew that several of the western clans–particularly the Campbells and MacLeans–might be receptive to an official anti-MacDonnell policy in the Hebrides. But Sorley Boy was also aware of Perrott's stormy relations with the queen. The Lord Deputy, after all, had borne sharp criticism for overestimating the Scottish threat. If the Scots left now, Perrott would have no justification for continuing a strong military presence in Ulster. Why, then, had Sorley launched an "invasion" in the winter of 1584–5 in the first place? Because he enjoyed the interior lines of communication and a simple logistical system, did Sorley wish to test Perrott's readiness and response and to demonstrate MacDonnell resilience to the Ulster Gaels? Or by withdrawing so suddenly did he hope to convince Elizabeth that Perrott indeed had made too much of the Scottish danger? Both reasons seem plausible.

Whatever the reasons for the MacDonnells' sudden departure from Ireland, their flight precipitated some salient changes in England's Ulster policy. Elizabeth had been quick to charge Perrott with overstating the Scottish threat.[40] When it was reported to Burghley in early April that the Scots were gone for good, "their hearts . . . broken, their goods preyed, and they shroud[ing] themselves in secret corners. . . ," the accusations against the Lord Deputy seemed credible.[41] After receiving reports that scattered pockets of MacDonnell resistance were being mopped up, the queen instructed Perrott to halt all military operations in Ulster.[42]

Elizabeth apparently believed that James VI had succeeded in halting the flow of redshanks to Ireland, and she urged him, for obvious reasons, to restrain Argyll and MacLean of Duart from interfering in Irish affairs. London now moved quickly to take advantage of a perceived weak point in the MacDonnells' position. Rather than bear the expense of keeping an English army in the field or risk furthering Argyll's and MacLean's aggrandizement in Ulster, Elizabeth preferred to pit one MacDonnell against another. Thus Angus was to be set at odds with Sorley and Donnell Gorme over royal recognition to the Glynnes. If the plan was to succeed, James VI would have to be trusted to play a central role in prying Angus away from his uncle and brother. The Scottish king summoned Angus and his mother, Lady Agnes, to court in late April. There the hereditary lord of Dunyveg received the king's protection. The central question now, however, turned on whether James would play his own hand or London's.[43]

Edinburgh continued to take a pro-English line, Angus promised to keep undesirable Scots from Ulster, and Turlough and many of the Irish chiefs stayed under English control, but the intractable problem of Sorley Boy's unresolved Irish claims remained. Until it was solved, little else mattered in England's attempt to pacify northern Ireland. In early August Sorley's redshanks began returning to Ulster. That the Antrim MacDonnells would absent themselves from March through July, the better part of the traditional campaigning season, suggests that they wished to again test England's resolve during a cold-weather campaign. As the MacDonnells returned to Ulster, Captain Nicholas Dawtrey, Perrott's agent in Edinburgh, reported that James VI's pro-English policy had been subverted. Dawtrey thought that the culprit was James Stewart, earl of Arran, who, in truth, had himself been double-crossed by London. Arran was charged with having conspired with Sorley and Angus MacDonnell. The king's and Argyll's positions on the issue, however, remained ambiguous.[44]

Disregarding support or opposition from the principal Scottish players, the dauntless Sorley quickly made his presence felt in Ulster. On 2 August he engaged the English in a sharp skirmish in Clandeboy. Sorley hurriedly brought together his Irish allies, including the MacNeills of Clandeboy (who had a history of preying on Carrickfergus), the O'Kellys, and the sons of Hugh MacFelim O'Neill, among others. Amid these ominous developments, Perrott had arranged a parley with Angus and Lady Agnes at Newry on 10 August concerning possession of the Glynnes. As if to reassure the Lord Deputy, James VI promised tó declare both Sorley and Angus traitors if they persisted in their invasion. James also considered granting a royal commission to Argyll to prosecute the MacDonnells. But for now, Angus would be no threat to Perrott. He did not appear at Newry, having been delayed by the renewal of the MacDonnell–MacLean feud over Islay.[45]

Sorley's invasion of Ulster in August 1585 prompted several members of the Dublin council to charge Perrott with incompetence. He had failed to banish the Scots, and the council hoped that the Lord Deputy might be persuaded to await a more propitious opportunity for renewing military action.[46] Returning from Edinburgh, Dawtrey lent support to the council's anti-Perrott faction:

> Notwithstanding the King's promise for the restraint of the Islanders your Lordship shall understand that there is 1500 of them passed into Ireland and hath done many great outrages and as I am informed whether by negligence of those that had the charge of the garrison at Carrickfergus (or otherwise) our men hath caught copper [had a difficult time] at their hands.[47]

James VI had promised to command the MacDonnells to return to Scotland, but English officials now understood that he had virtually no power over Sorley Boy. Sir Edward Wotton, an English agent in Scotland, informed Walsingham in late August that though he believed James sincere, "yet I cannot promise unto your honour that his letter [to the MacDonnells] will work the desired effect." Wotton was convinced that the Gaelic Scots cared "but little for the King, and will obey him at their own pleasure." He advocated employing the MacLeans against the MacDonnells. MacLean of

Duart, as Elizabeth's pensioner, "would be ready at all times, whensoever either Angus or Sorley should start into Ireland, to spoil and burn their countries. . . ."[48] England did not implement this plan in 1585, but London surely grabbed the MacDonnells' attention.

From August to November Sorley regained the initiative he had lost the previous spring. Though Angus's attention was drawn to the MacLean feud in Islay, the MacDonnells were able to sue for peace in Ulster under favorable terms. Walsingham, despite Wotton's insistence that London hire 2,500 MacLean redshanks, favored an agreement with Sorley before he overran the entire province. Fenton pleaded with Burghley that Sorley be placated by a grant of most of the Route. The English finally were forced to admit that their affairs in the north were in disarray.[49]

England was threatened in Ulster by the declining state of her Irish army and by persistent rumors of a Spanish invasion. Wotton informed Walsingham that Philip II's agents had already landed in the island. Moreover, Elizabeth had committed most of her first-rate officers and troops to the campaign in the Netherlands and had few to spare for Ireland. The army in the Low Countries enjoyed first call on victuals and clothing, two items of grave concern in Ireland with the approach of cold, wet weather. Through these difficulties, Perrott continued to make light of the Scots' landing, vowing to deal sternly with both Sorley and Angus at the appropriate time. But the queen grasped the gravity of the Ulster predicament, as is evinced by her controversial decision to create Hugh O'Neill, baron of Dungannon, second earl of Tyrone in 1585. She knew his loyalty would be critical in preserving England's presence in Ulster. Meanwhile, the decision not to employ the MacLeans in the Hebrides allowed Angus to recruit there with impunity. Wotton persisted in championing the MacLeans and informed Walsingham at the end of September that their chief had offered the queen his services in either Scotland or Ireland for the sum of £200 per annum. But to no avail. Nor was active resistance to the MacDonnells expected from James VI, even though Arran's fall in late October had removed the king from what London considered evil counsel. It appeared, then, that Scotland was descending into chaos at the end of 1585.[50]

Perrott being deprived of the proper means to resist Scottish inroads in Ulster, Sorley recaptured Dunluce Castle in early November. The constable and most of the garrison were slain. Captain Rich's company suffered a similar fate in O'Cahan's country. Amid this debacle, the Lord Deputy could only call for more troops and more money, a commitment Elizabeth was not prepared to make. As Perrott could not guarantee Ulster's security, English officials in Dublin and London saw no alternative to negotiating with Sorley Boy over his claim to the Glynnes and the Route.[51]

Sorley Boy finally received royal recognition of his long-standing claim to the Route in 1586. This grant, along with Angus MacDonnell's of the

Glynnes, was the culmination of a struggle that spanned four decades in which Sorley had fought tenaciously to hold the traditional MacDonnell lands in northeastern Ulster. English officers admitted the futility of trying any longer to subjugate Antrim, described as "the fastest and safest ground of Ireland." A report to Elizabeth revealed that none of the "disordered persons" of that region "were sure longer than her Majesty's forces contain them in obedience."[52] By early 1586, then, the queen was no longer motivated to contest the territory that Sir Henry Bagenal described as "a pleasant and fertile country. . . ."[53]

Perrott, his reputation already tarnished by the loss of Dunluce and his general ineffectiveness against the Scots, tried to redeem himself by setting Sorley and Angus against one another.[54] He had boasted to Walsingham the previous Christmas Eve: "I cast a bone a quarter of a year ago between Angus MacDonnell and Sorley Boy. I hear it hath wrought the effect I desired, and that Angus hath both taken him prisoner, and also intendeth to bring him shortly over to be delivered to me."[55] This outrageous claim was patently false and could have come only from a severely deluded mind. But Perrott realized that Clan Ian Mor's armor had a weak point–the southern Hebrides. In lieu of formulating discord between Sorley and Angus, Bagenal and Fenton advocated pensioning Archibald Campbell, seventh earl of Argyll, and Lachlan MacLean of Duart to serve against the MacDonnells.[56]

The deplorable state of the English army in Ulster in the winter of 1585–6 made difficult any sort of military action. A feeble sally by the Carrickfergus garrison against Alexander MacSorley, Sorley Boy's son, in Clandeboy drove home this point. There is no doubt that Sorley could have wreaked havoc against the English had he been so inclined. But by February he was already considering submission to Dublin. Consequently, the queen, anxious to be rid of the Scottish problem once and for all, circumvented Perrott and went directly to his council with instructions that a composition also be reached with Angus.[57] Fenton believed that "It will be needful that her Majesty do out of hand think of another choice [for Lord Deputy] thereby to stop the evils that are wont to ensue. . . ."[58] The very evils which Fenton feared had already materialized in late February. While Perrott had no idea of Angus's whereabouts, Captain John Price informed Walsingham on the 28th that the Dunyveg chief was about to land in Ireland with 2,000 redshanks. He also noted: "Sorley Boy and his son [i.e. Alexander MacSorley] I found [had] given their words to come in to the Lord Deputy but they say no they will not. . . ."[59]

Perrott's fortunes were declining until an English encounter with Alexander MacSorley presented an opportunity for him to mend his shattered reputation. But the subsequent killing of Alexander was a shameful spectacle and not the sort of deed to ennoble the perpetrators. In mid-March 500 Scots under Alexander and his cousin, MacDonnell Ballagh, were surprised in Tyrconnell by a comparable English force under a Captain Merriman.[60] Using his wits, Alexander,

> a lusty and tall young man, came in the head of his troops, and called for Captain Merriman with a loud voice: challenging him to come forth and fight singly. To whom a gallowglass (serving with the English and near at hand) made answer he was the man. They joined, and at the first the gallowglass struck a fierce blow at Alexander with his . . . axe . . . with which he drove the other's target [i.e. shield] unto his head, and had well near felled him to the ground. But Alexander, recovering himself, got within the gallowglasses' ward, and with his sword cleft him into the head, so leaving him for dead. . . . Captain Merriman (who was not far off), ran into Alexander; they both interconnected with sword and target. After the exchange of some few blows the captain cut Alexander over the leg; who, feeling himself hurt and not well able to stand, withdrew and was carried from his company. They, missing their captain, began to shift for themselves. When they were overthrown . . . Merriman made search for Alexander amongst the hurt men, knowing he was not able to go far. At length . . . he was found by the turning up of some turfs. . . . They struck off his head and sent it unto the Lord Deputy, who caused it to be set upon a pole in the castle of Dublin.[61]

Alexander MacSorley's death, so wrote Perrott, "hath greatly appalled Sorley and other ill disposed of this realm, for this eldest son of his was his only right arm." The young MacDonnell was described as "well akined and allied in Scotland, . . . withal as valiant . . . a fellow as was amongst all the Scots, [and] was the best killed man since Shane O'Neill."[62] The Lord Deputy's spirits were buoyed by this prize trophy. Fenton observed in mid-April that Perrott complained that "if he might have been suffered to prosecute them [i.e. the Scots] still with hostility, he would in short time have brought them to reason and ended that work with more honourable condition than now he can." But such optimistic reports had little basis in truth.[63] Sorley had lost his favourite son, but he and Angus still enjoyed a strong position from which to bargain with the queen.

Sorley, who had seen his wife Mary (daughter of Con Bacagh O'Neill), brothers, a son and several nephews go to the grave before him, was weary of the carnage and preferred to negotiate rather than fight from his strong position. In mid-April he wrote "an humble letter to the Lord Deputy not only for protection and to come to his Lordship to sue for it upon his knees as becometh an offender, but also to submit himself to such conditions as shall be imposed upon him." Fenton believed that Perrott would accept Sorley's offer because the MacDonnell leader was "now reduced to weakness and want of all things which in other times . . . he . . . had used."[64] But Fenton's and Archbishop Adam Loftus's belief that Sorley would prostrate himself before the Lord Deputy in Dublin was not mirrored by Wallop, who informed London that he doubted the Scot's word. He warned London that any articles to which the MacDonnells agreed, "they will not perform any length [other] than force shall make them."[65]

It is understandable why some members of the Irish council took a pessimistic view of Sorley's offer of submission. Wallop, for instance, believed that the only way Sorley and Angus could be brought to submit was through an English military buildup in Ulster. Loftus spoke for the more optimistic council members when he pronounced it likely that Sorley could be persuaded by Captain William Warren (who had conferred with the MacDonnell leader on several occasions) to come to Dublin.[66] But by early May Wallop's hard-line view appeared to have been confirmed by a report from Sir Edward Moore of Mellifont, a well-connected English captain, and the earl of Tyrone:

> We among others were used to deal with Sorley Boy MacDonnell to draw him to reasonable conformity and wishing him well so far . . . as he would show himself by duty to deserve. . . . But he most obstinately refusing all obedience and conformity, burst out into most despiteful . . . words which we then durst not utter for fear of increasing his Lordship [i.e. Perrott] too afar against him. Those speeches he used were these in effect and almost in word, viz. that he never hither came in to any Deputy, not so much as to the earl of Sussex, which was this man's better, and therefore he would not come in to him except he might have the earl of Ormond and some others of good account to be pledged for him. . . .[67]

Loftus, then, admitted the obvious when he told Burghley that Sorley, "notwithstanding his fair promises, faineth an excuse and deferreth his coming to my Lord Deputy, and it is now conceived that he will not come."[68]

Despite the difficulties in bringing Sorley Boy to submit, Perrott and the council arranged a deal with Angus MacDonnell (through Lady Agnes) on 16 May. Dunyveg would receive a grant to the Antrim Glynnes in return for his loyalty and service and a yearly rent to the queen. Only if Scotland and England went to war would Angus be exempted from his obligations. Now that one MacDonnell had come around, Perrott was confident that the other would submit shortly. By month's end even Wallop had changed his view of the situation.[69] Sorley Boy's health apparently was failing, and he believed he could no longer delay his submission. He preferred to bargain from a position of strength, and rumors of his declining condition would work against him. In late May Perrott wrote Elizabeth that Sorley "hath had incisions made in his forehead for the recovery of his sight which he hath almost lost, so as he was unable to travel. . . ." So anxious was the MacDonnell chief to get to Dublin that "he hath offered to be brought in a litter."[70]

206

It is unclear whether Angus's promise to submit forced Sorley's hand or whether the elder MacDonnell realized that at his age time was no longer an ally. In any case, the English were confident enough of Sorley's imminent submission to draft a set of instructions for the commissioners who would treat with him. It was revealed in these instructions that the queen intended to grant the Route to Sorley Boy while permitting him to hold part of the Glynnes with Angus's approval. But the commissioners were warned that if they "cannot drive him unto a deeper rent yearly, they shall do their best endeavours, taking from him the best pledges that might be gotten for the performance of the same."[71] The entire scheme had to be delicately balanced if it was to succeed.

Despite Sorley's age and obvious desire to reach an accord, some English officials still were not convinced of his sincerity. Fenton's optimism had faded, as he opined that Sorley's "coming is interrupted by some under-hand practice. . . ." Fenton also exhibited a deep-seated fear that the Scots might employ their military strength in lieu of negotiation: "It cannot be without suspicion of bad intention to stir some altercation in the north this summer if in the meanwhile he [i.e. Sorley] be not tempered withal by good means."[72] Showing the same caution, Sir Henry Bagenal advocated "that the Scots [should] be received into peace and . . . the lands they have usurped be divided . . . to them for rents. . . ."[73] The elder Bagenal informed Burghley on 9 June that the subjugated Irish chiefs wished to "shake off all English government. . . ." Moreover, he confirmed Donnell Gorme's recent landing in the Route with 300–400 redshanks, the subsequent spoiling of MacQuillin, and the more alarming prospect of Scots being drawn into Tyrconnell by Ineen Dubh O'Donnell. Perrott paid scant heed to these reports and seemed disgusted by the timorousness of his lieutenants.[74] He expected his MacDonnell nemesis in Dublin any day now.

Sorley Boy submitted to the queen's deputy in Dublin in June 1586. The English doubtless were relieved that he had finally come in, as they were in no position to force his hand. When the old man entered the city, he was greeted by the grim visage of Alexander MacSorley, whose head graced the walls of Dublin Castle. The story goes that Sorley reacted stoically to the grisly spectacle, remarking confidently that "my son hath many heads. . . ."[75] On 14 June Fenton reported to Burghley that Sorley Boy "is now come hither under protection, and having by public submission in writing acknowledged his disobedience, he seemeth likewise by words and speeches to make himself unworthy of all favour and forgiveness other than in such measure as it may please her Majesty. . . ."[76] The tenor of Sorley's submission is captured in a contrived letter presented to Perrott on 14 June. Sorley asked forgiveness for his numerous transgressions, cheerfully giving the lie of "being a man born out of this realm. . . ."[77] That he would utter, and the English accept, such a blatant falsehood points up the absurdity of the entire ceremony. Anxious to give a good performance, however, Sorley Boy did not stop with mere words. Rather he entered the cathedral and "there threw his sword down before your Majesty's picture, kissed the . . . same, [and] swore his allegiance to your Highness. . . ."[78] But Fenton cautioned that the sagacious warrior-statesman would demand reciprocity for his act: "Yet could he not omit to prefer demands for a great portion of the Route to be granted to him and his heirs male and looketh that it should be perfected to him presently, together with his pardon and a patent of denization." This led to the rather thorny problem of a counter-claim by Rory MacQuillin, who "opposeth himself against . . . [MacDonnell's] demand . . . , alleging that . . . Sorley . . . hath of long time disturbed his right by an injurious usurpation."[79]

Sorley and Perrott concluded a formal indenture on 18 June. The MacDonnell leader received a patent of denization, a royal pardon, the territories between the rivers Bush and Bann, the "toughs" (or *tuatha*) of Dunseverick, Loughgill, and Ballymonyre, and the constableship of Dunluce Castle. In return, he agreed to be a loyal subject, to assume responsibility for the behavior of his followers, to provide a rising out of twelve horse and forty foot, to pay an annual rent of fifty cattle, to oppose any rebellion or foreign invasion, and to refrain from subletting his lands without permission, among other things.[80] On the same day, the Route was formally divided between Sorley and MacQuillin, the former receiving "the best part" of the area. Rory MacQuillin, wrote Fenton, "showeth great discontentment therewith and is not as yet brought to allow of such partition. . . ."[81]

The agreements made in Dublin in 1586 were major pieces of diplomacy for both Clan Ian Mor and the English government. Besides the Irish indentures, Elizabeth concluded a defensive alliance–the Treaty of Berwick–with James VI in July.[82] England expected the Scottish king to restrict further passage of redshanks to Ulster, thus ensuring peace in that disturbed province. But Angus was in a somewhat less than conciliatory mood. It was not he, but his mother, who had actively sought the agreement with Perrott. Now that Angus faced a renewal of the MacLean feud, he might have pointed out that the English had done nothing to allay his fears that they might combine with the MacLeans against him.[83] Not surprisingly, then, Angus threatened the peace in summer 1586.

Angus MacDonnell gave every indication that he would not honor his indenture with Perrott. Whether Dunyveg was acting independently or under Sorley Boy's direction cannot be known. Sorley appeared satisfied with his own indenture, but England's decision to grant MacQuillin part of the Route must have cut him to the quick. It is curious that Angus, rumored in early July to be marshaling a formidable redshank army for Ulster, had already ventured far from the Glynnes and atttacked Sir John O'Dogherty in the Inishowen peninsula.[84] As the summer progressed,

Angus's intentions became clearer. Wallop reported on 12 August that Dunyveg still "hath not signified the acceptance of that agreement which his mother made in his name. . . ." More significantly, he "hath taken in hand MacQuillin . . . and killed sundry of his people very treacherously, by which I think he is assuredly practising some new mischief. . . ."[85] Indeed he was. Angus now commanded 1,400 Scots and had done his uncle Sorley a favor against Rory MacQuillin. But London received even more alarming news in mid-August. Angus had divided his army and despatched Donnell Gorme and fellow brother Alexander Carragh into Connacht to aid the rebellious MacWilliam Burkes. Angus himself returned to the Glynnes to store the plunder taken from O'Dogherty and MacQuillin.[86]

Angus being in the Glynnes and Sorley at his principal residence of Dunanynie Castle, the MacDonnell army met disastrous defeat at the hands of Sir Richard Bingham, governor of Connacht. The battle of Ardnary (23 September 1586) saw both Donnell Gorme and Alexander Carragh fall in one of the greatest overthrows the clan had ever suffered. Out of 2,300 troops, only one-quarter of whom were MacDonnell redshanks, more than half were lost.[87] A detailed description of the battle is beyond the scope of the present study; Ardnary, however, was a severe blow to MacDonnell prestige. But it did not negate the positive effects of Sorley Boy's and Angus's indentures to the Glynnes and the Route. For the elder MacDonnell, his lifelong struggle had finally ended.

Epilogue

The condition of man ... is a condition of war of everyone against everyone.

Thomas Hobbes, *Leviathan*

Sorley Boy's indenture with Lord Deputy Perrott in 1586 was a signal event in the history of the Antrim MacDonnells. For nearly a century Clan Ian Mor had struggled to extricate itself from the political turmoil in Scotland that followed the forfeiture of the lordship of the Isles. Central to this struggle was the establishment of a viable settlement beyond the reach of the political authority of the Scottish kings and their Campbell minions. By the late sixteenth century the family controlled both the Antrim Glynnes and the Route and had made some headway in re-establishing MacDonnell authority in the southwestern Highlands and Isles of Scotland. But Sorley's death in 1590 led to a split between the Antrim and Dunyveg branches of Clan Ian Mor. The next half-century would witness the deterioration of relations between the two branches. As a result of the family quarrel, the Dunyveg MacDonnells were virtually destroyed; however, the Antrim MacDonnells managed to weather several crises and play a prominent role in the War of the Three Kingdoms in the 1640s. The half-century between Sorley Boy's indenture in 1586 and the Antrim MacDonnells' adherence to the Royalist cause in the 1640s can be divided into three distict periods: 1) 1586 to the end of the Elizabethan era in 1603; 2) 1603 to the fall of the Dunyveg MacDonnells in 1615; and 3) 1615 to the landing of Alasdair MacColla's Irish army in the Scottish Highlands in mid-1644.

The first period is marked, of course, by the demise of Sorley Boy MacDonnell in early 1590. Not long thereafter, the emergence of a fateful breach between the Antrim and Dunyveg branches pointed up his most valuable contribution to Clan Ian Mor: the ability to keep the family united as a political and military force. A rupture within Clan Ian Mor had been avoided during Sorley's lifetime for two reasons: 1) his close relationship with his elder brother James MacDonnell, lord of Dunyveg and the Glynnes, and 2) his ability to dominate James's sons and their mother (Lady Agnes Campbell) after Dunyveg died in 1565. The 1586 indenture gave Sorley and his heirs title to most of the Route and part of the Glynnes. But there was no objection from Angus of Dunyveg. In fact, he sent a redshank army to wrest the remainder of the Route from the MacQuillins, thus giving the entire region to Sorley. That the Dunyveg branch of Clan Ian Mor did not protest the claims of the Antrim MacDonnells suggests Dunyveg's acknowledgment and acceptance of Sorley's leadership, not only in Ireland but Scotland as well. But the rift between the houses of Antrim and Dunyveg in the 1590s made it exceedingly difficult to keep open links between Ulster and the west of Scotland, thus inhibiting the all-important recruitment and transport of redshanks to Ireland. This situation obviously benefited the English in their attempts to subjugate Gaelic Ireland.

It still remained to be seen in the early 1590s what sort of relationship would develop between Sorley Boy's eldest surviving son and successor, James MacSorley (d. 1601), and Angus of Dunyveg. Since the early 1580s, Dunyveg's attention had been fixed on the MacDonnell–MacLean feud in the Hebrides. The resumption of that long-standing quarrel in 1581 had prompted James VI of Scotland finally to take a serious look at bringing the western Highlands and Isles under royal control. The king considered the western Gaels, especially the MacDonnells and their supporters, as barbarians "without any sort or show of civility."[1] In early 1588, James VI indeed seemed to be favoring a MacLean–Campbell combination against Clan Ian Mor. In response, Angus approached the English concerning a possible alliance against the king, the recent Treaty of Berwick notwithstanding. Because of festering Anglo-Spanish relations since 1584 and the problems that that situation posed in the Celtic fringe, Elizabeth could not dismiss Dunyveg's overtures out of hand. But as it turned out, there was to be no agreement between the MacDonnells and the English; London presumably thought it unwise to risk the ire of James VI. By the close of the year Clan Ian Mor was fortunate to be able to patch things up temporarily with the MacLeans, Sorley Boy and Angus having attended a so-called "parliament of peace" between concerned parties in the Isles.[2] This was to be old Sorley's last service for his family, as he died in late January or early February 1590.

Both the Dunyveg and Antrim branches of Clan Ian Mor were active in the affairs of Ulster in the early 1590s. The overriding political issue was the course of action that would be taken by the dynamic new chiefs of the Tyrone O'Neills and Tyrconnell O'Donnells.[3] In May 1593 Angus of Dunyveg met with James MacSorley to ascertain the current political situation in northern Ireland and how it might affect the clan. But before long the two MacDonnell chiefs were at odds. In early 1594 Angus sent his illegitimate son Ranald to Marshal Bagenal at Newry with a report that a large force of MacLean and Campbell redshanks would land at Lough Foyle and offer its services to Hugh Ruaidh O'Donnell and his allies, who included James MacSorley. Actually, Angus himself might have had a hand in raising these troops, as he had been discussing the employment of Scots mercenaries in Ulster with the O'Donnell chief for more than a year. For his part, MacSorley informed James VI that he would be willing to serve against Dunyveg. But neither the English nor the king of Scots proved willing to employ the MacDonnell chiefs at this point, even if they might be pitted one against the other. What shone clear in an otherwise muddled situation in mid-1594 is that the cooperation so carefully fostered by Sorley Boy between the two main branches of Clan Ian Mor had disappeared.[4]

Both Edinburgh and London had pressing problems in the mid-1590s that prevented them from taking full advantage of the discord between Angus of Dunyveg and James MacSorley. Though James VI's power and influence grew with his years on the throne, his realm was racked in the early 1590s by constant disorder throughout the western Highlands and Isles and political troubles within the influential families of Campbell and Huntly. For her part, Elizabeth faced the prospect of an Ulster rebellion fed by Spanish support. O'Donnell and a number of lesser chiefs had already taken up arms, and Hugh O'Neill, earl of Tyrone, was suspected of harboring sympathies for the rebels. Though there were obvious advantages for James VI and Elizabeth in widening the breach within Clan Ian Mor, neither monarch yet saw fit to deal directly with the MacDonnell chiefs.

The major issue within the Gaelic heartland centered on the flow of redshanks to Ireland. James VI presumably would have preferred that such troublesome men be as far from his kingdom as possible. Elizabeth surely desired that they remain in Scotland, far from the ranks of the upstart Ulster chiefs. Because many of the redshanks who made their way to Ireland were controlled by Clan Ian Mor, one might expect that both James VI and Elizabeth would have considered relations with Dunyveg and James MacSorley quite crucial. But the most important figure in the redshank trade was Archibald Campbell, the youthful seventh earl of Argyll.[5] On the one hand, if Argyll turned a blind eye to the mercenary traffic, there was virtually nothing that anyone could do to stop it, short of blockading the North Channel. But if Argyll decided to curtail the flow of redshanks, there were few men in the mid-1590s who could effectively challenge his authority. At this critical moment, O'Neill finally having thrown off his mask of loyalty to England, the Ulster chiefs needed military support from the Isles; but without Argyll's cooperation, Angus of Dunyveg and the others could not assure O'Neill and O'Donnell of a steady supply of troops. It is surely ironic that at the very moment when the O'Neills and O'Donnells had put aside their differences and made common cause against the Tudors, the situation in the Hebrides precluded the recruitment and transport of large numbers of redshanks to Ireland to assist them. Sorley Boy's demise had left the Islesmen and Ulster chiefs without an effective intermediary to coordinate the movement of Scottish troops to Ulster. Sorley's ability to control Angus of Dunyveg and to deal with the earls of Argyll and the MacLeans of Duart meant that the primary redshank recruiting grounds had been much more politically stable from 1560 to 1590 than they were at the time of the O'Neill–O'Donnell uprising.

The difficult position of the Dunyveg MacDonnells is demonstrated by the inability of Angus and Donald Gorme MacDonald of Sleat to mount an expedition to aid O'Neill and O'Donnell in 1595. Their fleet of galleys was intercepted by English patrol vessels off the coast of County Down. Driven ashore, Angus and Donald Gorme thus found themselves bottled up and forced to negotiate with the English. The Scottish chiefs did not hesitate to offer to employ their troops against the queen's Irish enemies. But Elizabeth did not trust Angus, and shortly, with her blessing, Argyll and MacLean moved to destroy the house of Dunyveg.[6] Indeed, Angus's conduct soon gave credence to the queen's opinion. In early autumn his son, Angus Oge, landed a 600-man force and joined O'Neill in an attack on the English near Newry. Fighting alongside O'Neill and Angus Oge was a body of redshanks sent by James MacSorley. Shortly after the attack, though, Angus Oge withdrew his men.[7] There are several possible explanations for this action: 1) that Angus of Dunyveg took seriously his pledge to aid the English; 2) that he wished to placate the queen in order that she might intercede on his behalf with Argyll and MacLean or with James VI; or 3) that he flatly refused to fight on the same side with his cousin, James MacSorley. In light of both Elizabeth's and James VI's preference for dealing with the Antrim rather than with the Dunyveg branch of Clan Ian Mor, it is unlikely that Angus expected much support from either London or Edinburgh. Having few options left, Dunyveg probably reasoned that he might be able to advance his own cause against James MacSorley in the Antrim Glynnes and the Route. G. A. Hayes-McCoy thinks that in the mid-1590s Angus had not yet lost his authority in Ireland to Sorley Boy's descendants.[8] Perhaps this assessment has some validity as long as James MacSorley headed the Antrim branch. But after his brother Ranald MacSorley, the future first earl of Antrim (1620), succeeded him in 1601, things began to change in favor of the Antrim MacDonnells.

While the Dunyveg MacDonnells found it increasingly difficult to influence affairs in northern Ireland, James MacSorley and his family were making trouble for the rebellious earl of Tyrone. MacSorley reiterated his pledge to serve the English against O'Neill and O'Donnell and claimed in late 1595 to have intercepted a shipment of munitions bound for Tyrone from Glasgow. In return for his support, James MacSorley hoped to free his younger brother Ranald from Dublin Castle and to receive recognition to the portion of the Route that remained in MacQuillin hands, but was now in danger of being snatched away by Tyrone. Not surprisingly, Angus of Dunyveg threw in his lot with the Irish rebels in spring 1596, informing Tyrone and O'Donnell that a redshank force was ready to set sail to assist them. Angus himself came to Ulster in June to confer with O'Neill and to reassert his claim to the Glynnes, where James MacSorley was threatening

213

to banish his remaining tenants. Dunyveg, though, found himself in a difficult position vis-à-vis the Ulster rebels, as Tyrone and MacSorley had recently come to an agreement and together persuaded the English to free Ranald MacSorley. Angus met O'Neill at Castle Roe, undoubtedly to discuss the prospect of his (Angus's) bringing over more redshanks. In return, Dunyveg probably requested Tyrone's help against the MacLeans and Campbells in the Isles.[9]

One need look no further than the period 1593–6 to discover the Machiavellian nature of Gaelic politics and diplomacy. During these three years the Dunyveg and Antrim MacDonnells had made "alliances" with both the English and the Irish rebels in Ulster. Such duplicity, of course, was not limited to Clan Ian Mor, as every major player in the archipelago resorted to such maneuverings. But the MacDonnells were particularly prone to such tactics. In the 1560s, it will be remembered, such ill-conceived diplomacy had prompted the short-lived Drum Cru alliance between Shane O'Neill and Elizabeth and the resulting disaster of Glentaisie. Only strong leadership from Colla and Sorley Boy had managed to put the family back on firm ground. Now, however, Clan Ian Mor lacked the requisite leadership to unify the two main branches and thus to overcome the disastrous consequences of political fragmentation.

Whitehall doubtless was dismayed by Tyrone's having conferred with both Angus of Dunyveg and James MacSorley. However, relations between the two MacDonnell chiefs were so strained that any sort of reconciliation leading to a united front with O'Neill and O'Donnell was unlikely. Angus of Dunyveg's attempt to hold his portion of the Glynnes was jeopardized by MacSorley, thus prompting Angus Oge's return to Scotland in summer 1596 to raise an army to retake the area. There were some doubts in English circles regarding the severity of the Antrim–Dunyveg breach. In fact, it was widely believed that Tyrone was behind the "quarrel," and that it was merely a stratagem designed to mask an O'Neill–O'Donnell–MacDonnell alliance to drive the English from Ulster.[10] The queen's government was mistaken, however. London's belief in a pan-Gaelic conspiracy was based on an inaccurate assessment of the degree of political unity extant, and possible, among the leading Irish and Scottish chiefs. That Tyrone and O'Donnell had overcome the traditional enmity between their families was remarkable enough; to have expected Clan Ian Mor at this point to put its own house in order and then to join the Irish rebels in a coordinated assault on English interests in Ireland bordered on pure fantasy.

Evidence of continued strain within Clan Ian Mor was revealed in an October 1596 letter from James MacSorley to James VI wherein the MacDonnell chief made an unsubstantiated charge that Angus of Dunyveg was illegitimate and thus had no legal claim to the family's Scottish lands. MacSorley undoubtedly hoped to take advantage of the king's anger against Dunyveg, who earlier in the year had refused to submit to James VI in response to a threatened expedition to the Isles. Indeed, Angus had visited Tyrone in hopes of gaining some advantage against the king. But the Scottish monarch was in no mood to entertain MacSorley and his wild charges against Dunyveg. However, this does not mean that James VI was unconcerned with Angus's, or for that matter, any recalcitrant chief's, behavior. In 1597 the Scottish parliament passed an act ordering all who claimed territory in the Highlands to produce title deeds on pain of forfeiture. Moreover, landowners were to pay all back-rents and taxes due the crown and vouch for the good behavior of their tenants. Edinburgh expected some chiefs to be unable to meet these requirements, thus making large tracts of land available to the crown. These forfeited lands then would be made over to subservient chiefs or planted with loyal Lowland colonists and thus "civilized."[11] The prospects of such legislation no doubt had made Sorley Boy anxious to secure a royal grant to the Glynnes and the Route. But now, Angus MacDonnell of Dunyveg seemed blind to the increased power of James VI in the western Highlands and Isles.

Angus of Dunyveg's refusal to submit to the king in 1596–7 was a foolhardy act, especially since the MacDonnell chief had no allies to turn to for support. Despite a temporary reconciliation with MacLean of Duart, that chief and Argyll still were very much his enemies. Tyrone and O'Donnell were in the midst of the most serious Irish uprising of the century and cared only for what they might get out of Dunyveg. And then there was his problem with James MacSorley's clan. As it turned out, Angus had nowhere to turn but to England, offering himself to Sir John Chichester, the new military governor at Carrickfergus.[12] Was his offer serious? Or was he merely buying time, waiting for a falling out between James MacSorley and Tyrone?

Dunyveg's offer to Chichester in all probability was not made in good faith. Nonetheless, his actions prompted James VI to begin negotiations with James MacSorley, whom the king saw as a more desirable tenant than Angus in Kintyre and Islay. London suspected that the Scottish king was meddling in Irish affairs; however, it appears that James VI was more concerned with displacing Dunyveg in favor of MacSorley than with aiding the rebellious Irish chiefs. It was not only the Scottish king who preferred dealing with the chief of the Antrim MacDonnells over Dunyveg; England did as well. In fact, London had proposed to set up James MacSorley in opposition to both Tyrone and Angus, but this plan had been shelved because of MacSorley's improved relations with James VI. Also, neither James nor Ranald MacSorley had lived up to the agreement made by their father Sorley in 1586. In late 1597 they abandoned all their castles barring Dunluce, where they concentrated their strength in advance of an apparent rapprochement with Tyrone and James VI.[13] A combination of the Irish chiefs, James VI, and the Antrim MacDonnells certainly would pose a considerable danger for the English in Ulster.

In early November 1597 a force of between 600 and 1,000 Antrim MacDonnells under James and Ranald MacSorley routed a comparable English contingent under Chichester just outside Carrickfergus. This defeat could hardly have come at a worse time for the English administration in Dublin. Tyrone's and O'Donnell's uprising was gathering steam, and any support by the MacDonnells in eastern Antrim and Down would draw precious forces away from the Blackwater–Erne line. It is impossible to determine whether the MacSorleys were acting in concert with Tyrone. Rumors abounded that James and Ranald had met with Tyrone a few days prior to the battle and that O'Neill had intimidated them into attacking Chichester. That the MacSorleys had been forced against their will to fight for Tyrone is unlikely. To alienate James MacSorley meant risking a valuable link between Tyrone and James VI and Scotland through which the O'Neill chief might secure redshanks. Shortly after the clash with Chichester, the Antrim chief went to Edinburgh to push his claim to Dunyveg lands in the western Highlands and Isles. Frustrated in his claim to Angus's territories, he was given a splendid sendoff by the king and left the royal presence as Sir James MacSorley MacDonnell of Dunluce.[14]

The rise of James MacSorley's star contrasted with the dark misfortune that befell Angus MacDonnell of Dunyveg in 1598. It is inscrutable why Dunyveg would continue to overlook the growth of royal authority in the Gaelic west. His eldest son and presumed heir, Sir James MacDonnell of Knockrinsay, who had been held hostage for several years in Edinburgh Castle, was allowed to travel to his father's house in Kintyre (near present-day Campbeltown) to warn him of the consequences of ignoring the king's writ. Once there, Knockrinsay set fire to his father's house, took him prisoner, and laid claim to the chiefship of the family. This audacious move resulted in an unfortunate sequence of events for the Dunyveg MacDonnells. Encouraged in particular by the fact that Knockrinsay's behavior put him in disfavor with James VI and in general by the confusion within Clan Ian Mor, Sir Lachlan Mor MacLean of Duart seized the opportunity to press his claim to the disputed Rhinns of Islay. After attempts to negotiate a settlement failed, the MacLeans suffered defeat at the battle of Loch Gruinart in August, losing Sir Lachlan in the action. To avenge his death, Hector MacLean put together a coalition that included MacLeod of Dunvegan, Cameron of Lochiel, MacNeill of Barra, and MacKinnon of MacKinnon, invaded Islay, and defeated Knockrinsay's forces. When in the following year Knockrinsay offered to give up Kintyre and appealed to the king for assistance in regaining part of Islay, he was rebuffed because of opposition from the earl of Argyll and Sir John Campbell of Calder. Argyll presumably opposed Knockrinsay's plan to withdraw from Kintyre to Islay because he himself hoped eventually to add both territories to his growing estates.[15]

Despite the Dunyveg MacDonnells' internal troubles between Knockrinsay and his father Angus and their recurring problems with Argyll, the

MacLeans, James VI, and the English, it seemed in 1598–9 that their luck was about to change for the better because of worsening relations between James MacSorley and Tyrone. In mid-1598 MacSorley was out with a force of 800 redshanks as far afield as Carrickfergus and Belfast. His operations against the English certainly proved beneficial to Tyrone and O'Donnell in preparing the way for their greatest victory at the Yellow Ford in August. In the first half of 1599 it was reported that the Antrim MacDonnells were actively watching the northeastern Ulster coastline to prevent an English landing in Tyrone's rear, having received a large supply of arms and ammunition from the O'Neill chief for this purpose. In April it was reported that James MacSorley had accompanied Hugh O'Donnell on a raid into Connacht and was preparing to send 500 troops to join Tyrone. But the apparent cooperation between the Antrim MacDonnells and the Irish chiefs amounted to little more than each side playing its own hand. Certainly the operations undertaken by MacSorley's clan benefited O'Neill and O'Donnell; but these actions were carried out solely to advance the cause of the MacDonnells. For instance, the MacSorleys were doubtless more than happy to stand guard along the coast from Dunluce to Carrickfergus in return for shipments of arms and ammunition from O'Neill. They also were not averse to extending their influence southward into County Down while England's main force was employed farther west against the Irish rebels.[16]

The fragile nature of the "alliance" between MacSorley and the Irish chiefs was finally revealed in mid 1599 when Angus of Dunyveg's sons, Sir James of Knockrinsay and Angus Oge, approached Hugh O'Donnell with an offer to provide him and O'Neill with redshanks. They had been reluctant to approach Tyrone because of his rumored close ties with James MacSorley. Tempted by the possibility of support from the Dunyveg MacDonnells, who, in truth, had no place else to turn and thus were likely to be serious in their offer, Tyrone decided to distance himself from the opportunistic MacSorleys. Thus when O'Neill mustered his forces in August, he did not send for James MacSorley. Tyrone's decision to treat with the Dunyveg MacDonnells in mid-1599 probably stemmed from his knowledge that Angus was about to regain control of the clan (which he did the following year). Neither he nor his son, Sir James of Knockrinsay, had been recognized by James VI as the legitimate head of the Dunyveg branch; therefore, Tyrone must have reasoned that old Angus, like his sons, had no place else to turn for succor. But the sagacious O'Neill leader did not make a clean break with MacSorley, just in case things went awry with Dunyveg.[17]

In early 1600 Tyrone for the moment abandoned any notion of risking an alliance with the Dunyveg MacDonnells. James MacSorley once again was assisting the O'Neill chief by watching the English garrison at Carrickfergus. The apparent resumption of good relations between MacSorley and Tyrone prompted Dublin officials to call on the queen to wage a force of redshanks against the Gaelic allies. While the English were trying to separate Tyrone and MacSorley, James VI was attempting to persuade the O'Neill earl to keep his distance from Angus of Dunyveg. Dunyveg had sent a messenger to Tyrone, requesting a meeting on Lough Foyle. Angus warned O'Neill that if the two could not reach an agreement, he would go to Carrickfergus and offer to serve the English. By April Dunyveg indeed had begun talks with Sir Arthur Chichester, who followed his brother as governor of Carrickfergus. But while Dunyveg might have been willing to come in to the new governor, James MacSorley feared that Sir Arthur would be looking to avenge the death of his brother. England undoubtedly preferred to keep both branches of Clan Ian Mor from aiding the Ulster rebels; however, it seemed that the younger Chichester's recent appointment and his willingness to negotiate with Dunyveg had driven the Antrim MacDonnells firmly into Tyrone's camp.[18]

England's two primary concerns regarding Clan Ian Mor during Tyrone's uprising were: 1) to keep the Antrim and Dunyveg branches apart; and 2) to prevent either or both of them from serving O'Neill and O'Donnell. While it was not difficult to keep Angus of Dunyveg and the MacSorleys at odds, it proved much more difficult to prevent the clan from giving aid, sporadic though it was, to Tyrone and O'Donnell. For instance, as Dunyveg talked with Chichester in spring 1600, his brother, Ranald MacDonnell of Smerby, landed a contingent of redshanks in the Inishowen peninsula to serve O'Donnell.[19] Since Lord Deputy Perrott's indenture with Sorley Boy and Angus of Dunyveg in 1586, England clearly had preferred dealing with the Antrim rather than the Dunyveg MacDonnells. It will be remembered that Angus was quite reluctant to abide by the agreement, doubtless because he believed that his uncle had gotten part of the Glynnes at his expense. Dunyveg, though, had had no choice but to subordinate himself to Sorley's authority. England had not forgotten which side of Clan Ian Mor was in the ascendancy in the late sixteenth century.

England's fears that Clan Ian Mor would unite and provide substantial military support for the Irish uprising were not realized. However, neither London nor Dublin had much to do with preventing a MacDonnell–O'Neill entente. Rather, the lack of MacDonnell cooperation with Tyrone stemmed from a much earlier episode–the row between James and Sorley Boy and Shane O'Neill in the 1560s. While Hugh O'Neill, Shane's nephew, certainly held no grudge against Clan Ian Mor for the tragedy at Cushendun in 1567 (in fact, he hated and feared his MacShane cousins), the descendants of James and Sorley MacDonnell had not forgotten the betrayal of the Drum Cru pact and the subsequent humiliation of Glentaisie. A lingering mistrust of O'Neill ambition surely must have tempered Clan Ian Mor's zeal for aiding Tyrone in his bid to banish the English and establish his own hegemony in Ulster.

At the turn of the century the Antrim MacDonnells understood that it was in their best interest to come to terms with London and Dublin. Elizabeth's days were short, and it appeared that James VI surely would succeed her as a result of the union of the Thistle and the Rose, the marriage of Henry VII's daughter Margaret to King James IV of Scotland in 1503. Henry had predicted that should one of his successors die without heirs and the English throne pass to the Stewarts, "Scotland would be an accession to England, and not England to Scotland, for the greater would draw the less."[20] It was not only Henry VII who realized that England would overshadow Scotland as the result of a personal union under a Stewart monarch; the Antrim MacDonnells knew that James VI of Scotland, when he became James I of England, would rule through the existing governmental apparatus in London. Thus James and Ranald MacSorley tried to cultivate good relations with London while at the same time they avoided provoking James VI in Edinburgh.[21]

Sir James MacSorley MacDonnell of Dunluce died suddenly in 1601 and was succeeded by his brother Ranald as chief of the Antrim branch of Clan Ian Mor. Ranald was in Scotland at the time of James's death. Upon returning to Ireland, he encountered Sir James of Knockrinsay, who was coming from a meeting with Tyrone. Both sides appealed to Chichester for assistance, but before he could decide with whom to side the two MacDonnells had joined battle. Victory went to Ranald, who carried Knockrinsay to Dunluce as a prisoner. Considering the bad blood between the Antrim and Dunyveg branches since Sorley Boy's death, it is surprising that this was the only major battle fought between the two sides of Clan Ian Mor. Shortly after his triumph, Ranald met with Chichester to cement favorable relations with England. Ranald doubtless wanted English recognition of his claim to the chiefship of the Antrim MacDonnells, especially since Sir James MacSorley of Dunluce had left behind several young sons as heirs. By coming to an agreement with Dublin and by controlling the fate of Knockrinsay, Ranald MacSorley hoped to establish sole dominance over both the Route and the Glynnes. But Chichester and Mountjoy put little faith in Ranald's promises, fearing that he would desert them for Tyrone at the first opportunity.[22]

In November 1601 Ranald MacSorley and most of his followers joined Tyrone and O'Donnell at what proved to be the most critical point in the Ulster uprising. The battle of Kinsale in the following month would determine the rising's fate. While the Antrim MacDonnells marched south to join the Irish chiefs, Sir James of Knockrinsay got control of Dunluce Castle and declared the house of Dunyveg to be the rightful possessor of the Glynnes and the Route. Knockrinsay appealed to Chichester to recognize his claims in northern Ireland, as Ranald MacSorley had proved to be untrustworthy. Thus the Dunyveg family appeared to be offering their services against their Antrim kinsmen. But Chichester had no desire to see the Dunyveg MacDonnells entrenched in Ulster in place of the Antrim branch, especially since Angus had used the occasion of Knockrinsay's imprisonment in Dunluce to raise his family's entire fighting strength and reassert his dominance within the family. Chichester warned Angus that if he came to Ireland and landed anywhere but Carrickfergus, it would be considered an act of war. But Sir Arthur did not wish to completely alienate the Dunyveg MacDonnells, fearing perhaps that Ranald MacSorley might just back the winning horse; thus instead of risking battle by trying to force Knockrinsay out of Dunluce, Chichester offered him supplies if he would abandon the stronghold. Shortly after Kinsale, Angus agreed to have Knockrinsay surrender Dunluce to the queen. But before he could do so, Ranald MacSorley had returned from Tyrone's campaign and laid claim to the castle. As the Irish uprising ran out of steam in early 1602, and the Antrim MacDonnells proved quick to distance themselves from Tyrone's and O'Donnell's lost cause, Chichester began to suspect that the Dunyveg MacDonnells' plans to bring a large redshank army to Ulster had less to do with any desire to subdue the queen's enemies than with their own desire to displace the Antrim MacDonnells.[23]

Ranald MacDonnell indeed seemed fortunate to have escaped serious punishment for supporting Tyrone's uprising; however, by no stretch of the imagination did he provide all that he might have to the rebels. Had the MacSorleys been serious in their support for the Irish chiefs, it is unlikely that Chichester and Mountjoy would have agreed to such lenient treatment, beginning with the restoration of Dunluce, their principal stronghold. Bolstering the Antrim MacDonnells' position as a stabilizing force in an otherwise chaotic province was the bizarre behavior of Sir James MacDonnell of Knockrinsay. He foolishly announced his intentions of marrying Tyrone's daughter even though he already had a wife in Scotland. At the same time he was busy telling Sir Henry Docwra at Derry that he detested the O'Neill chief. The purpose of such strange action simply is unfathomable, especially in light of the rather clear-cut political situation in 1602 Ulster. Knockrinsay soon left Ireland, returning to Scotland to join his father in defending Dunyveg lands against the encroaching Campbells. The departure of the Dunyveg MacDonnells left Ranald MacSorley as the dominant Clan Ian Mor leader in Ulster, despite the fact that James VI acknowledged in mid-year Dunyveg's claim to the Antrim Glynnes. But soon the Scottish king would head south for London to become James I of England, putting out of mind Clan Ian Mor's unresolved quarrels.[24]

After establishing himself upon the English throne in 1603, James VI and I appointed the earl of Argyll King's Lieutenant in the southwestern Highlands and Isles. The chiefs of that region, including Angus of Dunyveg, were brought to heel by several royal military expeditions that resulted in Campbell control of Kintyre and Jura by 1607. In the following year an obedient Angus surrendered Dunyveg Castle in Islay without a fight. To cap his campaign to bring the Gaelic chiefs of the west under royal control, King James enacted the Statutes of Iona in 1609.[25] Though most of the statutes were never put into effect, they symbolized what one historian has termed James I's resort to "government by pen."[26] Concurrently, and in much the same legalistic fashion, the new English monarch undertook the Plantation of Ulster, an endeavor that would have repercussions on the Antrim MacDonnell settlement.[27]

Thus by the end of the first decade of the seventeenth century, Clan Ian Mor faced an uncertain situation in both Scotland and Ireland. Angus and the Dunyveg MacDonnells seemed to understand that there was little hope of re-establishing their power in the face of determined Campbell resistance. In 1612 Angus agreed to relinquish Islay to Sir John Campbell of Calder in exchange for other lands and money to pay off his creditors. However, according to the agreement, if Dunyveg repaid the money received from Calder before a certain date he could reclaim possession of Islay. Before the year was out, Angus, with assistance from Sir Ranald MacSorley of Dunluce, had repaid the debt. Angus of Dunyveg died in early 1613, but Sir Ranald began to negotiate with the king's officials at Edinburgh for permission to take control of Islay.[28]

While James I raised no objections to Sir Ranald's occupation of Islay, the same cannot be said of the late Angus of Dunyveg's sons. It was not long before the inhabitants of the island were lodging complaints about their new landlord, many of which doubtless were the result of prodding by Dunyveg's dispossessed descendants. Rather than sit by and permit the Antrim MacDonnells to secure royal recognition to Islay, Ranald Oge, Angus's alleged bastard son, in March 1614 seized Dunyveg Castle from a small garrison holding it in the king's name under the bishop of the Isles. Whether Ranald Oge's actions were intended to further his own claim to the chiefship of the Dunyveg MacDonnells is unclear; however, he accomplished nothing for himself. Within a week he was driven off the island by his half-brother Angus Oge and his cousin Coll Ciotach MacDonnell, the latter being placed in command of the castle in James I's name. Angus Oge then offered to surrender the stronghold to the bishop of the Isles in return for a blanket pardon for his and Coll Ciotach's having forcibly taken it from Ranald Oge. But the Scottish Privy Council in Edinburgh suspected that Angus Oge's real intention was to keep Dunyveg Castle for himself, thus challenging Sir Ranald MacDonnell's claim to Islay.[29]

In mid-1614 the Scottish Privy Council agreed to pardon Angus Oge if he would surrender Dunyveg Castle to the bishop of the Isles. Angus Oge refused and the small force of Hebrideans under the bishop's command declined to take up arms against him. Attention in the Gaelic west now being focused on the Islay crisis, Coll Ciotach had no trouble in recruiting large numbers of islanders to support Angus Oge. Thus the

Privy Council, working through the bishop of the Isles, had little choice but to negotiate with the Dunyveg MacDonnells. Angus Oge, who claimed that Argyll had influenced his recent behavior, insisted that the bishop secure him a seven-year lease to Islay and, again, a full pardon for him and his supporters. In this way, Sir Ranald MacDonnell of Dunluce was to be dispossessed of the island. That Angus Oge blamed Argyll for forcing him to precipitate the Islay crisis in 1614 cannot be dismissed simply as an excuse put forth to cover the former's actions. Indeed, it is not difficult to see what might have motivated the Campbell chief to push Angus Oge into rebellion: the desire to keep Islay out of Antrim MacDonnell hands while at the same time ruining the Dunyveg MacDonnells in the process. This almost certainly would have opened the way for Campbell dominance of the island. But it is doubtful that Angus Oge had much faith in Argyll's promises to intercede with the king on his behalf should he (Angus Oge) refuse to surrender Dunyveg Castle. Thus Argyll's influence over Angus Oge, if indeed it existed at all, was not evident when the MacDonnell leader made the fateful decision to hold the fortress of Dunyveg against the government in late 1614.[30]

As it turned out, Sir John Campbell of Calder, rather than Argyll, stood to gain the most by the Dunyveg MacDonnells' Islay uprising. In October the Privy Council appointed Calder to lead an expedition against Angus Oge in return for which, if successful, he would receive Islay in feu from James I. The bishop of the Isles, who had been replaced as the king's agent by Calder, warned Edinburgh about the dangers of giving the Campbells too much power in the southwestern Highlands and Isles, but the council ignored his advice. In late 1614 the Scottish Privy Council appeared less concerned with Campbell aggrandizement in the west than with the possible reunion of Clan Ian Mor's Scottish and Irish territories under Sir Ranald MacDonnell of Dunluce; thus the decision was made to set Calder up in Islay to the exclusion of Sir Ranald.[31]

James I's policy toward the Gaelic heartland, like Elizabeth's before him, turned mainly on keeping the Scottish and Irish Celts separate. In 1614 James, it could be argued, was reluctant to allow Sir Ranald MacDonnell to take control over Clan Ian Mor's former Scottish lands–particularly Islay, Kintyre, and Jura–because of events in Ulster since the start of the plantations in 1609. With few exceptions, English and Lowland Scots settlements in the six escheated counties had failed to take root and prosper by 1614–15, leaving mainly those settlements dominated by Celtic Scots from the Borders–Southwest region of Scotland.[32] Those non-Celtic settlements that did thrive, especially Londonderry and Coleraine, were often the targets of Irish plots such as the one in 1614 involving the Tyrone O'Neills and Coll Ciotach MacDonnell. That the Ulster Plantation had failed to transform the province into an appendage of England and that the area remained a Celtic stronghold must have given the king second thoughts about permitting the most prominent Gaelic family in northern Ireland–the Antrim MacDonnells–to extend its influence across the North Channel, thus pulling even more territory under Ulster's control. James VI and I, like his Stewart predecessors, now faced the decision of which clan, MacDonnell or Campbell, to advance in the west. In 1614–15 there was little doubt that the king would decide in favor of the Campbells. To have done otherwise would have fostered conditions that might well have led to a revitalization of Clan Ian Mor on both sides of the North Channel reminiscent of the days of Sorley Boy.

The Dunyveg MacDonnells' Islay rising in 1614 and the government's decision to employ Campbell of Calder to suppress it eventually brought the Antrim MacDonnells into the struggle. The Antrim branch of Clan Ian Mor had not been involved in any sort of plot to seize Dunyveg Castle, but once Angus Oge was in possession of it he undoubtedly expected his Irish kinsmen to come to his aid. But he was to be disappointed. Having been left virtually alone on Islay, Angus quickly struck a deal with the Scottish chancellor, the earl of Dunfermline, to hand over the castle to the government in return for being appointed constable with authority to resist Calder's impending invasion.[33] The intent of such intrigue is difficult to determine. Was Dunfermline seeking to combat Campbell aggrandizement by employing the Dunyveg MacDonnells? Or was he trying to set up Angus Oge as a traitor by persuading him to resist a royal invasion force? Or, more likely, did Dunfermline understand that if Angus Oge managed to hold out against Calder, it perhaps would open the way for a counter-invasion of Islay by the Antrim MacDonnells, thus jeopardizing Edinburgh's attempt to control the southern Hebrides?

After having received a royal charter to Islay in late 1614, Calder began operations to reduce the stronghold early in the following year. Facing a superior Scottish-Irish force, Angus Oge lost his nerve and in a few days surrendered, despite the exhortations by his cousin Coll Ciotach to defend the fortress to the death. Coll Ciotach made a daring escape by galley, but Angus Oge and several of his followers were taken to Edinburgh and executed in July.[34]

Angus Oge's troubles aroused the interest of his brother, Sir James of Knockrinsay, who was being held prisoner in Edinburgh Castle. Knockrinsay had offered to go to Islay the previous autumn and persuade his recalcitrant brother to give up. His offer had been ignored and Calder proceeded to crush Angus Oge's resistance. In late May, however, Knockrinsay escaped to the Hebrides, seeking to rally MacDonnell opposition against Calder. By June he and about 300 followers, including the ubiquitous Coll Ciotach, had recaptured Dunyveg Castle and sought to bargain with the king from a position of strength. Indeed, Knockrinsay and Coll Ciotach went on the offensive and occupied parts of Kintyre and Jura. But the Scottish Privy Council refused to negotiate, instead putting a bounty on the MacDonnell leaders' heads and summoning a reluctant Argyll from the comforts of London to bring them to justice.[35]

Before Argyll arrived to lead the government expedition to the Isles, Knockrinsay and Coll Ciotach had pulled together a considerable force. However, the uprising collapsed when Argyll's lieutenant, Sir Dougal Campbell of Auchinbreck, prevented the MacDonnells from moving out of Kintyre and into Campbell territory. Knockrinsay fled to Islay, where he agreed to turn over Dunyveg Castle to Argyll; but Coll Ciotach, who also had reached Islay, took control of the stronghold and refused to surrender. Rather than try to deal with the impetuous Coll Ciotach, Knockrinsay sailed for Ulster, giving up the fight to reclaim his father's lands in Scotland. Knockrinsay's decision to flee to Ireland marked the end of the Dunyveg MacDonnells' Islay uprising and the disappearance of that branch of Clan Ian Mor as a political factor in the Gaelic heartland.[36]

If Sir James MacDonnell of Knockrinsay's flight to Ireland in 1615 denoted the demise of the Dunyveg MacDonnells, then the defiant resistance that Coll Ciotach (grandson of Colla MacDonnell, brother of Sorley Boy) put up to Argyll on Islay revealed the continued vigor of the Antrim side of Clan Ian Mor. But even the Antrim MacDonnells now had to contend with a changed political situation in the Gaelic west, one in which an intrusive royal government would figure prominently. Moreover, the attempt by the Scottish Privy Council in 1616 to enact various of the Statutes of Iona represented a conscious attempt to "civilize" the chiefs and their tacksmen and to bring them into a money economy that would eventually undermine the Gaelic way of life.[37]

The political situation that faced Clan Ian Mor's surviving Antrim branch from 1616 to 1645 certainly was complicated by the extension of the king's writ into the Hebrides and Gaelic Ulster. Though the MacDonnells (and Gaels in general) had resisted mightily control from Edinburgh and Dublin in practice, it must be pointed out that they were willing to acknowledge the theoretical overlordship of the Stewart or the Tudor monarchs. In Sorley Boy's day, for instance, they had frequently recognized the sovereignty of Mary, Queen of Scots, James VI, and Elizabeth I by entering into various *quid pro quo* agreements with them, usually consenting to provide services for tenurial rights. But on no account did the MacDonnells believe that they owed, as a matter of course, any practical obligations–including rents and taxes–to either Edinburgh or London. From the standpoint of practical politics, then, Clan Ian Mor saw itself as an autonomous entity that would obey the monarch only when it proved beneficial to do so.

If Clan Ian Mor was willing to accept the rightful overlordship of the Stewart kings in the early seventeenth century, it proved much less amenable to governance by royal officials. For instance, MacDonnell resistance to the Dublin government and to the Edinburgh–Campbell alliance is well documented. In fact, Clan Ian Mor's opposition to the aggrandizement of royal officials reflected a keen understanding of British politics from the mid-sixteenth to the mid-seventeenth century. In 1541 Henry VIII had established a kingdom in Ireland that was to be administered from Dublin Castle by English rather than by Irish lord deputies. In 1603 James VI moved his court to London, leaving behind a similar situation with a Scottish Privy Council sitting in Edinburgh Castle. Thus between the 1540s and 1640s, both Ireland and Scotland had ceased to be kingdoms governed strictly in the monarch's interest. Rather, they were kingdoms only in appearance, but in reality were ruled increasingly after 1560 for the benefit of either a Puritan "New English" colonial administration in Ireland or a related Presbyterian-Covenanting Assembly in Scotland. Sir Thomas Wentworth's attempt to govern Ireland once again in the king's name and the marquis of Montrose's championing of the royal prerogative in Scotland represented a conservative backlash against the political radicalism that would sweep over the "Three Kingdoms" from the 1640s to 1688-9. Clan Ian Mor did not always get on well with the likes of Wentworth,[38] but if forced to choose between supporting New English colonial officials in Dublin and Lowland Covenanters in Edinburgh that identified themselves with radical English Parliamentarians, or the Stewart dynasty, it was clear that the MacDonnells would favor the latter.

By the late 1630s Clan Ian Mor (like many Gaels in general) sided with Charles I because of its opposition to the traditional Campbell enemy. Lord Lorne, son of the elderly eighth earl of Argyll (d. 1638), publicly declared against Charles I in April 1638. Lorne, though himself nominally a Catholic, headed a family that supported the Presbyterian Covenanters and the emerging money economy of the Lowlands which brought that area within the ambit of London and the Parliamentarian southeast. That the ruling interests in the Lowlands in the 1630s were virulently anti-Gaelic (and anti-Catholic) resulted in a reconciliation between Clan Ian Mor and the crown. The king's problems with Lorne in Scotland drew the attention of Ranald MacDonnell, second earl of Antrim. In mid-1638 Antrim informed Charles that his branch of Clan Ian Mor opposed the Solemn League and Covenant. Indeed, Antrim intended to try to reunite the clan's Irish and Scottish elements in much the same way as his grandfather and father had done.[39]

Antrim's immediate plan to assist Charles I was based on a proposed invasion of Argyllshire in late 1638 or early 1639; however, his plans were scotched by none other than Wentworth, who did not trust the Antrim MacDonnells with government money and arms. Not surprisingly, Lorne got wind of Antrim's intentions and quickly prepared to repel the expedition. Sporadic fighting occurred between MacDonnell and Campbell forces in the southern Isles in 1639 as part of the First Bishops' War, but that was ended by a June treaty between king and Covenanters. While he negotiated with the Covenanters, Charles I appointed Antrim as King's Lieutenant in the Isles. But because of Wentworth's continued opposition to Antrim, fueled in part by Lorne's accusations of his (Antrim's) disloyalty, the MacDonnell chief found it difficult to secure the money and material to act in his new post. Such opposition between Royalist supporters in Ireland threatened to undo MacDonnell efforts to raise an army for the invasion of Scotland. In fact, because of the king's mounting problems within England itself, royal support for Antrim's Scottish expedition quickly faded in 1639–40.[40]

In the wake of Wentworth's removal and execution and the virtual disbanding of his Irish army in 1641, Ulster was shaken by a Catholic Irish uprising designed to drive out English and Lowland Scots settlers and to re-establish Celtic political control of the province. Though the rising was a blow against royal government in Ireland, the real target of the Irish Catholics was not the largely loyal non-Lowland Scots element in the north; rather, it was the pro-Covenanter/Parliamentarian faction. More than two years earlier, many of the Celtic Scottish settlers in Ulster had signed a petition pledging to support the king and to forswear all contrary "Covenants, Oaths, and Bands." Besides leaving most of the Celtic Scots estates unmolested, the October 1641 rising did not extend into the lands of the earl of Antrim. Antrim wished to remain loyal to Charles I, but his situation was made difficult by his Roman Catholicism and his kinship with many of the Gaelic Irish leaders. Thus he was reluctant to move too close to either side. Until the king raised his standard at Oxford in August 1642, the Antrim MacDonnells–including forces led by Alasdair MacColla–would change sides a number of times in what proved to be a most complex and confusing military situation in Ulster.[41]

The Antrim MacDonnells in early 1642 stood on the side of the Catholic Irish rebels. The earl of Argyll made much of Antrim's decision to allow his clansmen to join the Irish and prepared a 2,500-man army for despatch to Ulster. While the Covenanters prepared an army for service in Ireland, MacColla defeated a Protestant force at the Laney in February. Thereafter, Antrim himself returned to Dunluce Castle from Dublin and ordered his troops to immediately raise the siege of English-dominated Coleraine.[42] Antrim's actions suggest that he was wrestling with whether to back the king's government or the Irish Catholics amidst a highly charged political atmosphere. He returned to Dunluce as a loyal subject most assuredly to prevent Argyll's landing troops on his lands in the Glynnes and the Route. But to no avail. It was not long until a Covenanting army under Major-General Robert Munro landed in Ulster as the result of a treaty between Edinburgh and London. Charles I did not agree with the terms of this agreement and thus never signed it. But now that a Scots army was in northern Ireland, the question arose as to its mission: was it to defend the king's or the English/Lowland Scots' interests in Ulster against the Gaelic

Irish? That the earl of Antrim had professed himself a loyal subject, and that Munro had hunted him down, taken him into custody, and occupied his Dunluce residence as if he were in rebellion, suggests that the Covenanting army had no intention of doing the king's will.[43]

Antrim's imprisonment and the subsequent defeat of the Scottish-Irish Catholic forces under Sir Phelim O'Neill and Alasdair MacColla at Glenmaquin in mid-1642 put the Antrim MacDonnells' position in northeastern Ireland in jeopardy. Because most of the clan's lands in Ulster now were under Campbell control, it seemed that Antrim's plan to reunify and revive the fortunes of Clan Ian Mor had been shattered. After the debacle at Glenmaquin, a wounded Alasdair MacColla had obviously tried to make the best of a bad situation by approaching Sir Alexander Leslie, earl of Leven, the new Scottish commander in Ireland. The two men reached an accord in September whereby MacColla and his men would be pardoned in return for Alasdair's raising a regiment to serve against the Catholic Irish. However, it was not long until MacColla crossed west of the Bann, rejoining his former allies. At about the same time, Antrim escaped from Carrickfergus and fled to England, where civil war had already broken out. Soon the MacDonnell leader became deeply involved in various plots to enlist support for Charles I in the Celtic fringe. In return, he undoubtedly hoped to receive royal assistance in recovering Clan Ian Mor's lands in northeastern Ireland and the southern Hebrides.[44]

Antrim's escape to England in October 1642 plunged Clan Ian Mor squarely into the conflict between Charles I and Parliament. Once there, he presented to the king his plans for raising Irish and Scottish troops; however, Antrim received only a lukewarm reception from the Royalist brain's trust. To his credit, the proposal that the war be expanded under his (Antrim's) direction to include Ireland and Scotland revealed a sophisticated grasp of the geo-political significance of turning the conflict into a "War of the Three Kingdoms." As it turned out, the king's enemies were to suffer their worst defeats in Scotland and Ireland rather than in England, and though these Royalist victories alone were not enough to allow Charles to keep his crown, Antrim's plan to conduct the war outside of England proper doubtless should have received more attention than it did in late 1642. He envisioned English Royalists combining with Irish Catholic Confederates and Clan Ian Mor to first crush Parliamentary resistance in England before moving on the king's enemies in Ireland and Scotland. The plan was attractive, but likely would have exceeded the Royalists' logistical capabilities. But Charles I was too quick to dismiss the plan as foolhardy because it was overly ambitious; indeed, had Antrim's plan been scaled down to the size that it assumed in 1644, then the king might have won Scotland before the Covenanters were prepared to resist.[45]

The extent of Antrim's military planning became widely known in mid-1643. That he was taken seriously by the Scottish army in Ulster is pointed up by his arrest upon returning from his visit to Charles I. Interrogation revealed that Antrim had planned to raise MacDonnell and Irish reinforcements for the king in both Ireland and Scotland. Moreover, a Royalist army under Alasdair MacColla would be despatched to invade Campbell lands in Argyllshire. Though Charles I thus far had distanced himself from Antrim's schemes, the Covenanters feared that England, or, even worse, Scotland was to be the target of a fanatical Catholic Irish army. Thus the Covenanters threw in their lot with the English Parliamentarians by agreeing to a second Solemn League and Covenant in September and by subsequently sending a Scottish army south across the Tweed. By instilling fear of a Catholic invasion in the Covenanters, Antrim, instead of aiding the king, had brought a new and potent force into the field against him.[46]

Antrim escaped from his Scottish captors for a second time in late 1643, determined to revive his plans for a Royalist campaign. By now, however, his credibility was tarnished and few were willing to entertain his ideas. Antrim went to the king's headquarters at Oxford and offered to raise 10,000 Irish Catholic Confederates for service in England and 3,000 for Scotland. By this time Charles I had no choice but to accept help wherever he could find it; thus he issued appropriate royal instructions to Antrim. Besides the 13,000 men he had promised, the MacDonnell leader was asked to raise a further 2,000 for an invasion of Campbell lands in the southwestern Highlands and Isles. Moreover, Antrim was to cooperate with James Graham, marquis of Montrose, the king's Lieutenant-General in Scotland. Shortly after receiving Charles I's instructions, Antrim and Montrose signed an agreement to put a combined force in the field by 1 April 1644. Montrose would recruit in the northeast of Scotland and south of the Forth while Antrim worked Ulster and the Highlands and Isles. As it turned out, however, neither Montrose nor Antrim proved able to meet the deadline for beginning a Royalist campaign in Scotland. Instead of Antrim or his brother Alexander taking personal command of the Irish force, Alasdair MacColla received a royal commission as Major-General to lead the expedition. His 2,000 Ulster veterans finally left Ireland for the west coast of Scotland in July 1644.[47]

The campaigns of Montrose and MacColla in Scotland in 1644–5 marked Clan Ian Mor's re-entry into the affairs of Scotland through its Antrim branch. The half-century from 1590 to 1644 had witnessed the destruction of the Dunyveg MacDonnells and the temporary eclipse of the Antrim MacDonnells. When MacColla set foot in Morvern in early July 1644, he demonstrated not only his clan's loyalty to the Stewart dynasty, but its determination once more to influence the affairs of Scotland, especially in opposition to the hated Campbells. Despite the best efforts of Ranald MacDonnell, second earl of Antrim, and Major-General Alasdair MacColla, Clan Ian Mor's efforts in the 1640s would ultimately fall short of their objective. Thereafter the initiative within Clan Donald itself would pass to the northern septs of Sleat, Clanranald, Glencoe, Glengarry, and Keppoch.

The history of the Antrim and Dunyveg MacDonnells during the sixteenth century elucidates the significant role played by Clan Ian Mor in bringing the Gaelic heartland into the affairs of the entire British archipelago and ultimately into the affairs of continental Europe. The MacDonnells' success in northeastern Ireland before 1590 created "border-land" problems for England similar to those posed earlier by the Welsh marches, the English northern counties, and the Scottish Lowlands. That Sorley, his brothers, and their descendants, unlike earlier independent-minded frontier lords, succeeded in preserving until the mid-seventeenth century their own private rule in northeastern Ireland in opposition to the centralizing tendencies of an English-dominated government speaks well of Clan Ian Mor's military and political leadership. This indeed was the focus of Sorley Boy MacDonnell's life and legacy.

Notes

Prologue

1. Essex to Walsingham, 31 July 1575, London, Public Record Office, State Papers, Ireland, Elizabeth, SP 63/52/79.

2. In order to simplify the terminology associated with the main branches of Clan Ian Mor after 1493, I have chosen to refer to the MacDonnells in northeastern Ireland as the "Antrim MacDonnells" or the "MacDonnells of Antrim". In reality, the situation is somewhat more complicated. Until Sorley Boy's overwhelming domination of the Irish MacDonnells after 1565, the family was headed by his eldest brother James, the hereditary sixth lord of Dunyveg and the Glynnes. Thus the correct designation for the family would be the "MacDonnells of Dunyveg and the Glynnes". However, I have used the generic term "Antrim MacDonnells" to correspond with James's and his brothers' geographical location in Ulster. When referring to James and his Scottish possessions, I have used the title "of Dunyveg" or "of Dunyveg and the Glynnes". After James's death in 1565, his eldest son Angus inherited this title; but he was dominated by his uncle Sorley Boy until the latter's death in 1590. It was during this quarter-century that the actual (and official) split between the MacDonnells of Antrim (Sorley and his descendants) and the MacDonnells of Dunyveg and the Glynnes (the descendants of James MacDonnell) occurred. But as long as Sorley lived, the nominal division of Clan Ian Mor into two main branches did not have a negative effect on the family's affairs. It was only after his demise that the Antrim and Dunyveg branches fell out with one another, the latter suffering virtual complete destruction in the early seventeenth century.

3. Barnaby Rich, *A New Description of Ireland, wherein is described the disposition of the Irish* (London, 1610), 95.

4. Rev. George Hill, *An Historical Account of the MacDonnells of Antrim, Including Notices of some other Septs, Irish and Scottish* (Belfast, 1873); G.A. Hayes-McCoy, *Scots Mercenary Forces in Ireland (1565–1603)* (Dublin, 1937); Karl S. Bottigheimer, *Ireland and the Irish, A Short History* (New York, 1982); Ciaran Brady, "The Killing of Shane O'Neill: Some New Evidence", *Irish Sword* XV (1982–3): 116–23; Nicholas Canny, *The Elizabethan Conquest of Ireland: A Pattern Established, 1565–76* (Hassocks, Sussex and New York, 1976); *The Formation of the Old English Elite in Ireland* (Dublin, 1975); *Kingdom and Colony: Ireland in the Atlantic World, 1560–1800* (Baltimore, MD and London, 1988); *From Reformation to Restoration: Ireland, 1534–1660* (Dublin, 1987); Jane E. A. Dawson, "Two Kingdoms or Three?: Ireland in Anglo–Scottish Relations in the Middle of the Sixteenth Century", in Roger A. Mason, ed., *Scotland and England, 1286–1815* (Edinburgh, 1987); "The Fifth Earl of Argyle, Gaelic Lordship and Political Power in Sixteenth-Century Scotland," *Scottish Historical Review* LXVII, i, 183 (April 1988): 1–27; Steven G. Ellis, *Reform and Revival: English Government in*

Ireland, 1470–1534 (London, 1984); *Tudor Ireland: Crown, Community and the Conflict of Cultures, 1470–1603* (London and New York, 1985); Hiram Morgan, "The End of Gaelic Ulster: a Thematic Interpretation of Events between 1534 and 1610," *Irish Historical Studies* XXVI, 101 (May 1988): 8–32; David Stevenson, *Alasdair MacColla and the Highland Problem in the Seventeenth Century* (Edinburgh, 1980).

Chapter 1

1. John Bannerman, "The Lordship of the Isles", in Jennifer M. Brown, ed., *Scottish Society in the Fifteenth Century* (New York and London, 1977), 211; G. A. Hayes-McCoy, *Scots Mercenary Forces in Ireland (1565–1603)* (Dublin and London, 1937), 4–6; I. F. Grant, *The Lordship of the Isles, Wanderings in the Lost Lordship* (Edinburgh, 1935; reprint edn, Edinburgh, 1982); Thomas F. O'Rahilly, *Irish Dialects Past and Present* (Dublin, 1932; reprint edn, Dublin, 1976), 161–4, 260–3; David Mathew, *The Celtic Peoples and Renaissance Europe* (London and New York, 1933), 110. Indicative of the close relationship that existed between Gaelic Scotland and Ulster is a 1408 deed contained in Rev. William Reeves, *Account of an Ancient Scotch Deed* (Dublin, 1852), 1.

2. For a detailed study of the *gallóglaigh* ("foreign warriors") influence in Ireland, see Hayes-McCoy, *Scots Mercenary Forces*, 1–76. Also see Andrew McKerral, "West Highland Mercenaries in Ireland", *Scottish Historical Review* XXX (April 1951): 1–14; Sean O'Domhnaill, "Warfare in Sixteenth-Century Ireland", *Irish Historical Studies* V (1946–7): 29–54; G. A. Hayes-McCoy, "Strategy and Tactics in Irish Warfare, 1593–1601", *Irish Historical Studies* II (1940–1): 255–79; J. F. Lydon, "The Bruce Invasion of Ireland", *Historical Studies* IV (1963): 111–25; J. Michael Hill, "The Distinctiveness of Gaelic Warfare, 1400–1750", *European History Quarterly* XXII (July 1992) 323–46. For some standard descriptions of *gallóglaigh*, see Edmund Spenser, *A View of the Present State of Ireland*, ed. W. L. Renwick (Oxford, 1970), 117; John Dymmok, *A Treatice of Ireland*, ed. Rev. Richard Butler (Dublin, 1842), 7; Sir James Ware, *The Antiquities and History of Ireland*, 2 vols (London, 1714), II: 161; Barnaby Rich, *A New Description of Ireland, wherein is described the disposition of the Irish* (London, 1610), 37.

3. Bannerman, "Lordship of the Isles", 214; Colin MacDonald, *The History of Argyll up to the Beginning of the Sixteenth Century* (Glasgow, 1951), 188; A. MacDonald and A. MacDonald, *The Clan Donald*, 3 vols. (Inverness, 1896–1904), I: 150; Ranald Nicholson, *Scotland: The Later Middle Ages* (Edinburgh, 1974), 236–7.

4. Hayes-McCoy, *Scots Mercenary Forces*, 9, 37; W. C. MacKenzie, *The Highlands and Isles of Scotland: A Historical Survey* (Edinburgh and London, 1937; reprint edn., New York, 1977), 100–1; Donald Gregory, *The History of the Western Highlands and Isles of Scotland, from A.D. 1493 to A.D. 1625*, 2nd edn (Edinburgh, 1881; reprint edn, Edinburgh, 1975), 31–4; Jean Munro, "The Lordship of the Isles" in Loraine Maclean of Dochgarroch, ed., *The Middle Ages in the Highlands* (Inverness, 1981), 28–9; Rev. Alexander MacGregor, *The Feuds of the Clans* (Stirling, 1907), 15–21; William MacKay, *Sidelights on Highland History* (Inverness, 1925), 281–302.

5. MacKenzie, *Highlands and Isles*, 101–2; William Drummond-Norie, "Inverlochy, 1431–1645", *Celtic Monthly* V (1896–7): 84; Donald J. MacDonald, *Clan Donald* (Loanhead, Midlothian, 1978), 230; John S. Keltie, *A History of the Scottish Highlands, Highland Clans, and Regiments*, 2 vols. (Edinburgh and London, 1875), 72–3.

6. MacKenzie, *Highlands and Isles*, 102–3.

7. MacDonald, *History of Argyll*, 228–9; MacKenzie, *Highlands and Isles*, 102–3.

8. Bannerman, "Lordship of the Isles", 214; MacKenzie, *Highlands and Isles*, 104–5; MacDonald and MacDonald, *Clan Donald*, II: 502–6; Gregory, *Western Highlands and Isles*, 47–8; Munro, "Lordship of the Isles", 30–1; MacDonald, *History of Argyll*, 239–40.

9. Grant, "Lordship of the Isles", 200, 223; John MacKechnie, *The Clan MacLean: A Gaelic Sea Power* (Edinburgh and London, 1954), 8; MacKenzie, *Highlands and Isles*, 104–5; Gregory, *Western Highlands and Isles*, 50–3; Munro, "Lordship of the Isles", 32–3.

10. The first forfeiture had occurred in the mid-1470s when the Scottish crown first learned of the Westminster–Ardtornish treaty.

11. Bannerman, "Lordship of the Isles", 240; MacKenzie, *Highlands and Isles*, 105–6; MacDonald, *History of Argyll*, 275.

12. Alexander Grant, "Scotland's 'Celtic Fringe' in the Late Middle Ages: The MacDonald Lords of the Isles and the Kingdom of Scotland", in R. R. Davies, ed., *The British Isles 1100–1500, Comparisons, Contrasts and Connections* (Edinburgh, 1988), 134.

13. Rev. George Hill, *An Historical Account of the MacDonnells of Antrim, Including Notices of some other Septs, Irish and Scottish* (Belfast, 1873), 21–3; Rev. James O'Laverty, *An Historical Account of the Diocese of Down and Connor, Ancient and Modern*, 5 vols. (Dublin, 1878–95), I: xxii–xxiii, IV: 354, 356; Rev. George Hill, "Notices of the Clan Ian Vór, or Clan-Donnell Scots", *Ulster Journal of Archaeology* series I, IX (1861): 301–17; Hector MacLean, "A Sketch of the MacDonnells of Antrim", in *Transactions of the Gaelic Society of Inverness*, vol. XVII (Inverness, 1890–1), 85–8; MacDonald and MacDonald, *Clan Donald*, II: 490–3; Gregory, *Western Highlands and Isles*, 61–3; Hayes-McCoy, *Scots Mercenary Forces*, 12. From the early fourteenth through the sixteenth century, there were three main migrations of Scots to Ireland that corresponded roughly to the three centuries: 1) the *gallóglaigh*; 2) Clan Ian Mor, or Clan Donald South; and 3) the redshanks.

14. For a discussion of Irish succession and land-holding laws, see Kenneth Nicholls, *Land, Law and Society in Sixteenth-Century Ireland* (Cork, 1976); Laurence Ginnell, *The Brehon Laws* (London, 1894); G. A. Hayes-McCoy, "Gaelic Society in Ireland in the Late Sixteenth Century", *Historical Studies* IV (1963): 45–61; Nicholas P. Canny, "Hugh O'Neill, Earl of Tyrone, and the Changing Face of Gaelic Ulster", *Studia Hibernica* X (1970): 7–35; Eoin MacNeill, *Celtic Ireland* (Dublin and London, 1921); Constantia Maxwell, ed., *Irish History from Contemporary Sources (1509–1610)* (London, 1923), 352n.

15. MacDonald and MacDonald, *Clan Donald*, II: 490–1.

16. Ibid., 499–500; MacDonald, *History of Argyll*, 194; MacLean, "Sketch", 89–90; Donald J. MacDonald, *Clan Donald*, 230.

17. Hill, *MacDonnells of Antrim*, 35; Bannerman, "Lordship of the Isles", 216; MacDonald and MacDonald, *Clan Donald*, II: 500–2.

18. Hill, *MacDonnells of Antrim*, 33; MacDonald and MacDonald, *Clan Donald*, II: 510–11.

19. Hayes-McCoy, *Scots Mercenary Forces*, 11; Gregory, *Western Highlands and Isles*, 189; MacKenzie, *Highlands and Isles*, 119–20; MacDonald and MacDonald, *Clan Donald*,

II: 511–12; W. D. Lamont, *The Early History of Islay, 500–1726* (Dundee, Angus, 1966), 31; Hill, *MacDonnells of Antrim*, 33–4; Nicholson, *Scotland: The Later Middle Ages*, 542–3; Bannatyne Club, ed., *Origines Parochiales Scotiae*, 2 vols. (Edinburgh, 1850), I: 4.

20. Gregory, *Western Highlands and Isles*, 89–90; Hill, *MacDonnells of Antrim*, 34; MacKenzie, *Highlands and Isles*, 119–20; MacDonald and MacDonald, *Clan Donald*, II: 511–12; Lamont, *Early History of Islay*, 31; MacLean, "Sketch", 92; Nicholson, *Scotland: The Later Middle Ages*, 543; I. F. Grant, *Lordship of the Isles*, 373.

21. Hill, *MacDonnells of Antrim*, 34–5; MacDonald and MacDonald, *Clan Donald*, II: 511–12.

22. MacLean, "Sketch", 93; Donald J. MacDonald, *Clan Donald*, 233; Munro, "Lordship of the Isles", 33; MacDonald and MacDonald, *Clan Donald*, II: 512; Hill, *MacDonnells of Antrim*, 34–5; G. G. Smith, ed., *The Book of Islay* (privately printed, 1895), 24–6; I. F. Grant, *Lordship of the Isles*, 396, 402–3.

23. John O'Donovan, ed., *Annala Rioghachta Eireann, Annals of the Kingdom of Ireland, by the Four Masters, from the Earliest Period to the Year 1616*, 5 vols, (Dublin 1848), IV: 1213 (anno 1495).

24. Smith, ed., *Book of Islay*, 28.

25. Rev. George Hill, the most reliable nineteenth-century authority of the MacDonnells of Antrim, quickly dismisses the possibility of MacIan of Ardnamurchan's chief prisoner being John Mor, son of Donald Balloch. Several other sources, however, confuse John Mor MacDonnell with his son, John Cahanagh. Hill claims that it was the latter (and at least two of his sons) who was brought to Edinburgh by MacIan. One of the more recent examples of the confusion over this complex chain of events is contained in Donald J. MacDonald, *Clan Donald*, 233. MacDonald writes: "By some means which never have been satisfactorily explained, MacIan was able to seize Sir John in Finlaggan and convey him with his son, John Cathanach, and at least two of their associates, to the presence of the King." He continues: "Although the capture of Sir John and his son took place in 1494, the date of their execution has not been authoritatively established; but most historians agree that it must have taken place soon after their apprehension, and not later than the beginning of the year 1495." It appears that this erroneous account is derived from two otherwise rather dependable works – Gregory, *Western Highlands and Isles*, 89–90, and MacDonald and MacDonald, *Clan Donald*, II: 511–12. Hill's book, published in 1873, was sandwiched between these two studies, Gregory's having been first published in 1836, and the MacDonalds' toward the end of that century. Even Hill is not sure of the date of the execution of John Cahanagh and his sons, and simply drops the matter.

26. John Cahanagh MacDonnell had married Cecilia Savage, daughter of Robert Savage of Portaferry, Co. Down, by whom he had four sons, Alasdair Cahanagh was the eldest.

27. Bannerman, "Lordship of the Isles", 216; MacKenzie, *Highlands and Isles*, 120; Rev. George Hill, "Shane O'Neill's Expedition against the Antrim Scots, 1565", *Ulster Journal of Archaeology* series I, IX (1861): 122–41; MacDonald and MacDonald, *Clan Donald*, II: 512–13; Hill, *MacDonnells of Antrim*, 35.

28. Alexander MacBain and Rev. John Kennedy, eds., *Reliquiae Celticae: Texts, Papers, and Studies in Gaelic Literature and Philology left by the late Rev. Alexander Cameron, LL.D.*, 2 vols. (Inverness, 1892–4), II: 165.

29. MacDonald and MacDonald, *Clan Donald*, II: 514; Hill, "Shane O'Neill's Expedition".

30. The Ballycastle area evidently had served since time immemorial as the principal entrepôt for northeastern Ulster. Its position at the northern end of the Antrim Glynnes and on the eastern edge of that area known as the Route made Ballycastle the key to controlling both territories. The strategic importance of Ballycastle and its adjoining harbor Port Brittas (a part of Ballycastle Bay) was not lost upon Clan Ian Mor. That Alasdair Cahanagh's principal residence of Dunanynie Castle lay close to the port suggests that it was here that he and his bride established their household. Sorley Boy likely was born within the walls of Dunanynie Castle. Hill, *MacDonnells of Antrim*, 38–9; Hill, "Shane O'Neill's Expedition"; Hugh A. Boyd, "Ballycastle in Older Days", *The Glynns: Journal of the Glens of Antrim Historical Society* V (1977): 5–11; William Piers and Nicholas Malby to Queen, 30 January 1568, London, Public Record Office, State Papers, Ireland, Elizabeth, 63/23/32,i (hereafter cited as SP 63).

31. Hill, "Shane O'Neill's Expedition"; O'Laverty, *Down and Connor*, IV: 468; Rev. William Reeves, *Ecclesiastical Antiquities of Down, Connor, and Dromore* (Dublin, 1847), 282; C. Ardrigh, *The Ancient Franciscan Friary of Bun-na-mairge* (Dublin, 1908), passim.

32. K. A. Steer and J. W. M. Bannerman, *Late Medieval Monumental Sculpture in the West Highlands* (Edinburgh, 1977), 180n, states that both the *longfhada* and the *birlinn* were smaller than the war galley, the former usually having fewer than eighteen oars and the latter eighteen to twenty-four.

33. I. F. Grant, *Highland Folk Ways* (London and Boston, MA, 1961), 250–5; A. R. Cross, "Notes on Scottish Galleys", *Mariner's Mirror* XXXVI (1950): 270–1; MacKenzie, *Highlands and Isles*, 110; Hill, *MacDonnells of Antrim*, 169n; Bannerman, "Lordship of the Isles", 217.

34. Sir Henry Sidney, "Memoir of a Government in Ireland", *Ulster Journal of Archaeology* series I, III (1855): 33–44, 85–99, 336–57; V (1857): 299–315; VIII (1860): 179–95.

35. MacKenzie, *Highlands and Isles*, 121; Hill, "Shane O'Neill's Expedition"; Sidney, "Memoir"; Hill, *MacDonnells of Antrim*, 36; MacLean, "Sketch", 93–4.

36. Hill, *MacDonnells of Antrim*, 36–7; MacDonald and MacDonald, *Clan Donald*, II: 514–14; Lamont, *Early History of Islay*, 34–5; Gregory, *Western Highlands and Isles*, 114.

37. Bannatyne Club, ed., *Orig. Paroch. Scot.*, II: 4.

38. MacDonald and MacDonald, *Clan Donald*, II: 516; Hill, *MacDonnells of Antrim*, 36–7; MacKenzie, *Highlands and Isles*, 121–2.

39. For a contemporary description of the redshanks, see John Elder, "A proposal for uniting Scotland with England, addressed to King Henry VIII, 1542 or 1543", in Iona Club, ed., *Collectanea de Rebus Albanicis, consisting of original papers and documents relating to the history of the Highlands and Islands of Scotland* (Edinburgh, 1847), 28–9.

40. Gregory, *Western Highlands and Isles*, 114–15; MacDonald and MacDonald, *Clan Donald*, II: 514–14.

41. Bond of gossipry between Sir John Campbell of Cawdor and Alexander

MacDonnell of Dunyveg, 7 May 1520, in Spalding Club, ed., *The Book of the Thanes of Cawdor, 1236–1742* (Edinburgh, 1859), 133–5; Same contained in Smith, ed., *Book of Islay*, 35–7. Also see MacDonald and MacDonald, *Clan Donald*, II: 516–17; John de Vere Loder, *Colonsay and Oronsay in the Isles of Argyll: Their History, Flora, Fauna and Topography* (Edinburgh, 1935), 60–1; Lamont, *Early History of Islay*, 35.

42. Bannatyne Club, ed., *Orig. Paroch. Scot.*, II: 269.

43. O'Donovan, ed., *Four Masters*, IV: 1359 (anno 1522), 1371 (anno 1524), 1379 (anno 1525), 1395 (anno 1528); William M. Hennessy, ed., *The Annals of Loch Cé. A Chronicle of Irish Affairs from A.D. 1014 to A.D. 1590*, 2 vols. (London, 1871), II: 237–9 (anno 1522), 247 (anno 1524), 267 (anno 1528).

44. Lamont, *Early History of Islay*, 36; MacDonald and MacDonald, *Clan Donald*, II: 517–19; Gregory, *Western Highlands and Isles*, 132–3; MacLean, "Sketch", 94; Smith, ed., *Book of Islay*, 37–9.

45. Gregory, *Western Highlands and Isles*, 134–5; Hill, *MacDonnells of Antrim*, 157n; MacDonald and MacDonald, *Clan Donald*, II: 519–20; Lamont, *Early History of Islay*, 36–7.

46. Smith, ed., *Book of Islay*, 40–1; Gregory, *Western Highlands and Isles*, 136, 142–3; MacDonald and MacDonald, *Clan Donald*, II: 520–2; MacLean, "Sketch", 95.

47. Bannatyne Club, ed., *Orig. Paroch. Scot.*, II: 5; Smith, ed., *Book of Islay*, 41–3; Lamont, *Early History of Islay*, 37; MacDonald and MacDonald, *Clan Donald*, II: 522–3; Gregory, *Western Highlands and Isles*, 142–3.

48. MacLean, "Sketch", 94; MacDonald and MacDonald, *Clan Donald*, II: 523–4; Hill, "Clan Ian Vór"; Hennessy, ed., *Loch Cé*, II: 277 (1532); O'Donovan, ed., *Four Masters*, IV: 1413 (1532); William M. Hennessy and B. MacCarthy, eds., *Annals of Ulster, A Chronicle of Irish Affairs from A.D. 431 to A.D. 1540*, 4 vols. (Dublin, 1887–1901), III: 591 (1533).

49. Gregory, *Western Highlands and Isles*, 142–3; MacDonald and MacDonald, *Clan Donald*, II: 524–6; Hill, *McaDonnells of Antrim*, 37–8; Lamont, *Early History of Islay*, 37; Hennessy and MacCarthy, eds., *Annals of Ulster*, III: 609 (1536); Report by Robert Cowley, Master of the Rolls, on the state of Ireland, April 1538, London, Public Record Office, State Papers, Henry VIII, 60/6/53 (hereafter cited as SP 60). K. W. Nicholls, in "Notes on the Genealogy of Clann Eoin Mhoir", in *West Highland Notes & Queries* series II, 8 (November 1991): 11–24, posits that Alasdair Cahanagh MacDonnell died in 1536 rather than in 1538. In his opinion, Alasdair Cahanagh was succeeded in 1536 by his uncle and tanist (heir by election), Alexander Carrach MacDonnell. It is true that Alexander Carrach is mentioned several times in the Irish State Papers in 1538–9, and is identified in a letter from William Brabazon to Thomas Cromwell (26 May 1539, SP 60/8/19) as "Alexaunder Karrogh, otherwise called Macdonnell." But far from meaning that Alexander Carrach was actually "recognized as the overall head of Clann Donald" – as Nicholls writes – Brabazon's intent more likely was simply to identify this MacDonnell captain by his surname as a servant of the MacDonnells of Dunyveg. Another factor that suggests Nicholls is in error in writing that Alexander Carrach became lord of Dunyveg is that he and his sons regularly allied themsevles with the English and were banished finally from the southern Antrim Glynnes in the 1540s by James MacDonnell and his brothers (see Thomas Cusake, Chancellor of Ireland, to earl of Warwick, 27 September 1551, London, Public Record Office, State Papers, Ireland, Edward VI, 61/3/52). Indeed, Alexander Carrach might have tried to usurp the chiefship of Clan Ian Mor in 1538, but he certainly was never recognized by the MacDonnells of Dunyveg and

the Glynnes as their rightful head.

Chapter 2

1. Neither Sorley nor any of his brothers, except James, were taught to read or write. Rev. George Hill, "Notices of the Clan Ian Vór, or Clan-Donnell Scots," *Ulster Journal of Archaeology* series I, IX (1861): 301–17, notes that "few of the Scottish gentry aspired to such a high pitch of literary attainment as the simple act of writing implied; and as for the Island lords, they generally regarded the art as unworthy of anyone but a poor monk."

2. Donald Gregory, *The History of the Western Highlands and Isles of Scotland from A.D. 1493 to A.D. 1625*, 2nd edn. (Edinburgh, 1881; reprint edn., Edinburgh 1975), 143; Rev. George Hill, *An Historical Account of the MacDonnells of Antrim, Including Notices of some other Septs, Irish and Scottish* (Belfast, 1873), 41–2; Hill, "Ian Vór."

3. Gregory, *Western Highlands and Isles*, 143; Hill, *MacDonnells of Antrim*, 41–2; Hill, "Ian Vór."

4. See Chapter One.

5. Dioness Campbell, "Observations of Mr Dioness Campbell, Deane of Limerick, on the West Isles of Scotland," in Maitland Club, ed., *Miscellany of the Maitland Club*, 5 vols. (Glasgow, 1847), IV: 44; Hill, *MacDonnells of Antrim*, 41–2; Hill, "Ian Vór."

6. Hill, *MacDonnells of Antrim*, 142; Campbell, "Observations," 44.

7. Ibid.; Hill, *MacDonnells of Antrim*, 42.

8. Lord Deputy Gray's journey into Lecale, 1539, London, Public Record Office, State Papers, Ireland, Henry VIII, SP 60/8/33 (hereafter cited as SP 60). See also T. Alen to Cromwell, 20 October 1538, SP 60/7/50.

9. John O'Donovan, ed., *Annala Rioghachta Eireann, Annals of the Kingdom of Ireland, by the Four Masters, from the Earliest Period to the Year 1616*, 5 vols, (Dublin, 1848), passim; William M. Hennessy, ed., *The Annals of Loch Cé. A Chronicle of Irish Affairs from A.D. 1014 to A.D. 1590*, 2 vols. (London, 1871), passim; William M. Hennessy and B. MacCarthy, eds., *Annals of Ulster, A Chronicle of Irish Affairs from A.D. 431 to A.D. 1540*, 4 vols. (Dublin, 1887–1901), passim.

10. Steven G. Ellis, *Tudor Ireland: Crown, Community and the Conflict of Cultures, 1470–1603* (London and New York, 1985), 29–30; G. A. Hayes-McCoy, *Scots Mercenary Forces in Ireland (1565–1603)* (Dublin and London, 1937), 10; James Michael Hill, *Celtic Warfare, 1595–1763* (Edinburgh, 1986), 22–41.

11. John Andrews, *Ireland in Maps* (Dublin, 1961), 4. For contemporary descriptions of Ireland as a land in need of civilization (at least in English eyes), see Dublin, National Library of Ireland, MS 669; San Marino, CA, Huntington Library, Ellesmere MSS, EL 1701; Edmund Spenser, *A View of the Present State of Ireland*, ed. W. L. Renwick (Oxford, 1970).

12. Kenneth Nicholls, *Gaelic and Gaelicised Ireland in the Middle Ages* (Dublin, 1972), 24; David Beers Quinn, *The Elizabethans and the Irish* (Ithaca, NY and London, 1966), 15–16; Hayes-McCoy, *Scots Mercenary Forces*, 2–3, 10, 46–8; Ellis, *Tudor Ireland*, 30, 33, 40.

13. Ibid., 16–17, 22–3; Karl S. Bottigheimer, "Kingdom and Colony: Ireland in the Westward Enterprise, 1536–1660," in K. R. Andrews, N. P. Canny, and P. E. H. Hair,

eds., *The Westward Enterprise: English Activities in Ireland, the Atlantic, and America, 1480–1650* (Liverpool, 1978), 47; Hiram Morgan, "The End of Gaelic Ulster: a Thematic Interpretation of Events between 1534 and 1610," *Irish Historical Studies* XXVI, 101 (May 1988): 8–32.

14. David Beers Quinn, "Ireland and Sixteenth-Century European Expansion," *Historical Studies* I (1958): 20–32; Ellis, *Tudor Ireland*, 61, 90.

15. Articles concluded with Gillespick MacDonnell *ex parte* Con O'Neill, 1 July 1535, SP 60/2/56/i; Agreement between Lord Leonard Gray and Con O'Neill, 15 June 1536, SP 60/3/42/i; Manus O'Donnell to Gray, 20 August 1537, SP 60/5/6/i; Report by Robert Cowley, Master of the Rolls, on the state of Ireland, April 1538, SP 60/6/53; Brabazon, Aylmer, and Alen to Cromwell, 24 July 1538, SP 60/7/22; Brabazon, Aylmer, and Alen to Henry VIII, 22 August 1538, SP 60/7/35; Gray to Henry VIII, 19 May 1538; Brabazon to Aylmer and Alen, 1538, in Evelyn Philip Shirley, *The History of the County of Monaghan* (London, 1879), 33–4.

16. Walter Cowley to Cromwell, 18 February 1539, SP 60/8/7; Gerot Fleming to Cromwell, 27 April 1539, SP 60/8/13.

17. Quote from "Annales Hiberniae," in Shirley, *Monaghan*, 35. For a contemporary notice of the battle of Bellahoe, see O'Donovan, ed., *Four Masters*, IV (anno 1539).

18. Lord Deputy and Council to Henry VIII, 13 February 1540, SP 60/9/9; Con O'Neill to Henry VIII, 20 July 1540, SP 60/9/38; Henry VIII to Con O'Neill, 7 September 1540, SP 60/9/50; Indenture between Sir Anthony St. Leger and Manus O'Donnell, 6 August 1541, in Constantia Maxwell, ed., *Irish History from Contemporary Sources (1509–1610)* (London, 1923), 110; O'Donovan, ed., *Four Masters*, IV: 1463 (anno 1541); Privy Council to Henry VIII, 23 September 1541, SP 60/10/35; Sir Thomas Cusake to Privy Council, October 1541, SP 60/10/38.

19. St. Leger to Henry VIII, 9 October 1541, SP 60/10/39; Con O'Neill to Henry VIII, December 1541, SP 60/10/47; Henry VIII to St. Leger and Council, 14 April 1542, SP 60/10/55; Manus O'Donnell to Henry VIII, 22 April 1542, SP 60/10/56; St. Leger to Henry VIII, 22 May 1542, SP 60/10/60; St. Leger and Council to Henry VIII, 2 June 1542, SP 60/10/63; Henry VIII to St. Leger and Council, 5 July 1542, SP 60/10/65; St. Leger and Council to Henry VIII, 1 September 1542, SP 60/10/73; Submission of Con O'Neill, 24 September 1542, SP 60/10/78; Henry VIII to St. Leger and Council, 8 October 1542, SP 60/10/84.

20. For details of Con Bacagh O'Neill's submission to Henry VIII at Greenwich on 24 September 1542, see Maxwell, ed., *Irish History*, 110–11; James Morrin, ed., *Calendar of the Patent and Close Rolls of Chancery in Ireland*, 3 vols. (Dublin, 1861–3), I: 85–6. Con was the son of Con Mor ("the great") O'Neill and his wife, a daughter of Gerald, earl of Kildare, and the grandson of Henry O'Neill and another daughter of the Geraldine house.

21. Ellis, *Tudor Ireland*, 143–4.

22. Brendan Bradshaw, "The Elizabethans and the Irish," *Studies* (Spring 1977): 38–50; Nicholas P. Canny, *The Elizabethan Conquest of Ireland: A Pattern Established, 1565–76* (Hassocks, Sussex and New York, 1976), passim; *The Formation of the Old English Elite in Ireland* (Dublin, 1975), passim; "The Permissive Frontier: Social Control in English Settlements in Ireland and Virginia, 1550–1650," in Andrews *et al.*, eds., *Westward Enterprise*, 17–44; "Hugh O'Neill, Earl of Tyrone, and the Changing Face of Gaelic Ulster," *Studia Hibernica* X (1970): 7–35.

23. Bradshaw, "The Elizabethans and the Irish." See also G. R. Elton, *Reform and Renewal* (Cambridge, 1973), 46–50; Brendan Bradshaw, *The Irish Constitutional Revolution of the Sixteenth Century* (Cambridge, 1979), passim.

24. Bottigheimer, "Kingdom and Colony," 46, writes that "the promotion of Ireland to a Kingdom in 1541 was little more than an overzealous declaration of intent." Brendan Bradshaw, "The Beginnings of Modern Ireland," in Brian Farrell, ed., *The Irish Parliamentary Tradition* (Dublin and New York, 1973), 76, argues that the Irish Council drew the king into a situation in Ireland of which he was inadequately advised.

25. O'Donovan, ed., *Four Masters*, IV: 1469–71 (anno 1542); Hennessy, ed., *Loch Cé*, II: 335–7 (anno 1542).

26. The Route (Reuda or Reuta), a corruption of the original Gaelic *Riada* or *Righfada*, was considered MacQuillin's country. It lay between the rivers Bush and Bann, with it southern extremity extending between the Bann and the Glynnes. Hill, *MacDonnells of Antrim*, 46n; Rev. James O'Laverty, *An Historical Account of the Diocese of Down and Connor, Ancient and Modern*, 5 vols. (Dublin, 1878–95), IV: 11; O'Donovan, ed., *Four Masters*, IV: 1471–5 (anno 1542); Hennessy, ed., *Loch Cé*, II: 337 (anno 1542).

27. A. MacDonald and A. MacDonald, *The Clan Donald*, 3 vols. (Inverness, 1896–1904), W. D. Lamont, *The Early History of Islay, 500–1726* (Dundee, Angus, 1966), 40–1.

28. Lord Deputy St. Leger and Council in Ireland to Privy Council, 1 September 1542, in Maxwell, ed., *Irish History*, 108–9.

29. John Traver's plan for the reformation of Ireland, 1542, SP 60/10/85.

30. St. Leger to Henry VIII, 6 April 1543, SP 60/11/2.

31. St. Leger and Council to Henry VIII, 12 July 1542, SP 60/10/66; O'Laverty, *Down and Connor*, IV: 15–16; Richard Cox, *Hibernia Anglicana: or, the History of Ireland from the Conquest thereof by the English, to this present time*, 2nd edn., 2 vols. (London, 1692), II: 260; Hennessy, ed., *Loch Cé*, II: 329 (anno 1541); O'Donovan, ed., *Four Masters*, IV: 1461 (anno 1541). According to D. J. Shove, "Discussion: Post-Glacial Climatic Change," *Quarterly Journal of the Royal Meteorological Society* (April 1949): 175, Europe in the early modern period was in the grip of a "little ice age," which brought about severe climatic variations that adversely affected agricultural output. For more on the changing climate in Europe during this general period, see Emmanuel Le Roy Ladurie, *Times of Feast, Times of Famine: A History of the Climate since the Year 1000*, trans. B. Bray (London, 1971); Fernand Braudel, *The Structures of Everyday Life: Civilization and Capitalism, 15th–18th Century*, trans. Sian Reynolds (New York, 1981); Nels Winkless III and Iben Browning, *Climate and the Affairs of Men* (New York, 1975).

32. O'Donovan, ed., *Four Masters*, IV: 1489 (anno 1544); Hennessy, ed., *Loch Cé*, II: 345–7 (anno 1544).

33. O'Donovan, ed., *Four Masters*, IV: 1487 (anno 1544); M. Webb, "The Clan of the MacQuillins of Antrim," *Ulster Journal of Archaeology* series I, VIII (1860): 251–68.

34. Con O'Neill to Henry VIII, 1 May 1544, SP 60/11/41; Marquis of Kildare, *The Earls of Kildare and their Ancestors: from 1057 to 1773*, 2nd edn. (Dublin, 1858), 194–5.

35. St. Leger to Lord Chancellor Wriothesley, 26 February 1545, SP 60/12/1; St. Leger to Privy Council, 14 April 1545, SP 60/12/6; St. Leger and Council to Privy Council, 6 May 1545, SP 60/12/8; Hill, *MacDonnells of Antrim*, 42–3; Gregory, *Western Highlands and Isles*, 168–9.

36. Privy Council to St. Leger and Council, 4 June 1545, SP 60/12/10; Cox, *Hibernia Anglicana*, II: 278; Hill, "Ian Vór;" Raphael Holinshed, *Chronicles of England, Scotland, and Ireland*, ed. Henry Ellis, 6 vols. (London, 1808; reprint edn., New York, 1965), V: 539.

37. St. Leger and Council to Henry VIII, 12 August 1545, SP 60/12/18; St. Leger and Council to Privy Council, 13 August 1545, SP 60/12/19; Privy Council to St. Leger and Council, 5 September 1545, SP 60/12/20; Holinshed, *Chronicles*, V: 543.

38. Hill, "Ian Vór;" Gregory, *Western Highlands and Isles*, 171; Hill, *MacDonnells of Antrim*, 43; Lamont, *Islay*, 41; Holinshed, *Chronicles*, V: 543.

39. Hill, *MacDonnells of Antrim*, 43; Hill, "Ian Vór;" D. G. White, "Henry VIII's Irish Kerne in France and Scotland, 1544–1545," *Irish Sword* III (1957–8): 213–25; R. B. Wernham, *Before the Armada: The Emergence of the English Nation, 1485–1588* (New York, 1966), 149–63; Lamont, *Islay*, 41–2.

40. Bannatyne Club, ed., *Origines Parochiales Scotiae*, 2 vols. (Edinburgh, 1850), II: 5, 7, 259, 266, 270. See also Charter by Mary, Queen of Scots, in favor of James MacDonnell of Dunyveg and his heirs in Islay and elsewhere forming the barony of Bar in North Kintyre, 21 April 1545, G. G. Smith, ed., *The Book of Islay* (privately printed, 1895), 50–3.

41. MacDonald and MacDonald, *Clan Donald*, II: 529–30; Rev. George Hill, "Shane O'Neill's Expedition Against the Antrim Scots, 1565," *Ulster Journal of Archaeology* series I, IX (1861): 122–41.

42. James MacDonnell to Lord Deputy St. Leger, 24 January 1546, SP 60/12/29/i.

43. Ibid.

44. Hill, *MacDonnells of Antrim*, 44–6.

45. MacDonald and MacDonald, *Clan Donald*, II: 530.

46. Wernham, *Before the Armada*, 161–3; James Hogan, *Ireland in the European System, 1500–1557* (London, 1920), 74–5.

47. "Wait Quha" to Wharton, 28 June 1547, London, Public Record Office, State Papers, Scotland, Edward VI, 1/24 (hereafter cited as SP Scot. Ed. VI); "Ye Wait Quha" to Wharton, 5 July 1547, SP Scot. Ed. VI, 1/28; Wernham, *Before the Armada*, 170; John Prebble, *The Lion in the North* (London, 1971), 184–6; Sir Charles Oman, *A History of the Art of War in the Sixteenth Century* (London, 1937), 358–67.

48. Lord Chancellor Alen to Sir William Paget, Comptroller, 23 November 1548, London, Public Record Office, State Papers, Ireland, Edward VI, SP 61/1/129 (hereafter cited as SP 61).

49. O'Donovan, ed., *Four Masters*, IV: 1513 (anno 1548).

50. Calvagh O'Donnell to Lord Deputy Bellingham, 4 January 1549, SP 61/2/2; Privy Council to Bellingham, 6 January 1549, SP 61/2/3.

51. Sir James Melville of Halhill, *Memoirs of his own Life*, ed. Bannatyne Club (Edinburgh, 1827), 11–12.

52. Cox, *Hibernia Anglicana*, II: 286; Andrew Brereton to Bellingham, 14 June 1549, SP 61/2/41; Hill, "Ian Vór;" Con O'Donnell to Lord Deputy Bellingham and Council, 4 March 1550, and George Dowdall, archbishop of Armagh, to Sir John Alen, Chancellor, and Irish Council, 22 March 1550, in Evelyn Philip Shirley, ed., *Original Letters and Papers in Illustration of the History of the Church in Ireland, during the reigns of Edward IV, Mary, and Elizabeth* (London, 1851), 37–9; Manus O'Donnell to Lord Deputy and Council, 4 March 1550, SP 61/2/52/i; Con O'Neill to George Dowdall, archbishop of Armagh, 7 March 1550, SP 61/2/52/ii; Sir William Brabazon, Lord Justice, to Privy Council, 26 March 1550, SP 61/2/52.

53. MacDonald and MacDonald, *Clan Donald*, II: 531–2; "Pardon of Alexander Oge, son of Alexander Carraghe. . . ." quoted in Morrin, ed., *Patent and Close Rolls*, no. 91, 8 July 1550, I: 208.

54. O'Donovan, ed., *Four Masters* IV: 1521 (anno 1551); Cox, *Hibernia Anglicana*, II: 291; Hill, *MacDonnells of Antrim*, 122.

Chapter 3

1. John O'Donovan, ed., *Annala Rioghachta Eireann, Annals of the Kingdom of Ireland, by the Four Masters, from the Earliest Period to the Year 1616*, 5 vols. (Dublin, 1848), IV: 1521 (anno 1551).

2. Richard Cox, *Hibernia Anglicana: or, the History of Ireland from the Conquest thereof by the English, to this present time*, 2nd edn., 2 vols. (London, 1692), II: 282; David Beers Quinn, "Ireland and Sixteenth-Century European Expansion," *Historical Studies* I (1958): 20–32; Steven G. Ellis, *Tudor Ireland: Crown, Community and the Conflict of Cultures, 1470–1603* (London and New York, 1985), 230–2; Rev. George Hill, *An Historical Account of the MacDonnells of Antrim, Including Notices of some other Septs, Irish and Scottish* (Belfast, 1873), 46–7.

3. Lord Deputy St. Leger to Lord Protector Somerset, 18 February 1551, London, Public Record Office, State Papers, Ireland, Edward VI, SP 61/3/9 (hereafter cited as SP 61). Carrickfergus (Knockfergus) Castle anchored the eastern flank of the English line of advance into Ulster and served as their most important port in that province until the establishment of a tenable position at Derry early in the seventeenth century. G. A. Hayes-McCoy, *Ulster and other Irish Maps, c. 1600* (Dublin, 1964), 5–6; Ellis, *Tudor Ireland*, 231; Gilbert Camblin, *The Town in Ulster* (Belfast, 1951), 14; Philip H. Bagenal, *Vicissitudes of an Anglo-Irish Family, 1530–1800* (London, 1925), 24–5; Edmund Campion, *A Historie of Ireland, written in the Yeare 1571*, ed. James Ware (Dublin, 1633; reprint edn. Dublin, 1809), 187-8; James Wills, *Lives of Illustrious and Distinguished Irishmen from the Earliest Times to the Present Period*, 6 vols. (Dublin, Edinburgh, and London, 1847), I: 464.

4. Lord Deputy and Council to Privy Council, 2 September 1551, SP 61/3/51; Ellis, *Tudor Ireland*, 230; D. G. White, "The Reign of Edward VI in Ireland: Some Political, Social and Economic Aspects," *Irish Historical Studies* XIV (1956–7): 204–6; D. Potter, "French Intrigue in Ireland during the Reign of Henri II, 1547–1559," *International History Review* V (1983): 168–76.

5. Thomas Cusake, Chancellor of Ireland, to earl of Warwick, 27 September 1551, SP 61/3/52; Instructions to Mr. Wood, 29 September 1551, SP 61/3/54; Bagenal, *Vicissitudes*, 6; A. MacDonald and A. MacDonald, *The Clan Donald*, 3 vols. (Inverness, 1896–1904), II: 530–2; O'Donovan, ed., *Four Masters*, IV: 1521 (anno 1551); Cox, *Hibernia Anglicana*, II: 291; Sir James Ware, *The Antiquities and History of Ireland*, 2

vols. (London, 1714), I: 124; Hill, *MacDonnells of Antrim*, 47; Dugald Mitchell, *A Popular History of the Highlands and Gaelic Scotland* (Paisley, Renfrew, 1900), 396; Rev. E. A. D'Alton, *History of Ireland from the Earliest Times to the Present Day*, 3 vols. (London, 1904–8), II: 8–9, 34.

6. Cusake to Warwick, 27 September 1551, SP 61/3/52.

7. Ibid.

8. Hill, *MacDonnells of Antrim*, 51n–2; Cusake to Warwick, 27 September 1551, SP 61/3/52.

9. Ibid.; Rev. George Hill, "Notices of the Clan Ian Vór, or Clan-Donnell Scots", *Ulster Journal of Archaeology* series I, IX (1861): 301–17.

10. Cusake to Warwick, 27 September 1551, SP 61/3/52.

11. MacDonald and MacDonald, *Clan Donald*, II: 530–1.

12. Council in Dublin to Privy Council, 20 May 1551, SP 61/3/25; O'Donovan, ed., *Four Masters*, IV: 1521 (anno 1551); Sean O'Faolain, *The Great O'Neill* (New York, 1942), 45; Philip Wilson, *The Beginnings of Modern Ireland* (Dublin and London, 1912), 380–1.

13. Sir Henry Sidney, "Memoir of a Government in Ireland," *Ulster Journal of Archaeology* series I, III (1855): 33–44, 85–96, 336–57; V (1857): 299–315; VIII (1860): 179–95; John J. Marshall, *History of Dungannon* (Dungannon, Tyrone, 1929), 19; R. Barry O'Brien, *Irish Memories* (London, 1904), 24–5; J. J. O'Connell, *The Irish Wars: A Military History of Ireland from the Norse Invasions to 1798* (Dublin, n.d.), 10–11; James Michael Hill, *Celtic Warfare, 1595–1763* (Edinburgh, 1986), 22–44.

14. Marshal Nicholas Bagenal to Lord Deputy Crofts, 11 November 1551, SP 61/3/65,i; Con O'Neill to Sir Anthony St. Leger, 9 February 1552, SP 61/4/9.

15. Hill, *MacDonnells of Antrim*, 52–3.

16. Privy Council to Lord Deputy Crofts, 23 February 1552, SP 61/4/11; J. H. Andrews, "Geography and Government in Elizabethan Ireland", in Nicholas Stephens and Robin E. Glasscock, eds., *Irish Geographical Studies in honour of E. Estyn Evans* (Belfast, 1970), 181–2.

17. For changes in England's Irish policy in the 1550s, see Quinn, "Ireland and Sixteenth-Century European Expansion;" Brendan Bradshaw, "Native reaction to the Westward Enterprise: a case-study in Gaelic ideology", in K. R. Andrews, N. P. Canny, and P. E. H. Hair, eds., *The Westward Enterprise: English Activities in Ireland, the Atlantic, and America, 1480–1650* (Liverpool, 1978), 67.

18. Ellis, *Tudor Ireland*, 177; Karl S. Bottigheimer, "Kingdom and colony: Ireland in the Westward Enterprise, 1536–1660" in Andrews *et al.*, *Westward Enterprise*, 47.

19. William Piers to Lord Justice, 14 February 1558, London, Public Record Office, State Papers, Ireland, Mary, SP 62/2/13,i (hereafter cited as SP 62).

20. Sir Thomas Cusake's book of the State of Ireland, sent to the duke of Northumberland, 8 May 1552, London, Lambeth Palace Library, Carew MSS, vol. 611, f. 112. Also see same report, SP 61/4/43.

21. Cusake's book of the State of Ireland, 8 May 1552, Carew MSS, vol. 611, f. 112; Hill, *MacDonnells of Antrim*, 122.

22. Piers to Lord Justice, 14 February 1558, SP 62/2/13,i; Hill, *MacDonnells of*

Antrim, 122; Lord Deputy St. Leger to Secretary Sir William Petre, 18 December 1555, SP 62/1/8; MacDonald and MacDonald, *Clan Donald*, II: 675.

23. Privy Council to Lord Deputy and Council, 29 May 1552, SP 61/4/48.

24. MacDonald and MacDonald, *Clan Donald*, II: 674-5.

25. Cusake's book of the State of Ireland, 8 May 1552, Carew MSS, vol. 611, f. 112.

26. O'Donovan, ed., *Four Masters*, IV: 1525, 1527 (anno 1552); Rev. James O'Laverty, *An Historical Account of the Diocese of Down and Connor, Ancient and Modern*, 5 vols. (Dublin, 1878–95), II: 169.

27. Sidney, "Memoir;" Ware, *Antiquities*, 127; Cox, *Hibernia Anglicana*, II: 293; Memorandum concerning Con O'Neill, earl of Tyrone, 30 December 1552, Carew MSS, vol. 603, f. 49.

28. Ibid.

29. Ellis, *Tudor Ireland*, 317–18.

30. Ibid.

31. O'Laverty, *Down and Connor*, II: 170; O'Donovan, ed., *Four Masters*, IV: 1539 (anno 1555).

32. T. Bedford Franklin, *A History of Scottish Farming* (London, 1952), 102–3.

33. Cox, *Hibernia Anglicana*, II: 302; O'Laverty, *Down and Conner*, III: 27.

34. Edward Walshe, "'Conjectures' Concerning the State of Ireland [1552]," *Irish Historical Studies* V (1946–7): 303–22.

35. Ellis, *Tudor Ireland*, 232–4.

36. T. W. Moody, F. X. Martin, and F. J. Byrne. eds., *A New History of Ireland*, 9 vols. (Oxford, 1976–84), vol. III, *Early Modern Ireland, 1534–1691*, 76 (hereafter cited as NHI); Lord Ernest Hamilton, *Elizabethan Ulster* (London, 1919), 11; Historical Manuscripts Commission, *The Manuscripts of Charles Haliday, Esq., of Dublin. Acts of the Privy Council in Ireland, 1556-1571*, fifteenth report, appendix, part III, ed. John T. Gilbert (London, 1897), 2; Margaret MacCurtain, *Tudor and Stuart Ireland* (Dublin, 1972), 59.

37. A present remedy for the reformation of the North and the rest of Ireland, April 1556, SP 62/1/13.

38. "An Act against bringing in of Scots, retaining of them, and marrying with them," 3 and 4 Philip and Mary, in Great Britain, *The Statutes at Large passed in the Parliaments held in Ireland, 1310–1786*, 2 vols. (Dublin, 1786), II: 10.

39. Ibid.

40. Fitzwalter to Queen, 31 December 1556, SP 62/1/22,ii; Instructions to Sir Thomas Challoner, February 1556, London, Public Record Office, State Papers, Scotland, Mary (hereafter cited as SP Scot. Mary); "Obligation by James, Duke of Chastellaurault, Earl of Arran, and Lord Hamilton, to James MacDonnell of Dunyveg, in reference to the Duke's Isle of Arran," 12 May 1556, in Iona Club, ed., *Collectanea de Rebus Albanicis, consisting of original papers and documents relating to the history of the Highlands and Islands of Scotland* (Edinburgh, 1847), 88–9.

41. Sidney, "Memoir;" O'Donovan, ed., *Four Masters*, IV: 1539 (anno 1555 or 1556).

42. Cox, *Hibernia Anglicana*, II: 303; Book of Howth, 1556, Carew MSS, ff. 121–2.

43. Descriptions of the battle of Ballohe M'Gille Corrough are found in Book of Howth, 1556, Carew MSS, ff. 121–2; Instructions from Sussex, 12 June 1556, in *Haliday MSS*, 3–4; Cox, *Hibernia Anglicana*, II: 303; O'Laverty, *Down and Connor*, III: 27; Ware, *Antiquities*, 139; Hill, *MacDonnells of Antrim*, 129n; Lord Deputy Sussex's journey, 8 August 1556, Carew MSS, vol. 621, f. 15.

44. Sidney, "Memoir."

45. Lord Deputy Sussex's journey, 8 August 1556, Carew MSS, vol. 621, f. 15.

46. Book of Howth, 1556, Carew MSS, ff. 121v–2; Lord Deputy Sussex's journey, 8 August 1556, Carew MSS, vol. 621, f. 15.

47. According to Hill, *MacDonnells of Antrim*, 138n, besides Glenarm, the family had nine other castles in the Glynnes and Route in the sixteenth century: Dunluce, Dunseverick, Dunanynie, Deffrick, Clough, Clare, New Castle (Ballycastle), Red Bay, and Castle MacMartin.

48. O'Laverty, *Down and Connor*, I: xxiii; Hill, *MacDonnells of Antrim*, 124n–5n.

49. Cusake's book of the State of Ireland, 8 May 1552, Carew MSS, vol. 611, f. 112.

50. Thomas Radcliffe, Lord Fitzwalter, Lord Deputy, to Queen, 2 January 1557, SP 62/1/22; Cox, *Hibernia Anglicana* II: 306; Hamilton, *Elizabethan Ulster*, 12; Cusake's book of the State of Ireland, 8 May 1552, Carew MSS, vol. 611, f. 112; O'Donovan, ed., *Four Masters*, IV: 1541 (anno 1555).

51. Ibid.

52. John T. Gilbert, ed., *Account of Facsimiles of National Manuscripts of Ireland* (London, 1884), 153; O'Donovan, ed., *Four Masters*, IV: 1551, 1553 (anno 1557).

53. Ibid.

54. Ibid., IV: 1553, 1555 (anno 1557). Shane's personal guard was known as his *Luchdtach*, a group of young warriors chosen from the leading families of the clan and expertly trained in the use of the sword and target, Lochaber axe, bow, and in horsemanship and other military and athletic skills. Young men usually were initiated into this elite circle by participating in a cattle raid on a neighboring clan or family. Hill, *MacDonnells of Antrim*, 131n. Also see a description in Martin Martin, *A Description of the Western Islands of Scotland circa 1695*, ed. Donald J. MacLeod, 4th edn. (Stirling, 1934), 167.

55. O'Donovan, ed., *Four Masters*, IV: 1555, 1557, 1559 (anno 1557).

56. Philip and Mary to Lord Deputy Sussex, 23 June 1557, SP 62/1/44.

57. Marquis of Kildare, *The Earls of Kildare and Their Ancestors: From 1057 to 1773*, 2nd edn. (Dublin, 1858), 202; Cox, *Hibernia Anglicana*, II: 305; Ware, *Antiquities*, 142; Mitchell, *History of the Highlands*, 397.

58. Quoted in Hill, *MacDonnells of Antrim*, 129n.

59. Alice Stopford Green, *The Making of Ireland and its Undoing* (London, 1909), 92; Ellis, *Tudor Ireland*, 235.

60. George Dowdall, archbishop of Armagh, to Nicholas Heath, archbishop of York, and Lord Chancellor and Privy Council, 17 November 1557, SP 62/1/61.

61. Ellis, *Tudor Ireland*, 235–6; Brendan Bradshaw, *The Irish Constitutional Revolution of the Sixteenth Century* (Cambridge, 1979), 286–75; Nicholas P. Canny, *The Formation of the Old English Elite in Ireland* (Dublin, 1975), 15, 21.

62. Sir Charles Oman, *A History of the Art of War in the Sixteenth Century* (London, 1937), 254–73; J. J. Silke, *Ireland and Europe, 1559–1607* (Dundalk, 1966), 4–5.

63. Lord Justice Sir Henry Sidney and Council to Privy Council, 8 February 1558, SP 62/2/10; Ellis, *Tudor Ireland*, 237.

64. Hill, *MacDonnells of Antrim*, 39–40; Charter by Francis and Mary, regranting to MacDonald of Dunivaig certain lands in Islay forming part the barony of Bar, the said MacDonald having lost his writs by war and fire, in G. G. Smith, ed., *The Book of Islay* (privately printed, 1895), 62–5; Bannatyne Club, ed., *Origines Parochiales Scotiae*, 2 vols. (Edinburgh, 1850), II: 6, 24.

65. Lord Deputy Sussex to Mr. Secretary Boxoll, 3 June 1558, SP 62/2/49. Colla Dubh ("the dark-haired") MacDonnell, also known as na-g Capul ("of the horses"), was the third son of Alasdair Cahanagh.

66. Lord Deputy Sussex to Boxoll, 3 June 1558, SP 62/2/49. Colla left two sons, Gillaspick and Ranald. Gillaspick was the father of Coll Keitache mac Gillaspick MacColla of Colonsay, who himself was the father of the famous Alasdair MacColla, who fought beside Montrose in the Scottish Highlands in the 1640s. Sorley Boy, then, was Coll Keitache's great-uncle and Alasdair MacColla's great-grand-uncle.

67. Lord Deputy Sussex to Boxoll, 3 June 1558, SP 62/2/49.

68. Ibid.

69. Sidney, "Memoir;" Ware, *Antiquities*, 145.

70. Rev. George Hill, "Shane O'Neill's Expedition Against the Antrim Scots, 1565," *Ulster Journal of Archaeology* series I, IX (1861): 122–41.

71. Campion, *Historie of Ireland*, 187–9; Sidney, "Memoir."

72. O'Donovan, ed., *Four Masters*, IV: 1563, 1565 (anno 1558).

73. Sidney, "Memoir;" Con Bacagh O'Neill to Queen Mary [I], June 1558, SP 62/2/56.

74. Raphael Holinshed, *Chronicles of England, Scotland, and Ireland*, ed. Henry Ellis, 6 vols. (London, 1808; reprint edn. New York, 1965), V: 586; Campion, *Historie of Ireland*, 185; Sidney, "Memoir;" Ware, *Antiquities*, 145; Cox, *Hibernia Anglicana*, II: 307; MacDonald and MacDonald, *Clan Donald*, II: 534; Hill, "Shane O'Neill's Expedition;" Ellis, *Tudor Ireland*, 237; Wilson, *Beginnings of Modern Ireland*, 424–5; Extract from a letter from Sussex to Mary, Queen of England, 6 October 1558, in Smith, ed., *Book of Islay*, 66–7.

75. Holinshed, *Chronicles*, V: 586.

76. Ellis, *Tudor Ireland*, 238; Charles O'Mahony, *The Viceroys of Ireland* (London, 1912), 67–8.

77. O'Laverty, *Down and Connor*, IV: 19; Hill, *MacDonnells of Antrim*, 123–4.

78. Ibid.; M. Webb, "The Clan of the MacQuillins of Antrim," *Ulster Journal of Archaeology* series I, VIII (1860): 251–68.

79. Ibid.; Hill, *MacDonnells of Antrim*, 125n.

80. Hector MacLean, "A Sketch of the MacDonnells of Antrim", in *Transactions of the Gaelic Society of Inverness,* vol. XVII (Inverness, 1890–91), 95–6; Webb, "MacQuillins of Antrim;" Hill, *MacDonnells of Antrim,* 123n; O'Laverty, *Down and Connor,* IV: 16. Hill, "Shane O'Neill's Expedition," identified one John Magee, whose family settled near Ballycastle and who followed Sorley Boy at the battle of Aura. Afterwards he was granted lands near Fairhead. For Magee's role at Slieve-an-Aura, also see Rev. William Reeves, *Account of an Ancient Scotch Deed* (Dublin, 1852), 3–4.

81. Cox, *Hibernia Anglicana,* II: 313; Ellis, *Tudor Ireland,* 238–9.

82. Hill, *MacDonnells of Antrim,* 125.

83. Disposition of Mary of Guise, queen regent, to James MacDonnell of Dunyveg and the Glynnes, of the said ward, non-entries, relief, and marriage of Mary MacLeod, heiress of Dunvegan, 27 June 1559, in Iona Club, ed., *Collectanea de Rebus Albanicis,* 141–3.

84. Argyll's influence on affairs in Ulster between 1560 and 1563 will be discussed in Chapter Four below.

85. Instructions to the earl of Sussex, May 1559, Carew MSS, vol. 628, f. 82.

86. Queen to James MacDonnell, June 1559, London, Public Record Office, State Papers, Ireland, Elizabeth, SP 63/1/38 (hereafter cited as SP 63); Hill, *MacDonnells of Antrim,* 125–6.

87. Instructions from the Queen to Lord Deputy Sussex, 16 July 1559, SP 63/1/60.

88. Ibid.

89. Ibid.

90. Instructions to the earl of Sussex, 17 July 1559, Carew MSS, vol. 628, f. 69 (same as SP 63/1/60, except for date of 16 July 1559).

91. Ibid.

Chapter 4

1. G. A. Hayes-McCoy, *Scots Mercenary Forces in Ireland (1565–1603)* (Dublin and London, 1937), 88; Jane E. A. Dawson, "Two Kingdoms or Three?: Ireland in Anglo-Scottish Relations in the Middle of the Sixteenth Century," in Roger A. Mason, ed., *Scotland and England, 1286–1815* (Edinburgh, 1987), 114, 118.

2. Steven G. Ellis, *Tudor Ireland: Crown, Community and the Conflict of Cultures, 1470–1603* (London and New York, 1985), 15, 239; J. H. Elliott, *Europe Divided, 1559–1598* (New York, 1968), 11–12; Dawson, "Two Kingdoms or Three?," 119; J. J. Silke, *Ireland and Europe, 1559–1607* (Dundalk, Louth, 1966), 8–9; T. W. Moody, F. X. Martin, and F. J. Byrne, eds., *A New History of Ireland,* 9 vols. (Oxford, 1976–84), vol. III, *Early Modern Ireland, 1534–1691,* 80 (hereafter cited as NHI).

3. Quoted in Dawson, "Two Kingdoms or Three?," 119.

4. Ibid., 119–20.

5. Sir William Fitzwilliam, Lord Justice, to Lord Deputy Sussex, 8 March 1560, London, Public Record Office, State Papers, Ireland, Elizabeth, SP 63/2/7 (hereafter cited as SP 63).

6. William Cecil's Articles declaring both the state of the North part of Ireland and what is required of the part of Scotland to help the same be set in good order, 2 April 1560, Belfast, Public Record Office of Northern Ireland, MS T530. II.

7. Ibid.

8. Maitland to Cecil, 10 April 1560, London, Public Record Office, State Papers, Scotland, Elizabeth, 3/16 (hereafter cited as SP Scot. Eliz.); Fitzwilliam to Cecil, 20 April 1560, SP 63/2/12.

9. Richard Cox, *Hibernia Anglicana: or, the History of Ireland from the Conquest thereof by the English, to this present time*, 2nd edn., 2 vols. (London, 1692), II: 315.

10. Ellis, *Tudor Ireland*, 15, 239–40.

11. Fitzwilliam to Sussex, 8 March 1560, SP 63/2/7; Memorial to the earl of Sussex, 27 May 1560, London, Lambeth Palace Library, Carew MSS, vol. 628, f. 88; Shane O'Neill to Argyll, 19 July 1560, SP 63/2/26; Argyll to the Queen, 19 July 1560, SP 63/2/27; List of disloyal subjects in Ulster, July 1560, SP 63/2/28; Dawson, "Two Kingdoms or Three?," 121.

12. Queen Elizabeth to Argyll, 4 August 1560, in Alexander MacDonald, ed., *Letters to the Argyll Family* (Edinburgh, 1839; reprint edn., New York, 1973), 4.

13. Argyll to Cecil, 20 August 1560, SP Scot. Eliz. 5/12; Thomas Randolph to Cecil, 25 August 1560, SP Scot. Eliz. 5/16.

14. Gilbert Gerrard, Attorney General, to Cecil, 5 September 1560, SP 63/2/33.

15. Sir Henry Sidney, "Memoir of a Government in Ireland," *Ulster Journal of Archaeology* series I, III (1855): 33–44, 85–99, 336–57; V (1857): 299–315; VIII (1860): 179–95; Queen to Sussex, 15 August 1560, SP 63/2/30.

16. Ellis, *Tudor Ireland*, 240. For an expert and lucid treatment of the military aspects of the French Religious Wars, see Sir Charles Oman, *A History of the Art of War in the Sixteenth Century* (London, 1937), 393–533.

17. The general hosting northward against Shane O'Neill, 12 September 1560, in Historical Manuscripts Commission, *The Manuscripts of Charles Haliday, Esq., of Dublin. Acts of the Privy Council in Ireland, 1556–1571*, fifteenth report, appendix, part III, ed. John T. Gilbert (London, 1897), 88–9; Dawson, "Two Kingdoms or Three?," 122.

18. Bannatyne Club, ed., *Origines Parochiales Scotiae*, 2 vols. (Edinburgh, 1850), I: 6–7; W. C. MacKenzie, *The Highlands and Isles of Scotland: A Historical Survey* (Edinburgh and London, 1937; reprint edn., New York, 1977), 154–5.

19. Indenture between the Queen and James MacDonnell, 20 January 1561, SP 63/3/4.

20. Ibid.

21. James Hogan, "Shane O'Neill comes to the Court of Elizabeth," in Seamus Pender, ed., *Féilscríbhinn Torna: Essays and Studies Presented to Professor Tadhg Ua Donnchadha (Torna)* (Cork, 1947), 155; Shane O'Neill to Queen, 8 February 1561, SP 63/3/14.

22. Hogan, "Shane O'Neill," 155.

23. Sussex to Cecil, 19 August 1561, SP 63/4/37.

24. Sussex and Council to Queen, 26 January 1561, SP 63/3/7.

25. Sir George Stanley to Sussex, 28 February 1561, London, British Library, Cottonian MSS, Titus. B. XIII f. 27.

26. Captain William Piers, constable of Carrickfergus, to Sir William Fitzwilliam, 28 April 1561, SP 63/3/64,i; Rev. C. H. Forde, *Round the Coast of Northern Ireland* (Belfast, 1928), 48; Rev. James O'Laverty, *An Historical Account of the Diocese of Down and Connor, Ancient and Modern*, 5 vols. (Dublin, 1878–95), IV: 545; Rev. George Hill, *An Historical Account of the MacDonnells of Antrim, Including Notices of some other Septs, Irish and Scottish* (Belfast, 1873), 188n. Several times between 1559 and 1564 Sussex left Ireland for England, Lord Justice Fitzwilliam usually ruling in his place. F. S. Thomas, ed., *Historical Notes, 1509–1603*, 3 vols. (London, 1856), I: 467.

27. Instructions to Sussex, 22 May 1561, Carew MSS, vol. 628, f. 90.

28. Ibid.

29. Instructions to Sussex, 24 May 1561, SP 63/3/78.

30. Fitzwilliam to Cecil, 30 May 1561, SP 63/3/84; Fitzwilliam to Sussex, 30 May 1561, SP 63/3/85; Cecil to Sussex, 19 June 1561, Cottonian MSS, Titus. B. XIII f. 38.

31. John O'Donovan, ed., *Annala Rioghachta Eireann, Annals of the Kingdom of Ireland, by the Four Masters, from the Earliest Period to the Year 1616*, 5 vols. (Dublin, 1848), IV: 1587 (anno 1561).

32. Sussex to Cecil, 23 June 1561, SP 63/4/13.

33. Sussex and Council to Queen, 16 July 1561, SP 63/4/22; James Stuart, *Historical Memoirs of the City of Armagh* (Newry, 1819), 256.

34. Cecil to Sussex, 25 July 1561, Cottonian MSS, Titus. B. XIII f. 42.

35. Sussex and Council to Queen, 31 July 1561, SP 63/4/24; Hogan, "Shane O'Neill," 156; Sussex and Council to Queen, 31 July 1561, SP 63/4/24; O'Donovan, ed., *Four Masters*, IV: 1585–7 (anno 1561); Herbert F. Hore, "The Ulster State Papers," *Ulster Journal of Archaeology* series I, VIII (1859): 45–65; Sussex to Cecil, 31 July 1561, SP 63/4/25.

36. Sidney, "Memoir."

37. Hogan, "Shane O'Neill," 156.

38. Instructions to William Cantwell concerning Shane O'Neill, 6 August 1561, SP 63/4/29.

39. Sussex to Cecil, 14 August 1561, SP 63/4/35. For Irish chiefs on the English payroll against O'Neill in the autumn of 1561, see Irish Manuscripts Commission, ed., *Fitzwilliam Accounts, 1560–65 (Annesley Collection)*, ed. A. K. Longfield (Dublin, 1960), 61; Ellis, *Tudor Ireland*, 240.

40. Cecil to Sussex, 21 August 1561, Cottonian MSS, Titus. B. XIII f. 48.

41. Dawson, "Two Kingdoms or Three?," 123; Hogan, "Shane O'Neill," 156.

42. Ibid.; Queen to Sussex, 25 August 1561, SP 63/4/39.

43. Ibid.

44. Ibid.

45. Hogan, "Shane O'Neill," 160.

46. Randolph to Cecil, 12 September 1561, Cottonian MSS, Calig. B. IX f. 167; Randolph to Cecil, 24 September 1561, Cottonian MSS, Calig. B. X f. 184; Randolph to Cecil, 7 September 1561, Cottonian MSS, Calig. B. X f. 151; Randolph to Cecil, 10 September 1561, SP Scot. Eliz. 6/66; O'Donovan, ed., *Four Masters*, IV: 1587–9 (anno 1561); Marquis of Kildare, *The Earls of Kildare and their Ancestors: from 1057 to 1773*, 2nd edn. (Dublin, 1858), 203–4.

47. Elizabeth to Mary, Queen of Scots, December 1561, SP Scot. Eliz. 6/87; Hayes-McCoy, *Scots Mercenary Forces*, 81; A. MacDonald and A. MacDonald, *The Clan Donald*, 3 vols. (Inverness, 1896–1904), II: 537.

48. John Willock to Randolph, 30 January 1562, Great Britain, *Calendar of State Papers, Foreign Series, of the reign of Elizabeth, 1558–1603*, 23 vols., ed. Rev. Joseph Stevenson *et al.* (London, 1863–1950), IV (1561–2) (hereafter cited as *CSP For. Eliz.*): 513; W. D. Lamont, *The Early History of Islay, 500–1726* (Dundee, Angus, 1966), 42; J. P. MacLean, *History of the Island of Mull*, 2 vols. (San Mateo, CA, 1925), 46; Hayes-McCoy, *Scots Mercenary Forces*, 86–7; Donald Gregory, *The History of the Western Highlands and Isles of Scotland from A.D. 1493 to A.D. 1625* (Edinburgh, 1881; reprint edn., Edinburgh, 1975), 191; Dugald Mitchell, *A Popular History of the Highlands and Gaelic Scotland* (Paisley, Renfrew, 1900), 397; MacDonald and MacDonald, *Clan Donald*, II: 538.

49. Randolph to Cecil, 15 January 1562, *CSP For. Eliz.*, IV (1561–2): 492; Dawson, "Two Kingdoms or Three?," 123–4; Randolph to Cecil, 15 January 1562, SP Scot. Eliz. 7/10.

50. Robert Chambers, ed., *Domestic Annals of Scotland from the Reformation to the Revolution*, 3 vols. (Edinburgh and London, 1874), I: 25n–6n; Ollamh, *The Story of Shane O'Neill, Hereditary Prince of Ulster* (Dublin, n.d.), 40–4; Hayes-McCoy, *Scots Mercenary Forces*, 82; Indenture between Elizabeth and Shane O'Neill, 30 April 1562, Carew MSS, vol. 614, f. 137; Randolph to Cecil, 31 March 1562, SP Scot. Eliz. 7/31. For land grants made by Mary, Queen of Scots, to James MacDonnell in 1562, see Bannatyne Club, ed., *Orig. Paroch. Scot.*, I: 6–7, 266; A letter of tack by Mary, Queen of Scots, to James MacDonnell, 24 September 1562, in G. G. Smith, ed., *The Book of Islay* (privately printed, 1895), 67–9.

51. Proclamation by the Queen in favour of Shane O'Neill, 5 May 1562, SP 63/6/6; Shane O'Neill to Privy Council, March 1562, SP 63/5/61; Dawson, "Two Kingdoms or Three?," 124; Hogan, "Shane O'Neill," 164–5.

52. James MacDonnell to Sussex, 18 July 1562, SP 63/6/66,i; Kildare, *Earls of Kildare*, 204; Ellis, *Tudor Ireland*, 240–1; M. Dillon, "Ceart Ui Néill," *Studia Celtica* I (1966): 1–18; J. B. Black, *The Reign of Elizabeth, 1558–1603* (Oxford, 1959), 469; Sussex to Queen, concerning articles with James and Sorley Boy MacDonnell, 12 August 1562, SP 63/6/66; Sussex to James MacDonnell, 13 August 1562, SP 63/6/66,ii.

53. Sussex to Cecil, 26 July 1562, SP 63/6/58; Instructions from Sussex to Terence Daniel, dean of Armagh and archdeacon of Meath, 31 July 1562, SP 63/6/60; Sussex to Cecil, 1 August 1562, SP 63/6/62; Alexander G. Richey, *Lectures on the History of Ireland from A.D. 1534 to the Date of the Plantation of Ulster* (London and Dublin, 1870), 297.

54. Sussex to Queen, concerning articles with James and Sorley Boy MacDonnell, 12 August 1562, SP 63/6/66.

55. Sussex to James MacDonnell, 13 August 1562, SP 63/6/66,ii.

56. Shane Maguire to Sussex, 15 August 1562, Cottonian MSS, Vesp. F. XII f. 67; Sussex to Queen, 27 August 1562, SP 63/6/75; Sussex to Cecil, 21 September 1562, SP 63/7/16.

57. James MacDonnell to Sussex, 31 August 1562, Cottonian MSS, Vesp. F. XII f. 81; Sorley Boy MacDonnell to Sussex, 9 September 1562, Cottonian MSS, Vesp. F. XII f. 85.

58. James MacDonnell to Sussex, 28 September 1562, SP 63/7/29,iii. The same letter is also located in Cottonian MSS, Vesp. F. XII f. 78.

59. Sussex to Queen, 29 September 1562, SP 63/7/19.

60. Ibid.

61. Con O'Donnell to Queen, 30 September 1562, SP 63/7/21; Sussex to Queen, 1 October 1562, SP 63/7/22; Sussex to James MacDonnell, 16 October 1562, SP 63/7/29,iv. The same letter is also located in Cottonian MSS, Vesp. F. XII f. 77.

62. Shane Maguire to Sussex, 20 October 1562, Cottonian MSS, Vesp. F. XII f. 92. In Shane Maguire to Sussex, 25 November 1562, Cottonian MSS, Vesp. F. XII f. 47, he lamented that "the last journey that Shane . . . made into this country with the help of Hugh O'Donnell, . . . they left neither house nor corn in all my country upon the main land unwasted, neither church nor sentory unrobbed. . . ." Memorandum from Sussex, 26 October, 1562, in Historical Manuscripts Commission, *Haliday MSS*, 127, addresses the weak state of English defenses in Ireland.

63. Sorley Boy MacDonnell to Sussex, 17 November 1562, Cottonian MSS, Vesp. F. XII f. 58. O'Neill's spy network proved so effective that the editor of Sidney, "Memoir," was moved to admit "that no affair was deliberated in Council in Dublin, but O'Neill knew of it before the matter was concluded. He had many friends in the metropolis, and moreover frequently sent messengers thither as spies. Old Sir Turlough Luineach used to complain that he could not have a carouse of sack but it was known in Dublin in four-and-twenty hours."

64. Instructions from Sussex to William Piers, 10 December 1562, SP 63/7/56.

65. Randolph to Cecil, 16 December 1562, SP Scot. Eliz. 7/91; Sussex to Privy Council, 28 December 1562, SP 63/7/58.

66. Hayes-McCoy, *Scots Mercenary Forces*, 81.

67. Sussex to Privy Council, 28 December 1562, SP 63/7/58; William Cecil, Lord Burghley, *A Collection of State Papers, 1542–1570*, ed. Samuel Haynes (London, 1740), 387–8.

68. Randolph to Cecil, 22 January 1563, SP Scot. Eliz. 8/6; Randolph to Cecil, 31 January 1563, SP Scot. Eliz. 8/7; Randolph to Cecil, 6 February 1563, SP Scot. Eliz. 8/9.

69. Ibid.

70. Depositions of John English, concerning Thomas Phettiplace and William Johnson, before the Privy Council, 23 March 1563, SP Scot. Eliz. 8/28; Privy Council to Phettiplace and Johnson, 1 April 1563, SP Scot. Eliz. 8/29; James MacDonnell to Sussex, 4 April 1563, SP 63/8/27.

71. Sussex and Council to Privy Council, 24 April 1563, SP 63/8/34; R. Barry

O'Brien, *Irish Memories* (London, 1904), 42–3; Myles V. Ronan, *The Reformation in Ireland under Elizabeth, 1558–1580* (London and New York, 1930), 87.

72. Piers to Sussex, 11 April 1563, SP 63/8/34,i.

73. Sussex and Council to James MacDonnell, 14 April 1563, SP 63/8/34,iii.

74. James MacDonnell to Randolph, 16 April 1563, SP Scot. Eliz. 8/35,i.

75. Sussex and Council to Sorley Boy MacDonnell, 20 April 1563, SP 63/8/34, vi; Sussex and Council to Privy Council, 24 April 1563, SP 63/8/34; Randolph to Cecil, 1 May 1563, SP Scot. Eliz. 8/35.

76. A journey by Sussex in 1563, Carew MSS, vol. 621, f. 23a; John J. Marshall, *Benburb: Its Battlefields and History* (Dungannon, Tyrone, 1924), 4; O'Brien, *Irish Memories*, 42–3; Sussex and Council to Privy Council, 11 May 1563, SP 63/8/45; John J. Marshall, *History of Dungannon* (Dungannon, Tyrone, 1929), 21.

77. Sussex complained about being sent into the field without money or munitions. Sussex to Cecil, 24 April 1563, SP 63/8/33. See also *NHI*, III: 84–5.

78. Extract from a letter from Randolph to Sussex, 15 May 1563, SP 63/8/46,i; MacDonald and MacDonald, *Clan Donald*, II: 679.

79. Sussex to Cecil, 20 May 1563, SP 63/8/46; Extract from a letter from Randolph to Sussex, 15 May 1563, SP 63/8/46,i.

80. Queen to Sussex and Chancellor, 25 May 1563, SP 63/8/48; Randolph to Cecil, 13 June 1563, SP Scot. Eliz. 8/42.

81. Report by Piers, intended for Sussex or Cecil, 1563, SP 63/9/83.

82. Ibid.; Hill, *MacDonnells of Antrim*, 148n, notes that Donnell Gorme MacDonald of Sleat believed himself the rightful heir to the lordship of the Isles, as he was fourth in descent from Hugh MacDonald of Sleat, a younger brother of John, fourth lord of the Isles.

83. Report by Piers, intended for Sussex or Cecil, 1563, SP 63/9/83.

84. Ibid.

85. J. H. Andrews, "Geography and Government in Elizabethan Ireland," in Nicholas Sephens and Robin E. Glasscock, eds., *Irish Geographical Studies in honour of E. Estyn Evans* (Belfast, 1970), 178, contends that "Ireland presented a cheerless picture to the Elizabethans, under-improved, under-populated (except perhaps for the mountains) and under-exploited." The country was "bleakly deficient in towns and villages, and [a place] where the 'mere' Irishman was an elusive and barbarous figure with an apparent lack of locational roots. . . . Economic assets in these Irish heartlands consisted principally of livestock, more mobile than any force that could be sent to seize them; houses were flimsy, squalid, and so easily rebuilt that burning them down could never constitute much of a punishment."

86. Shane O'Neill's answer to the Queen, 10 September 1563, SP 63/9/6; Petitions from Shane O'Neill sent by Sir Thomas Cusake and Robert Fleming, 11 September 1563, SP 63/9/7; Peace made at Drum Cru between Gerald, earl of Kildare and Sir Thomas Cusake, the Queen's Commissioner, and Shane O'Neill, 11 September 1563, Carew MSS, vol. 611, f. 130. This last letter is also located in SP 63/9/9.

87. Despite the provisions of the Peace of Drum Cru, Sussex had sent one John Smith to assassinate Shane with poisoned wine. The attempt failed. Elizabeth was

extremely upset with Sussex over his lack of success. Queen to Sussex, 15 October 1563, SP 63/9/34; Richey, *Lectures*, 301; W. F. Collier, *The Central Figures of Irish History from 400 A.D. to 1603 A.D.* (London, 1891), 142–3.

88. Articles contained in the Peace of Drum Cru, concluded between Sir Thomas Cusake and Shane O'Neill, 8 November 1563, Carew MSS, vol. 614, f. 172.

89. Articles of Agreement between Sir Thomas Cusake, knight, one of the Privy Council, and Shane O'Neill, 18 November 1563, no. 12, in James Morrin, ed., *Calendar of the Patent and Close Rolls of Chancery in Ireland*, 3 vols. (Dublin, 1861–3), I: 485; Hill, *MacDonnells of Antrim*, 130.

90. Brendan Bradshaw, "The Elizabethans and the Irish," *Studies* (Spring 1977): 38–50; Ellis, *Tudor Ireland*, 180, 228, 246; David Beers Quinn, "Ireland and Sixteenth-Century European Expansion," *Historical Studies* I (1958): 20–32; Sidney, "Memoir,"

Chapter 5

1. Report by William Piers, intended for Sussex or Cecil, 1563, London, Public Record Office, State Papers, Ireland, Elizabeth, SP 63/9/83 (hereafter cited as SP 63).

2. "The opinion of the earl of Sussex, 11 September 1560," quoted in Jane E. A. Dawson, "Two Kingdoms or Three?: Ireland in Anglo-Scottish Relations in the Middle of the Sixteenth Century," in Roger A. Mason, ed., *Scotland and England, 1286–1815* (Edinburgh, 1987), 131n.

3. "He that will England win, let him in Ireland begin," was a sound bit of geo-political advice in the sixteenth century. Quoted in Cyril Falls, *Elizabeth's Irish Wars* (London, 1950; reprint edn. New York, 1970), 9. Steven G. Ellis, *Tudor Ireland: Crown, Community and the Conflict of Cultures, 1470–1603* (London and New York, 1985), 180, 246, 278; Dawson, "Two Kingdoms or Three?," 114; R. B. Wernham, *The Making of Elizabethan Foreign Policy, 1558–1603* (Berkeley, CA and London, 1980), 23.

4. David Beers Quinn, "Sir Thomas Smith (1513–1577) and the Beginnings of English Colonial Theory," *Proceedings of the American Philosophical Society* LXXXIX, 4 (10 December 1945): 543–60; Ellis, *Tudor Ireland*, 248–9.

5. Thomas Smith, "Information for Ireland (1561)," quoted in Constantia Maxwell, ed., *Irish History from Contemporary Sources (1509–1603)*, (London, 1923), 341–2. For some interesting contemporary observations of the Irish military character, see Edmund Spenser, *A View of the Present State of Ireland*, ed. W. L. Renwick (Oxford, 1970), 12, 70, 72, 98; and Barnaby Rich, *A New Description of Ireland, wherein is described the disposition of the Irish* (London, 1610), 95–6.

6. James Michael Hill, *Celtic Warfare, 1595–1763* (Edinburgh, 1986), 22–44; J. Michael Hill, "The Distinctiveness of Gaelic Warfare, 1400–1750," *European History Quarterly* XXII, (July 1992), 323–45; John Dymmok, *A Treatice of Ireland*, ed. Rev. Richard Butler (Dublin, 1842), 7–8; James Morrin, ed., *Calendar of the Patent and Close Rolls of Chancery in Ireland*, 3 vols. (Dublin, 1861), I: 298n; John T. Gilbert, ed., *Account of Facsimiles of National Manuscripts of Ireland* (London, 1884), 184–5; Sir Henry Sidney, "Memoir of a Government in Ireland," *Ulster Journal of Archaeology* series I, III (1855): 33–44, 85–99, 336–57; V (1857): 299–315; VIII (1860): 179–95; Rev. George Hill, *An Historical Account of the MacDonnells of Antrim, Including Notices of some other Septs, Irish and Scottish* (Belfast, 1873), 168n; Rich, *New Description of*

Ireland, 37; Iona Club, ed., *Collectanea de Rebus Albanicis, consisting of original papers and documents relating to the history of the Highlands and Islands of Scotland* (Edinburgh, 1847), 27–8, 32–3, 36–7; G. A. Hayes-McCoy, *Irish Battles* (London, 1969), 1–11; Andrew McKerral, "West Highland Mercenaries in Ireland," *Scottish Historical Review* XXX (April 1951): 1–14; Sean O'Domhnaill, "Warfare in Sixteenth-Century Ireland," *Irish Historical Studies* V (1946–7): 29–54; Katherine Simms, "Warfare in the Medieval Gaelic Lordships," *Irish Sword* XII (1975–6): 98–108; R. R. Davies, *Domination and Conquest: The Experience of Ireland, Scotland and Wales 1100–1300* (Cambridge and New York, 1990), passim.

7. Simms, "Warfare in the Medieval Gaelic Lordships." For a study of the military importance of the castle in Irish warfare, see W. A. McComish, "The Survival of the Irish Castle in an Age of Cannon," *Irish Sword* IX, 34 (Summer 1969): 16–21.

8. Hill, *Celtic Warfare,* 1–8, *et seq.*

9. John Hooker, alias Vowell, *The Irish Chronicle from the death of King Henry VIII until 1586,* in Raphael Holinshed, *Chronicles of England, Scotland, and Ireland,* 6 vols. (London, 1808; reprint edn., New York, 1965), VI: 333; Dymmok, *Treatice of Ireland,* 70; Sir Henry Sidney to the earl of Leicester, 1 March 1566, SP 63/16/35 (see also Sidney, "Memoir"); Edmund Campion, *A Historie of Ireland, written in the Yeare 1571,* ed. James Ware (Dublin, 1633; reprint edn., Dublin, 1809), 189; Richard Cox, *Hibernia Anglicana: or, the History of Ireland from the Conquest thereof by the English, to this present time,* 2nd edn., 2 vols. (London, 1692), II: 321. For the fascinating career of Alasdair MacColla, see David Stevenson, *Alasdair MacColla and the Highland Problem in the Seventeenth Century* (Edinburgh, 1980).

10. Quoted in Hill, *MacDonnells of Antrim,* 135n.

11. Ibid.

12. Quoted in ibid., 143n.

13. Ibid.

14. Terence Daniel, dean of Armagh, to Cecil, 10 March 1564, SP 63/10/28; Robert Fleming to Cecil, 15 April 1564, SP 63/10/48; Ellis, *Tudor Ireland,* 242, 249.

15. John O'Donovan, ed., *Annala Rioghachta Eireann, Annals of the Kingdom of Ireland, by the Four Masters, from the Earliest Period to the Year 1616,* 5 vols. (Dublin, 1848), IV: 1599, 1601 (anno 1564); Ellis, *Tudor Ireland,* 249; Lord Ernest Hamilton, *Elizabethan Ulster* (London, 1919), 23–5; Terence Daniel to Cecil, 25 May 1564, SP 63/10/69; Shane O'Neill to Queen, 23 May 1564, SP 63/10/66; Sir Thomas Cusake to Privy Council, 8 June 1564, SP 63/11/1.

16. Daniel to Cecil, 25 May 1564, SP 63/10/69; Robert Chambers, ed., *Domestic Annals of Scotland from the Reformation to the Revolution,* 3 vols. (Edinburgh and London, 1874), I: 25–6; T. Bedford Franklin, *A History of Scottish Farming* (London, 1952), 102–3; Shane O'Neill to Queen, 23 May 1564, SP 63/10/66.

17. Sir Thomas Cusake to Privy Council, 8 June 1564, SP 63/11/1; Cusake to Lord Robert Dudley, 9 June 1564, SP 63/11/3; Mary, Queen of Scots, to Elizabeth, 2 June 1564, London, Public Record Office, State Papers, Scotland, Elizabeth, 9/32 (hereafter cited as SP Scot. Eliz.); Sir Andrew Agnew, *The Hereditary Sheriffs of Galloway,* 2 vols. (Edinburgh, 1893), I: 386–7.

18. Hill, *MacDonnells of Antrim,* 130–1; Cusake to Dudley, 9 June 1564, SP 63/11/3; Rev. George Hill, "Shane O'Neill's Expedition Against the Antrim Scots, 1565,"

Ulster Journal of Archaeology series I, IX (1861): 122–41; Lord Justice Arnold and Council to Shane O'Neill, 22 August 1564, SP 63/11/80; Shane O'Neill to Arnold and Council, 18 August 1564, SP 63/11/76; Daniel to Arnold, 21 August 1564, SP 63/11/79.

19. Arnold and Council to Shane O'Neill, 22 August 1564, SP 63/11/80; Hill, *MacDonnells of Antrim*, 131; Shane O'Neill to Arnold and Council, 18 August 1564, SP 63/11/76.

20. Daniel to Arnold, 21 August 1564, SP 63/11/79.

21. Arnold and Council to Shane O'Neill, 22 August 1564, SP 63/11/80; Hill, *MacDonnells of Antrim*, 131.

22. Daniel to Arnold, 21 August 1564, SP 63/11/79; Hill, "Shane O'Neill's Expedition;" J. Michael Hill, "Shane O'Neill's Campaign Against the MacDonnells of Antrim, 1564–5," *Irish Sword* XVIII, 71 (Summer 1992), 129–38; E. O. James, *Seasonal Feasts and Festivals* (New York, 1961), 312, 316.

23. Shane O'Neill to Arnold and Council, 5 September 1564, SP 63/11/83; Daniel to Arnold, 10 September 1564, SP 63/11/84; Rev. James O'Laverty, *An Historical Account of the Diocese of Down and Connor, Ancient and Modern*, 5 vols. (Dublin, 1878–5), IV: 19–20; Hill, *MacDonnells of Antrim*, 131.

24. Daniel to Arnold, 10 September 1564, SP 63/11/84.

25. Ibid.

26. Ibid.

27. J. J. O'Connell, *The Irish Wars: A Military History of Ireland from the Norse Invasions to 1798* (Dublin, n.d.), 15–17; Hill, *MacDonnells of Antrim*, 131.

28. Shane O'Neill to Arnold and Council, 5 September 1564, SP 63/11/83; Hill, *MacDonnells of Antrim*, 131; Arnold and Council to Shane O'Neill, 14 September 1564, SP 63/11/87.

29. Randolph to Cecil, 24 October 1564, SP Scot. Eliz. 9/62; Robert Fleming, mayor of Drogheda, to Cecil, February 1565, SP 63/12/48; Hill, *MacDonnells of Antrim*, 131.

30. Randolph to Cecil, 24 December 1564, SP Scot. Eliz. 9/80; Bannatyne Club, ed., *Origines Parochiales Scotiae*, 2 vols. (Edinburgh, 1850), II: 7. According to tradition, Catherine fell in love with Shane and bore him several children.

31. Sir William Fitzwilliam to Cecil, 7 January 1565, SP 63/12/4.

32. Dawson, "Two Kingdoms or Three?," 124; Randolph to Cecil, 13 January 1565, SP Scot. Eliz. 10/4.

33. Robert Fleming to Cecil, February 1565, SP 63/12/48; Hill, "Shane O'Neill's Expedition."

34. A. MacDonald and A. MacDonald, *The Clan Donald*, 3 vols. (Inverness, 1896–1904), II: 680–1.

35. Robert Fleming to Cecil, February 1565, SP 63/12/48.

36. Gerot Fleming to Cusake, June 1565, SP 63/13/82; Shane O'Neill to Arnold, 2 May 1565, SP 63/13/34.

37. Gerot Fleming to Cusake, June 1565, SP 63/13/82.

Fire and Sword

38. Ibid.

39. Shane O'Neill to Arnold, 2 May 1565, SP 63/13/34.

40. Hill, *MacDonnells of Antrim*, 132; MacDonald and MacDonald, *Clan Donald*, II: 540–1, 680–1; Shane O'Neill to Arnold, 2 May 1565, SP 63/13/34; Gerot Fleming to Cusake, June 1565, SP 63/13/82; O'Laverty, *Down and Connor*, IV: 520.

41. Shane O'Neill to Arnold, 2 May 1565, SP 63/13/34; Hill, *MacDonnells of Antrim*, 188n.

42. Shane O'Neill to Arnold, 2 May 1565, SP 63/13/34; Gerot Fleming to Cusake, June 1565, SP 63/13/82; Hill, *MacDonnells of Antrim*, 132–4n; MacDonald and MacDonald, *Clan Donald*, II: 680–1; Hill, "Shane O'Neill's Expedition."

43. Shane O'Neill to Arnold, 2 May 1565, SP 63/13/34.

44. Hill, *MacDonnells of Antrim*, 133; Hill, "Shane O'Neill's Expedition."

45. For a discussion of the salient points of Celtic generalship and tactics, see Hill, *Celtic Warfare*, passim; Hill, "Distinctiveness of Gaelic Warfare."

46. Shane O'Neill to Arnold, 2 May 1565, SP 63/13/34; Gerot Fleming to Cusake, June 1565, SP 63/13/82.

47. Hill, "Shane O'Neill's Expedition;" Gerot Fleming to Cusake, June 1565, SP 63/13/82.

48. Shane O'Neill to Arnold, 2 May 1565, SP 63/13/34.

49. Gerot Fleming to Cusake, June 1565, SP 63/13/82.

50. Hayes-McCoy, *Irish Battles*, 82.

51. The Book of Howth, in Great Britain, *Calendar of the Carew Manuscripts, Preserved in the Archiepiscopal Library at Lambeth*, 6 vols., ed. J. S. Brewer and William Bullen (London, 1867–71), VI: 127.

52. Dioness Campbell, "Observations of Mr Dioness Campbell, Deane of Limerick, on the West Isles of Scotland," in Maitland Club, ed., *Miscellany of the Maitland Club*, 5 vols. (Glasgow, 1847), IV: 45.

53. Hayes-McCoy, *Irish Battles*, 75, 82; Hill, *Celtic Warfare*, 1–8, 22–44.

54. Gerot Fleming to Cusake, June 1565, SP 63/13/82; Hill, *MacDonnells of Antrim*, 134n; Hill, "Shane O'Neill's Expedition."

55. Shane O'Neill to Arnold, 2 May 1565, SP 63/13/34; Fitzwilliam to Cecil, 16 May 1565, SP 63/13/38; Fitzwilliam to Cecil, 18 May 1565, SP 63/13/44; Shane O'Neill to Cusake, 22 May 1565, SP 63/13/48; Daniel to Cecil, 24 June 1565, SP 63/13/77; William M. Hennessy, ed., *The Annals of Loch Cé. A Chronicle of Irish Affairs from A.D. 1014 to A.D. 1590*, 2 vols. (London, 1871), II: 389 (anno 1565); Rev. George Hill, "Notices of the Clan Ian Vór, or Clan-Donnell Scots," *Ulster Journal of Archaeology* series I, IX (1861): 301–17.

56. Fitzwilliam to Cecil, 18 May 1565, SP 63/13/44.

57. Shane O'Neill to Arnold, 2 May 1565, SP 63/13/34; Gerot Fleming to Cusake, June 1565, SP 63/13/82.

58. Ibid.; O'Donovan, ed., *Four Masters*, IV: 1605–7 (anno 1565); Sidney, "Memoir."

254

59. Gerot Fleming to Cusake, June 1565, SP 63/13/82.

60. Hill, "Shane O'Neill's Expedition;" Gerot Fleming to Cusake, June 1565, SP 63/13/82.

61. For a discussion of the period 1586 to 1644, see Epilogue below.

62. Gerot Fleming to Cusake, June 1565, SP 63/13/82.

63. Hill, *MacDonnells of Antrim*, 138n.

64. Gerot Fleming to Cusake, June 1565, SP 63/13/82; Hill, *MacDonnells of Antrim*, 138n.

65. Fitzwilliam to Cecil, 18 May 1565, SP 63/13/44; Shane O'Neill to Privy Council, 25 August 1565, SP 63/14/50; Randolph to Throckmorton, 3 June 1565, SP Scot. Eliz. 10/61.

66. Daniel to Cecil, 24 June 1565, SP 63/13/77; Randolph to Cecil, 11 May 1565, SP Scot. Eliz. 10/44.

67. Hugh Brady, bishop of Meath, to Cecil, 16 May 1565, SP 63/13/39.

68. Fitzwilliam to Cecil, 30 May 1565, SP 63/13/50; Shane O'Neill to Cecil, 18 June 1565, SP 63/13/66.

69. Fitzwilliam to Cecil, 16 May 1565, SP 63/13/38.

70. Fitzwilliam to Cecil, 23 August 1565, SP 63/14/44.

71. Cecil to Sir Thomas Smith, 3 June 1565, London, British Library, Lansdowne MSS, 102, f. 60.

72. Shane O'Neill to Queen, 28 July 1565, SP 63/14/32; Hill, *MacDonnells of Antrim*, 137n; Privy Council to Arnold, 22 June 1565, SP 63/13/69; Privy Council to Shane O'Neill, 22 June 1565, SP 63/13/71.

73. Daniel to Cecil, 24 June 1565, SP 63/13/77.

74. Queen to Sidney, 9 July 1565, SP 63/14/8; F. S. Thomas, ed., *Historical Notes, 1509–1603*, 3 vols. (London, 1856), I: 465.

75. MacDonald and MacDonald, *Clan Donald*, II: 545.

76. Queen to Sidney, 9 July 1565, SP 63/14/8.

77. Calvagh O'Donnell to Queen, 29 October 1564, SP 63/11/96.

78. Queen to Sidney, 9 July 1565, SP 63/14/8.

79. Ibid.

80. Morrin, ed., *Patent and Close Rolls*, I: 495–6.

81. Queen to Sidney, 9 July 1565, SP 63/14/8.

82. Ibid.

83. Ibid.

84. Fitzwilliam to Cecil, 23 August 1565, SP 63/14/44; Counterfeit letter from Arnold and Council to Argyll, 4 August 1565, SP 63/15/63, iii; Randolph to Cecil, 4 September 1565, SP Scot. Eliz. 11/29.

85. Cusake to Cecil, 23 August 1565, in Evelyn Philip Shirley, ed., *Original Letters and*

Papers in Illustration of the History of the Church in Ireland, during the reigns of Edward VI, Mary, and Elizabeth (London, 1851), 222–4.

86. Shane O'Neill to Privy Council, 25 August 1565, SP 63/14/50; Shane O'Neill to Cecil, 25 August 1565, SP 63/14/51; Arnold to Privy Council, 31 August 1565, SP 63/14/57; Queen to Sidney, 12 November 1565, SP 63/15/42.

87. Quoted in R. Barry O'Brien, *Irish Memories* (London, 1904), 50.

88. Fitzwilliam to Cecil, 23 August 1565, SP 63/14/44; O'Brien, *Irish Memories*, 52.

89. Randolph to Cecil, 4 September 1565, SP Scot. Eliz. 11/29.

90. O'Donovan, ed., *Four Masters*, IV: 1605–7 (anno 1565).

91. Campbell, "Observations," 45; Randolph to Cecil, 2 September 1565, SP Scot. Eliz. 11/28.

Chapter 6

1. Sir Henry Sidney to earl of Leicester, 1 March 1566, London, Public Record Office, State Papers, Ireland, Elizabeth, SP 63/16/35 (hereafter cited as SP 63); Ciaran Brady, "The Killing of Shane O'Neill: Some New Evidence," *Irish Sword* XV (1982–3): 116–23; Thomas Wright, ed., *Queen Elizabeth and Her Times*, 2 vols. (London, 1838), I: 213n.

2. Randolph to Cecil, 13 October 1565, London, Public Record Office, State Papers, Scotland, Elizabeth, 11/65 (hereafter cited as SP Scot. Eliz.); Earl of Clanrickard to Sussex, 15 October 1565, London, British Library, Cottonian MSS, Titus. B. XIII f. 154. For a similar report, see Clanrickard to Fitzwilliam, 15 October 1565, SP 63/15/15,i.

3. Earl of Argyll to Adam Loftus, archbishop of Armagh, 18 November 1565, SP 63/15/63,i.

4. Jane Dawson, "The Fifth Earl of Argyle, Gaelic Lordship and Political Power in Sixteenth-Century Scotland," *Scottish Historical Review* LXVII, i, 183 (April, 1988): 1–27; G. A. Hayes-McCoy, *Scots Mercenary Forces in Ireland, (1565–1603)* (Dublin and London, 1937), 89; Brady, "Killing of Shane O'Neill."

5. Dawson, "Fifth Earl of Argyle;" Brady, "Killing of Shane O'Neill."

6. Cecil to Sir Thomas Smith, 26 March 1566, London, British Library, Lansdowne MSS, 102, f. 71.

7. Queen to Sidney, 12 November 1565, SP 63/15/42; Sidney to Leicester, 1 March 1566, SP 63/16/35.

8. Ibid.

9. Ibid.

10. David B. Quinn, "Ireland and Sixteenth Century European Expansion," *Historical Studies* I (1958): 20–32. For the changes in England's Irish policy in the mid-1560s, see also Nicholas P. Canny, *The Elizabethan Conquest of Ireland: A Pattern Established, 1565–76* (Hassocks, Sussex and New York, 1976).

11. Steven G. Ellis, *Tudor Ireland: Crown, Community and the Conflict of Cultures, 1470–1603* (London and New York, 1985), 169, 217, 248–50; Penry Williams, *The Council in the Marches of Wales under Elizabeth I* (Cardiff, 1958), 251–2; Canny, *Elizabethan Conquest of Ireland*, 45. Both Luther and Calvin, much like

Sidney, arrived at a view of government, starting from man's "innate viciousness and irrationality," that emphasized its "coercive authority, symbolized by the sword." Brendan Bradshaw, "The Elizabethans and the Irish," *Studies* (Spring 1977): 38–50.

12. Queen to Sidney, 28 March 1566, SP 63/16/69.

13. Sir Henry Sidney, "Memoir of a Government in Ireland," *Ulster Journal of Archaeology* series I, III (1855): 33–44, 85–99, 336–57; V (1857): 299–315; VIII (1860): 179–95; Queen to Sidney, 28 March 1566, SP 63/16/69; Ellis, *Tudor Ireland*, 251.

14. Ibid.; Sidney to Privy Council, 15 April 1566, SP 63/17/13.

15. Sidney to Cecil, 17 April 1566, in Arthur Collins, ed., *Letters and Memorials of State*, 2 vols. (London, 1746; reprint edn., New York, 1973), I: 10.

16. Hugh Brady, bishop of Meath, to Cecil, 29 April 1566, in Evelyn Philip Shirley, ed., *Original Letters and Papers in Illustration of the History of the Church in Ireland, during the reigns of Edward VI, Mary, and Elizabeth* (London, 1851), 244–5; Bishop of Meath to Sussex, 27 April 1566, Cottonian MSS, Titus. B. XII f. 149.

17. R. B. Wernham, *The Making of Elizabethan Foreign Policy, 1558–1603* (Berkeley, CA and London, 1980), 23; Ellis, *Tudor Ireland*, 254, 278; O'Neill to King Charles IX of France, 25 April 1566, SP 63/17/34. For an interesting point of view on the connections between Gaelic Ulster and the continent during the sixteenth century, see Brendan Bradshaw, "Manus 'The Magnificent': O'Donnell as Renaissance Prince," in Art Cosgrove and Donal McCartney, eds., *Studies in Irish History, Presented to R. Dudley Edwards* (Dublin, 1979), 15–36.

18. Randolph to Cecil, 4 May 1566, SP Scot. Eliz. 12/55; Randolph to Cecil, 13 May 1566, SP Scot. Eliz. 12/56.

19. Queen to Randolph, 23 May 1566, Lansdowne MSS, 9, f. 20; Sir Francis Knollys to Cecil, 19 May 1566, SP 63/17/56.

20. Queen to Randolph, 23 May 1566, SP Scot. Eliz. 12/60; Brady, "Killing of Shane O'Neill;" Randolph to Cecil, 26 May 1566, SP Scot. Eliz. 12/65; T. Waldegrave to T. Clopton, date doubtful (1566), in Wright, ed., *Queen Elizabeth*, I: 240; Henry Killigrew to Cecil, 28 June 1566, SP Scot. Eliz. 12/77; Sidney, "Memoir."

21. Sidney to Cecil, 3 June 1566, SP 63/18/1.

22. Knollys to Cecil, 29 May 1566, SP 63/17/67; Tom Glasgow, Jr., "The Elizabethan Navy in Ireland (1558-1603)," *Irish Sword* VII, 39 (1974–5): 291–307; Ellis, *Tudor Ireland*, 254.

23. Sidney to Cecil, 9 June 1566, SP 63/18/9.

24. Memorial for Henry Killigrew from Queen, 13–15 June 1566, SP Scot. Eliz. 12/72; Ellis, *Tudor Ireland*, 254.

25. Randolph to Cecil, 13 June 1566, SP Scot. Eliz. 12/70; Randolph to Cecil, 14 June 1566, SP Scot. Eliz. 12/71.

26. Queen to Sidney, 15 or 16 June 1566, SP 63/18/17.

27. Killigrew to Cecil, 24 June 1566, SP Scot. Eliz. 12/75; Ellis, *Tudor Ireland*, 254.

28. Sidney to Cecil, 24 June 1566, SP 63/18/25.

29. Queen to Sidney, 5 July 1566, SP 63/18/41.

30. Killigrew to Cecil, 4 July 1566, SP Scot. Eliz. 12/80; William Rogers to Cecil, 5 July 1566, SP Scot. Eliz. 12/82.

31. Thomas Lancaster to Cecil, 16 August 1566, SP 63/18/89; Sidney to Leicester, 19 August 1566, in Collins, ed., *Letters and Memorials of State*, I: 15; Earl of Murray to Cecil, 11 July 1566, SP Scot. Eliz. 12/85; Sidney, "Memoir;" Sidney to Privy Council, 9 and 14 September 1566, SP 63/19/11; Archbishop of Armagh to Sussex, 3 September 1566, Cottonian MSS, Titus. B. XIII f. 159.

32. Sidney to Leicester, 19 August 1566, in Collins, ed., *Letters and Memorials of State*, I: 16.

33. Sidney to Privy Council, 9 and 14 September 1566, SP 63/19/11.

34. Queen to Sidney, 5 July 1566, SP 63/18/41; Queen to Sidney, 8 July 1566, SP 63/18/46.

35. Queen to Sidney, 5 July 1566, SP 63/18/41; Sidney, "Memoir."

36. Ellis, *Tudor Ireland*, 254–5; Sidney, "Memoir."

37. Ibid.; Ellis, *Tudor Ireland*, 254.

38. James Michael Hill, *Celtic Warfare, 1595–1763* (Edinburgh, 1986), 30–2; Sidney, "Memoir;" Sidney to Cecil, 21 September 1566, SP 63/19/14; Ellis, *Tudor Ireland*, 254.

39. Sidney, "Memoir;" Ellis, *Tudor Ireland*, 254.

40. Sidney, "Memoir."

41. Captain Thomas Browne to Sidney, 8 November 1566, SP 63/19/36; Hayes-McCoy, *Scots Mercenary Forces*, 93.

42. Captain Thomas Browne to Sidney, 8 November 1566, SP 63/19/36.

43. Ibid.

44. Examination of Richard Creagh, taken before Cecil, 1567, in Shirley, ed., *Original Letters and Papers*, 326–8; Sidney to Privy Council, 12 November 1566, SP 63/19/44; Captain Thomas Wilsford to Cecil, 15 November 1566, SP 63/19/47; Sidney, earl of Kildare, Sir Nicholas Bagenal, and Francis Agarde to Queen, 12 November 1566, SP 63/19/43; Thomas Lancaster to Cecil, 23 November 1566, SP 63/19/57; Raphael Holinshed, *Chronicles of England, Scotland and Ireland*, 6 vols., ed. Henry Ellis (London, 1808; reprint edn., New York, 1965), V: 334–5; Ellis, *Tudor Ireland*, 254–5; Sidney, "Memoir."

45. Sidney to Privy Council, 12 December 1566, SP 63/19/71.

46. Alasdair Oge MacDonnell to William Piers, 10 December 1566, SP 63/19/73,ii; Piers to Sidney, 15 December 1566, SP 63/19/73,i.

47. Ibid.

48. Sidney to Privy Council, 25 December 1566, in Shirley, ed., *Original Letters and Papers*, 288; Sidney, "Memoir;" Geoffrey Vaughn to William Winter and Edward Baeshe, 13 January 1567, SP 63/20/5.

49. O'Neill to Sidney and Council, 29 December 1566, SP 63/20/13,i.

50. Queen to Sidney, 16 January 1567, SP 63/20/8.

51. Ibid.

52. Ibid.

53. Brady, "Killing of Shane O'Neill."

54. Sidney to Privy Council, 18 January 1567, SP 63/20/13.

55. Sidney, "Memoir;" Sidney to Privy Council, 18 January 1567, SP 63/20/13; O'Neill to the Cardinals of Guise and Lorraine, 1 February 1567, SP 63/20/22. Black dice were the symbol of the Geraldine family.

56. Report from Derry, March 1567, SP 63/20/54,i; Privy Council to Sidney, 3 April 1567, SP 63/20/60.

57. Cecil to Sidney, 25 February 1567, SP 63/20/36; Cecil to Sidney, 11 March 1567, SP 63/20/44; Queen to Sidney, 16 January 1567, SP 63/20/8; Report from Derry, March 1567, SP 63/20/54,i. For a report that O'Neill had requested shipping from the French monarch, see Lord Treasurer Winchester to Sidney, 4 April 1567, SP 63/20/61; Sidney to Cecil, 4 March 1567, SP 63/20/41.

58. Privy Council to Sidney, 3 April 1567, SP 63/20/60; Hayes-McCoy, *Scots Mercenary Forces*, 95; Rev. George Hill, *An Historical Account of the MacDonnells of Antrim, Including Notices of some other Septs, Irish and Scottish* (Belfast, 1873), 130n.

59. Hugh MacManus O'Donnell to Sidney, 28 April 1567, SP 63/20/69.

60. Sidney to Queen, 20 April 1567, in Collins, ed., *Letters and Memorials of State*, I: 30; Privy Council to Sidney, 12 May 1567, SP 63/20/83; Sidney, "Memoir."

61. Statement by Thomas Phettiplace, 16 May 1567, SP 63/20/92.

62. G. A. Hayes-McCoy, *Irish Battles* (London, 1969) 80-4; Sidney, "Memoir;" John O'Donovan, ed., *Annala Rioghachta Eireann, Annals of the Kingdom of Ireland, by the Four Masters, from the Earliest Period to the Year 1616*, 5 vols. (Dublin, 1848), IV: 1615–17 (anno 1567).

63. Ibid.

64. Edmund Campion, *A Historie of Ireland, written in the Yeare 1571*, ed. James Ware (Dublin, 1633; reprint edn., Dublin, 1809), 190.

65. Brady, "Killing of Shane O'Neill," has shed fresh light on Shane's death by the discovery of a letter from William Fitzwilliam (not Sir William of Milton, but his third cousin who served in Ireland as Vice-Treasurer in 1559–73) to Hugh Fitzwilliam, 11 June 1567, Northamptonshire Record Office, Fitzwilliam [Milton] Correspondence, no. 27.

66. Alasdair Oge to Sidney, 20 May 1567, SP 63/20/93.

67. Sidney, "Memoir."

68. Alasdair Oge to Sidney, 20 May 1567, SP 63/20/93.

69. Sidney, "Memoir;" F. S. Thomas, ed., *Historical Notes, 1509–1603*, 3 vols. (London, 1856), III: 1184.

70. Rev. James O'Laverty, *An Historical Account of the Diocese of Down and Connor, Ancient and Modern*, 5 vols. (Dublin, 1878–95), IV: 528; Sidney, "Memoir;" John T. Gilbert, ed., *Account of Facsimiles of National Manuscripts of Ireland* (London, 1884),

157–8; Campion, *Historie,* 191–2; Rev. George Hill, "Shane O'Neill's Expedition Against the Antrim Scots, 1565," *Ulster Journal of Archaeology* series I, IX (1861): 122–41.

71. William Fitzwilliam to Hugh Fitzwilliam, 11 June 1567, Fitzwilliam Correspondence, no. 27, in Brady, "Killing of Shane O'Neill."

72. Act of Attainder against Shane O'Neill, 1569–71, in Great Britain, *The Statutes at Large passed in the Parliaments held in Ireland, 1310–1786,* 2 vols. (Dublin, 1786), I: 322–38; Brady, "Killing of Shane O'Neill."

73. Act of Attainder against Shane O'Neill, 1569–71, in Irish Statutes, I: 322–38.

74. William Fitzwilliam to Hugh Fitzwilliam, 11 June 1567, Fitzwilliam Correspondence, no. 27, in Brady, "Killing of Shane O'Neill."

75. The traditional version of Shane's death is contained in, among many others, Campion, *Historie,* 191–2; Sir James Ware, *The Antiquities and History of Ireland,* 2 vols. (London, 1714): II: 10–11; William Camden, *Britannia: or, a Chorographical Description of the Flourishing Kingdoms of England, Scotland, and Ireland, and the Islands Adjacent; from the Earliest Antiquity,* ed. Richard Gough, 2nd edn., 4 vols. (London, 1806), IV: 457; Holinshed, *Chronicles,* V: 337–8; Denis Taaffe, *An Impartial History of Ireland,* 4 vols. (Dublin, 1809–11), I: 385–6; Thomas Leland, *The History of Ireland from the Invasion of Henry II,* 3 vols. (London, 1773), II: 236; J. A. Froude, *The Reign of Queen Elizabeth,* 5 vols. (London, 1912), II: 177; Hill, *MacDonnells of Antrim,* 92, 140–3; Donald J. MacDonald, *Clan Donald* (Loanhead, Midlothian, 1978), 265–6; Lord Ernest Hamilton, *Elizabethan Ulster* (London, 1919), 39.

76. O'Donovan, ed., *Four Masters,* IV: 1617–19 (anno 1567).

77. Sidney, "Memoir."

78. Fitzwilliam to Cecil, 10 June 1567, SP 63/21/8.

79. William Fitzwilliam to Hugh Fitzwilliam, 11 June 1567, Fitzwilliam Correspondence, no. 27, in Brady, "Killing of Shane O'Neill."

80. Hill, *MacDonnells of Antrim,* 140–3; Hill, "Shane O'Neill's Expedition."

81. Brady, "Killing of Shane O'Neill;" Sidney, "Memoir."

82. O'Donovan, ed., *Four Masters,* IV: 1621 (anno 1567).

83. The Book of Howth, in Great Britain, *Calendar of the Carew Manuscripts, Preserved in the Archiepiscopal Library at Lambeth,* 6 vols., ed. J. S. Brewer and William Bullen (London, 1867–71), VI: 120.

84. Sidney, "Memoir."

85. Quoted in O'Laverty, *Down and Connor,* V: 351. Concerning Shane's death, Sidney wrote Cecil: "I would the rebel might have been taken, to the end that he might in other sort have received his just desert. . . ." Sidney, "Memoir."

86. Hayes-McCoy, *Scots Mercenary Forces,* 94–5; James Stuart, *Historical Memoirs of the City of Armagh* (Newry, 1819), 261; Hill, *MacDonnells of Antrim,* 143-6; O'Laverty, *Down and Connor,* IV: 524–5; Dioness Campbell, "Observations of Mr Dioness Campbell, Deane of Limerick, on the West Isles of Scotland," in Maitland Club, ed., *Miscellany of the Maitland Club,* 5 vols. (Glasgow, 1847), IV: 45.

87. Fitzwilliam to Cecil, 10 June 1567, SP 63/21/8.

88. Queen to Sidney, 11 June 1567, SP 63/21/10.

89. Lord Treasurer Winchester to Sidney, 24 June 1567, SP 63/21/28; Lord Chancellor and Privy Council of Ireland to Queen, 28 June 1567, SP 63/21/34; Memorandum concerning Sidney's letters to the Privy Council, 5 July 1567, SP 63/21/48; Brady, "Killing of Shane O'Neill."

90. Queen to Sidney, 6 July 1567, SP 63/21/49.

91. Ibid.

92. Ibid.

93. Ellis, *Tudor Ireland*, 255–6; Brady, "Killing of Shane O'Neill;" Bradshaw, "Elizabethans and the Irish."

94. According to Bradshaw, Sidney believed that the Irish "must first be dealt with by sharp and relentless severity before they could be brought to that degree of civility that would make it feasible to govern them by normal civilized procedures." And because the English did not understand (nor attempt to understand) the Celtic Christian tradition, "they felt free to treat the Irish as heathens. . . ." But despite Sidney's "dynamic approach to political affairs and . . . [his support for] the protestant ideology which is clearly expressed in his correspondence," he failed to advance the Reformation in Ireland. Brendan Bradshaw, "Sword, Word and Strategy in the Reformation in Ireland," *The Historical Journal* XXI, 3 (1978): 475–502. For supporting views of the faliure of Reformation policies in sixteenth-century Ireland, see Quinn, "Ireland and Sixteenth Century European Expansion;" David Beers Quinn, "'A Discourse of Ireland' (circa 1599): a Sidelight on English Colonial Policy," in *Proceedings of the Royal Irish Academy* XLVII, sec. C, no. 3 (1942): 151–66; Karl Bottigheimer, "Kingdom and Colony: Ireland in the Westward Enterprise, 1536–1660," in K. R. Andrews, N. P. Canny, and P. E. H. Hair, eds., *The Westward Enterprise: English Activities in Ireland, the Atlantic, and America, 1480–1650* (Liverpool, 1978), 51.

95. Queen to Sidney, 22 July 1567, SP 63/21/65; Piers and Malby to Fitzwilliam and Weston, 3 November 1567, 63/22/25,i; Brady, "Killing of Shane O'Neill;" O'Laverty, *Down and Connor*, IV: 20–1.

Chapter 7

1. Queen to Sir Henry Sidney, 11 June 1567, London, Public Record Office, State Papers, Ireland, Elizabeth, SP 63/21/10 (hereafter cited as SP 63).

2. Rev. George Hill, *An Historical Account of the MacDonnells of Antrim, Including Notices of some other Septs, Irish and Scottish* (Belfast, 1873), 146; G. A. Hayes-McCoy, *Scots Mercenary Forces in Ireland, (1565–1603)* (Dublin and London, 1937), 117–18; Rev. George Hill, "Notices of the Clan Ian Vór, or Clan-Donnell Scots," *Ulster Journal of Archaeology* series I, IX (1861): 301–17.

3. Sir Francis Knollys's opinion concerning Turlough Luineach O'Neill, 7 July 1567, SP 63/21/56; Hill, *MacDonnells of Antrim*, 146.

4. Queen to Sidney, 6 July 1567, SP 63/21/49.

5. Ibid.

6. Hill, *MacDonnells of Antrim*, 146; Queen to Sidney, 22 July 1567, SP 63/21/65. See also Irish Manuscripts Commission, *Sidney State Papers, 1565–70*, ed. Tómas O'Laidhin (Dublin, 1962), 79.

7. Piers and Malby to Lords Justice, 3 November 1567, SP 63/22/25,i.

8. Fitzwilliam to Cecil, 24 November 1567, SP 63/22/26; Piers and Malby to Lords Justice, 18 November 1567, SP 63/22/28,i; A. MacDonald and A. MacDonald, *The Clan Donald*, 3 vols. (Inverness, 1896–1904), II: 684; Memorandum concerning the Scots in Ulster before the arrival of Sorley Boy MacDonnell, January 1568, SP 63/23/15,i; Hayes-McCoy, *Scots Mercenary Forces*, 96–7.

9. Lords Justice and Council to Queen, 27 November 1567, SP 63/22/28; Fitzwilliam to Cecil, 27 November 1567, SP 63/22/29; Hector MacLean, "A Sketch of the MacDonnells of Antrim", in *Transactions of the Gaelic Society of Inverness*, vol. XVII (Inverness, 1890–1): 98–9; Turlough O'Neill to Lords Justice and Council, 24 November 1567, SP 63/22/36,viii; Daniel to Commissioners, 27 November 1567, SP 63/22/36,iv; Lord Louth, James Dowdall, and William Bathe to Lords Justice, 29 November 1567, SP 63/22/36,i.

10. Hill, *MacDonnells of Antrim*, 147; Piers and Malby to Lords Justice and Council, 21 November 1567, SP 63/22/36,vi; Fitzwilliam to Cecil, 27 November 1567, SP 63/22/29.

11. Daniel to Lords Justice, 10 December 1567, SP 63/22/57,ii. Though he clearly was writing of Sorley Boy, Daniel's words "his goodwill" are somewhat ambiguous. Thus it was Sorley Boy who made the oath never to leave Ireland against his own will. During the remainder of his life he frequently returned to Scotland to make alliances or to recruit redshanks; however, he always returned to Antrim to hold his lands against all opposition.

12. Daniel to Lords Justice, 10 December 1567, SP 63/22/57,ii; Piers and Malby to Lords Justice, 6 December 1567, SP 63/22/57,i.

13. Daniel to Lords Justice, 10 December 1567, SP 63/22/57,ii; Sir Nicholas Bagenal to Lords Justice and Council, 2 December 1567, SP 63/22/36,v.

14. Sorley Boy MacDonnell to Piers and Malby, 16 December 1567, SP 63/23/10,iii.

15. Ibid.

16. Piers and Malby to Sorley Boy MacDonnell, 20 December 1567, SP 63/23/10,iv.

17. Malby to Lords Justice, 19 December 1567, SP 63/23/10,ii.

18. Sorley Boy MacDonnell to Piers and Malby, 23 December 1567, SP 63/23/10,v.

19. Hayes-McCoy, *Scots Mercenary Forces*, 99.

20. Queen to Lords Justice, 10 December 1567, SP 63/22/37; Lords Justice to Queen, 24 December 1567, SP 63/22/57; Queen to Lords Justice, 24 December 1567, SP 63/22/58; MacDonald and MacDonald, *Clan Donald*, II: 684–5.

21. Piers and Malby to Lords Justice, 2 January 1568, SP 63/23/10,i.

22. G. A. Hayes-McCoy, *Ulster and other Irish Maps c. 1600* (Dublin, 1964), 5–6; Bagenal to Lords Justice, 3 January 1568, SP 63/23/11,i; Bagenal, Louth, *et al.* to Lords Justice, 3 January 1568, SP 63/23/11,ii; Daniel to Lords Justice, 22 January 1568, SP 63/23/20,ii.

23. Hill, *MacDonnells of Antrim*, 147.

24. Fitzwilliam to Cecil, 17 January 1568, SP 63/23/11.

25. Ibid.

26. Fitzwilliam to Cecil, 17 January 1568, SP 63/23/11; Fitzwilliam to Queen, 22 January 1568, SP 63/23/13.

27. Piers and Malby to Lords Justice, 18 January 1568, SP 63/23/24,i; Lords Justice to Queen, 29 January 1568, SP 63/23/24; Hill, *MacDonnells of Antrim*, 150n; Robert Chambers, ed., *Domestic Annals of Scotland from the Reformation to the Revolution*, 3 vols. (Edinburgh and London, 1874), I: 56; Bagenal to Lords Justice, 22 January 1568, SP 63/23/20,i.

28. Fitzwilliam to Cecil, 22 January 1568, SP 63/23/15; Fitzwilliam to Cecil, 29 January 1568, SP 63/23/25; Lords Justice to Piers and Malby, 23 January 1568, SP 63/23/74,xi; Piers and Malby to Lords Justice, 30 January 1568, SP 63/23/32,i. Sir Henry Sidney, "Memoir of a Government in Ireland," *Ulster Journal of Archaeology* series I, III (1855): 33–44, 85–99, 336–57; V (1857): 299–315; VIII (1860): 179–95, elaborated on the state of English military affairs in Ulster in 1567: "I planted three garrisons in Clandeboy and the Glynnes, namely . . . Piers, with a company of footmen, in the castle and town of Carrickfergus; the renowned soldier . . . Malby with a company of horsemen in Belfast; and the lusty young Captain William Horsey in Glenarm. . . ."

29. Lords Justice and Council to Queen, 23 January 1568, SP 63/23/16; Turlough O'Neill to Piers and Malby, 20 January 1568, SP 63/23/32,ii; John J. Marshall, *Lough Neagh in Legend and History* (Dungannon, Tyrone, 1934), 36.

30. Piers and Malby to Lords Justice, 30 January 1568, SP 63/23/32,i; Piers and Malby to Lords Justice, 2 February 1568, SP 63/23/32,iii.

31. Bagenal to Lords Justice, 5 February 1568, SP 63/23/32,iv.

32. Daniel to Lord Justice Weston, 11 March 1568, SP 63/23/74,ix; Lord Justice Fitzwilliam to Queen, 8 February 1568, SP 63/23/32; Hayes-McCoy, *Scots Mercenary Forces*, 101; Piers and Malby to Lords Justice, 15 February 1568, SP 63/23/74,i; Malby to Lord Deputy Sidney, 13 February 1568, SP 63/23/39; Sidney to Edward Clinton, earl of Lincoln, Lord High Admiral of England, March 1568, in Arthur Collins, ed., *Letters and Memorials of State*, 2 vols. (London, 1746; reprint edn., New York, 1973), I: 33–4; Malby to Cecil, 12 February 1568, SP 63/23/37; Fitzwilliam to Cecil, 8 February 1568, SP 63/23/36.

33. Lords Justice to Piers and Malby, 3 March 1568, SP 63/23/74,xiii.

34. Ibid.; Malby to Lords Justice, 5 March 1568, SP 63/23/74,iii; Captain Thomas Cheston to Piers and Malby, 5 March 1568, SP 63/23/74,iv.

35. Piers and Malby to Lords Justice, 9 March 1568, SP 63/23/74,v.

36. Sorley Boy MacDonnell to Malby, 16 March 1568, SP 63/24/4,i.

37. Ibid.

38. Turlough O'Neill to Fitzwilliam and Council, 19 March 1568, SP 63/24/9,iii.

39. Bagenal to Lords Justice, 20 March 1568, SP 63/23/74,viii; Malby to Cecil, 19 March 1568, SP 63/23/73; Fitzwilliam and Bagenal to Queen, 14 April 1568, SP 63/24/4; Hill, *MacDonnells of Antrim*, 149–50; Hayes-McCoy, *Scots Mercenary Forces*, 100–1; MacDonald and MacDonald, *Clan Donald*, II: 686; Tom Glasgow, Jr., "The Elizabethan Navy in Ireland, (1558–1603)," *Irish Sword* VII, 39 (1974–5): 291–307.

40. Captain Cheston to Piers and Malby, 3 April 1568, SP 63/24/4,ii; Weston to Cecil, 3 April 1568, SP 63/24/2; Fitzwilliam and Bagenal to Queen, 14 April 1568,

SP 63/24/4; Fitzwilliam to Cecil, 14 April 1568, SP 63/24/5; Weston to Queen, 18 April 1568, SP 63/24/9.

41. Fitzwilliam, Bagenal, Piers, and Malby to Queen, 21 April 1568, SP 63/24/13.

42. Ibid.

43. Bagenal to Sidney, 3 May 1568, SP 63/24/31; Fitzwilliam and Bagenal to Queen, 1 May 1568, SP 63/24/28; Fitzwilliam and Bagenal to Weston, 23 April 1568, SP 63/24/38,ii.

44. Piers to Fitzwilliam, 26 April 1568, SP 63/24/28,ii; Hayes-McCoy, *Scots Mercenary Forces*, 101–2; Thomas Lancaster, archbishop of Armagh, *et al.* to Robert Weston, 20 May 1568, in Historical Manuscripts Commission, *The Manuscripts of Charles Haliday, Esq., of Dublin. Acts of the Privy Council in Ireland, 1556–1571*, ed. John T. Gilbert (London, 1897), 224–5.

45. Louth, Bagenal, Daniel, and Thomas Fleming to Lords Justice, 24 May 1568, SP 63/24/38,iii; Hayes-McCoy, *Scots Mercenary Forces*, 102; Fitzwilliam to Cecil, 26 May 1568, SP 63/24/38; Daniel and Fleming to Lords Justice and Council, June 1568, SP 63/25/45,ii.

46. Thomas Lancaster, archbishop of Armagh, to Queen, 15 June 1568, SP 63/25/5.

47. Fitzwilliam to Cecil, 26 May 1568, SP 63/24/38; Fitzwilliam to Queen, 5 July 1568, SP 63/25/21.

48. Edward Waterhouse to Lords Justice, 4 August 1568, SP 63/25/70,i; MacDonald and MacDonald, *Clan Donald*, II: 684–5; Hayes-McCoy, *Scots Mercenary Forces*, 103; Hill, *MacDonnells of Antrim*, 147–8. Donald Gorme MacDonald of Sleat was the rightful representative of the lord of the Isles as he was fourth in descent from Hugh of Sleat, a younger brother of John, fourth (and last) lord of the Isles. When John's descendants in the male line became extinct after 1493, Donald Gorme's father made a bid to become lord of the Isles, but was killed in 1539. By his wife, Margaret MacLeod, he left one son–Donald Gorme–named Sassenach, or "the Englishman," because he received an English education and was much favored by Elizabeth. Donald Gorme died in 1585. Hill, *MacDonnells of Antrim*, 148n. See also Donald Gregory, *The History of the Western Highlands and Isles of Scotland from A.D. 1493 to A.D. 1625* (Edinburgh, 1881; reprint edn., Edinburgh, 1975), 145.

49. Piers and Malby to Queen, 7 July 1568, SP 63/25/23.

50. Hill, "Clan Ian Vór;" Waterhouse to Lords Justice, 4 August 1568, SP 63/25/70,i.

51. John Willock to Cecil, 8 July 1568, London, Public Record Office, State Papers, Scotland, Elizabeth, 15/45 (hereafter cited as SP Scot. Eliz.); Hayes-McCoy, *Scots Mercenary Forces*, 103.

52. Great Britain, *The Register of the Privy Council of Scotland*, ed. J. H. Burton *et al.*, 38 vols. (Edinburgh, 1877–1970), I (1545–71): 616; Bannatyne Club, *A Diurnal of Remarkable Occurants that have passed within the Country of Scotland since the death of King James the Fourth till the year MDLXXV* (Edinburgh, 1833), 131; Hayes-McCoy, *Scots Mercenary Forces*, 102–4. Mary, Queen of Scots, to Argyll, 7 July 1568, in Alexander MacDonald, ed., *Letters to the Argyll Family* (Edinburgh, 1839; reprint edn., New York, 1973), 6–7, notes that "our sister the Queen [i.e. Elizabeth] . . .

has written to my lord of Moray expressly that he use no further extremitie against you. . . ."

53. Sidney to earl of Leicester, 8 August 1568, and Sidney to Cecil, 8 August 1568, in Collins, ed., *Letters and Memorials of State*, I: 34–6.

54. Queen to Argyll, 14 August 1568, SP Scot. Eliz. 15/61.

55. Argyll to Queen, 24 August 1568, in Collins, ed., *Letters and Memorials of State*, I: 36-7.

56. Daniel to Lords Justice, 20 August 1568, SP 63/25/70,ii; Lords Justice to Queen, 4 September 1568, SP 63/25/77; Fitzwilliam to Cecil, 5 September 1568, SP 63/25/78; Lords Justice to Privy Council, 6 September 1568, SP 63/25/79; Steven G. Ellis, *Tudor Ireland: Crown, Community and the Conflict of Cultures, 1470–1603* (London and New York, 1985), 256; Raphael Holinshed, *Chronicles of England, Scotland, and Ireland*, ed. Henry Ellis, 6 vols. (London, 1808; reprint edn., New York, 1965), V: 340; Hill, *MacDonnells of Antrim*, 150; Sidney to Cecil, 12 November 1568, SP 63/26/18; Hayes-McCoy, *Scots Mercenary Forces*, 104.

57. Bannatyne Club, ed., *Diurnal of Remarkable Occurants*, 330; MacDonald and MacDonald, *Clan Donald*, II: 547; Sidney to Cecil, 17 November 1568, in Collins, ed., *Letters and Memorials of State*, I: 39, revealed that "I cannot well spare the shipping here already, from attending the Scots upon the coast of Ulster." Thomas Lancaster, archbishop of Armagh, to Cecil, 12 November 1568, SP 63/26/20; Hill, *MacDonnells of Antrim*, 147-8.

58. Great Britain, *The Statutes at Large passed in the Parliaments held in Ireland, 1310–1786*, 2 vols. (Dublin, 1786), I: 347; Hayes-McCoy, *Scots Mercenary Forces*, 43.

59. John Smith's advice for the realm of Ireland, April 1569, SP 63/28/10.

60. Ibid.

61. Queen to Sidney, 6 June 1569, in Irish Manuscripts Collection, *Sidney State Papers*, 108; Malby to Cecil, 21 June 1569, SP 63/28/45; Sidney to Cecil, 30 June 1569, SP 63/28/58.

62. Piers to Lord Chancellor, 5 August 1569, SP 63/29/30; Caher MacSeain to dean of Armagh, 7 August 1569, SP 63/29/32; Edward Moore to earl of Kildare, 11 August 1569, SP 63/29/36; Fitzwilliam to Cecil, 12 September 1569, SP 63/29/61; Hill, *MacDonnells of Antrim*, 148–52; Hayes-McCoy, *Scots Mercenary Forces*, 105–6.

63. Information from Leonard Sumpter, Bristol merchant, 13 August 1569, SP 63/29/38; Patrick Cullen to Daniel, 24 August 1569, SP 63/29/43; Daniel to Lord Chancellor and Council, 26 August 1569, SP 63/29/44; Turlough Braselagh O'Neill of Clandeboy to Daniel, 26 August 1569, SP 63/29/45.

64. Turlough Braselagh O'Neill to Daniel, 27 August 1569, SP 63/29/48,i; MacDonald and MacDonald, *Clan Donald*, II: 686–7.

65. Turlough Braselagh O'Neill to Daniel, 27 August 1569, SP 63/29/48,i. According to Hill, "Clan Ian Vór," it does not appear that Alasdair Oge MacDonnell "ever returned again to the Antrim coast. . . . He died probably in 1569, or the year following, as no later mention of him occurs in either the Irish or Scottish State Papers."

66. Turlough Braselagh O'Neill to Daniel, 27 August 1569, SP/63/29/48,i.

67. Louth to Lord Chancellor and Privy Council, 29 August 1569, SP 63/29/51;

Fleming to Lord Chancellor, 29 August 1569, SP 63/29/52; Daniel and John Sankye to Lord Chancellor and Council, 30 August 1569, SP 63/29/53; Hayes-McCoy, *Scots Mercenary Forces*, 106–7; Fitzwilliam to Cecil, 2 September 1569, SP 63/29/56; Fitzwilliam to Cecil, 12 September 1569, SP 63/29/61; John Douglas to Cecil, 15 August 1569, London, British Library, Cottonian MSS, Calig. C. I f. 441.

68. According to Hayes-McCoy, *Scots Mercenary Forces*, 107–9, Turlough's major difficulties were "the maintaining of himself in Ulster, the working of his scheme for Scottish aid through his wife and her relations, and the quartering of and provision for what Scots mercenaries he employed." Hill, *MacDonnells of Antrim*, 152.

69. Katherine Simms, "Warfare in the Medieval Gaelic Lordships," *Irish Sword* XII (1975–6): 98–108.

70. Memorial of things to be advised for answering to the articles upon the treaty, 1570, in Great Britain, *Calendar of State Papers Relating to Scotland and Mary, Queen of Scots, 1547–1603*, ed. Joseph Bain *et al.*, 13 vols. (Edinburgh, 1898–1969), III: 371 (hereafter cited as CSP Scot.); Articles to be performed by the Queen of Scots, 7 May 1570, Cottonian MSS, Calig. C. II f. 23; Hayes-McCoy, *Scots Mercenary Forces*, 3, 114; Articles presented to Mary, Queen of Scots, by Lord Burghley, in Great Britain, *Calendar of State Papers, Relating to English Affairs, preserved principally at Rome*, ed. J. M. Rigg, 2 vols. (London, 1916–26), I: 355–9; Sir Thomas Gerrard's book for planting the Glynnes and Clandeboy, 15 March 1570, SP 63/30/32.

71. Rev. James O'Laverty, *An Historical Account of the Diocese of Down and Connor, Ancient and Modern*, 5 vols. (Dublin, 1878–95), II: 171–2; Gerrard's book for planting the Glynnes and Clandeboy, 15 March 1570, SP 63/30/32; George Benn, *A History of the Town of Belfast from the Earliest Times to the Close of the Eighteenth Century* (London, 1877), 22.

72. Queen to Sidney, 17 May 1570, in Irish Manuscripts Commission, *Sidney State Papers*, 126–7.

73. Sidney to Cecil, 8 November 1570, in William Cecil, Lord Burghley, *A Collection of State Papers, 1542–1570*, ed. Samuel Haynes (London, 1740), 622–3; Ellis, *Tudor Ireland*, 264; Fitzwilliam to William Cecil, Lord Burghley, 15 March 1570, SP 63/31/21; Malby to Burghley, 8 April 1570, SP 63/30/37; Fitzwilliam to Burghley, 5 and 11 February 1571, SP 63/31/8; Sir Brian MacFelim O'Neill to Sidney and Council, 19 March 1571, SP 63/32/2,iv; Chambers, ed., *Domestic Annals*, I: 72.

74. Sir Brian MacFelim O'Neill to Sidney and Council, 19 March 1571, SP 63/32/2,iv.

75. Peace between the Queen's Commissioners and Turlough O'Neill, 20 January 1571, London, Lambeth Palace Library, Carew MSS, vol. 611, f. 168.

76. Hayes-McCoy, *Scots Mercenary Forces*, 115.

77. Lady Agnes Campbell to Queen, March 1571, SP 63/31/25. See also Agnes Campbell, lady of Dunyveg, to earl of Morton, 17 March 1571, SP 63/31/24; Lord Chancellor and Council to Queen, 23 March 1571, SP 63/31/33. According to Sidney, "Memoir," Lady Agnes "ruled . . . Turlough completely. In one instance she would not allow "the O'Neill" to keep a meeting appointed with . . . Sidney for conference on some political matters, lest some step should be urged on him for resisting the settling of the Scots in Ulster, a settlement of which she was most desirous. . . ." Turlough O'Neill to Queen, 19 April 1571, SP 63/32/11.

78. Fitzwilliam to Burghley, 5 and 11 February 1571, SP 63/31/8; Mary, Queen of

Scots, to bishop of Ross, 4 March 1571, Cottonian MSS, Calig. C. II f. 158; Piers to Burghley, 25 March 1571, SP 63/31/41; Fitzwilliam to Privy Council, 12 April 1571, SP 63/32/9; Bagenal to Fitzwilliam, 14 and 17 April 1571, SP 63/32/13,i.

79. Piers to Queen, 6 July 1571, SP 63/33/1; Hill, *MacDonnells of Antrim*, 147n.

80. Sir Brian MacFelim O'Neill to Sidney and Council, 19 March 1571, SP 63/32/2,iv.

81. Sir Brian MacFelim O'Neill to Queen, 6 July 1571, SP 63/33/3; Hayes-McCoy, *Scots Mercenary Forces*, 116–7; Ellis, *Tudor Ireland*, 265.

82. Piers to Fitzwilliam, 8 February 1572, SP 63/35/23,vi; Hayes-McCoy, *Irish Maps*, 31; Tract by Sir Thomas Smith on the colonization of the Ardes, 1572, in Hill, *MacDonnells of Antrim*, 405–15; O'Laverty, *Down and Connor*, II: 172–3; David Beers Quinn, "Sir Thomas Smith (1513–77) and the Beginnings of English Colonial Theory," *Proceedings of the American Philosophical Society* LXXXIX, 4 (10 December 1945): 543–60; Moritz Julius Bonn, *Die Englische Kolonisation in Irland*, 2 vols. (Stuttgart and Berlin, 1906), 273–4; Fitzwilliam to Queen, 27 February 1572, SP 63/35/23; Advertisements from Scotland, 26 February 1572, SP Scot. Eliz. 22/24.

83. Piers to Queen, 6 July 1571, SP 63/33/1.

84. Instructions for Lord Hunsdon, 22 October 1571, SP Scot. Eliz. 21/74; Hayes-McCoy, *Scots Mercenary Forces*, 118.

85. Sir Brian MacFelim O'Neill to Fitzwilliam, 6 March 1572, SP 63/35/32,i; Sir Brian MacFelim O'Neill to Queen, 27 March 1572, SP 63/35/44; Sir Brian MacFelim O'Neill to Privy Council, 27 March 1572, SP 63/35/45.

86. Sir Thomas Smith to Sir Brian MacFelim O'Neill, 20 May 1572, SP 63/36/22; Sir Thomas Smith to Burghley, 10 September 1572, SP 63/37/54; O'Laverty, *Down and Connor*, I: 386.

87. Fitzwilliam to Burghley, 14 March 1572, SP 63/35/32; Piers to Fitzwilliam, 16 April 1572, SP 63/36/6; Fitzwilliam to Privy Council, 27 February 1572, SP 63/35/24; Fitzwilliam and Council to Privy Council, 6 May 1572, SP 63/36/16; Memorandum concerning the delivery of Mary, Queen of Scots, 12 March 1572, Cottonian MSS, Calig. C. III f. 235.

88. Piers to Malby, 13 June 1572, SP 63/36/46,i.

89. Nicholas Canny, "The Permissive Frontier: Social Control in English Settlements in Ireland and Virginia, 1550–1650," in K. R. Andrews, N. P. Canny, and P. E. H. Hair, eds., *The Westward Enterprise: English Activities in Ireland, the Atlantic, and America, 1480–1650*, (Liverpool, 1978) 18–20; MacDonald and MacDonald, *Clan Donald*, II: 687–8.

90. Fitzwilliam to Burghley, 4 October 1572, SP 63/38/4.

91. Hayes-McCoy, *Scots Mercenary Forces*, 119–20.

92. Malby to Fitzwilliam, 14 October 1572, SP 63/38/12; Turlough O'Neill to Fitzwilliam, 10 October 1572, SP 63/38/10.

93. Turlough O'Neill to Fitzwilliam and Council, 10 October 1572, SP 63/38/11; Malby to Fitzwilliam, 14 October 1572, SP 63/38/12; Hayes-McCoy, *Scots Mercenary Forces*, 119–20; O'Laverty, *Down and Connor*, II: 173–4; The Lord Deputy's letter, 25 September 1572, *CSP Scot.*, IV: 403; Fitzwilliam to Burghley, 21 October 1572, SP 63/38/20; Benn, *History of Belfast*, 30–1.

94. Fitzwilliam to Burghley, 26 October 1572, SP 63/38/24; Sir Thomas Smith to Burghley, 28 October 1572, SP 63/38/26; Fitzwilliam and Council to Queen, 7 December 1572, SP 63/38/49; Henry Killigrew to Burghley, 10 December 1572, SP Scot. Eliz. 23/119; Chambers, ed., *Domestic Annals,* I: 84; Sir Thomas Smith to Fitzwilliam, 8 November 1572, SP 63/38/30.

Chapter 8

1. Essex's offer touching the inhabiting in the north of Ireland, May 1573, London, Lambeth Palace Library, Carew MSS, vol. 635, f. 102.

2. Sir Thomas Smith to Lord Burghley, 20 February 1573, London, British Library, Lansdowne MSS, 16, f. 45; Smith to Burghley, 27 February 1573, London, British Library, Harleian MSS, 6991, f. 16.

3. Terence Daniel to Fitzwilliam, 30 March 1573, SP 63/40/52,vi; Fitzwilliam and Council to Queen, 7 April 1573, SP 63/40/2; Bagenal and Daniel to Fitzwilliam, April 1573, SP 63/40/2,i; Malby to Burghley, 10 April 1573, London, Public Record Office, State Papers, Ireland, Elizabeth, SP 63/40/9 (hereafter cited as SP 63).

4. James Morrin, ed., *Calendar of the Patent and Close Rolls of Chancery in Ireland,* 3 vols. (Dublin, 1861–3), I: 553, no. 12; Turlough Luineach O'Neill to Fitzwilliam and Council, 21 April 1573, SP 63/40/52,iii.

5. Essex's offer touching the inhabiting in the north of Ireland, May 1573, Carew MSS, vol. 635, f. 102.

6. A breviate of the patent to be granted by the queen to Essex, May 1573, Carew MSS, vol. 635, f. 104; Essex's offer touching the inhabiting in the north of Ireland, May 1573, Carew MSS, vol. 635, f. 102.

7. Bagenal and Dowdall to Fitzwilliam and Council, 20 May 1573, SP 63/40/52,v; Fitzwilliam to Burghley, 20 May 1573, SP 63/40/48; Fitzwilliam and Council to Queen, 25 May 1573, SP 63/40/52; Rev. James O'Laverty, *An Historical Account of the Diocese of Down and Connor, Ancient and Modern,* 5 vols. (Dublin, 1878–95), III: 28.

8. Fitzwilliam and Council to Queen, 25 May 1573, SP 63/40/52.

9. Killigrew to Burghley, 14 April 1573, London, Public Record Office, State Papers, Scotland, Elizabeth, 25/11 (hereafter cited as SP Scot. Eliz.); Bagenal to Fitzwilliam, n.d., SP 63/40/52,iv.

10. O'Laverty, *Down and Connor,* II: 174; Smith to Burghley, 29 May 1573, SP 63/40/76; Thomas Smith's interview with Sorley Boy MacDonnell, 29 May 1573, SP 63/40/77; Dispatch from Anthony de Guaras to Ulster rebels, May 1573, SP 63/40/80.

11. Essex's demands for Ireland, 19 June 1573, SP 63/41/46; Piers to Burghley, 28 June 1573, SP 63/41/56; Fitzwilliam to Burghley, 30 June 1573, SP 63/41/61; Rev. George Hill, *An Historical Account of the MacDonnells of Antrim, Including Notices of some other Septs, Irish and Scottish* (Belfast, 1873), 154–5; Sir Thomas Smith to Burghley, 2 June 1573, Lansdowne MSS, 18, f. 6.

12. Instructions for Edward Tremaine, sent to Fitzwilliam by the Lord Treasurer, June 1573, Carew MSS, vol. 600, f. 43a.

13. Steven G. Ellis, *Tudor Ireland: Crown, Community and the Conflict of Cultures, 1470–1603* (London and New York, 1985), 267; John Smith of the Ardes to

Burghley, 18 July 1573, SP 63/41/86; Instructions for Edward Tremaine, sent to Fitzwilliam by the Lord Treasurer, June 1573, Carew MSS, vol. 600, f. 43a; Hill, *MacDonnells of Antrim*, 155.

14. Essex to Burghley, 20 July 1573, Harleian MSS, 6991, f. 23. According to Richard Cox, *Hibernia Anglicana: or, the History of Ireland from the Conquest thereof by the English, to this present time*, 2nd edn., 2 vols. (London, 1692), II: 340, Essex was to "repel the Scots, and not . . . hurt the Irish."

15. Bagenal to Fitzwilliam, 25 July 1573, SP 63/41/91.

16. Ellis, *Tudor Ireland*, 267; Privy Council to Fitzwilliam, 10 August 1573, SP 63/42/4.

17. Essex to Turlough O'Neill, 6 September 1573, SP 63/42/18,i; Essex to Privy Council, 10 September 1573, SP 63/42/18; Essex to Burghley, 10 September 1573, SP 63/24/19; Essex to Privy Council, 16 September 1573, 63/42/58.

18. Hill, *MacDonnells of Antrim*, 152; Ellis, *Tudor Ireland*, 267; Essex to earl of Leicester, 15 September 1573, SP 63/42/22; Bagenal to Fitzwilliam and Council, 27 September 1573, SP 63/42/29; Essex to Privy Council, 29 September 1573, SP 63/42/32; Queen to Fitzwilliam, 29 September 1573, SP 63/42/31; John Strype, *The Life of the Learned Sir Thomas Smith* (Oxford, 1820), 135–6.

19. Edward Waterhouse to Burghley, 29 September 1573, SP 63/42/34; Sir Thomas Smith to Burghley, 13 October 1573, SP 63/42/50; Essex to Privy Council, 4 October 1573, SP 63/42/38.

20. Memorandum of Sorley Boy MacDonnell's letters and petitions to the Lord Deputy, 19 October 1573, SP 63/42/54.

21. Essex to Waterhouse, 2 November 1573, SP 63/42/66.

22. Essex to Privy Council, 28 October 1573, SP 63/42/58.

23. Essex to Waterhouse, 2 November 1573, SP 63/42/66.

24. Hill, *MacDonnells of Antrim*, 153.

25. Essex to Waterhouse, 2 November 1573, SP 63/42/66.

26. Essex to Queen, 2 November 1573, SP 63/42/64.

27. Ibid.; Essex to Burghley, 2 November 1573, SP 63/42/68; Thomas Wilsford to Burghley, 1 December 1573, SP 63/43/1; Essex to Waterhouse, 2 November 1573, SP 63/42/66.

28. Essex to Burghley, 2 December 1573, SP 63/43/2; Articles between Essex and the adventurers, January 1574, SP 63/44/23; G. A. Hayes-McCoy, *Scots Mercenary Forces in Ireland (1565–1603)* (Dublin and London, 1937), 120; Queen to Fitzwilliam, 18 January 1574, Carew MSS, vol. 628, f. 162a; Privy Council to Fitzwilliam and Council, 17 January 1574, Carew MSS, vol. 628, f. 161.

29. Ibid.

30. Essex to Privy Council, 9 February 1574, SP 63/44/58; Regent Morton to Queen Elizabeth, 21 January 1574, in Great Britain, *Calendar of the State Papers Relating to Scotland and Mary, Queen of Scots, 1547–1603*, ed. Joseph Bain *et al.*, 13 vols. (Edinburgh, 1898–1969), IV: 638; Ellis, *Tudor Ireland*, 267–8; Essex to Burghley, 9 February 1574, SP 63/44/34; Essex to Fitzwilliam and Council, 6 March 1574, SP 63/45/21,i.

31. Ibid.; Essex's offer to surrender his patent in Clandeboy, 8 March 1574, SP 63/45/8; Essex to Privy Council, 8 March 1574, SP 63/45/7; Essex to Queen, 7 March 1574, SP 63/48/58; Memorial concerning Ireland, 10 March 1574, SP 63/45/10.

32. Notes touching the pacifying of the present trouble in Ireland, 21 March 1574, Carew MSS, vol. 628, f. 157; Articles of truce between Essex and Turlough O'Neill, 16 March 1574, SP 63/45/11; Turlough O'Neill to Queen, 23 March 1574, SP 63/45/19; Barnaby Gooch to Burghley, 2 April 1574, SP 63/45/53,i; Sir Edward Fitton to Burghley, 27 March 1574, SP 63/45/34; Fitzwilliam and Council to Queen, 24 March 1574, SP 63/45/21.

33. Queen to Fitzwilliam, 30 March 1574, SP 63/45/39; Instructions for Essex, 30 March 1574, SP 63/45/42,i; Queen to Essex, 30 March 1574, SP 63/45/42; Burghley, Sussex, and Leicester to Essex, 30 March 1574, SP 63/45/43; Queen to Essex, 30 March 1574, Carew MSS, vol. 628, f. 201.

34. Burghley, Sussex, and Leicester to Essex, 30 March 1574, SP 63/45/43; Queen to Fitzwilliam, 30 March 1574, SP 63/45/39.

35. Ibid.

36. Instructions for Fitzwilliam, 30 March 1574, Carew MSS, vol. 628, f. 198.

37. Queen to Fitzwilliam, 30 March 1574, Carew MSS, vol. 628, f. 165a; Instructions for Fitzwilliam, 30 March 1574, Carew MSS, vol. 628, f. 198.

38. Essex to Queen, 2 April 1574, SP 63/48/58; Essex to Privy Council, 2 April 1574, SP 63/48/58; Essex to Burghley, 2 April 1574, SP 63/45/50; Essex to Privy Council, 6 April 1574, SP 63/48/58; Barnaby Gooch to Burghley, 7 April 1574, SP 63/45/60; Essex to Privy Council, 15 April 1574, SP 63/45/66; Essex to Burghley, 15 April 1574, SP 63/45/67.

39. Barnaby Gooch to Burghley, 15 April 1574, SP 63/45/69; Burghley's Memorial for the Government of Ireland, 20 April 1574, SP 63/45/77; Privy Council to Fitzwilliam, 26 April 1574, SP 63/45/84; Essex to Privy Council, 21 April 1574, SP 63/45/78; Privy Council to Essex, 26 April 1574, SP 63/45/85.

40. Ibid.; Privy Council to Fitzwilliam, 26 April 1574, SP 63/45/84.

41. Queen to Essex, 27 April 1574, SP 63/45/86; Waterhouse to Burghley, 29 April 1574, SP 63/45/89; Sir Brian MacFelim O'Neill to Queen, 8 May 1574, SP 63/46/5; Essex to Queen, 13 May 1574, SP 63/46/11; Essex to Queen, 13 May 1574, SP 63/46/10; Essex to Privy Council, 13 May 1574, SP 63/46/12.

42. Essex to Sir Francis Walsingham, 13 May 1574, SP 63/46/14; Essex to Burghley, 13 May 1574, SP 63/46/13; T. W. Moody, F. X. Martin, and F. J. Byrne, eds., *A New History of Ireland*, 9 vols. (Oxford, 1976–84), vol. III, *Early Modern Ireland, 1534–1691*, (Oxford, 1976), 99 (hereafter cited as *NHI*); George Benn, *A History of the Town of Belfast* (London, 1877), 46–9; Edward Barkley to Burghley, 14 May 1574, SP 63/46/15; Essex to Turlough O'Neill, 10 June 1574, SP 63/46/58; Fitzwilliam to Queen, 10 June 1574, SP 63/46/54.

43. Essex to Lord Treasurer, Chamberlain, Leicester, and Walsingham, 14 June 1574, SP 63/46/61.

44. Essex to Burghley, 14 June 1574, SP 63/46/62.

45. Essex to Privy Council, 14 June 1574, SP 63/48/58; Fitzwilliam and Essex to

Privy Council, 20 June 1574, SP 63/46/70; Robert Chambers, ed., *Domestic Annals of Scotland from the Reformation to the Revolution*, 3 vols. (Edinburgh and London, 1874), I: 94; Essex to Burghley, 24 June 1574, SP 63/46/74; Articles between Essex and Francis Laney, 25 June 1574, SP 63/47/4,i; Fitzwilliam to Privy Council, 20 June 1574, SP 63/46/61; Essex to Privy Council, 10 July 1574, SP 63/47/3.

46. Privy Council to Essex, 11 July 1574, Carew MSS, vol. 628, f. 208.

47. Queen to Essex, 13 July 1574, SP 63/47/12; Fitzwilliam to Privy Council, 18 July 1574, SP 63/48/61; Fitzwilliam to Privy Council, 18 July 1574, SP 63/47/23,i; Essex to Fitzwilliam, 30 July 1574, SP 63/47/40,i; Earl of Argyll's progress, July 1574, SP Scot. Eliz. 26/39.

48. Fitzwilliam and Council to Essex, 2 August 1574, SP 63/47/40,ii; Burghley's points for Ireland, 12 September 1574, SP 63/47/59; Waterhouse to Burghley, 23 September 1574, SP 63/47/65; Essex to Privy Council, 8 October 1574, SP 63/48/3; Essex to Burghley, 8 October 1574, SP 63/48/4; Walter Bourchier Devereux, ed., *Lives and Letters of the Devereux, Earls of Essex, in the Reigns of Elizabeth, James I, and Charles I, 1540–1646*, 2 vols. (London, 1853), I: 80–8.

49. Fitzwilliam to Burghley, 11 October 1574, SP 63/48/6; Fitzwilliam to Walsingham, 11 October 1574, SP 63/48/7; Essex to Walsingham, 12 October 1574, SP 63/48/10; Auditor Jenison to Burghley, 13 October 1574, SP 63/48/14; Essex to Privy Council, 16 October 1574, SP 63/48/16; Essex to Privy Council, 23 October 1574, SP 63/48/20; Privy Council to Essex, 8 November 1574, SP 63/48/46; Essex to Queen, 12 October 1574, SP 63/48/58; Essex to Privy Council, 12 October 1574, SP 63/48/58.

50. Fitzwilliam and Council to Privy Council, 25 October 1574, SP 63/48/22; Waterhouse to Burghley, 16 October 1574, SP 63/48/17; Essex to Burghley, 23 October 1574, SP 63/48/21; John Symcott to Burghley, 27 October 1574, SP 63/48/28; Queen to Essex, 9 November 1574, SP 63/48/47; Privy Council to Fitzwilliam, 9 November 1574, SP 63/48/48.

51. Privy Council to Essex, 9 November 1574, Carew MSS, vol. 628, f. 211a.

52. Privy Council to Fitzwilliam, 9 November 1574, Carew MSS, vol. 628, f. 213a; Privy Council to Essex, 9 November 1574, Carew MSS, vol. 628, f. 211a.

53. Privy Council to Fitzwilliam, 9 November 1574, Carew MSS, vol. 628, f. 213a; Privy Council to Essex, 9 November 1574, Carew MSS, vol. 628, f. 211a.

54. Proclamation by Essex concerning the apprehension of Sir Brian MacFelim O'Neill, November 1574, SP 63/48/57,i; Essex to Fitzwilliam, 14 November 1574, SP 63/48/52,iii; Essex to Privy Council, 24 November 1574, SP 63/48/57.

55. Essex to Fitzwilliam, 14 November 1574, SP 63/48/52,iii; John O'Donovan, ed., *Annala Rioghachta Eireann, Annals of the Kingdom of Ireland, by the Four Masters, from the Earliest Period to the Year 1616*, 5 vols. (Dublin, 1848), V: 1677–9 (anno 1574).

56. Essex to Privy Council, 24 November 1574, SP 63/48/57; Waterhouse to Walsingham, 18 November 1574, SP 63/48/55; Essex to Burghley, 4 December 1574, SP 63/48/68; Essex to Burghley, 2 December 1574, SP 63/48/58; Articles by Captain Piers for the reformation of the north of Ireland, November 1574, Carew MSS, vol. 616, f. 141.

57. O'Laverty, *Down and Connor*, II: 177–8; Essex to Burghley, 3 December 1574, SP 63/48/66.

58. Articles by Captain Piers for the reformation of the north of Ireland, November 1574, Carew MSS, vol. 616, f. 141.

59. Essex to Burghley, 2 December 1574, SP 63/48/58; Articles by Captain Piers for the reformation of the north of Ireland, November 1574, Carew MSS, vol. 616, f. 141; Piers to Privy Council, November 1574, Carew MSS, vol. 616, f. 143.

60. Memorandum by Burghley concerning Essex's plat and intentions for Ulster, 2 February 1575, SP 63/49/51; John Crawford of Ayr to Essex, 5 February 1575, SP 63/50/32,iii; Queen to Fitzwilliam and Essex, 24 February 1575, SP 63/49/69; Queen to Fitzwilliam and Essex, 24 February 1575, SP 63/49/71.

61. Essex to Privy Council, 10 March 1575, SP 63/50/4; Essex to Burghley, 11 March 1575, SP 63/50/8.

62. Privy Council to Fitzwilliam, 14 March 1575, SP 63/50/15.

63. Queen to Fitzwilliam and Essex, 15 March 1575, in Arthur Collins, ed., *Letters and Memorials of State*, 2 vols. (London, 1746; reprint edn., New York, 1973), I: 64.

64. Ibid., 63–4; Fitzwilliam to Privy Council, 31 March 1575, SP 63/50/28.

65. Sir Hugh O'Donnell to Essex, 18 March 1575, SP 63/50/32,i; Owen O'Gallagher to Essex, 18 March 1575, SP 63/50/32,ii.

66. Essex to Privy Council, 29 March 1575, in Collins, ed., *Letters and Memorials of State*, I: 70.

67. Essex to Queen, 31 March 1575, SP 63/50/32.

68. Queen to Fitzwilliam and Essex, 8 April 1575, SP 63/50/49; Queen to Fitzwilliam and Essex, 11 April 1575, SP 63/50/56; Hayes-McCoy, *Scots Mercenary Forces*, 120; Burghley, Sussex, and Leicester to Fitzwilliam and Essex, 9 April 1575, SP 63/50/53; Queen to Essex, 5 May 1575, SP 63/51/4; Lord Keeper archbishop of Dublin and Vice-Treasurer Fitton to Burghley, 14 April 1575, SP 63/50/68; Essex to Privy Council, 15 April 1575, SP 63/50/69; Lord Keeper archbishop of Dublin to Burghley, 1 May 1575, SP 63/51/1; Queen to Fitzwilliam, 5 May 1575, SP 63/51/3; Chambers, ed., *Domestic Annals*, I: 99; Memorandum concerning supplies for Ulster, 15 April 1575, SP 63/50/70; Fitzwilliam to Burghley, 3 May 1575, SP 63/51/2; O'Donovan, ed., *Four Masters*, V: 1681 (anno 1575); Malby to Walsingham, 25 April 1575, SP 63/50/74; Essex to Privy Council, 28 April 1575, SP 63/50/77.

69. Memorandum concerning Ulster, April 1575, SP 63/50/87; Memorandum concerning troop strength of Ulster chiefs, April 1575, Carew MSS, vol. 616, f. 80; Turlough O'Neill to Fitzwilliam, 29 April 1575, SP 63/52/23,i; Malby to Burghley, 14 May 1575, SP 63/51/22.

70. Essex to Burghley, 8 May 1575, SP 63/51/9; Malby to Burghley, 14 May 1575, SP 63/51/22; Malby to Privy Council, 9 May 1575, SP 63/51/11; Essex to Walsingham, 9 May 1575, SP 63/51/10; O'Donovan, ed., *Four Masters*, V: 1681 (anno 1575); Sir James Ware, *The Antiquities and History of Ireland*, 2 vols. (London, 1714), II: 17; Essex to Walsingham, 9 May 1575, SP 63/51/10; Fitzwilliam to Burghley, 15 May 1575, SP 63/51/29; Queen to Fitzwilliam, 22 May 1575, SP 63/51/38; Queen to Essex, 22 May 1575, SP 63/51/39.

71. Ibid.7

72. Instructions for Essex via Ashton, 22 May 1575, Carew MSS, vol. 628, f. 225a.

73. Queen to Fitzwilliam, 22 May 1575, SP 63/51/38; Instructions for Essex via Ashton, 22 May 1575, Carew MSS, vol. 628, f. 225a; Queen to Essex, July 1575, Carew MSS, vol. 628, f. 228a; Queen to Fitzwilliam and Essex, July 1575, Carew MSS, vol. 628, f. 227a.

74. Fitzwilliam to Privy Council, 25 May 1575, SP 63/51/41; Instruction from Essex to Queen and Privy Council via Ashton, 1 June 1575, SP 63/52/5; Fitzwilliam to Queen, 14 June 1575, SP 63/52/23; Fitzwilliam to Privy Council, 20 June 1575, SP 63/52/27; Fitzwilliam to Burghley, 20 June 1575, SP 63/52/29; Waterhouse to Burghley, 24 June 1575, SP 63/52/32; Waterhouse to Walsingham, 24 June 1575, SP 63/52/33.

75. Waterhouse to Walsingham, 24 June 1575, SP 63/52/33; Extract of Essex's instructions to Ashton, 25 June 1575, SP 63/52/34; Articles of peace between Turlough O'Neill and Essex, 27 June 1575, SP 63/52/44,i; Articles between Turlough O'Neill and Essex, 27 June 1575, SP 63/52/45 and 63/52/48,xviii; Essex's proclamation, 28 June 1575, SP 63/52/48,xvii; Essex to Fitzwilliam, 29 June 1575, SP 63/52/48,xvi.

76. Extract of Essex's instructions to Ashton, 25 June 1575, SP 63/52/34; Essex's considerations concerning peace with Turlough O'Neill, June 1575, SP 63/52/48,xix; A. MacDonald and A. MacDonald, *The Clan Donald*, 3 vols. (Inverness, 1896–1904), II: 689; Essex to Queen, 22 July 1575, SP 63/52/67.

77. Essex to Privy Council, 5 July 1575, SP 63/52/44; Malby to Walsingham, 5 July 1575, SP 63/52/46; Waterhouse to Walsingham, 9 July 1575, SP 63/52/51.

78. Essex to Queen, 22 July 1575, SP 63/52/67.

79. Ibid.

80. Ibid.; Essex to Walsingham, 23 July 1575, SP 63/52/70.

81. Hill, *MacDonnells of Antrim*, 183; Essex to Queen, 31 July 1575, SP 63/52/77.

82. Ibid.

83. Ibid.

84. Ibid.

85. Ellis, *Tudor Ireland*, 268; David Beers Quinn, "Ireland and Sixteenth Century European Expansion," *Historical Studies* I (1958): 20–32.

86. Quoted in Hill, *MacDonnells of Antrim*, 158n.

Chapter 9

1. Essex to Privy Council, 31 July 1575, London, Public Record Office, State Papers, Ireland, Elizabeth, SP 63/52/78 (hereafter cited as SP 63). Instructions from Queen for Sidney, 2 August 1575, SP 63/53/2; Richard Cox, *Hibernia Anglicana: or, the History of Ireland from the Conquest thereof by the English, to this present time*, 2nd edn., 2 vols. (London, 1692), II: 342.

2. Queen to Essex, 6 August 1575, London, Lambeth Palace Library, Carew MSS, vol. 628, f. 231a; Walsingham to Burghley, 7 August 1575, London, British Library, Harleian MSS, 6992, f. 3; Queen to Essex, 12 August 1575, Carew MSS, vol. 628, f. 230a.

3. Advertisements from Scotland, August 1575, London, British Library, Cottonian

MSS, Calig. C. V. f. 29; Essex to Lord Deputy Fitzwilliam and Council, 16 August 1575, SP 63/53/11; Essex to Queen, 16 August 1575, SP 63/53/10; Malby to Queen, 18 August 1575, SP 63/53/13; Rev. James O'Laverty, *An Historical Account of the Diocese of Down and Connor, Ancient and Modern*, 5 vols. (Dublin, 1878–95), IV: 21–2; Rev. George Hill, *An Historical Account of the MacDonnells of Antrim, Including Notices of some other Septs, Irish and Scottish* (Belfast, 1873), 155.

4. Vice-Treasurer Fitton to Burghley, 29 August 1575, SP 63/53/18; Francis Lany to Sidney, 16 September 1575, SP 63/53/22; Essex to Walsingham, 28 September 1575, SP 63/53/33; O'Laverty, *Down and Connor*, III: 28; Cox, *Hibernia Anglicana*, II: 342–3; Sir James Ware, *The Antiquities and History of Ireland*, 2 vols. (London, 1714), II: 18; Sidney to Lords of the Council, 28 September 1575, in Arthur Collins, ed., *Letters and Memorials of State*, 2 vols. (London, 1746; reprint edn., New York, 1973), I: 73.

5. Cox, *Hibernia Anglicana*, II: 342–3.

6. Fitton to Burghley, 27 September 1575, SP 63/53/26; Sidney to Cecil, 28 September 1575, in Collins, ed., *Letters and Memorials of State*, I: 72; John O'Donovan, ed., *Annala Rioghachta Eireann, Annals of the Kingdom of Ireland, by the Four Masters, from the Earliest Period to the Year 1616*, 5 vols. (Dublin, 1848), V: 1681 (anno 1575); Steven G. Ellis, *Tudor Ireland: Crown, Community and the Conflict of Cultures, 1470–1603* (London and New York, 1985), 269–70.

7. Ware, *Antiquities*, II: 18; G. A. Hayes-McCoy, *Scots Mercenary Forces in Ireland, (1565–1603)* (Dublin and London, 1937), 120–1; A. MacDonald and A. MacDonald, *The Clan Donald*, 3 vols. (Inverness, 1896–1904), II: 691.

8. Sidney to Lords of the Council, 28 September 1575, in Collins, ed., *Letters and Memorials of State*, I: 73.

9. Sir Henry Sidney, "Memoir of a Government in Ireland," *Ulster Journal of Archaeology* series I, III (1855): 33–44, 85–99, 336–57; V (1857): 299–315; VIII (1860): 179–95; Hill, *MacDonnells of Antrim*, 155.

10. Sidney to Lords of the Council, 15 November 1575, in Collins, ed., *Letters and Memorials of State*, I: 77.

11. Sidney, "Memoir;" Sidney to Lords of the Council, 15 November 1575, in Collins, ed., *Letters and Memorials of State* I: 77, 79; Hill, *MacDonnells of Antrim*, 156; Hayes-McCoy, *Scots Mercenary Forces*, 120–1.

12. Truce and composition between Sidney and Council and Sorley Boy MacDonnell, 19 October 1575, SP 63/53/52; Memorandum concerning letters to Sidney from Sorley Boy, 19 October 1575, Carew MSS, vol. 632, f. 9a; Sidney to Burghley, 22 December 1575, SP 63/54/22.

13. Sidney, "Memoir."

14. Ibid.; Turlough Luineach O'Neill's petitions to Sidney, 3 November 1575, SP 63/53/56; Cox, *Hibernia Anglicana*, II: 343; Turlough O'Neill to Queen, 10 November 1575, SP 63/53/61; Sidney to Burghley, 22 December 1575, SP 63/54/22; Privy Council to Sidney, 23 January 1576, SP 63/55/5; Sidney to Lords of the Council, 15 November 1575, in Collins, ed., *Letters and Memorials of State*, I: 77–8.

15. Ibid., 78.

16. Ibid., 77; Ralph Bagenal to Burghley, 24 November 1575, SP 63/53/69.

17. Hayes-McCoy, *Scots Mercenary Forces*, 122, 126.

18. Sidney, "Memoir."

19. Edmund Tremayne to Sidney, 24 January 1576, SP 63/55/6; Privy Council to Sidney, 24 January 1576, Carew MSS, vol. 628, f. 293.

20. Sir Thomas Smith to Burghley, 4 December 1575, London, British Library, Lansdowne MSS, 21, f. 21.

21. Sidney to Lords of the Council, 16 June 1576, in Collins, ed., *Letters and Memorials of State*, I: 115; Privy Council to Sidney, 13 July 1576, Carew MSS, vol. 628, f. 295; Sidney to Walsingham, 15 August 1576, SP 63/56/19; Sidney to Lords of the Council, 15 August 1576, in Collins, ed., *Letters and Memorials of State*, I: 126.

22. Sidney to Privy Council, 27 January 1577, Carew MSS, vol. 601, f. 63; Sidney to Lords of the Council, 27 January 1577, in Collins, ed., *Letters and Memorials of State*, I: 155; Sidney, "Memoir."

23. Hayes-McCoy, *Scots Mercenary Forces*, 125; Sidney to Privy Council, 17 March 1577, Sidney to Lords of the Council, 27 January 1577, in Collins, ed., *Letters and Memorials of State*, I: 164, 151; Sidney, "Memoir;" Sidney to Privy Council, 17 March 1577, SP 63/57/39.

24. Sidney to Lords of the Council, 17 March 1577, in Collins, ed., *Letters and Memorials of State*, I: 164.

25. Ibid., I: 165.

26. Sidney to Queen, 15 September 1577, in Collins, ed., *Letters and Memorials of State*, I: 218. See also O'Donovan, ed., *Four Masters*, V: 1693 (anno 1577).

27. Irish Council to Queen, 12 September 1577, in Collins, ed., *Letters and Memorials of State*, I: 216.

28. MacDonald and MacDonald, *Clan Donald*, II: 548; Instructions to Thomas Randolph in Scotland, 30 January 1578, London, Public Record Office, State Papers, Scotland, Elizabeth, 27/28 (hereafter cited as SP Scot. Eliz.); Hayes-McCoy, *Scots Mercenary Forces*, 126; Sidney to Lords of the Council, February 1578, in Collins, ed., *Letters and Memorials of State*, I: 243.

29. Sidney and Irish Council to Queen, 20 April 1578, in Collins, ed., *Letters and Memorials of State*, I: 249.

30. Ellis, *Tudor Ireland*, 274.

31. Memorials and Notes for Mr Lodovicke Briskett, 14 June 1578, in Collins, ed., *Letters and Memorials of State*, I: 261.

32. Irish Council to Queen, 12 September 1578, SP 63/62/8; Dungannon to Lord Justice William Drury, 22 December 1578, SP 63/65/4,ii; Turlough O'Neill to Drury, 18 December 1578, SP 63/65/4,i.

33. Robert Bowes to Walsingham, 24 November 1578, Cottonian MSS, Calig. C. V. f. 110.

34. Act by Privy Council of Scotland to keep the peace between MacLean of Duart and MacDonnell of Dunyveg, 12 January 1579, and Complaint by MacLean of Duart against Argyll, 29 December 1578, in G. G. Smith, ed., *The Book of Islay* (privately printed, 1895), 74–5.

35. Ellis, *Tudor Ireland,* 278; R. Trevor Davies, *The Golden Century of Spain, 1501–1621* (London, 1964), 210–11; R. B. Wernham, *The Making of Elizabethan Foreign Policy, 1558–1603* (Berkeley, CA and London, 1980), 25–6; Fitton to Burghley, 8 January 1579, SP 63/65/12; Drury to Privy Council, 6 January 1579, SP 63/65/4; Memorandum concerning Dungannon's creation as earl of Tyrone on Turlough Luineach's death, January 1579, SP 63/65/7; Drury to Burghley, 6 January 1579, SP 63/65/5.

36. Drury to Burghley, 11 February 1579, SP 63/65/36.

37. Drury to Walsingham, 11 February 1579, SP 63/65/38; Fitton to Burghley, 12 February 1579, SP 63/65/40; Fitton to Burghley, 22 February 1579, SP 63/65/44; Drury to Privy Council, 30 March 1579, SP 63/66/14.

38. Drury to Privy Council, 30 March 1579, SP 63/66/14.

39. Bowes to earl of Leicester, 20 February 1579, Cottonian MSS, Calig. C. III. f. 534; Hugh O'Donnell to Sidney, April 1579, SP 63/66/50,ii.

40. Edward Waterhouse to Walsingham, 3 August 1579, SP 63/68/2; J. J. Silke, *Ireland and Europe, 1559–1607* (Dundalk, Louth, 1966), 13–14; James Fitzmaurice to Alexander Kittaghe MacDonnell, July 1579, SP 63/67/34; Fitzmaurice to Ustainn MacDonnell, July 1579, SP 63/67/35; Fitzmaurice to Ranald MacColla MacDonnell, July 1579, SP 63/67/36; Drury and Council to Privy Council, 22 July 1579, SP 63/67/40; Captain William Piers, the younger, to Walsingham, 5 July 1579, SP 63/67/24; Ellis, *Tudor Ireland,* 278–9.

41. William Gerrard, Lord Chancellor of Ireland, to Leicester, 28 July 1579, and Excerpt of a letter from Thomas Sackford to Lord Chancellor Gerrard, 16 August 1579, in James Hogan and N. MacNeill O'Farrell, eds., *The Walsingham Letter-Book or Register of Ireland, May, 1578 to December, 1579* (Dublin, 1959), 102, 134; Justice James Dowdall to Lord Chancellor, 3 August 1579, SP 63/68/7,i; Orders taken by Lord Chancellor and Irish Council, 9 August 1579, SP 63/68/23; Proceedings of the Chancellor of Ireland, 21 August 1579, SP 63/69/6,i; Lord Chancellor to Walsingham, 5 September 1579, SP 63/69/6.

42. Christopher Fleming to Gerrard, 5 September 1579, SP 63/69/7; Turlough O'Neill to Gerrard, 8 September 1579, SP 63/69/13; Fleming to Gerrard and archbishop of Dublin, 6 September 1579, SP 63/69/8; Turlough O'Neill to Drury, 8 September 1579, SP 63/69/14; Gerrard to Dowdall and Terence Daniel, 9 September 1579, SP 63/69/15; Fleming to Gerrard, 9 September 1579, SP 63/69/16; Malby to Walsingham, 10 September 1579, SP 63/69/17; Dowdall and Daniel to Gerrard, 10 September 1579, SP 63/69/21; Gerrard to Turlough O'Neill, 11 September 1579, SP 63/69/23; Gerrard, bishop of Meath, and William Pelham to Sir Hugh O'Reilly, 12 September 1579, SP 63/69/25.

43. Thomas Woodhouse to Malby, 12 September 1579, SP 63/69/26; Gerrard to Burghley, 10 and 16 September 1579, SP 63/69/30; Gerrard to Walsingham, 10 and 16 September 1579, SP 63/69/31; Agreement of Gerrard and Council to Queen's instructions, September 1579, SP 63/69/31,i; Drury to Walsingham, 17 September 1579, SP 63/69/33; Wallop to Walsingham, 20 September 1579, SP 63/69/36; Drury to Walsingham, 17 September 1579, SP 63/69/34.

44. Declaration of Thomas Stevenson to the Irish Council, 25 September 1579, in Hogan and O'Farrell, eds., *Walsingham Letter-Book,* 187–8.

45. Ibid.

46. Present Occurants in Scotland, October 1579, Cottonian MSS, Calig. C. V. f. 170; Declaration of Thomas Stevenson to the Irish Council, 25 September 1579, in Hogan and O'Farrell, eds., *Walsingham Letter-Book*, 187–8.

47. Patrick Cullen to Bagenal, 14 November 1579, in Hogan and O'Farrell, eds., *Walsingham Letter-Book*, 224.

48. Dungannon to Lord Justice Pelham, 22 November 1579, Carew MSS, vol. 597, f. 112a; Dungannon to Pelham, 24 November 1579, SP 63/70/22; Hayes-McCoy, *Scots Mercenary Forces*, 129–30.

49. Pelham to Queen, 23 November 1579, Carew MSS, vol. 597, f. 115. See also, Waterhouse to Gerrard, 26 November 1579, SP 63/70/27; Malby to Burghley, 27 November 1579, SP 63/70/30.

50. Ibid.; Extracts of letters from Dungannon, Nicholas Walshe, earl of Ormond, and Sir Warham St. Leger, 9 through 24 November 1579, SP 63/70/23; Pelham to Burghley, 28 November 1579, SP 63/70/35; Wallop to earl of Sussex, 28 November 1579, SP 63/70/36; Malby to Walsingham, 10 December 1579, SP 63/70/51; Pelham and Council to Privy Council, 15 December 1579, Carew MSS, vol 597, ff. 147, 150–1a; Pelham to Queen, 28 December 1579, Carew MSS, vol. 597, f. 167; Fitton to Walsingham, 3 January 1580, SP 63/71/2.

51. Hayes-McCoy, *Scots Mercenary Forces*, 130; Tom Glasgow, Jr., "The Elizabethan Navy in Ireland (1558–1603)," *Irish Sword* VII, 39 (1974–5): 291–307; Pelham to Walsingham, 6 January 1580, SP 63/71/8; Pelham to Sorley Boy MacDonnell, 20 January 1580, Carew MSS, vol. 597, f. 206; Pelham and Council to Privy Council, 17 January 1580, Carew MSS, vol. 597, f. 202; Hayes-McCoy, *Scots Mercenary Forces*, 130; Bowes to Leicester, 20 February 1580, Cottonian MSS, Calig. C. III. f. 582.

52. Nicholas White, Master of the Rolls, to Burghley, 20 April 1580, SP 63/72/53.

53. White to Walsingham, 20 April 1580, SP 63/72/54; Waterhouse to Walsingham, 24 April 1580, SP 63/72/65; Hayes-McCoy, *Scots Mercenary Forces*, 130–1; Waterhouse to Walsingham, 30 April 1580, SP 63/72/74; Malby to Burghley, 26 April 1580, SP 63/72/68; Irish Council to Privy Council, 9 March 1580, SP 63/72/9; Pelham to Bagenal, 14 March 1580, Carew MSS, vol. 597, f. 284.

54. Hayes-McCoy, *Scots Mercenary Forces*, 131–2; Malby to Leicester, 10 May 1580, Carew MSS, vol. 619, f. 46; Bowes to Burghley and Walsingham, 10 May 1580, SP Scot. Eliz. 26/83.

55. Malby to Leicester, 12 July 1580, Carew MSS, vol. 619, f. 37.

56. Hayes-McCoy, *Scots Mercenary Forces*, 132–3; Bagenal to Piers, the elder, 25 May 1580, SP 63/73/54,i; Piers, the elder, to Walsingham, 12 June 1580, SP 63/73/54; Piers, the elder, to Walsingham, 29 May 1580, SP 63/73/36.

57. Lord Grey de Wilton to Queen, 12 August 1580, Cottonian MSS, Titus. B. XIII. f. 305.

58. Grey and Council to Privy Council, 14 August 1580, SP 63/75/40.

59. Malby to Walsingham, 17 August 1580, SP 63/75/54; Malby to Leicester, 17 August 1580, Carew MSS, vol. 607, f. 68.

60. Ibid.; Hayes-McCoy, *Scots Mercenary Forces*, 135–6.

61. Piers, the elder, to Walsingham, 18 August 1580, SP 63/75/58; Examination of

Sir James Fitzgerald, August 1580, SP 63/76/25,i; Bagenal to Grey, 2 September 1580, SP 63/76/1; Viscount Gormanstown to Grey, 4 September 1580, SP 63/76/9; Dungannon to Grey, 3 September 1580, SP 63/76/6; Dungannon to Grey, 4 September 1580, SP 63/76/7; Malby to Walsingham, 7 September 1580, SP 63/76/15.

62. Silke, *Ireland and Europe*, 15; Malby to Leicester, 7 September 1580, Carew MSS, vol. 619, f. 48; Wallop to Walsingham, 9 September 1580, SP 63/76/21; Grey to Burghley, 12 September 1580, SP 63/76/27; Grey to Walsingham, 12 September 1580, SP 63/76/28; Hayes-McCoy, *Scots Mercenary Forces*, 130; Gerrard to Burghley, 14 September 1580, SP 63/76/30; Geoffrey Fenton to Walsingham, 28 September 1580, SP 63/76/69; Fenton to Burghley, 30 September 1580, SP 63/76/77; Turlough O'Neill's petitions to Queen, via Piers, the elder, September 1580, SP 63/76/77,i; Bagenal to Leicester, 3 October 1580, Cottonian MSS, Titus. B. XIII. f. 307.

63. Grey to Queen, 5 October 1580, SP 63/77/12; Bowes to Burghley and Walsingham, 18 October 1580, Cottonian MSS, Calig. C. VI. f. 102.

64. Bowes to Burghley and Walsingham, 24 October 1580, Cottonian MSS, Calig. C. VI. f. 93.

65. Gerrard to Burghley, 18 October 1580, SP 63/77/37; Bagenal to Walsingham, 3 November 1580, SP 63/78/2; Gerrard and Council to Privy Council, 3 November 1580, SP 63/78/4; Grey to Walsingham, 9 December 1580, SP 63/79/5.

66. Advice to Walsingham, January 1581, SP Scot. Eliz. 29/22.

67. Hayes-McCoy, *Scots Mercenary Forces*, 137, 143; Wallop to Burghley, 13 January 1581, SP 63/80/4; William Byrd, mayor of Chester, to Burghley, 20 January 1581, SP 63/80/20; Advice to Walsingham, January 1581, SP Scot. Eliz. 29/22.

68. Piers, the elder, to Walsingham, 16 January 1581, SP 63/80/13; Waterhouse to Walsingham, 25 January 1581, SP 63/80/28.

69. Wallop to Leicester, 26 January 1581, Cottonian MSS, Titus. B. XIII. f. 319.

70. Grey to Walsingham, 27 January 1581, SP 63/80/32; Malby to Leicester, 29 January 1581, Carew MSS, vol. 619, f. 42; Ciaran Brady, "Conservative Subversions: the Community of the Pale and the Dublin Administration, 1556–86," in P. J. Corish, ed., *Radicals, Rebels and Establishments* (Belfast, 1985), 25.

71. Elizabeth's intentions toward James VI, 17 February 1581, SP Scot. Eliz. 29/35; Order appointing Sir Nicholas Bagenal Governor of Ulster, 1 March 1581, in Hogan and O'Farrell, eds., *Walsingham Letter-Book*, 109.

72. Malby to Leicester, 23 March 1581, Carew MSS, vol. 607, f. 58.

73. Walsingham to Randolph, 7 March 1581, SP Scot. Eliz. 29/44; Walsingham to Randolph, 15 March 1581, SP Scot. Eliz. 29/47; Fenton to Walsingham, 16 April 1581, SP 63/82/30; Privy Council to Lord Deputy, 19 April 1581, SP 63/82/39; Hayes-McCoy, *Scots Mercenary Forces*, 138.

74. Privy Council to Grey, 19 April 1581, SP 63/82/41; Wallop to Walsingham, 23 April 1581, 63/82/47; Grey to Walsingham, 24 April 1581, 63/82/48; Grey to Queen, 26 April 1581, SP 63/82/54; Bagenal to Walsingham, 25 April 1581, SP 63/82/52.

75. Grey to Walsingham, 12 May 1581, SP 63/83/6; Wallop to Burghley, 13 May

1581, SP 63/83/12; David Beers Quinn, "Ireland and Sixteenth Century European Expansion," *Historical Studies* I (1958): 20–32; Malby to Walsingham, 6 July 1581, SP 63/84/8; Grey to Privy Council, 10 July 1581, SP 63/84/12.

76. Hayes-McCoy, *Scots Mercenary Forces*, 138–9; Malby and Waterhouse to Walsingham, 9 July 1581, SP 63/84/11; Grey to Privy Council, 10 July 1581, SP 63/84/13; Waterhouse to Walsingham, 17 July 1581, SP 63/84/24; Waterhouse to Walsingham, 23 July 1581, SP 63/84/44; Malby to Leicester, 18 July 1581, Carew MSS, vol. 619, f. 40; Wallop to Walsingham, 10 July 1581, SP 63/84/16.

77. Sir William Stanley to Walsingham, 26 April 1581, SP 63/82/57.

78. Wallop and Waterhouse to Burghley, 26 April 1581, SP 63/82/56; Wallop to Burghley, 6 July 1581, SP 63/84/4; Grey to Walsingham, 18 July 1581, SP 63/84/26; Thomas Sackford to Burghley, 25 July 1581, SP 63/84/49; Irish Council to Privy Council, 31 July 1581, SP 63/84/53.

79. Instructions from Grey to Justice Dowdall and Lodowick Briskett concerning Turlough O'Neill, 1 August 1581, SP 63/85/13,i; Ellis, *Tudor Ireland*, 284; Grey to Queen, 10 August 1581, SP 63/85/5; Articles ratifying peace between Grey and Turlough O'Neill made near Benburb in September 1580, 2 August 1581, SP 63/85/13,ii; Grey to Privy Council, 12 August 1581, SP 63/85/13; Grey to Sir Christopher Hatton, 12 August 1581, in Thomas Wright, ed., *Queen Elizabeth and Her Times*, 2 vols. (London, 1838), II: 147.

80. Articles for the reformation of the north, by Piers, the elder, 10 August 1581, SP 63/85/7; Wallop to Walsingham, 11 August 1581, SP 63/85/9; Andrew Trollope to Walsingham, 12 September 1581, SP 63/85/39.

81. Hayes-McCoy, *Scots Mercenary Forces*, 139; Patrick Cullen to Bagenal, 30 November 1581, SP 63/87/31,i; MacDonald and MacDonald, *Clan Donald*, II: 549–50; Edward White's notes concerning Malby, 1 May 1582, SP 63/92/2.

82. Waterhouse to Walsingham, 5 July 1582, SP 63/94/7; William Clifford to Malby, 6 July 1582, SP 63/94/15,ii; Thomas Woodhouse to Captain Anthony Brabazon, 7 July 1582, SP 63/94/15,iii; Waterhouse to Walsingham, 9 July 1582, SP 63/94/13; Grey and Council to Privy Council, 10 July 1582, SP 63/94/15; Malby to Walsingham, 12 July 1582, SP 63/94/20; Malby to Grey, 8 July 1582, SP 63/94/15,i; Malby to Waterhouse and Fenton, 8 July 1582, SP 63/94/13,i; Chancellor Adam Loftus to Walsingham, 28 May 1582, SP 63/92/87; Grey to Walsingham, 16 July 1582, SP 63/94/28; Malby to Burghley, 19 July 1582, SP 63/94/32; Malby to Walsingham, 19 July 1582, SP 63/94/33; Turlough O'Neill's petitions to Queen, 5 July 1582, SP 63/94/9; Malby to Leicester, 20 July 1582, Carew MSS, vol. 619, f. 54.

83. Malby to Walsingham, 27 August 1582, SP 63/94/100; Malby to Walsingham, 28 August 1582, SP 63/94/102; Malby to Walsingham, 1 September 1582, SP 63/95/5; Lords Justice to Turlough O'Neill, 4 November 1582, SP 63/97/15,iv; Lords Justice to Privy Council, 5 November 1582, SP 63/97/15; Piers, the elder, to Lords Justice, 10 December 1582, SP 63/98/49,i; Lords Justice to Walsingham, 20 December 1582, SP 63/98/49; Lords Justice to Privy Council, 7 December 1582, SP 63/98/20; Hayes-McCoy, *Scots Mercenary Forces*, 145.

84. Memorials of certain special matters recommended by Her Majesty unto Colonel Stewart and Mr Colville, May 1583, in John Colville, *Original Letters of Mr John Colville, 1582–1603*, ed. Bannatyne Club (Edinburgh, 1858), 228–9; Advice from Elizabeth to James VI, May 1583, SP Scot. Eliz. 32/29.

85. O'Laverty, *Down and Connor*, III: 64.

86. O'Donovan, ed., *Four Masters*, V: 1811 (anno 1583); William M. Hennessy, ed., *The Annals of Loch Cé. A Chronicle of Irish Affairs from A.D. 1014 to A.D. 1590*, 2 vols. (London, 1871), II: 453 (anno 1583); Malby to Walsingham, 16 April 1583, SP 63/101/29.

87. Instructions to captains Nicholas Dawtrey and William Chatterton, 1583, in Irish Manuscripts Commission, *Calendar of the Irish Council Book, 1581–1586*, in *Analecta Hibernica*, vol. 24, ed. David B. Quinn (Dublin, 1967), 138 (hereafter cited as IMC, *Irish Council Book*); Lords Justice to Walsingham, March 1583, SP 63/100/20.

88. O'Donovan, ed., *Four Masters*, V: 1811 (anno 1583).

89. Piers, the elder, to Walsingham, 11 April 1583, SP 63/101/20; Malby to Walsingham, 7 April 1583, SP 63/101/16; Malby to Burghley, 24 March 1583, SP 63/100/45; Malby to Walsingham, 4 April 1583, SP 63/101/7; Lords Justice to Privy Council, 29 April 1583, SP 63/101/43; Bowes to Walsingham, 1 May 1583, SP Scot. Eliz. 32/1; Hayes-McCoy, *Scots Mercenary Forces*, 146.

90. Turlough O'Neill to Lords Justice, 1 May 1583, SP 63/102/21,i; Lords Justice to Turlough O'Neill, 8 May 1583, SP 63/102/21,ii; Fleming to Malby, 2 May 1583, SP 63/102/4,i.

91. Dungannon to Lords Justice, 11 May 1583, SP 63/102/71,i; Sir Edward Moore to Lords Justice, 12 May 1583, SP 63/102/29,i; Lords Justice to Privy Council, 14 May 1583, SP 63/102/29; Malby to Walsingham, 13 May 1583, SP 63/102/28; Hayes-McCoy, *Scots Mercenary Forces*, 146-7; Dungannon to Lords Justice, 13 May 1583, SP 63/102/30,i; Sir Henry Bagenal to Lords Justice, 13 May 1583, SP 63/102/30,ii; Lords Justice to Walsingham, 14 May 1583, SP 63/102/30; Malby to Walsingham, 13 May 1583, SP 63/102/27; Bowes to Walsingham, 9 July 1583, Cottonian MSS, Calig. C. VII. f. 263; A Discourse for the reformation of Ireland, 1583, Carew MSS, vol. 621, f. 97.

92. Hayes-McCoy, *Scots Mercenary Forces*, 148; Sorley Boy and Alexander MacDonnell to Sir Henry Bagenal, 4 July 1583, in IMC, *Irish Council Book*, 143-4; Wallop to Burghley, 13 July 1583, SP 63/103/20.

93. Articles of truce between Turlough O'Neill, O'Donnell, and Dungannon, 22 October 1583, Carew MSS, vol. 600, f. 79; Articles of peace between O'Neill, O'Donnell, and Dungannon, 22 October 1583, SP 63/105/58,i; Lords Justice to Privy Council, 7 November 1583, SP 63/105/58; Proposed treaty between Elizabeth and Mary, Queen of Scots, 2 October 1583, in Great Britain, *Calendar of the State Papers Relating to Scotland and Mary, Queen of Scots, 1547–1603*, ed. Joseph Bain *et al.*, 13 vols. (Edinburgh, 1898–1969), VI: 629; Lady Agnes Campbell (O'Neill) to Lords Justice, 4 November 1583, SP 63/105/62; Lords Justice to Walsingham, 12 November 1583, SP 63/105/61.

Chapter 10

1. Rev. George Hill, *An Historical Account of the MacDonnells of Antrim, Including Notices of some other Septs, Irish and Scottish* (Belfast, 1873), 159; Steven G. Ellis, *Tudor Ireland: Crown, Community and the Conflict of Cultures, 1470–1603* (London and New York, 1985), 285; Extract of letters, January 1584, in Great Britain, *Calendar of the State Papers Relating to Scotland and Mary, Queen of Scots, 1547–1603*, ed. Joseph Bain *et al.*, 13 vols. (Edinburgh, 1898–1969), VII: 8; Sir Christopher Nugent, Baron Delvin,

to Queen, 1584, in John T. Gilbert, ed., *Account of Facsimiles of National Manuscripts of Ireland* (London, 1884), 192.

2. Robert Bowes to Walsingham, 13 February 1584, 34/20, Walsingham to William Davison, 22 August 1584, 36/40, London, Public Record Office, State Papers, Scotland, Elizabeth (hereafter cited as SP Scot. Eliz.); Bowes to Walsingham, 24 February 1584, Walsingham to Lord Hunsdon, 24 August 1584, London, British Library, Cottonian MSS, Calig. C. VII f. 275, VIII, f. 99v; Lords Justice Adam Loftus and Henry Wallop to Walsingham, 26 March 1584, SP 63/108/56, Sir Henry Bagenal to Walsingham, 15 April 1584, London, Public Record Office, State Papers, Ireland, Elizabeth, SP 63/109/37 (hereafter cited as SP 63).

3. John O'Donovan, ed., *Annala Rioghachta Eireann, Annals of the Kingdom of Ireland, by the Four Masters, from the Earliest Period to the Year 1616*, 5 vols. (Dublin, 1848), V: 1817–19 (anno 1584); William Johns to Walsingham, 14 July 1584, SP 63/111/31; Oliver Eustace to Sir Lucas Dillon, 26 July 1584, SP 63/111/39,iii; Hugh O'Donnell to Perrott, 27 July 1584, SP 63/111/39,i; G. A. Hayes-McCoy, *Scots Mercenary Forces in Ireland (1565–1603)* (Dublin and London, 1937), 148–9.

4. Ibid.; Perrott to Walsingham, 6 August 1584, SP 63/111/45.

5. Captain Joshua Mince to Perrott, 3 August 1584, SP 63/111/39,ii.

6. Davison to Walsingham, 4 August 1584, SP Scot. Eliz. 36/10; Hayes-McCoy, *Scots Mercenary Forces*, 153; Memorials from Edward Norris to Privy Council on the present state of Ireland, 6 August 1584, SP 63/111/43; Perrott and Council to Privy Council, 6 August 1584, SP 63/111/39; Perrott to Queen, 6 August 1584, SP 63/111/38; Sir Richard Bingham to Burghley, 7 August 1584, SP 63/111/52.

7. Privy Council to Perrott, 15 August 1584, SP 63/111/64; Sir Geoffrey Fenton to Burghley, 19 August 1584, SP 63/111/67; William M. Hennessy, ed., *The Annals of Loch Cé. A Chronicle of Irish Affairs from A.D. 1014 to A.D. 1590*, 2 vols. (London, 1871), II: 461 (anno 1584); Hill, *MacDonnells of Antrim*, 159; Hayes-McCoy, *Scots Mercenary Forces*, 153–4; Perrott to Privy Council, 21 August 1584, SP 63/111/70; Declaration of Gerald Hay, Waterford merchant, 21 August 1584, SP 63/111/70,i; O'Donovan, ed., *Four Masters*, V: 1817 (anno 1584).

8. Bingham to Burghley, 7 August 1584, SP 63/111/52; Fenton to Walsingham, 22 August 1584, SP 63/111/73; Wallop to Walsingham, 23 August 1584, SP 63/111/74; Hayes-McCoy, *Scots Mercenary Forces*, 153-54; Hill, *MacDonnells of Antrim*, 160-61.

9. Sir Nicholas Bagenal to Leicester, 24 August 1584, London, Lambeth Palace Library, Carew MSS, vol. 619, f. 14; Hayes-McCoy, *Scots Mercenary Forces*, 154; Walsingham to Davison, 29 August 1584, SP Scot. Eliz. 36/53; Bingham to Walsingham, 30 August 1584, SP 63/111/81.

10. Privy Council to Perrott, 31 August 1584, SP 63/111/82.

11. Nicholas Skiddy to Walsingham, 4 September 1584, SP 63/111/84; Fenton to Walsingham, 14 September 1584, SP 63/111/85; Richard Cox, *Hibernia Anglicana: or, the History of Ireland from the Conquest thereof by the English, to this present time*, 2nd edn., 2 vols. (London, 1692), II: 381; Sir Henry Sidney, "Memoir of a Government in Ireland," *Ulster Journal of Archaeology* series I, III (1855): 33–44, 85–99, 336–57; V (1857): 299–315, VIII (1860): 179–95; Hayes-McCoy, *Scots Mercenary Forces*, 155; O'Donovan, ed., *Four Masters*, V: 1821 (anno 1584).

12. Sidney, "Memoir;" A. MacDonald and A. MacDonald, *The Clan Donald*, 3

vols. (Inverness, 1896–1904), II: 693; O'Donovan, ed., *Four Masters*, V: 1821 (anno 1584); Perrott to Privy Council, 15 September 1584, SP 63/111/88; Perrott to Privy Council, 17 September 1584, Carew MSS, vol. 632, f. 73a; Perrott to Walsingham, 18 September 1584, SP 63/111/94; Hill, *MacDonnells of Antrim*, 162–3.

13. Hayes-McCoy, *Scots Mercenary Forces*, 157–8; Articles between Perrott and Council and Donnell Gorme MacDonnell, 18 September 1584, Carew MSS, vol. 611, f. 225; Indenture between Perrott and Donnell Gorme MacDonnell, 18 September 1584, Irish Manuscripts Commission, *Calendar of the Irish Council Book, 1581–1586*, in *Analecta Hibernica*, vol. 24, ed. David B. Quinn (Dublin, 1967), 159 (hereafter cited as IMC, *Irish Council Book*); Cox, *Hibernia Anglicana*, II: 381; O'Donovan, ed., *Four Masters*, V: 1895n–96n; Articles of Agreement between Perrott and Council and Donnell Gorme MacDonnell, 18 September 1584, SP 63/112/41,xii.

14. Hayes-McCoy, *Scots Mercenary Forces*, 157–8; Articles of indenture between Perrott and the Ulster Lords, 18 September 1584, Carew MSS, vol. 611, f. 145; Articles of agreement by Turlough Luineach O'Neill, 18 September 1584, SP 63/112/41,ii; Articles of agreement by Sir Hugh O'Donnell, 20 September 1584, SP 63/112/41,iii; Indenture between O'Neill and O'Donnell before Perrott, 20 September 1584, Carew MSS, vol. 611, f. 144; Articles of agreement by Theobald MacQuillin, 20 September 1584, SP 63/112/41,iv; Articles of agreements of Hugh Oge MacFelim O'Neill, Cormac MacNeill MacBrian, Ever MacRory MacBrian, Aghowly MacCartan, and Sir Hugh Magennis, 6 and 7 October 1584, SP 63/112/41,vii–xi; Articles of agreement by Con MacNeill Oge, 6 October 1584, SP 63/112/41,v; Articles of agreement of Shane MacBrian MacFelim, 6 October 1584, SP 63/112/41,vi; Perrott to Privy Council, 20 October 1584, in IMC, *Irish Council Book*, 9.

15. Cox, *Hibernia Anglicana*, II: 382.

16. Perrott to Privy Council, October 1584, Carew MSS, vol. 632, f. 74a; Hill, *MacDonnells of Antrim*, 163n.

17. Perrott to Privy Council, 25 October 1584, SP 63/112/41; Bingham to Walsingham, 14 October 1584, SP 63/112/7; Perrott to Privy Council, October 1584, Carew MSS, vol. 632, f. 74a; John Norris, President of Munster, to Burghley, 16 October 1584, SP 63/112/11.

18. Captain Christopher Carlyle to Walsingham, 17 October 1584, SP 63/112/14.

19. Perrott to Walsingham, 20 October 1584, SP 63/112/22.

20. Ibid.; Perrott to Burghley, 22 October 1584, SP 63/112/28.

21. Perrott to Lord Treasurer, 20 October 1584, in Irish Manuscripts Commission, *The Perrott Papers*, in *Analecta Hibernica*, vol. 12, ed. C. MacNeill (Dublin, 1943), 12 (hereafter cited as IMC, *Perrott Papers*); George Beverley to Burghley, 24 October 1584, SP 63/112/38; Sir Edward Waterhouse to Burghley, 23 October 1584, SP 63/112/30; Waterhouse to Walsingham, 24 October 1584, SP 63/112/37. In early November, Perrott finally admitted the need to station vessels on Lough Erne. Perrott to Privy Council, 6 November 1584, SP 63/112/66.

22. James Michael Hill, *Celtic Warfare, 1595–1763* (Edinburgh, 1986), 22–44.

23. Walsingham to Perrott, 26 and 28 October 1584, SP 63/112/49.

24. John Norris to Walsingham, 31 October 1584, SP 63/112/61; Perrott to

Walsingham, 16 November 1584, SP 63/112/72; Hayes-McCoy, *Scots Mercenary Forces*, 158.

25. Captain William Bowen to Perrott, 17 November 1584, SP 63/112/90,iii; Sir Henry Bagenal to Perrott, 16 November 1584, SP 63/112/90,i; Martin Couche to Walsingham, 2 December 1584, SP 63/113/5.

26. Ibid.

27. Captain Nicholas Dawtrey to Perrott, 18 November 1584, in John Dawtrey, *The Falstaff Saga, being the Life and Opinions of Captain Nicholas Dawtrey* (London, 1927), 180; Sir William Stanley to Burghley, 2 December 1584, SP 63/113/2; Perrott to Walsingham, 4 December 1584, SP 63/113/10; Bagenal to Perrott, 16 November 1584, SP 63/112/90,i; Martin Couche to Walsingham, 2 December 1584, SP 63/113/5; Hill, *MacDonnells of Antrim*, 166.

28. Captain Carlyle to Burghley, 19 November 1584, SP 63/112/77; Dawtrey to Perrott, 18 November 1584, SP 63/112/90,ii; Perrott to Walsingham, 27 November 1584, SP 63/112/90; Hill, *MacDonnells of Antrim*, 166; Hayes-McCoy, *Scots Mercenary Forces*, 158–9.

29. Bagenal to Perrott, 7 January 1585, SP 63/114/29,i.

30. Hayes-McCoy, *Scots Mercenary Forces*, 159; Stanley to Bagenal, 5 January 1585, SP 63/114/29,ii.

31. Stanley to Bagenal, 5 January 1585, SP 63/114/29,ii; Stanley to Burghley, 22 March 1585, SP 63/115/34; Launcelot Clayton to Walsingham, 12 June 1585, SP 63/117/21; Perrott to Privy Council, October 1585, SP 63/120/18.

32. Stanley to Bagenal, 5 January 1585, SP 63/114/29,ii.

33. Ibid.; Bagenal to Perrott, 7 January 1585, SP 63/114/29,i; Beverley to Walsingham, 5 January 1585, SP 63/114/11; Hayes-McCoy, *Scots Mercenary Forces*, 159.

34. Bagenal to Perrott, 7 January 1585, SP 63/114/29,i; Perrott to Walsingham, 11 January 1585, SP 63/114/19; Perrott to Burghley, 15 January 1585, SP 63/114/29; Perrott to Walsingham, 17 January 1585, SP 63/114/32; Beverley to Burghley, 20 January 1585, SP 63/114/40; Privy Council to Perrott, January 1585, SP 63/114/52; Perrott to earl of Leicester, 7 March 1585, in IMC, *Perrott Papers*, 16; Hayes-McCoy, *Scots Mercenary Forces*, 159–60. The Scots' success contradicted Captain Henry Lee's claim of a breach between Sorley and Angus. Lee to Walsingham, 2 February 1585, SP 63/114/62.

35. Hill, *MacDonnells of Antrim*, 167; Wallop to Walsingham, 20 January 1585, SP 63/114/42; Wallop to Walsingham, 18 and 25 January 1585, SP 63/114/47; Sorley Boy MacDonnell to Perrott, 5 February 1585, SP 63/114/67; Sorley Boy to Captain Carlyle, 5 February 1585, SP 63/114/68–9.

36. Perrott to Burghley, 31 January 1585, SP 63/114/50; Perrott to Walsingham, 31 January 1585, SP 63/114/51; Walsingham to Perrott, 1 February 1585, SP 63/114/59; Instructions to Sir Lewis Bellenden, 16 February 1585, Edinburgh, University of Edinburgh Library, Laing MSS, I: 10; Hayes-McCoy, *Scots Mercenary Forces*, 161–3.

37. Captain Edward Barkley to Perrott, 26 February 1585, SP 63/114/82; Rhys ap Hugh to Perrott, 1 March 1585, SP 63/115/5; Hennessy, ed., *Loch Cé*, II: 467 (anno 1585); Hayes-McCoy, *Scots Mercenary Forces*, 163.

38. Fenton to Walsingham, 7 March 1585, SP 63/115/21.

39. Bagenal, Stanley, and Barkley to Perrott, 22 March 1585, SP 63/115/37; Wallop to Walsingham, 22 March 1585, SP 63/115/33; Bagenal to Burghley, 22 March 1585, SP 63/115/35; Bagenal to Walsingham, 22 March 1585, SP 63/115/36; Bagenal, Stanley, and Barkley to Perrott, 26 March 1585, SP 63/115/39; Perrott and Council to Privy Council, 12 June 1585, in IMC, *Perrott Papers*, 19–20.

40. Queen to Perrott, 14 April 1585, SP 63/116/12.

41. Beverley to Burghley, 1 April 1585, SP 63/116/2.

42. Sir Nicholas Bagenal to Burghley, 24 May 1585, SP 63/116/51; John Price to Walsingham, 1 May 1585, SP 63/116/34; Perrott and Council to Privy Council, June 1585, Carew MSS, vol. 632, f. 79a; Hill, *MacDonnells of Antrim*, 177–8; Hayes-McCoy, *Scots Mercenary Forces*, 163–4.

43. Perrott and Council to Privy Council, June 1585, Carew MSS, vol. 632, f. 79a; Hill, *MacDonnells of Antrim*, 177–8; Hayes-McCoy, *Scots Mercenary Forces*, 163–5; Walsingham to Perrott, 14 April 1585, SP 63/116/13; Sir Nicholas White, Master of the Rolls, to Burghley, 20 April 1585, SP 63/116/19; Perrott to Walsingham, 24 April 1585, SP 63/116/22; MacDonald and MacDonald, *Clan Donald*, II: 695–6.

44. Dr. John Long, archbishop of Armagh, to Walsingham, 4 June 1585, SP 63/117/7; Henry Hovenden's petition on the part of Hugh O'Neill, June 1585, SP 63/117/53; Wallop to Burghley, 21 May 1585, SP 63/116/46; Hill, *MacDonnells of Antrim*, 167n–8n; Hayes-McCoy, *Scots Mercenary Forces*, 165–7; Edward Wotton to Walsingham, 30 July 1585, SP Scot. Eliz. 37/103; Charges brought against the earl of Arran, August 1585, SP Scot. Eliz. 38/9.

45. Captain Stafford to Wallop, 2 August 1585, SP 63/118/54,i; Wallop to Burghley, 4 August 1585, SP 63/118/48; Perrott to Walsingham, 10 August 1585, SP 63/118/58; Advertisements from Ulster, 6 August 1585, SP 63/118/78,i; James VI of Scotland to Perrott, 8 August 1585, Carew MSS, vol. 632, f. 81a; J. P. MacLean, *History of the Island of Mull*, 2 vols. (San Mateo, CA, 1925), 48–50; Hayes-McCoy, *Scots Mercenary Forces*, 165; Sir James Perrott, *A Chronicle of Ireland, 1584–1608*, ed. Herbert Wood (Dublin 1933), 44–5.

46. Loftus and Wallop to Burghley, 13 August 1585, SP 63/118/64.

47. Dawtrey to Wotton, 14 August 1585, London, British Library, Add. MSS, 32657, f. 153.

48. Wotton to Walsingham, 22 August 1585, SP Scot. Eliz. 38/32.

49. Fenton to Burghley, 23 August 1585, SP 63/118/75; Fenton to Burghley, 30 August 1585, SP 63/118/78; Hayes-McCoy, *Scots Mercenary Forces*, 169–70; Hill, *MacDonnells of Antrim*, 178–80.

50. Wotton to Walsingham, 19 August 1585, SP Scot. Eliz. 38/25; Beverley to Burghley, 10 September 1585, SP 63/119/19; Wallop to Burghley, October 1585, SP 63/120/19; Perrott to Burghley, 24 September 1585, SP 63/119/32; Wotton to Walsingham, 30 September 1585, SP Scot. Eliz. 38/71; Wotton to Walsingham, 7 October 1585, SP Scot. Eliz. 38/78; Queen to Perrott, November 1585, Carew MSS, vol. 632, f. 82; Hayes-McCoy, *Scots Mercenary Forces*, 171; Bagenal to Perrott, 3 November 1585, SP 63/121/4,i.

51. Hayes-McCoy, *Scots Mercenary Forces*, 169; Wallop to Walsingham, 18 November

1585, SP 63/121/10; Hill, *MacDonnells of Antrim*, 180n; Perrott's project for the reformation of Ireland, 1585, Carew MSS, vol. 614, f. 254; Perrott to Walsingham, 11 November 1585, SP 63/121/4.

52. Dublin, National Library of Ireland, MS 669, ff. 46v–7.

53. Marshal Bagenal's description of Ulster, 1586, in Constantia Maxwell, ed., *Irish History from Contemporary Sources (1509–1610)* (London, 1923), 265–6.

54. Perrott to Lord Treasurer, 25 January 1586, in IMC, *Perrott Papers*, 35.

55. Perrott to Walsingham, 24 December 1585, in IMC, *Perrott Papers*, 36–7.

56. Fenton's notes concerning Ireland, January 1586, SP 63/122/60.

57. Wallop to Walsingham, 6 January 1586, SP 63/122/15; Hill, *MacDonnells of Antrim*, 181; Queen to Lord Chancellor and Council, 26 February 1586, SP 63/122/81.

58. Fenton to Burghley, 15 April 1586, SP 63/123/36.

59. Perrott to Walsingham, 20 February 1586, SP 63/122/77; Captain John Price to Walsingham, 28 February 1586, SP 63/122/90.

60. Price to Walsingham, 31 March 1586, SP 63/123/20; Briefs of letters, January–April 1586, Carew MSS, vol. 632. f. 85a; Hayes-McCoy, *Scots Mercenary Forces*, 175–6; O'Donovan, ed., *Four Masters*, V: 1855 (anno 1586).

61. Perrott, *Chronicle*, 46–7. This story is substantiated by Cox, *Hibernia Anglicana*, II: 386.

62. Perrott to Lords of the Council, 15 April 1586, in IMC, *Perrott Papers*, 54.

63. Fenton to Burghley, 15 April 1586, SP 63/123/36. Wallop noted that "Since the death of Alexander MacSorley . . . [Ulster] seemeth to be in all reasonable quiet. . . ." Wallop to Burghley, 26 April 1586, SP 63/123/52; Sir Nicholas White to Burghley, 12 April 1586, SP 63/123/31.

64. Fenton to Burghley, 19 April 1586, SP 63/123/46.

65. Wallop to Burghley, 26 April 1586, SP 63/123/52; Loftus to Burghley, 26 April 1586, SP 63/123/54.

66. Wallop to Burghley, 26 April 1586, SP 63/123/52; Loftus to Burghley, 26 April 1586, SP 63/123/54.

67. Certificate under the hands of Hugh O'Neill, earl of Tyrone, and Sir Edward Moore, 7 May 1586, SP 63/124/6.

68. Loftus to Burghley, 12 May 1586, SP 63/124/14.

69. Grant of the Glynnes to Angus MacDonnell, 16 May 1586, Carew MSS, vol. 632, f. 89; Indenture between Perrott and Council and Angus MacDonnell of Dunyveg, 16 May 1586, SP 63/124/29; Perrott to Sir George Carew, 28 May 1586, Carew MSS, vol. 605, f. 78; Wallop to Burghley, 30 May 1586, SP 63/124/47.

70. Perrott to Queen, 26 May 1586, in IMC, *Perrott Papers*, 61. Perrott reiterated this same message two days later. See Perrott and Council to Queen, 28 May 1586, in ibid., 62.

71. Instructions for commissioners to deal with the Scots in Clandeboy, May 1586, SP 63/124/62.

72. Fenton to Burghley, 1 June 1586, SP 63/124/63.

73. Sir Henry Bagenal's information on the north of Ireland, 7 June 1586, SP 63/124/66.

74. Sir Nicholas Bagenal to Burghley, 9 June 1586, SP 63/124/70.

75. Perrott, *Chronicle*, 47.

76. Fenton to Burghley, 14 June 1586, SP 63/124/76.

77. Sorley Boy's submission to Perrott, 14 June 1586, SP 63/124/77.

78. A brief declaration of part of the services done to your Majesty by Sir John Perrott, 14 December 1588, SP 63/139/7. See also William Camden, *Britannia: or, a Chorographical Description of the Flourishing Kingdoms of England, Scotland, and Ireland, and the Islands Adjacent; from the Earliest Antiquity*, ed. Richard Gough, 2nd. edn., 4 vols. (London, 1806), IV: 431.

79. Fenton to Burghley, 14 June 1586, SP 63/124/76.

80. Sorley Boy MacDonnell's patent of denization, 18 June 1586, Oxford, Bodleian Library, MS Laud Misc., 613, ff. 302–5; Indenture between Perrott and Sorley Boy, 18 June 1586, SP 63/124/83. For copies of the same document, see SP 63/150/77,iv and SP 63/151/7,v.

81. Abstract of the division of the Route between Rory MacQuillin and Sorley Boy MacDonnell, 18 June 1586, SP 63/124/85; Fenton to Burghley, 23 June 1586, SP 63/124/90.

82. J. J. Silke, *Ireland and Europe, 1559–1607* (Dundalk, Louth, 1966), 15–16.

83. Hayes-McCoy, *Scots Mercenary Forces*, 181; Narrative of the feud between the Clandonald and the Clanlean and of the events which came to pass in the island of Islay, July 1586, in G. G. Smith, ed., *The Book of Islay* (privately printed, 1895), 79–86. For further details of the MacDonnell–MacLean feud, see Observations of Dioness Campbell, Dean of Limerick, 1586, SP Scot. Eliz. 58/72, and Bannatyne Club, ed., *The Historie and Life of King James the Sext: Being an account of the affairs of Scotland, from the year 1566, to the year 1596; with a short continuation to the year 1617* (Edinburgh, 1825), 217–23.

84. Wallop to Walsingham, 8 July 1586, SP 63/125/10; Roger Wilbraham to Burghley, 9 July 1586, SP 63/125/11.

85. Wallop to Burghley, 12 August 1586, SP 63/125/47.

86. Price to Burghley, 15 August 1586, SP 63/125/56; Wallop to Walsingham, 23 August 1586, SP 63/125/62.

87. Walsingham to Sir Edward Stafford, 27 October 1586, Cottonian MSS, Galba. E. VI f. 309; Services done by Sir Richard Bingham, governor of Connacht, against the Scots, Carew MSS, September 1586, vol. 632, f. 12; Answer of Donnell Gorme and Alexander Carragh MacDonnell to Bingham, 22 September 1586, SP 63/126/17; Names of Scots slain at Ardnary, 23 September 1586, SP 63/126/18; Captain Thomas Woodhouse to Fenton, 23 September 1586, SP 63/126/31,iv; Fenton to Walsingham, 29 September 1586, SP 63/126/32; Bingham to Loftus, 23 September 1586, SP 63/126/34,i; Bingham to Perrott, 23 September 1586, SP 63/126/34,ii; Bingham's discourse of his services in Connacht, October 1586, SP 63/126/53,i; Notes concerning Bingham's service in Ireland, 1586, SP 63/127/78; William Davison to Burghley, 8 October 1586, London, British Library, Harleian MSS,

290, f. 189; Hennessy, ed., *Loch Cé*, II: 473–5 (anno 1586); O'Donovan, ed., *Four Masters*, V: 1849–55 (anno 1586).

Epilogue

1. C. H. McIlwain, ed., *The Political Works of James I* (New York, 1965), 22.

2. Captain Charles Eggarton to Sir William Fitzwilliam, January 1589, London, Public Record Office, State Papers, Ireland, Elizabeth, SP 63/141/19,iv (hereafter cited as SP 63).

3. Rory MacQuillin to Fitzwilliam, 4 February 1590, SP 63/150/77,i; MacQuillin to Fitzwilliam, 13 February 1590, SP 63/150/77,ii; G. A. Hayes-McCoy, *Scots Mercenary Forces in Ireland (1565–1603)* (Dublin and London, 1937), 203; William M. Hennessy, ed., *The Annals of Loch Cé. A Chronicle of Irish Affairs from A.D. 1014 to A.D. 1590*, 2 vols. (London, 1871), II: 509 (anno 1590); John O'Donovan, ed., *Annala Rioghachta Eireann, Annals of the Kingdom of Ireland, by the Four Masters, from the Earliest Period to the Year 1616*, 5 vols. (Dublin, 1848), V: 1893 (anno 1590).

4. Hugh O'Donnell to Angus MacDonnell, September 1593, SP 63/172/18,i; Hugh O'Neill, earl of Tyrone, to Lord Deputy and Council, 14 May 1593, SP 63/169/49,ii; Lord Deputy and Council to Privy Council, 28 February 1594, SP 63/173/64; Declaration of Ranald Oge MacDonnell before Sir Henry Bagenal *et al.*, 17 February 1594, SP 63/173/64,x.

5. Elizabeth I to James VI, 25 October 1594, 54/73, Elizabeth I to earl of Argyll, 25 October 1594, 54/74, London, Public Record Office, State Papers, Scotland, Elizabeth (hereafter cited as SP Scot. Eliz.).

6. Lord Deputy Russell's Journal, 1595, London, British Library, Additional Manuscripts, 4728, ff. 33–4 (hereafter cited as BL, Add. MSS); Roger Aston to Robert Bowes, 15 August 1595, SP Scot. Eliz. 56/89; Lachlan MacLean of Duart to Bowes, 22 August 1595, SP Scot. Eliz. 56/94; John Auchinross to George Nicolson, 22 August 1595, SP Scot. Eliz. 56/96; George Erskine to Bowes, 24 August 1595, SP Scot. Eliz. 56/98; Donald Gorme MacDonnell to Lord Deputy, 3 August 1595, SP 63/182/9; Letter written by John Morgan, 1 August 1595, SP 63/182/10,i; Rowland Savage to Captain Izod, 1 August 1595, SP 63/182/26,i; Captain George Thornton to Bagenal, 16 August 1595, SP 63/182/43,i; Angus MacDonnell and Donald Gorme MacDonnell to Captain Thornton and Captain Riggs, 28 July 1595, SP 63/182/43,ii.

7. Sir Henry Bagenal to Burghley, 9 and 12 September 1595, SP 63/183/19; Sir John Norris to Cecil, 10 September 1595, SP 63/183/21.

8. Hayes-McCoy, *Scots Mercenary Forces*, 259.

9. Russell's Journal, 1596, BL, Add. MSS, 4728, f. 63; Bowes to Sir Robert Cecil, 30 April 1596, SP Scot. Eliz. 58/71; Hugh O'Neill, earl of Tyrone, to Norris, 16 June 1596, SP 63/191/6,vi; Tyrone to Hugh O'Donnell, 16 June 1596, SP 63/191/6,vii; Eggarton to Burghley, 7 October 1595, SP 63/183/78; Agreement between Eggarton and James MacSorley MacDonnell, 3 October 1595, SP 63/183/78,ii; James MacSorley to Lord Deputy, 4 October 1595, SP 63/183/80,ii; Lord Deputy to Burghley, 15 February 1596, SP 63/186/66; James MacSorley to Lord Deputy, 13 April 1596, SP 63/188/67,iv; Captain Rice Mansell to Lord Deputy, 20 May 1596, SP 63/189/46,vii; Eggarton to Lord Deputy, 27 May 1596, SP 63/190/11,xi;

Eggarton to Lord Deputy, 7 June 1596, SP 63/190/30,vi; Francis Stafford to Lord Deputy, 10 July 1596, SP 63/191/19; Eggarton to Lord Deputy, 26 June 1596, SP 63/191/15,x; Thomas Stevenson, mayor of Carrickfergus, and Captain Mansell to Lord Deputy, 26 June 1596, SP 63/191/15,x(a); Stafford to Lord Deputy, 10 July 1596, SP 63/191/19.

10. John Eliot to Lord Deputy, 21 July 1596, SP 63/191/37,vii; Instructions from Sir John Norris to Queen and Privy Council, 27 July 1596, SP 63/191/45; Lord Deputy and Council to Privy Council, 13 August 1596, SP 63/192/7; Eggarton to Lord Deputy, 31 July 1596, SP 63/192/7,iii; Mansell to Lord Deputy, 31 July 1596, SP 63/192/7,iv.

11. Hayes-McCoy, *Scots Mercenary Forces*, 278–9; Great Britain, *The Acts of the Parliaments of Scotland*, ed. Thomas Thomson and Cosmo Innes, 12 vols. (Edinburgh, 1814–75), IV: 138–9 (hereafter cited as *APS*); Spottiswoode Society, *The Spottiswoode Miscellany: A Collection of Original Papers and Tracts, Illustrative Chiefly of the Civil and Ecclesiastical History of Scotland*, ed. James Maidment, 2 vols. (Edinburgh, 1845), II: 372; Bowes to Cecil, 11 April 1597, SP Scot. Eliz. 60/56; Bowes to Lord Burghley, 21 April 1597, SP Scot. Eliz. 60/58.

12. Bowes to Cecil, 20 September 1597, SP Scot. Eliz. 61/33; Donald Gregory, *The History of the Western Highlands and Isles of Scotland from A.D. 1493 to A.D. 1625* (Edinburgh, 1881; reprint edn., Edinburgh, 1975), 274; Sir John Chichester to Burghley, 16 September 1597, SP 63/200/125.

13. Bowes to Burghley, 11 May 1597, SP Scot. Eliz. 60/68; Chichester to Burghley, 16 September 1597, SP 63/200/125; Extracts from letters sent by Richard Weston to Sir Geoffrey Fenton, 6 November 1597, SP 63/201/67,ii.

14. Aston to Cecil, 21 December 1597, SP Scot. Eliz. 61/63; Nicolson to Cecil, 23 December 1597, SP Scot. Eliz. 61/65; Cecil to Sir William Bowes, 4 January 1598, SP Scot. Eliz. 52/198; Aston to Cecil, 20 January 1598, SP Scot. Eliz. 62/2,i; Gregory, *Western Highlands and Isles*, 273–4; A certificate of the overthrow of Sir John Chichester, 4 November 1597, SP 63/201/63,i; Eggarton to Burghley, 7 November 1597, SP 63/201/63; Eggarton to Sir Thomas Norris, Lord Justice, 5 November 1597, SP 63/201/64,i.

15. Nicolson to Cecil, 25 February 1598, SP Scot. Eliz. 62/6; Nicolson to Burghley, 5 March 1598, SP Scot. Eliz. 62/8; Nicolson to Cecil, 2 August 1598, SP Scot. Eliz. 62/57; Nicolson to Cecil, 9 August 1598, SP Scot. Eliz. 62/62; Laird of Glenorchy to Nicolson, 9 August 1598, SP Scot. Eliz. 62/59; Nicolson to Cecil, 10 August 1598, SP Scot. Eliz. 62/63; Cecil to Nicolson, 10 August 1598, SP Scot. Eliz. 52/221; Nicolson to Cecil, 16 August 1598, SP Scot. Eliz. 62/67; Nicolson to Cecil, 12 August 1599, SP Scot. Eliz. 65/11; MacNeil of Barra, *The Clan MacNeil* (New York, 1923), 62; David Stevenson, *Alasdair MacColla and the Highland Problem in the Seventeenth Century* (Edinburgh, 1980), 26.

16. Auchinross to Nicolson, 30 June 1598, SP Scot. Eliz. 62/43,ii; Intelligences sent to Fenton, 6 February 1599, SP 63/203/38; Fenton to Cecil, 22 June 1598, SP 63/202/2/82; Earl of Essex and Council to Privy Council, 28 April 1599, SP 63/205/38; Essex to Privy Council, 29 April 1599, SP 63/205/42; Letter to Sir George Carey, 23 May 1599, SP 63/205/68,i; Advertisements from Dundalk, 19 June 1599, SP 63/205/84; Sir Ralph Lane to Essex, June 1599, SP 63/205/100.

17. Nicolson to Cecil, 9 June 1599, SP Scot. Eliz. 64/81; Nicolson to Cecil, 28 July 1599, SP Scot. Eliz. 65/8; Nicolson to Cecil, 12 November 1599, SP Scot. Eliz.

65/64; Lane to Essex, June 1599, SP 63/205/100; Richard Weston to Essex, 28 August 1599, SP 63/205/156.

18. Nicolson to Cecil, 16 February 1600, SP Scot. Eliz. 66/11; Nicolson to Cecil, 23 February 1600, SP Scot. Eliz. 66/13; Nicolson to Cecil, 2 May 1600, SP Scot. Eliz. 66/25; Intelligences from the north to Fenton, 7 January 1600, SP 63/207/1/11,i; Intelligences to Fenton, 19 January 1600, SP 63/207/1/30; Lord Justice Loftus to Cecil, 20 January 1600, SP 63/207/1/34; Lane to Cecil, 1 February 1600, SP 63/207/1/82; Sir Arthur Chichester to Sir Geoffrey Fenton, 22 May 1600, SP 63/207/3/54; Chichester to Sir George Carey, 21 May 1600, SP 63/207/3/64,ii.

19. Captain Humphrey Willis to Cecil, 29 October 1600, SP 63/207/5/127; Sir Henry Docwra to Privy Council, 2 November 1600, SP 63/207/6/9; Hugh O'Donnell to O'Connor Sligo, 16 November 1600, SP 63/207/6/75,vii.

20. Quoted in Maurice Ashley, *Great Britain to 1688: A Modern History* (Ann Arbor, MI, 1961), 200.

21. Chichester to Cecil, 16 December 1600, SP 63/207/6/78; Articles between Chichester and Ranald MacSorley, 16 December 1600, SP 63/207/6/78,i; Docwra to Cecil, 19 December 1600, SP 63/207/6/84; Chichester to Cecil, 12 January 1601, SP 63/208/1/5; Willis to Cecil, 24 January 1601, SP 63/208/1/18; Sir James MacSorley to Sir Francis Stafford, 6 January 1601, SP 63/208/2/7,i; Lord Deputy Mountjoy to Sir James MacSorley, 31 January 1601, SP 63/208/2/7,ii; Chichester to Angus MacDonnell, 24 March 1601, SP 63/208/2/7,ii; Chichester to Sir James MacSorley, 5 April 1601, SP 63/208/2/7,iv; Sir James MacSorley to Chichester, 11 April 1601, SP 63/208/2/7,v; Fynes Moryson, *Itinerary*, 4 vols. (Glasgow, 1908), II: 308.

22. Chichester to Cecil, 12 April 1601, SP 63/208/2/7; Chichester to Cecil, 15 May 1601, SP 63/208/2/68; Chichester to Privy Council, 8 July 1601, SP 63/208/3/59; Chichester to Cecil, 20 October 1601, SP 63/209/154; O'Donovan, ed., *Four Masters* (anno 1590); Rev. George Hill, *An Historical Account of the MacDonnells of Antrim, Including Notices of some other Septs, Irish and Scottish* (Belfast, 1873), 192.

23. Extract of a letter showing Tyrone's forces, 29 October 1601, SP 63/209/169; Chichester to Privy Council, 6 November 1601, SP 63/209/175; Willis to Cecil, 15 November 1601, SP 63/209/186; Chichester to Cecil, 22 November 1601, SP 63/209/196; Sir Francis Stafford to Cecil, 7 December 1601, SP 63/209/222; Chichester to Privy Council, 9 December 1601, SP 63/209/227; Chichester to Cecil, 29 December 1601, SP 63/209/264; Chichester to Cecil, 15 January 1602, SP 63/210/24; Fenton to Cecil, 5 February 1602, SP 63/210/37; Docwra to Cecil, 12 March 1602, SP 63/210/58; Chichester to Cecil, 14 March 1602, SP 63/210/64; Hill, *MacDonnells of Antrim*, 194; Nicolson to Cecil, 3 and 4 December 1601, SP Scot. Eliz. 67/136.

24. Auchinross to Nicolson, 13 February 1602, SP Scot. Eliz. 68/18; Auchinross to Nicolson, 21 February 1602, SP Scot. Eliz. 68/23; Captain Thomas Phillips to Cecil, 11 March 1602, SP 63/210/57; Chichester to Cecil, 18 March 1602, SP 63/210/68; Lord Deputy and Council to Privy Council, 19 July 1602, SP 63/211/87.

25. Gregory, *Western Highlands and Isles*, 305–7, 322–6; Great Britain, *The Register of the Privy Council of Scotland*, ed. J. H. Burton *et al.*, 38 vols. (Edinburgh, 1877–1970), IX (1610–13): 25–30 (hereafter cited as *RPCS*).

26. Maurice Lee, Jr., *Government by Pen: Scotland under James VI and I* (Chicago, 1980).

27. J. Michael Hill, "The Scottish Plantations in Ulster to 1625: A Reinterpretation," *Journal of British Studies* XXXII (January 1993): 24–43.

28. Gregory, *Western Highlands and Isles*, 326–8; *RPCS* (1613–16), 818; A. MacDonald and A. MacDonald, *The Clan Donald*, 3 vols. (Inverness, 1896–1900), II: 586; Stevenson, *Alasdair MacColla*, 30–1.

29. *RPCS* (1613–16), 13–14; Gregory, *Western Highlands and Isles*, 349–53; MacDonald and MacDonald, *Clan Donald*, II: 582–3; John de Vere Loder, *Colonsay and Oronsay in the Isles of Argyll: Their History, Flora, Fauna and Topography* (Edinburgh, 1935), 108–29; Scottish History Society, *Highland Papers*, ed. J. R. N. MacPhail, 3 vols. (Edinburgh, 1920), III: 144–5.

30. *RPCS* (1613–16), 695–7; Scottish History Society, *Highland Papers*, III: 149–52; Gregory, *Western Highlands and Isles*, 353–5; Stevenson, *Alasdair MacColla*, 36–8.

31. *RPCS* (1613–16), 716–24; Gregory, *Western Highlands and Isles*, 356.

32. Hill, "Scottish Plantations."

33. Great Britain, *Calendar of State Papers Relating to Ireland, 1509–1670*, ed. H. C. Hamilton *et al.*, 24 vols. (London, 1860–1911), 1615–25: 42–3; M. A. Hickson, ed., *Ireland in the Seventeenth Century*, 2 vols. (London, 1884), I: 15–17, 20; II: 260; Stevenson, *Alasdair MacColla*, 39–40; Gregory, *Western Highlands and Isles*, 359–61.

34. Great Britain, *Registrum magni sigilli regum Scotorum: The Register of the Great Seal of Scotland*, 11 vols. (Edinburgh, 1882–1914), 1609–20: no. 1137; R. Pitcairn, ed., *Ancient Criminal Trials in Scotland*, 3 vols. (Edinburgh, 1833), III: 364–5; Scottish History Society, *Highland Papers*, III: 176–86; Gregory, *Western Highlands and Isles*, 361–6.

35. Stevenson, *Alasdair MacColla*, 44–5; Scottish History Society, *Highland Papers*, III: 165–6, 243, 254–6, 260, 262–70; Gregory, *Western Highlands and Isles*, 367–78.

36. Ibid., 378–80; Scottish History Society, *Highland Papers*, III: 276–8.

37. *RPCS* (1613–16), 671–2; Gregory, *Western Highlands and Isles*, 392–7; Stevenson, *Alasdair MacColla*, 47.

38. Wentworth to King James I, 28 July 1638, in William Knowler, ed., *The Earl of Strafford's Letters and Dispatches*, 2 vols. (London, 1739), II: 187–8.

39. Hill, *MacDonnells of Antrim*, 245; Edinburgh, Scottish Record Office (hereafter cited as SRO), Campbell of Stonefield Papers, GD. 14/19, ff. 135–7.

40. SRO, Breadalbane Muniments (mounted letters), GD. 112/39/777; Hill, *MacDonnells of Antrim*, 441–6; Earl of Antrim to Wentworth, 17 July 1638, Lord Lorne to Wentworth, 25 July 1638, in Knowler, ed., *Strafford's Letters and Dispatches*, II: 184, 187.

41. The humble petition of divers Lords Spiritual and Temporal, Knights, Gentlemen, and others of the Scottish nation, inhabiting the Kingdom of Ireland, 16 May 1639, in Knowler, ed., *Strafford's Letters and Dispatches*, II: 344–5.

42. *RPCS* (1638–43), 185; Hill, *MacDonnells of Antrim*, 72–4; Hickson, ed., *Ireland in the Seventeenth Century*, I: 246; Edmund Hogan, ed., *The history of the warr of Ireland from 1641 to 1653. By a British Officer* (Dublin, 1873), 23; J. T. Gilbert, ed., *History of the Irish Confederation and the War in Ireland, 1641–9*, 7 vols. (Dublin, 1882–91), I: 33.

43. Stevenson, *Alasdair MacColla*, 85; Hill, *MacDonnells of Antrim*, 261–2; John Spalding, *Memorialls of the Trubles in Scotland and in England, A.D. 1624–A.D. 1645*, ed. Spalding Club, 2 vols. (Aberdeen, 1850–1), II: 257.

44. James Hogan, ed., *Letters and Papers relating to the Irish Rebellion* (Dublin, 1936), 45–51; Stevenson, *Alasdair MacColla*, 86–7; Hogan, ed., *History of the warr*, 23–4; Hill, *MacDonnells of Antrim*, 74–5; Oxford, Bodleian Library, Carte MSS, 4, f. 230.

45. Historical Manuscripts Commission, *Portland MSS*, 10 vols. (London, 1892–1931), I: 120–3; *RPCS* (1638–43), 436, 442–4; Spalding, *Memorialls*, II: 242–50; David Stevenson, *The Scottish Revolution 1637–44: The Triumph of the Covenanters* (New York, 1973), 270–5.

46. Ibid., 276–98; *APS*, VI, i: 47–9; Spalding, *Memorialls*, II: 242–50.

47. J. Lowe, "The Earl of Antrim and Irish Aid to Montrose in 1644," *Irish Sword* VI (1959–60): 191–8; Hill, *MacDonnells of Antrim*, 266–7; Stevenson, *Alasdair MacColla*, 102–3.

Selected Bibliography

Unpublished Primary Sources

Belfast. Public Record Office, Northern Ireland. MS T530: II.
Dublin. National Library of Ireland. MS 669.
Edinburgh. Edinburgh University Library. Laing MSS.
Edinburgh. Scottish Record Office. Breadalbane Muniments.
Edinburgh. Scottish Record Office. Campbell of Stonefield Papers.
London. British Library. Additional MSS.
London. British Library. Cottonian MSS.
London. British Library. Harleian MSS.
London. British Library. Lansdowne MSS.
London. Lambeth Palace Library. Carew MSS.
London. Public Record Office. State Papers. Ireland. Henry VIII–Elizabeth.
London. Public Record Office. State Papers. Scotland.
Oxford. Bodleian Library. MS Laud Misc., 613.
Oxford. Bodleian Library. Carte MSS.
San Marino, CA. Huntington Library. Ellesmere MSS.

Printed Primary Sources

Anderson, Alan Orr, ed. *Early Sources of Scottish History, 500 to 1286.* 2 vols. Edinburgh, 1922.

Bain, Joseph, ed. *The Hamilton Papers.* 2 vols. Edinburgh, 1890–2.
Bannatyne Club, ed. *A Diurnal of Remarkable Occurants that have passed within the Country of Scotland since the death of King James the Fourth till the year MDLXXV.* Edinburgh, 1833.
———. *The Historie and Life of King James the Sext: Being an account of the affairs of Scotland, from the year 1566 to the year 1596; with a short continuation to the year 1617.* Edinburgh, 1825.
———. *Origines Parochiales Scotiae.* 2 vols. Edinburgh, 1850.
Bannatyne, Richard, ed. *Journal of the Transactions in Scotland, 1570–1573.* Edinburgh, 1806

Bowes, Robert. *The Correspondence of Robert Bowes of Aske, Esquire, the Ambassador of the Queen Elizabeth in the Court of Scotland.* Edited by Surtees Society. London and Edinburgh, 1842.

Buchanan, George. *The History of Scotland.* 4 vols. Edited and translated by James Aikman. Glasgow, 1827.

Burghley, William Cecil, Lord. *A Collection of State Papers, 1542–1570.* Edited by Samuel Haynes. London, 1740.

Camden Society. *The Egerton Papers.* Edited by J. Payne Collier. London, 1840; reprint edn., New York, 1968.

Camden, William. *Britannia: or, a Chorographical Description of the Flourishing Kingdoms of England, Scotland, and Ireland, and the Islands Adjacent; from the Earliest Antiquity.* 2nd edn. 4 vols. Edited by Richard Gough. London, 1806.

Campbell, Dioness. "Observations of Mr Dioness Campbell, Deane of Limerick, on the West Isles of Scotland." In *Miscellany of the Maitland Club.* Edited by Maitland Club. 5 vols. Vol. IV. Glasgow, 1847.

Campion, Edmund. *A Historie of Ireland, written in the Yeare 1571.* Edited by James Ware. Dublin, 1633; reprint edn., Dublin, 1809.

Chambers, Robert, ed. *Domestic Annals of Scotland from the Reformation to the Revolution.* 3 vols. Edinburgh and London, 1874.

Collins, Arthur, ed. *Letters and Memorials of State.* 2 vols. London, 1746; reprint edn., New York, 1973.

Colton, John. *Acts of Archbishop Colton in his Metropolitan Visitation of the Diocese of Derry, A.D. 1397.* Edited by Rev. William Reeves. Dublin, 1850.

Colville, John. *Original Letters of Mr John Colville, 1582–1603.* Edited by Bannatyne Club. Edinburgh, 1858.

Cox, Richard. *Hibernia Anglicana: or, the History of Ireland from the Conquest thereof by the English, to this present time.* 2nd edn. 2 vols. London, 1692.

Cuellar, Don Francisco. *Captain Cuellar's Narrative of the Spanish Armada and of his Wanderings and Adventures in Ireland.* Translated by Robert Crawford. Madrid, 1884–5.

Devereux, Walter Bourchier, ed. *Lives and Letters of the Devereux, Earls of Essex, in the Reigns of Elizabeth, James I, and Charles I, 1540–1646.* 2 vols. London, 1853.

Dewar, John. *The Dewar Manuscripts.* Vol. I: *Scottish West Highland Folktales.* Edited by Rev. John Mackechnie. Glasgow, 1964.

Dubourdieu, Rev. John. *Statistical Survey of the County of Antrim.* 2 vols. Dublin, 1812.

Dymmok, John. *A Treatice of Ireland.* Edited by Rev. Richard Butler. Dublin, 1842.

Gilbert, J. T., ed. *History of the Irish Confederation and the War in Ireland, 1641–9.* 7 vols. Dublin, 1882–91.

Great Britain. *Accounts of the Lord High Treasurer of Scotland.* 10 vols. Edited by Thomas Dickson and James Balfour Paul. Edinburgh, 1902.

————. *The Acts of the Parliaments of Scotland.* 12 vols. Edited by Thomas Thomson and Cosmo Innes. Edinburgh, 1814–75.

————. *Calendar of the Carew Manuscripts, Preserved in the Archiepiscopal Library at Lambeth.* 6 vols. Edited by J. S. Brewer and William Bullen. London, 1867–71.

————. *Calendar of State Papers, Foreign Series, of the reign of Elizabeth, 1588–1603.* 23 vols. Edited by Rev. Joseph Stevenson *et al.* London, 1863–1950.

————. *Calendar of State Papers, Relating to English Affairs, preserved principally at Rome.* 2 vols. Edited by J. M. Rigg. London, 1916–26.

————. *Calendar of State Papers Relating to Ireland, 1509–1670.* 24 vols. Edited by H. C. Hamilton *et al.* London, 1860–1911.

————. *Calendar of the State Papers Relating to Scotland and Mary, Queen of Scots, 1547–1603.* 13 vols. Edited by Joseph Bain *et al.* Edinburgh, 1898–1969.

————. *Calendar of the State Papers, Relating to Scotland.* Vol. 1: *The Scottish Series, of the reigns of Henry VIII, Edward VI, Mary, Elizabeth, 1509–1589.* 2 vols. Edited by M. J. Thorpe. London, 1858.

————. *The Register of the Privy Council of Scotland.* 38 vols. Edited by J. H. Burton *et al.* Edinburgh, 1877–1970.

————. *Registrum magni sigilli regum Scotorum: The Register of the Great Seal of Scotland.* 11 vols. Edinburgh, 1882–1914.

————. *The Statutes at Large passed in the Parliaments held in Ireland, 1310–1786.* 2 vols. Dublin, 1786.

Hall, Edward. *Hall's Chronicles: Containing the History of England, During the Reign of Henry the Fourth, and the succeeding Monarchs, to the end of the reign of Henry the Eighth, in which are particularly described the manners and customs of those periods. Carefully collated with the editions of 1548 and 1550.* London, 1809.

Hall, Spencer, ed. *Documents from Simancas relating to the Reign of Elizabeth (1558–1568).* London, 1865.

Hamilton, Sir James, Viscount Clandeboye. *The Hamilton Manuscripts.* Edited by T. K. Lowry. Belfast, 1867.

Hanmer, Meredith, Campion, Edmund, and Spenser, Edmund. *The Historie of Ireland, Collected by three learned authors.* Edited by Sir James Ware. Dublin, 1633.

Hardwicke, Philip York, 2nd earl of, ed. *Miscellaneous State Papers from 1501 to 1726.* 2 vols. London, 1778.

Harris, Walter, ed. *Hibernica: or, some antient pieces relating to Ireland.* 2 vols. Dublin, 1747–50.

Hennessy, William M., ed. *The Annals of Loch Cé. A Chronicle of Irish Affairs from A.D. 1014 to A.D. 1590.* 2 vols. London, 1871.

Hennessy, William M., and MacCarthy, B., eds. *Annals of Ulster, A Chronicle of Irish Affairs from A.D. 431 to A.D. 1540.* 4 vols. Dublin, 1887–1901.

Hickson, M. A., ed. *Ireland in the Seventeenth Century.* 2 vols. London, 1884.

Hill, Rev. George, ed. *The Montgomery Manuscripts, 1603–1706.* Belfast, 1869.

Historical Manuscripts Commission. *The Manuscripts of Charles Haliday, Esq., of Dublin. Acts of the Privy Council in Ireland, 1556–1571.* Fifteenth report, appendix, part III. Edited by John T. Gilbert. London, 1897.

———. *Portland MSS.* 10 vols. London, 1892–1931.

Hogan, Edmund. *The Description of Ireland, 1598.* Dublin, 1878.

———, ed. *The History of the warr of Ireland from 1641 to 1653. By a British Officer.* Dublin, 1873.

Hogan, James, ed. *Letters and Papers relating to the Irish Rebellion.* Dublin, 1936.

Hogan, James, and O'Farrell, N. MacNeill, eds. *The Walsingham Letter-Book or Register of Ireland, May, 1578 to December, 1579.* Dublin, 1959.

Holinshed, Raphael. *Chronicles of England, Scotland, and Ireland.* 6 vols. London, 1808; reprint edn., New York, 1965.

Hooker, John, alias Vowell. *The Irish Chronicle from the death of King Henry VIII until 1586.* In *Chronicles of England, Scotland, and Ireland,* vol. VI. Edited by Raphael Holinshed. London, 1808; reprint edn., New York, 1965.

Iona Club, ed. *Collectanea de Rebus Albanicis, consisting of original papers and documents relating to the history of the Highlands and Islands of Scotland.* Edinburgh, 1847.

Ireland. Public Record Office. *Account of Facsimiles of National Manuscripts of Ireland.* 4 vols. Edited by John T. Gilbert. London, 1874–84.

Irish Manuscripts Commission. *Calendar of the Irish Council Book, 1581–1586.* In *Analecta Hibernica,* vol. 24. Edited by David B. Quinn. Dublin, 1967.

———. *Catalogue of Publications, 1928–1957.* Dublin, 1957.

———. *Fitzwilliam Accounts, 1560–65 (Annesley Collection).* Edited by A. K. Longfield. Dublin, 1960.

———. *List from the Ellesmere Collection.* In *Analecta Hibernica,* vol. 8. Dublin, 1938.

———. *The Perrott Papers.* In *Analecta Hibernica,* vol. 12. Edited by C. MacNeill. Dublin, 1943.

———. *Sidney State Papers, 1565–70.* Edited by Tómas O'Laidhin. Dublin, 1962.

———. *Wild Geese in Spanish Flanders, 1582–1700.* Edited by Brendan Jennings. Dublin, 1964.

Keating, Geoffrey. *Foras feasa ar Éirinn: the history of Ireland.* 4 vols. Edited by D. Comyn and P. S. Dineen. London, 1902–14.

Knowler, William, ed. *The Earl of Strafford's Letters and Dispatches.* 2 vols. London, 1739.

Lynch, John. *Cambrensis Eversus.* 3 vols. Edited by Rev. Matthew Kelly. Dublin, 1848–52.

MacBain, Alexander, and Kennedy, Rev. John, eds. *Reliquiae Celticae: Texts, Papers, and Studies in Gaelic Literature and Philology left by the late Rev. Alexander Cameron, LL.D.* 2 vols. Inverness, 1892–4.

MacDonald, Alexander, ed. *Letters to the Argyll Family.* Edinburgh, 1839; reprint edn., New York, 1973.

MacDonald, Colin M., ed. *The Third Statistical Account of Scotland, The County of Argyll.* Glasgow, 1961.

Machyn, Henry. *The Diary of Henry Machyn, 1550–1563.* Edited by John Gough Nichols. London, 1848.

McIlwain, C. H., ed. *The Political Works of James I.* New York, 1965.

MacLauchlan, Rev. Thomas, and Skene, William F., eds. *The Dean of Lismore's Book.* Edinburgh, 1862.

Maidment, James, ed. *Analecta Scotica: Collections illustrative of the Civil, Ecclesiastical, and Literary History of Scotland.* Edinburgh, 1834.

Maitland Club, ed. *Selections from Unpublished Manuscripts in the College of Arms and the British Museum illustrating the Reign of Mary Queen of Scotland, MDXLIII–MDLXVIII.* Glasgow, 1837.

Martin, Martin. *A Description of the Western Islands of Scotland circa 1695.* 4th edn. Edited by Donald J. MacLeod. Stirling, 1934.

Maxwell, Constantia, ed. *Irish History from Contemporary Sources (1509–1610).* London, 1923.

Melville, Sir James, of Halhill. *Memoirs of his own Life.* Edited by Bannatyne Club. Edinburgh, 1827.

Monro, Sir Donald. *Description of the Western Isles of Scotland, 1549.* Glasgow, 1884.

Morley, Henry, ed. *Ireland under Elizabeth and James the First.* London, 1890.

Morrin, James, ed. *Calendar of the Patent and Close Rolls of Chancery in Ireland.* 3 vols. Dublin, 1841–3.

Moryson, Fynes. *Itinerary.* 4 vols. Glasgow, 1908.

———. *Shakespeare's Europe: A Survey of the Condition of Europe at the end of the 16th century.* Edited by Charles Hughes. London, 1903; reprint edn., New York, 1967.

O'Daly, Aenghus. *The Tribes of Ireland.* Edited by John O'Donovan. Dublin, 1852; reprint edn., Cork, 1976.

O'Donovan, John, ed. *Annala Rioghachta Eireann, Annals of the Kingdom of*

Ireland, by the Four Masters, from the Earliest Period to the Year 1616. 5 vols. Dublin, 1848.

Payne, Robert. "A Brief Description of Ireland made in this yeere 1589." London, 1590. In *Tracts Relating to Ireland.* 2 vols. Edited by the Irish Archaeological Society. Dublin, 1841–3.
Perrott, Sir James. *A Chronicle of Ireland, 1584–1608.* Edited by Herbert Wood. Dublin, 1933.
Pitcairn, R., ed. *Ancient Criminal Trials in Scotland.* 3 vols. Edinburgh, 1833.
Pittscottie, Robert Lindsay of. *The Historie and Chronicles of Scotland.* Edited by A. J. G. MacKay. Edinburgh, 1899.

Reeves, Rev. William, ed. *Account of an Ancient Scotch Deed.* Dublin, 1852.
Rich, Barnaby. *A New Description of Ireland, wherein is described the Disposition of the Irish.* London, 1610.

Scottish History Society. *Acts of the Lords of the Isles, 1336–1493.* Edited by Jean Munro and R. W. Munro. Edinburgh, 1986.
———. *Highland Papers.* Vol. III. Edited by J. R. N. MacPhail. Edinburgh, 1920.
Shirley, Evelyn Philip, ed. *Original Letters and Papers in Illustration of the History of the Church in Ireland, during the reigns of Edward VI, Mary, and Elizabeth.* London, 1851.
Smith, G. G., ed. *The Book of Islay.* Privately printed, 1895.
Spalding Club, ed. *The Book of the Thanes of Cawdor, 1236–1742.* Edinburgh, 1859.
Spalding, John. *Memorialls of the Trubles in Scotland and in England, A.D. 1624–A.D. 1645.* 2 vols. Edited by Spalding Club. Aberdeen, 1850–1.
Spenser, Edmund. *A View of the Present State of Ireland.* Edited by W. L. Renwick. Oxford, 1970.
Spottiswoode Society. *The Spottiswoode Miscellany: A Collection of Original Papers and Tracts, Illustrative Chiefly of the Civil and Ecclesiastical History of Scotland.* 2 vols. Edited by James Maidment. Edinburgh, 1845.

Teignmouth, Lord. *Sketches of the Coasts and Islands of Scotland and the Isle of Man.* 2 vols. London, 1836.
Thomas, F. S., ed. *Historical Notes, 1509–1603.* 3 vols. London, 1856.

Ware, Sir James. *The Antiquities and History of Ireland.* 2 vols. London, 1714.
Wright, Thomas, ed. *Queen Elizabeth and Her Times.* 2 vols. London, 1838.

Young, Robert M., ed. *Historical Notices of Old Belfast and its Vicinity.* Belfast, 1895.

Printed Secondary Sources

Agnew, Sir Andrew. *The Hereditary Sheriffs of Galloway.* 2 vols. Edinburgh, 1893.

Allingham, Hugh. *Captain Cuellar's Adventures in Connacht and Ulster, A.D. 1588.* London, 1897.

Andrews, J. H. "Geography and Government in Elizabethan Ireland." In *Irish Geographical Studies in honour of E. Estyn Evans.* Edited by Nicholas Stephens and Robin E. Glasscock. Belfast, 1970.

Andrews, John. *Ireland in Maps.* Dublin, 1961.

Andrews, K. R. *Elizabethan privateering, 1585–1603.* Cambridge, 1964.

Andrews, K. R., Canny, N. P., and Hair, P. E. H., eds. *The Westward Enterprise: English Activities in Ireland, the Atlantic, and America, 1480–1650.* Liverpool, 1978.

Ardrigh, C. *The Ancient Franciscan Friary of Bun-na-mairge.* Dublin, 1908.

Ashley, Maurice. *Great Britain to 1688: A Modern History.* Ann Arbor, MI, 1961.

Bagenal, Philip H. *Vicissitudes of an Anglo-Irish Family, 1530–1800.* London, 1925.

Bagwell, Richard. *Ireland under the Tudors.* 3 vols. London, 1890–5.

Bannerman, John. "The Lordship of the Isles." In *Scottish Society in the Fifteenth Century.* Edited by Jennifer M. Brown. New York and London, 1977.

———. *Studies in the History of Dalriada.* Edinburgh and London, 1974.

Barrett, E. Boyd. *The Great O'Neill.* Boston, MA, 1939.

Beeler, John. *Warfare in Feudal Europe, 730–1200.* Ithaca, NY and London, 1971.

Belmore, Somerset. *Descriptive Notes on the Irish Historical Atlas.* Belfast, 1903.

Benn, George. *A History of the Town of Belfast from the Earliest Times to the Close of the Eighteenth Century.* London, 1877.

Blácam, Aodh de. *Gaelic Literature Surveyed.* Dublin, 1929; reprint edn., Dublin, 1973.

Black, J. B. *The Reign of Elizabeth, 1558–1603.* Oxford, 1959.

Black, Jeremy. *A Military Revolution?: Military Change and European Society, 1550–1800.* London, 1991.

Bonn, Moritz Julius. *Die Englische Kolonisation in Irland.* 2 vols. Stuttgart and Berlin, 1906.

Bottigheimer, Karl S. *Ireland and the Irish, A Short History.* New York, 1982.

———. "Kingdom and Colony: Ireland in the Westward Enterprise, 1536–1660." In *The Westward Enterprise.* Edited by K. R. Andrews, N. P. Canny, and P. E. H. Hair. Liverpool, 1978,

Boyd, Hugh A. *Rathlin Island, North of Antrim.* Ballycastle, Antrim, 1947.

Boylan, Henry. *A Dictionary of Irish Biography.* New York, 1978.

Bradshaw, Brendan. "The Beginnings of Modern Ireland." In *The Irish Parliamentary Tradition.* Edited by Brian Farrell. Dublin and New York, 1973.

———. *The Irish Constitutional Revolution of the Sixteenth Century.* Cambridge, 1979.

———. "Manus 'The Magnificent': O'Donnell as Renaissance Prince." In *Studies in Irish History presented to R. Dudley Edwards.* Edited by Art Cosgrove and Donal MacCartney. Dublin, 1979.

———. "Native Reaction to the Westward Enterprise: a Case-Study in Gaelic Ideology." In *The Westward Enterprise.* Edited by K. R. Andrews, N. P. Canny, and P. E. H. Hair. Liverpool, 1978.

Brady, Ciaran. "Conservative Subversives: the Community of the Pale and the Dublin Administration, 1556–85." In *Radicals, Rebels and Establishments.* Edited by P. J. Corish. Belfast, 1985.

Braudel, Fernand. *The Structures of Everyday Life: Civilization and Capitalism, 15th–18th Century.* Translated by Sian Reynolds. New York, 1981.

Breffny, Brian de. *Castles of Ireland.* London, 1977.

Brenan, Rev. M. J. *An Ecclesiastical History of Ireland.* Dublin and London, 1864.

Brown, Jennifer M., ed. *Scottish Society in the Fifteenth Century.* New York and London, 1977.

Brown, Keith M. *Bloodfeud in Scotland, 1573–1625.* Edinburgh, 1986.

Butler, William F. T. *Gleanings from Irish History.* London, 1925.

Byrne, Matthew J. *Ireland under Elizabeth.* Dublin, 1903.

Caldwell, David H., ed. *Scottish Weapons and Fortifications, 1100–1800.* Edinburgh, 1981.

Camblin, Gilbert. *The Town in Ulster.* Belfast, 1951.

Campbell, Lord Archibald. *Records of Argyll, Legends, Traditions, and Recollections of Argyllshire Highlanders.* Edinburgh and London, 1885.

Canny, Nicholas P. *The Elizabethan Conquest of Ireland: A Pattern Established, 1565–76.* Hassocks, Sussex and New York, 1976.

———. *The Formation of the Old English Elite in Ireland.* Dublin, 1975.

———. *From Reformation to Restoration: Ireland, 1534–1600.* Dublin, 1987.

———. *Kingdom and Colony: Ireland in the Atlantic World, 1560–1800.* Baltimore, MD and London, 1988.

———. "The Permissive frontier: Social Control in English Settlements in Ireland and Virginia, 1550–1650." In *The Westward Enterprise.* Edited by K. R. Andrews, N. P. Canny, and P. E. H. Hair. Liverpool, 1978.

Carmichael, Alasdair. *Kintyre, Best of All the Isles.* London, 1974.

Clapperton, Chalmers M., ed. *Scotland: A New Study.* Newton Abbot, Devon and London, 1983.

Colles, Ramsay. *The History of Ulster from the Earliest Times to the Present Day.* 4 vols. London, 1919.

Collier, W. F. *The Central Figures of Irish History from 400 A.D. to 1603 A.D.* London, 1891.

Corish, Patrick J., ed. *A History of Irish Catholicism.* Dublin, 1967.

Cosgrove, Art. *Late Medieval Ireland.* Dublin, 1981.

Cowan, Ian B. *The Parishes of Medieval Scotland.* Edinburgh, 1967.

Cromb, James. *The Highlands and Highlanders of Scotland.* Dundee and Edinburgh, 1883.

Cruden, Stewart. *Scottish Abbeys.* Edinburgh, 1960.

———. *The Scottish Castle.* London, 1960.

Cruickshank, C. G. *Elizabeth's Army.* 2nd edn. London, 1966.

Cunningham, Audrey. *The Loyal Clans.* Cambridge, 1932.

Curtis, Edmund. *A History of Medieval Ireland from 1110 to 1513.* New York and Dublin, 1923.

Cusack, M. F. *An Illustrated History of Ireland from the Earliest Period.* New York, 1868.

D'Alton, Rev. E. A. *History of Ireland from the Earliest Times to the Present Day.* 3 vols. London, 1904–8.

Davies, R. R. *Domination and Conquest: The Experience of Ireland, Scotland and Wales 1100–1300.* Cambridge and New York, 1990.

Davies, R. Trevor. *The Golden Century of Spain, 1501–1612.* London, 1964.

Dawson, Jane E. A. "Two Kingdoms or Three?: Ireland in Anglo-Scottish Relations in the Middle of the Sixteenth Century." In *Scotland and England, 1286–1815.* Edited by Roger A. Mason. Edinburgh, 1987.

Dawtrey, John. *The Falstaff Saga, being the Life and Opinions of Captain Nicholas Dawtry.* London, 1927.

Dean, James. *Catalogue of Manuscripts in the Public Library of Armagh.* Dundalk, 1928.

Donaldson, Gordon, and Morpeth, Robert S. *A Dictionary of Scottish History.* Edinburgh, 1977.

DuPuy, R. Ernest, and DuPuy, Trevor N. *The Encyclopedia of Military History from 3500 B.C. to the present.* 2nd edn. New York, 1986.

Edwards, R. Dudley. *An Atlas of Irish History.* 2nd edn. London, 1981.

———. *Ireland in the Age of the Tudors.* London, 1977.

Edwards, R. W. Dudley, and O'Dowd, Mary. *Sources for Early Modern Irish History, 1534–1641.* Cambridge, 1985.

Elliott, J. H. *Europe Divided, 1559–1598.* New York, 1968.

Ellis, Steven G. *The Pale and the Far North: Government and society in two early Tudor borderlands.* Galway, 1988.

———. *Reform and Revival: English Government in Ireland, 1470–1534.* London, 1984.

———. *Tudor Ireland: Crown, Community and the Conflict of Cultures, 1470–1603.* London and New York, 1985.

Elton, G. R. *Reform and Renewal.* Cambridge, 1973.

Falls, Cyril. *Elizabeth's Irish Wars.* London, 1950; reprint edn., New York, 1970.

Farrell, Brian, ed. *The Irish Parliamentary Tradition.* Dublin and New York, 1973.

Flowers, Robin, and Dillon, Myles. *Catalogue of Irish Manuscripts in the British Museum.* 3 vols. London, 1953.

Forde, Rev. C. H. *Round the Coast of Northern Ireland.* Belfast, 1928.

Franklin, T. Bedford. *A History of Scottish Farming.* London, 1952.

Froude, J. A. *The Reign of Queen Elizabeth.* 5 vols. London, 1912.

Gilbert, John T., ed. *Account of Facsimiles of National Manuscripts of Ireland.* London, 1884.

Ginnell, Laurence. *The Brehon Laws.* London, 1894.

Grant, Alexander. "Scotland's 'Celtic Fringe' in the Late Middle Ages: The MacDonald Lords of the Isles and the Kingdom of Scotland." In *The British Isles 1100–1500, Comparisons, Contrasts and Connections.* Edited by R. R. Davies. Edinburgh, 1988.

Grant, I. F. *Highland Folk Ways.* London and Boston, MA 1961.

———. *The Lordship of the Isles, Wanderings in the Lost Lordship.* Edinburgh, 1935; reprint edn., Edinburgh, 1982.

———. *The Social and Economic Development of Scotland before 1603.* Edinburgh, 1930.

Green, Alice Stopford. *The Making of Ireland and its Undoing.* London, 1909.

———. *The Old Irish World.* Dublin and London, 1912.

Gregory, Donald. *The History of the Western Highlands and Isles of Scotland from A.D. 1493 to A.D. 1625.* Edinburgh, 1881; reprint edn., Edinburgh, 1975.

Grimble, Ian. *Scottish Islands.* London, 1985.

Gwynn, Rev. Aubrey. *The Medieval Province of Armagh, 1470–1545.* Dundalk, 1946.

Hamilton, Lord Ernest. *Elizabethan Ulster.* London, 1919.

Hamilton, Rev. William. *Letters Concerning the Northern Coast of Antrim.* Dublin, 1790.

Hayes-McCoy, G. A. *Irish Battles.* London, 1969.

———. *Scots Mercenary Forces in Ireland (1565–1603).* Dublin and London, 1937.

———. *Sixteenth-Century Irish Swords in the National Museum of Ireland.* Dublin, 1977.

———. *Ulster and other Irish Maps c. 1600.* Dublin, 1964.

Healy, T. M. *Stolen Waters: A Page in the Conquest of Ulster.* London, 1913.

Hechter, Michael. *Internal Colonialism: The Celtic Fringe in British National Development, 1536–1966.* Berkeley, CA, 1975.

Henderson, George. *The Norse Influence on Celtic Scotland.* Glasgow, 1910.

Hill, Rev. George. *An Historical Account of the MacDonnells of Antrim, Including Notices of some other Septs, Irish and Scottish.* Belfast, 1873.

———. *An Historical Account of the Plantation in Ulster, 1608–1620.* Belfast, 1877.

Hill, James Michael. *Celtic Warfare, 1595–1763.* Edinburgh, 1986.

Hinton, Edward M. *Ireland through Tudor Eyes.* Philadelphia, PA, 1935.

Hogan, Rev. Edmund. *Distinguished Irishmen of the Sixteenth Century.* London, 1894.

Hogan, James. *Ireland in the European System, 1500–1557.* London, 1920.

———. "Shane O'Neill Comes to the Court of Elizabeth." In *Féilscríbhinn Torna: Essays and Studies Presented to Professor Tadhg Ua Donnchadha (Torna).* Edited by Seamus Pender. Cork, 1947.

Innes, Cosmo. *Sketches of Early Scotch History and Social Progress.* Edinburgh, 1861.

Ireland, John de Courcy. *Ireland and the Irish in Maritime History.* Dún Laoghaire, Dublin, 1986.

James, E. I. *Seasonal Feasts and Festivals.* New York, 1961.

Johnston, Edith M. *Irish history: A Select Bibliography.* Dublin, 1968.

Jones, Frederick M. "The Counter-Reformation." In *A History of Irish Catholicism.* Edited by Patrick J. Corish. Dublin, 1967.

Jones, Howard Mumford. *Ideas in America.* Cambridge, MA, 1944.

———. *O Strange New World. American Culture: The Formative Years.* New York, 1964.

Keltie, John S. *A History of the Scottish Highlands, Highland Clans, and Regiments.* 2 vols. Edinburgh and London, 1875.

Kermack, W. R. *Historical Geography of Scotland.* Edinburgh and London, 1926.

———. *The Scottish Highlands: A Short History, c. 300–1746.* Edinburgh and London, 1957.

Kildare, the Marquis of. *The Earls of Kildare and their Ancestors: from 1057 to 1773.* 2nd edn. Dublin, 1858.

Knox, Alexander. *A History of the County of Down.* Dublin, 1875.

Ladurie, Emmanual Le Roy. *Times of Feast, Times of Famine: A History of the Climate since the Year 1000.* Translated by B. Bray. London, 1971.

Lamont, W. D. *Ancient and Mediaeval Sculptured Stones of Islay.* Edinburgh and London, 1968.

————. *The Early History of Islay, 500–1726.* Dundee, Angus, 1966.

Leask, Harold G. *Irish Castles and Castellated Houses.* Dundalk, Louth, 1946.

Lee, J., ed. *Irish Historiography, 1970–1979.* Cork, 1981.

Lee, Jr., Maurice. *Government by Pen: Scotland under James VI and I.* Chicago, 1980.

Leland, Thomas. *The History of Ireland from the Invasion of Henry II.* 3 vols. London, 1773.

Lethbridge, Thomas C. *Herdsmen and Hermits: Celtic Seafarers in the Northern Seas.* Cambridge, 1950.

Lewis, Samuel. *A Topographical Dictionary of Ireland.* 2 vols. 2nd edn. London, 1847.

Lindsay, Ian G., and Cosh, Mary. *Inveraray and the Dukes of Argyll.* Edinburgh, 1973.

Loder, John de Vere. *Colonsay and Oronsay in the Isles of Argyll: Their History, Flora, Fauna and Topography.* Edinburgh, 1935.

Lombard, Peter. *The Irish War of Defence, 1598–1600.* Translated and edited by Matthew J. Byrne. Dublin and Cork, 1930.

Longfield, Ada K. *Anglo-Irish Trade in the Sixteenth Century.* London, 1929.

Lydon, J. F. *The Lordship of Ireland in the Middle Ages.* Toronto, 1972.

McClintock, H. F. *Old Irish and Highland Dress.* Dundalk, Louth, 1943.

McCracken, Eileen. *The Irish Woods since Tudor Times: Distribution and Exploitation.* Newton Abbot, Devon, 1971.

MacCulloch, John. *The Highlands and Western Isles of Scotland.* 4 vols. London, 1824.

MacCurtain, Margaret. *Tudor and Stuart Ireland.* Dublin, 1972.

MacDonald, A., and MacDonald, A. *The Clan Donald.* 3 vols. Inverness, 1896–1904.

————, eds. *The MacDonald Collection of Gaelic Poetry.* Inverness, 1911.

MacDonald, Colin. *The History of Argyll up to the Beginning of the Sixteenth Century.* Glasgow, 1951.

MacDonald, Donald J. *Clan Donald.* Loanhead, Midlothian, 1978.

MacGregor, Alasdair A. *The Western Isles.* London, 1949.

MacGregor, Rev. Alexander. *The Feuds of the Clans.* Stirling, 1907.

MacKay, William. *Sidelights on Highland History.* Inverness, 1925.

MacKechnie, John. *The Clan MacLean: A Gaelic Sea Power.* Edinburgh and London, 1954.

MacKenzie, W. C. *The Highlands and Isles of Scotland: A Historical Survey.* Edinburgh and London, 1937; reprint edn., New York, 1977.

————. *History of the Outer Hebrides.* Paisley, 1903; reprint edn., Edinburgh, 1974.

MacKenzie, W. M. *The Mediaeval Castle in Scotland.* London, 1927.

MacKinnon, Donald. *A Descriptive Catalogue of Gaelic Manuscripts in the Advocates' Library.* Edinburgh, 1912.

MacLauchlan, Rev. Thomas. *Celtic Gleanings; or, Notices of the History and Literature of the Scottish Gael.* Edinburgh, 1857.

MacLean, Fitzroy. *A Concise History of Scotland.* London, 1970.

MacLean, Hector. "A Sketch of the MacDonnells of Antrim." In *Transactions of the Gaelic Society of Inverness,* vol. XVII. Inverness, 1890–1.

MacLean, J. P. *History of the Island of Mull.* 2 vols. San Mateo, CA, 1925.

MacLean, Loraine, of Dochgarroch, ed. *The Middle Ages in the Highlands.* Inverness, 1981.

MacNeice, John F. *Carrickfergus and its Contacts: Some Chapters in the History of Ulster.* London and Belfast, 1928.

MacNeil of Barra. *The Clan MacNeil.* New York, 1923.

MacNeill, Eoin. *Celtic Ireland.* Dublin and London, 1921.

———. *Phases of Irish History,* Dublin, 1937.

McSkimin, Samuel. *The History and Antiquities af the County of the town of Carrickfergus from the earliest records till 1839.* 2nd edn. Belfast, 1909.

Marshall, John J. *Benburb: Its Battlefields and History.* Dungannon, Tyrone, 1924.

———. *History of Dungannon.* Dungannon, Tyrone, 1929.

———. *Lough Neagh in Legend and History.* Dungannon, Tyrone, 1934.

Martin, F. X., and Moody, T. W., eds. *The Course of Irish History.* Cork, 1967.

Mason, Roger A., ed. *Scotland and England, 1286–1815.* Edinburgh, 1987.

Mathew, David. *The Celtic Peoples and Renaissance Europe.* London and New York, 1933.

Maxwell, Constantia. *The Stranger in Ireland from the Reign of Elizabeth to the Great Famine.* London, 1954.

Meehan, Rev. C. P. *The Fate and Fortunes of Hugh O'Neill, Earl of Tyrone, and Rory O'Donnell, Earl of Tyrconnell.* New York, 1868.

———. *The Rise and Fall of the Irish Franciscan Monasteries, and Memoirs of the Irish Hierarchy in the Seventeenth Century.* Dublin, 1869.

Menzies, Gordon, ed. *Who Are the Scots?* London, 1971.

Mitchel, John. *The Life and Times of Aodh O'Neill, Prince of Ulster; called by the English, Hugh, Earl of Tyrone, with some account of his predecessors, Con, Shane and Tirlough.* New York, 1868.

Mitchell, Dugald. *A Popular History of the Highlands and Gaelic Scotland.* Paisley, Renfrew, 1900.

Moody, T. W., ed. *Irish Historiography, 1936–1970.* Dublin, 1971.

Moody, T. W., Martin, F. X., and Byrne, F. J., eds. *A New History of Ireland.* 9 vols. Vol. III: *Early Modern Ireland, 1534–1691.* Oxford, 1976.

Morris, William O'Connor. *Ireland, 1494–1868.* Cambridge, 1898.

Munro, Jean. "The Lordship of the Isles." In *The Middle Ages in the Highlands.* Edited by Loraine MacLean. Inverness, 1981.

Neilson, George. *Trial by Combat.* New York, 1891.

Nicholls, Kenneth. *Gaelic and Gaelicised Ireland in the Middle Ages*. Dublin, 1972.

———. *Land, Law and Society in Sixteenth-Century Ireland*. Cork, 1976.

Nicholson, Ranald. *Scotland: The Later Middle Ages*. Edinburgh, 1974.

Norman, A. V. B., and Pottinger, Don. *English Weapons and Warfare, 449–1660*. New York, 1985.

O'Brien, R. Barry. *Irish Memories*. London, 1904.

O'Callaghan, John C. *The Green Book*. Dublin, 1841.

O'Ceallaigh, Seamus. *Gleanings from Ulster History*. Cork and Oxford, 1951.

O'Connell, J. J. *The Irish Wars: A Military History of Ireland from the Norse Invasions to 1798*. Dublin, n.d.

O'Conor, Matthew. *The Irish Brigades*. Dublin, 1855.

———. *Military History of the Irish Nation*. Dublin, 1845.

O'Cuiv, Brian, ed. *Seven Centuries of Irish Learning, 1000–1700*. Dublin, 1971.

O'Dell, A. C., and Walton, K. *The Highlands and Islands of Scotland*. London and Edinburgh, 1962.

O'Donovan, John. *The Economic History of Live Stock in Ireland*. Dublin and Cork, 1940.

O'Faolain, Sean. *The Great O'Neill*. New York, 1942.

O'Flaherty, Roderick. *Ogygia, or a Chronological Account of Irish Events*. 2 vols. Translated by Rev. James Hely. Dublin, 1793.

O'Grady, Standish, ed. *Pacata Hibernia, or a History of the Wars in Ireland during the Reign of Queen Elizabeth*. 2 vols. London, 1896.

O'Hegarty, P. S. *The Indestructible Nation, A Survey of Irish History from the English Invasion*. Dublin and London, 1918.

O'Laverty, Rev. James. *An Historical Account of the Diocese of Down and Connor, Ancient and Modern*. 5 vols. Dublin, 1878–95.

Ollamh. *The Story of Shane O'Neill, Hereditary Prince of Ulster*. Dublin, n.d.

O'Mahony, Charles. *The Viceroys of Ireland*. London, 1912.

Oman, Sir Charles. *A History of the Art of War in the Sixteenth Century*. London, 1937.

O'Rahilly, Thomas F. *Irish Dialects Past and Present*. Dublin, 1932; reprint edn., Dublin, 1976.

Orel, Harold, ed. *Irish History and Culture: Aspects of a People's Heritage*. Lawrence, KS, 1976.

Otway-Ruthven, A. J. *A History of Medieval Ireland*. London, 1968.

Parker, Geoffrey, *The Military Revolution: Military Innovation and the Rise of the West, 1500–1800*. Cambridge, 1988.

Parry, J. H. "Introduction: the English in the New World." In *The Westward Enterprise*. Edited by K. R. Andrews, N. P. Canny, and P. E. H. Hair. Liverpool, 1978.

Perceval-Maxwell, Michael. *The Scottish Migration to Ulster in the Reign of James I.* London, 1973.

Piggott, Stuart. *The Druids.* Harmondsworth, Middlesex, 1974.

Plowden, Francis. *The history of Ireland from its invasion under Henry II to its union with Great Britain.* 2 vols. London, 1809.

Prebble, John. *The Lion in the North.* London, 1971.

Quinn, David Beers. *The Elizabethans and the Irish.* Ithaca, NY and London, 1966.

Ranelagh, John O'Beirne. *A Short History of Ireland.* Cambridge, 1983.

Reeves, Rev. William. *Ecclesiastical Antiquities of Down, Connor, and Dromore.* Dublin, 1847.

Reid, James Seaton. *History of the Presbyterian Church in Ireland.* 3 vols. 3rd edn. London, 1853.

Richey, Alexander G. *Lectures on the History of Ireland from A.D. 1534 to the Date of the Plantation of Ulster.* London and Dublin, 1870.

Roberts, Michael. *The Military Revolution, 1560–1660.* Belfast, 1956.

Rogers, Rev. Charles. *Social Life in Scotland from Early to Recent Times.* Edinburgh, 1884–6.

Ronan, Myles V. *The Reformation in Ireland under Elizabeth, 1558–1580.* London and New York, 1930.

Rushe, Denis Carolan. *Historical Sketches of Monaghan from the Earliest Records to the Fenian Movement.* Dublin, 1895.

Shearman, Hugh. *Ulster.* London, 1949.

Shirley, Evelyn Philip. *The History of the County of Monaghan.* London, 1879.

Silke, J. J. *Ireland and Europe, 1559–1607.* Dundalk, Louth, 1966.

Simpson, Grant G. *Scottish Handwriting, 1150–1650.* Edinburgh, 1973.

Simpson, W. Douglas. *The Highlands of Scotland.* London, 1976.

———. *Scottish Castles.* Edinburgh, 1959.

Skene, W. F. *Celtic Scotland.* 3 vols. Edinburgh 1876–80.

———. *The Highlanders of Scotland.* 2nd edn. Edited by Alexander MacBain. Stirling, 1902.

Steer, K. A., and Bannerman, J. W. M. *Late Medieval Monumental Sculpture in the West Highlands.* Edinburgh, 1977.

Stephen, Sir Leslie, and Lee, Sir Sidney, eds. *The Dictionary of National Biography.* 22 vols. Oxford and London, 1885–90.

Stevenson, David. *Alasdair MacColla and the Highland Problem in the Seventeenth Century.* Edinburgh, 1980.

———. *The Scottish Revolution 1637–44: The Triumph of the Covenanters.* New York, 1973.

Storrie, Margaret C. *Islay: Biography of an Island.* Port Ellen, Islay, 1981.

Strype, John. *The Life of the Learned Sir Thomas Smith.* Oxford, 1820.

Stuart, James. *Historical Memoirs of the City of Armagh*. Newry, 1819.

Taaffe, Denis. *An Impartial History of Ireland*. 4 vols. Dublin, 1809–11.
Taylor, E. G. R. *Late Tudor and Early Stuart Geography, 1583–1650*. London, 1934; reprint edn., New York, 1968.
———. *Tudor Geography, 1485–1583*. London, 1930.
Thirsk, Joan. "The Farming Regions of England." In *The Agrarian History of England and Wales, 1500–1640*. Edited by Joan Thirsk. Cambridge, 1967.
Tindall, Jemima. *Scottish Island Hopping*. London and New York, 1981.

Walker, John. *An Economical History of the Hebrides and Highlands of Scotland*. 2 vols. Edinburgh, 1808.
Warrack, John. *Domestic Life in Scotland, 1488–1688*. New York, 1920.
Watson, William J. *The History of the Celtic Place-Names of Scotland*. Edinburgh and London, 1926.
———, ed. *Rosg Gaidhlig*. Inverness, 1915.
Webb, Henry J. *Elizabethan Military Science: The Books and the Practice*. Madison, WI, 1965.
Weller, Jac. *Weapons and Tactics, Hastings to Berlin*. New York and London, 1966.
Wernham, R. B. *Before the Armada: The Emergence of the English Nation, 1485–1588*. New York, 1966.
———. *The Making of Elizabethan Foreign Policy, 1558–1603*. Berkeley, CA and London, 1980.
Williams, Penry. *The Council in the Marches of Wales under Elizabeth I*. Cardiff, 1958.
Wills, James, ed. *Lives of Illustrious and Distinguished Irishmen from the Earliest Times to the Present Period*. 6 vols. Dublin, Edinburgh, and London, 1847.
Willson, D. Harris. *King James VI and I*. New York, 1956.
Wilson, Philip. *The Beginnings of Modern Ireland*. Dublin and London, 1912.
Winkless, Nels, III, and Browning, Iben. *Climate and the Affairs of Men*. New York, 1975.
Wood-Martin, W. G. *The Lake Dwellings of Ireland*. Dublin and London, 1886.
Wormald, Jenny. *Court, Kirk, and Community: Scotland, 1470–1625*. Toronto and London, 1981.

Journal Articles

Boyd, Hugh A. "Ballycastle in Older Days." *The Glynnes: Journal of the Glens of Antrim Historical Society* V (1977): 5–11.
Bradshaw, Brendan. "The Elizabethans and the Irish." *Studies* (Spring 1977): 38–50.
———. "Sword, Word and Strategy in the Reformation in Ireland." *The Historical Journal* XXI, 3 (1978): 475–502.

Brady, Ciaran. "The Killing of Shane O'Neill: Some New Evidence." *Irish Sword* XV (1982–3): 116–23.

Brown, A. L. "The Cistercian Abbey of Saddell." *Innes Review* XX (1969): 129–37.

Canny, Nicholas P. "Hugh O'Neill, Earl of Tyrone, and the Changing Face of Gaelic Ulster." *Studia Hibernica* X (1970): 7–35.

Celoria, Francis. "Notes on Lore and Customs in the District near Portnahaven, Rhinns of Islay, Argyll, Scotland." *Folklore* LXXVI (1965): 39–47.

Cross, A. R. "Notes on Scottish Galleys." *Mariner's Mirror* XXXVI (1950): 270–1.

Dawson, Jane. "The Fifth Earl of Argyle, Gaelic Lordship and Political Power in Sixteenth-Century Scotland." *Scottish Historical Review* LXVII, i, 183 (April 1988): 1–27.

Dillon, M. "Ceart Ui Néill." *Studia Celtica* I (1966): 1–18.

Drummond-Norie, William. "Inverlochy, 1431–1645." *Celtic Monthly* V (1896–7): 84.

Duncan, A. A. M., and Brown, A. L. "Argyll and the Isles in the Earlier Middle Ages." *Proceedings of the Society of Antiquaries of Scotland* XC (1956–7): 192–220.

Falls, Cyril. "The Elizabethan Soldier in Ireland." *History Today* I (February 1951): 40–5.

Glasgow, Jr, Tom. "The Elizabethan Navy in Ireland (1558–1603)." *Irish Sword* VII, 39 (1974–5): 291–307.

Green, William S. "The Wrecks of the Spanish Armada on the Coast of Ireland." *The Geographical Journal* V, xxvii (May 1906): 429–51.

Hayes-McCoy, G. A. "Gaelic Society in Ireland in the Late Sixteenth Century." *Historical Studies* IV (1963): 45–61.

———. "The Making of an O'Neill: A View of the Ceremony at Tullaghoge, Co. Tyrone." *Ulster Journal of Archaeology* series III, XXXIII (1970): 89–94.

———. "Strategy and Tactics in Irish Warfare, 1593–1601." *Irish Historical Studies* II (1940–1): 250–79.

Hill, Rev. George. "Notices of the Clan Ian Vór, or Clan-Donnell Scots." *Ulster Journal of Archaeology* series I, IX (1861): 301–17.

———. "Shane O'Neill's Expedition Against the Antrim Scots, 1565." *Ulster Journal of Archaeology* series I, IX (1861): 122–41.

Hill, J. Michael. "The Distinctiveness of Gaelic Warfare, 1400–1750." *European History Quarterly* XXII (July 1992): 323–46.

———. "The Rift within Clan Ian Mor: The Antrim and Dunyveg

MacDonnells, 1590–1603." *The Sixteenth Century Journal* (forthcoming, 1993).

———. "The Scottish Plantations in Ulster to 1625: A Reinterpretation." *Journal of British Studies* XXXII (January 1993): 24–43.

———. "Shane O'Neills's Campaign Against the MacDonnells of Antrim, 1564–5." *Irish Sword* XVIII, 71 (Summer 1991): 129–38.

Hore, Herbert F. "Irish Bardism in 1561." *Ulster Journal of Archaeology* series I, vi (1858): 165–7.

———. "The Ulster State Papers." *Ulster Journal of Archaeology* series I, VII (1859): 45–65.

———. "Woods and Fastnesses and their Denizens, in Ancient Leinster." *Kilkenny and S. E. Ireland Archaeology Society Journal* I (1856–7): 229–40.

Lowe, J. "The Earl of Antrim and Irish Aid to Montrose in 1644." *Irish Sword* IV (1959–60): 191–8.

Lydon, J. F. "The Bruce Invasion of Ireland." *Historical Studies* IV (1963): 111–25.

McComish, W. A. "The Survival of the Irish Castle in an Age of Cannon." *Irish Sword* IX, 34 (Summer 1969): 16–21.

McKerral, Andrew. "West Highland Mercenaries in Ireland." *Scottish Historical Reviw* XXX (April 1951): 1–14.

Morgan, Hiram. "The End of Gaelic Ulster: a Thematic Interpretation of Events between 1534 and 1610." *Irish Historical Studies* XXVI, 101 (May 1988): 8–32.

Nicholls, K. W. "Notes on the Genealogy of Clann Eoin Mhoir." *West Highland Notes & Queries* series II, 8 (November 1991): 11–24.

O'Doibhlin, Eamon. "O'Neill's 'Own Country' and its Families." *Seanchas Ard Mhacha* VI, 1 (1971): 3–23.

O'Domhnaill, Sean. "Warfare in Sixteenth-Century Ireland." *Irish Historical Studies* V (1946–7): 29–54.

Pocock, J. G. A. "British History. A Plea for a New Subject." *Journal of Modern History* 47 (1975): 601–28.

Potter, D. "French Intrigue in Ireland during the Reign of Henri II, 1547–1559." *International History Review* V (1983): 168–76.

Quinn, David Beers. "'A Discourse of Ireland' (circa 1599): a Sidelight on English Colonial Policy." *Proceedings of the Royal Irish Academy* XLVII, sec. C, no. 3 (1942): 151–66.

———. "Ireland and Sixteenth-Century European Expansion." *Historical Studies* I (1958): 20–32.

———. "Sir Thomas Smith (1513–1577) and the Beginnings of English Colonial Theory." *Proceedings of the American Philosophical Society* LXXXIX, 4 (10 December 1945): 543–60.

Scott, William W. "John of Fordun's Description of the Western Isles." *Scottish Studies* XXIII (1979): 1–13.

Shove, D. J. "Discussion: Post-Glacial Climatic Change." *Quarterly Journal of the Royal Meteorological Society* (April 1949): 175.

Sidney, Sir Henry. "Memoir of a Government in Ireland." *Ulster Journal of Archaeology* series I, III (1855): 33–44, 85–99, 336–57; V (1857): 299–315; VIII (1860): 179–95.

Simms, Katherine. "Warfare in the Medieval Gaelic Lordships." *Irish Sword* XII (1975–6): 98–108.

Walshe, Edward. "'Conjectures' Concerning the State of Ireland [1552]." *Irish Historical Studies* V (1946–7): 303–22.

Webb, M. "The Clan of the MacQuillins of Antrim." *Ulster Journal of Archaeology* series I, VIII (1860): 251–68.

White D. G. "Henry VIII's Irish Kerne in France and Scotland, 1544–1545." *Irish Sword* III (1957–8): 213–25.

———. "The Reign of Edward VI in Ireland: Some Political Social and Economic Aspects." *Irish Historical Studies* XIV (1956–7): 204–6.

Index